Louis Zukofsky and the Poetry of Knowledge

Modern and Contemporary Poetics

Louis Zukofsky and the Poetry of Knowledge

Mark Scroggins

The University of Alabama Press
Tuscaloosa and London

∞
The paper on which this book is printed meets the minimum requirements of American National Standard for Information Science-Permanence of Paper for Printed Library Materials, ANSI Z39.48-1984.

Library of Congress-in-Publication Data

Scroggins, Mark.
Louis Zukofsky and the poetry of knowledge / Mark Scroggins.
p. cm.
Includes bibliographical references (p.) and index.
ISBN 0-8173-0907-1 (cloth); ISBN 0-8173-0957-8 (paper)
1. Zukofsky, Louis, 1904–1978—Criticism and interpretation.
I. Title.
PS3549.U47Z83 1998
811′.52—dc21 98–8879
CIP

British Library Cataloguing-in-Publication Data available

For my mother,
Nelle Walker Scroggins,
And in memory of my father,
Herman Wardell Scroggins

Contents

Acknowledgments

I love the work of Louis Zukofsky in much the same way that I love the work of Ben Jonson, and I would have Zukofsky escape the plight in which T. S. Eliot found Jonson: "to be damned by the praise that quenches all desire to read the book; to be afflicted by the imputation of the virtues that excite the least pleasure; and to be read only by historians and antiquaries" (*Sacred Wood* 104). In Eliot's eyes, "No critic has succeeded in making [Jonson] appear pleasurable or even interesting." Eliot's Jonson is in many ways like Zukofsky: "the polished veneer of Jonson reflects only the lazy reader's fatuity; unconscious does not respond to unconscious; no swarms of inarticulate feelings are aroused. The immediate appeal of Jonson is to the mind; his emotional tone is not in the single verse, but in the design of the whole" (105–6). The solution, Eliot proposes, is "intelligent saturation in his work as a whole" (106). I have tried to saturate myself in Zukofsky's writings—however intelligently my readers can judge—and in so doing have found models in two very different, but both quite extraordinary, studies of twentieth-century poets: Richard Poirier's *Robert Frost: The Work of Knowing* and Peter Makin's *Bunting: The Shaping of His Verse.*

This book has been long in the making, and owes whatever value it may have to any number of hands. In its earliest stages as a Cornell University doctoral dissertation, this work benefitted from keen readings by Debra Fried, Roger Gilbert, and Joel Porte. Colleagues in the graduate program at Cornell, especially Oliver

Buckton, Patricia P. Chu, and Srinivas Aravamudan, provided support both emotional, critical, and culinary. Fellowships from the Andrew Mellon Foundation and Cornell University enabled me to complete the dissertation in Reston, Virginia. During the three years I worked at this book without formal institutional support, a ring of friends and colleagues at the Catholic University of America and the George Washington University provided constant encouragement. Eric Murphy Selinger is no doubt the dearest friend I made at George Washington. We share I think a fundamental love of and delight in poetry itself, and although our specific tastes may diverge, his continual smiling skepticism and willingness to be persuaded have done much to shape this volume's rhetoric.

Various sections of this book have been road tested as conference papers. I thank the organizers of the Twentieth-Century Literature Conference at the University of Louisville, where I presented papers derived from this manuscript in 1992, 1993, and 1996—two of them on panels organized by Burton Hatlen. I presented the nucleus of one chapter at the landmark 1993 "The First Postmodernists: American Poets of the 1930s" conference at the University of Maine, Orono. I also thank Thomas Gardner and Norman Finkelstein, who organized panels at the 1992 and 1993 Modern Language Association conferences at San Francisco and Toronto respectively. Several sections of this book were previously published in earlier forms. I thank Burt Hatlen and Roy Miki, editors respectively of *Sagetrieb* and *West Coast Line,* for allowing parts of Chapters 2, 3, and 10 to appear in their journals. I thank Joseph M. Conte for commissioning an earlier version of Chapter 1 for the *Dictionary of Literary Biography: American Poets Since World War II.* And I thank the University of Alabama Press for publishing *Upper Limit Music,* in which Chapter 6 and some paragraphs of my introduction first appeared.

During my undergraduate years at Virginia Polytechnic Institute and State University, Thomas Gardner and Alison Sulloway showed me what it means to write about a poet with both passion and critical distance. They are two of the readers to whom this book is most especially addressed. Although it may not seem evident from the academic boilerplate that characterizes too much of my prose, I write as one poet addressing another. I have found from the beginning of my reading of Zukofsky that his best readers have been poets. John Taggart and Ted Pearson, in conversations and letters, have offered insights into Zukofsky's work that I could never have obtained from books. Other poet friends, while not directly involved in the study of Louis Zukofsky, have provided a sense of the high seriousness of writing poetry that is so much a part of Zukofsky's work. Among them, C. S. Giscombe and E. A. Miller remain in some sense my ideal audience. I hope this book to some degree pleases all of these most stringent readers.

My attention was first drawn to Zukofsky by Guy Davenport's essays, and a longstanding correspondence with Guy, seasoned with very occasional conversations, has been one of the consistent pleasures of this task. I hope this book at least in part amuses him. Joseph M. Conte, Burton Hatlen, Hank Lazer, Jennifer A. Low, Ira B. Nadel, and Peter Quartermain all read portions of the manuscript and made useful suggestions. Other critics, scholars, and poets have contributed to my work, among them Barry Ahearn, Charles Bernstein, Robert Creeley, Theodore Enslin, Norman Finkelstein, Benjamin Friedlander, Andrew Levy, Jerome J. McGann, Marnie Parsons, and Marjorie Perloff. Ronald Johnson, in conversations and letters, enlightened me as to his intentions in *ARK*. A prominent Language poet's suggestion (retailed to me at second hand) that my *Bottom* chapter ought to be entitled "Spanking Zukofsky's *Bottom*" is one that I fear I did not have the temerity to accept, though I admire its chutzpah and its very Zukofskyan sense of humor.

Paul Zukofsky has taken much time from his own multifarious pursuits to read and comment on the manuscript as a whole, as he did for the collection *Upper Limit Music*. Had I taken all his suggestions, this book would have no doubt been far shorter and considerably more graceful. Although I have indeed picked and chosen among them, his comments have again proved indispensable.

A circle of family and friends has supported and encouraged this work. Richard and Nancy Belt, Belinda and Jeff Oswalt, and Martha Belt all sustained to this work while I was in Reston, while Laurice Campbell and Olly Buckton have made Delray Beach as welcoming a new home as could be imagined. My parents, given any number of opportunities to despair at the wayward progress of a career that took its own sweet time getting off the ground, remained as loving and present as could be imagined. My father died while this book was in the final stages of preparation. He would have been its most attentive reader; without his example and encouragement, it would never have been written.

I would like to thank the following publishers and individuals for permission to reprint from these materials:

Complete Poems, by Basil Bunting. Copyright © 1994 by The Estate of Basil Bunting. Reprinted by permission of Oxford University Press.

Ground Work II: In the Dark, by Robert Duncan. Copyright © 1987 by Robert Duncan. Reprinted by permission of New Directions Publishing Corporation.

ARK, by Ronald Johnson. Copyright © 1996 by Ronald Johnson. Reprinted by permission of Living Batch Press.

"Shake, Quoth the Dove House," copyright © 1964 by Ronald Johnson, from *Valley of the Many-Colored Grasses* by Ronald Johnson. Reprinted by permission of W. W. Norton & Company, Inc.

Notes for Echo Lake, by Michael Palmer. Copyright © 1981 by Michael Palmer. Reprinted by permission of Michael Palmer.

Without Music, by Michael Palmer. Copyright © 1977 by Michael Palmer. Reprinted by permission of Michael Palmer.

The Cantos, by Ezra Pound. Copyright © 1934, 1938 by Ezra Pound. Reprinted by permission of New Directions Publishing Corporation.

Collected Poems, by Wallace Stevens. Copyright © 1954 by Wallace Stevens. Reprinted by permission of Alfred A. Knopf, Inc.

Opus Posthumous, by Wallace Stevens. Copyright © 1957 by Elsie Stevens and Holly Stevens. Reprinted by permission of Alfred A. Knopf, Inc.

Loop, by John Taggart (Los Angeles: Sun & Moon Press, 1991), pp. 137, 178, 216. Copyright © 1991 by John Taggart. Reprinted by permission of the publisher.

Collected Earlier Poetry, by William Carlos Williams. Copyright © 1938 by New Directions Publishing Corporation. Reprinted by permission of New Directions Publishing Corporation.

Pictures from Brueghel and Other Poems, by William Carlos Williams. Copyright © 1962 by William Carlos Williams. Reprinted by permission of New Directions Publishing Corporation.

"A", by Louis Zukofsky. Copyright © 1978 by Celia Zukofsky and Louis Zukofsky. Reprinted by permission of the Johns Hopkins University Press.

Bottom: On Shakespeare, by Louis Zukofsky. Copyright © 1996 by Paul Zukofsky. Reprinted by permission of Paul Zukofsky.

Complete Short Poetry, by Louis Zukofsky. Copyright © 1991 by Celia Zukofsky and Louis Zukofsky. Reprinted by permission of the Johns Hopkins University Press.

Prepositions: The Collected Critical Essays of Louis Zukofsky, by Louis Zukofsky. Copyright © 1996 by Paul Zukofsky. Reprinted by permission of Paul Zukofsky.

Abbreviations

References in my text to the most frequently cited of Zukofsky's works will be signaled by the following abbreviations, except for references to *"A"*, which, for the convenience of those who might be consulting earlier publications of the various movements, will include both movement and page numbers of the 1993 Johns Hopkins University Press edition: for instance, "A"-12, 239. A full bibliography of Zukofsky works referred to can be found in Works Cited.

A	*"A"* (1978; reprint, Baltimore: Johns Hopkins UP, 1993)
Auto	*Autobiography* (New York: Grossman, 1970)
B	*Bottom: On Shakespeare* (1963; reprint, Berkeley: U of California P, 1987)
CF	*Collected Fiction* (Elmwood Park, IL: Dalkey Archive P, 1990)
CSP	*Complete Short Poetry* (Baltimore: Johns Hopkins UP, 1991)
P	*Prepositions: The Collected Critical Essays*, expanded ed. (Berkeley: U of California P, 1981)
P/Z	*Pound/Zukofsky: Selected Letters of Ezra Pound and*

Louis Zukofsky, ed. Barry Ahearn (New York: New Directions, 1987)

TP A *Test of Poetry* (1948; reprint, New York: C.Z. Publications, 1980)

References to critical, biographical, and bibliographical articles in Carroll F. Terrell's indispensable *Louis Zukofsky: Man and Poet* will use the abbreviation *LZMP* and will also be listed separately in Works Cited. My few quotations from Shakespeare will follow the text of the *Riverside Shakespeare*, although I would note that Zukofsky himself for the most part used William Allen Neilson's *Complete Works of William Shakespeare* (Cambridge, MA: Riverside P, 1947).

Louis Zukofsky and the Poetry of Knowledge

Introduction

The 1930s announced themselves at their very outset as a tumultuous decade, a moment of political struggle and literary guard-changing. In 1931 the Second Spanish Republic was proclaimed, and Japan invaded Manchuria. In both Europe and Asia, the world propelled itself so many steps further toward world war; in the realm of letters, English novelist Arnold Bennett and Austrian playwright Arthur Schnitzler died, American critic Edmund Wilson produced the first major evaluation of modernism in *Axel's Castle,* and a relatively unknown New York poet guest-edited an issue of Harriet Monroe's Chicago periodical *Poetry: A Magazine of Verse.* That same year the Englishman Stephen Spender, five years younger than his transatlantic colleague Louis Zukofsky, and already known in British literary circles as something of a bright young man, published a poem in which he moodily reflected, "I think continually of those who were truly great." Part of Spender's point, of course, was that it is men of action, like the fighters in the late war—for which he and his public school peers had been too young to enlist—rather than poets, who achieve an authentic greatness in a world in which, as his friend Wystan Auden would write in 1939, "poetry makes nothing happen." But how, one may reflect sixty-five years later in our own age of anxiety, does one recognize the truly great figures of one's own literary day? Two-thirds of a century, the better part of a person's life, still seems all too short a distance from which to make authoritative pronouncements—either in history or in literary history.

Bennett, who dominated British writing to such an extent that Ezra Pound devoted an entire poem of his 1920 sequence *Hugh Selwyn Mauberley* to attacking him, is now rarely read by any but scholars of literary history. Even the Spender/Auden/Isherwood phalanx, once so prominent in English letters that Samuel Hynes would title his study of the English 1930s *The Auden Generation,* has begun to be brusquely shuffled out of its comfortable critical centrality.[1] In our own moment, and in the increasingly balkanized and autistic field of American poetry—a field in which a shrinking pie of public recognition, institutional support, and cultural prestige seems to be divided among more and more poets each year; in which movements, cliques, and coteries spring up like toadstools, their partisans far more anxious to demonize other factions than actually to *read* their poetry—what sense does it make to speak of a poet like Zukofsky, reaching his own maturity in the troubled 1930s, as *great?*

There are two paradigms at odds here. One, which carries an air of sturdy commonsense, proposes that greatness is in part a measure of a figure's impact on the larger culture. Irving's Rip Van Winkle and Ichabod Crane, for instance, have become figures of American secular scripture, while the gnomic aphorisms of Emerson's essays—"hitch your wagon to a star," "a foolish consistency is the hobgoblin of little minds"—are nearly as widespread as the sayings of that earlier sage, Poor Richard. Whitman, perhaps most iconoclastic of the writers of the American Renaissance and now universally recognized as the most "American" poet of his day, encapsulated the ideal relationship of the great bard and his public in the 1855 preface to his first *Leaves of Grass:* "The proof of a poet is that his country absorbs him as affectionately as he has absorbed it" (*Poetry and Prose* 26). Whitman of course was wrong, even (or perhaps especially) in the case of his own reception. His embarrassing status as an American prophet without honor, fired from his government job on account of his scandalous poems, taken up not by his countrymen but by the English, fits better a second paradigm: the model of the unrecognized poet of greatness, what Jerome McGann calls "that familiar trope of romantic ideology, the neglected genius" (*New Oxford Book* xxii). Thomas Chatterton is of course the archetypal example, and it is of him that Wordsworth writes in his "Resolution and Independence": "By our own spirits are we deified; / We Poets in our youth begin in gladness; / But thereof comes in the end despondency and madness" (Wordsworth 262). The twenty-six-year-old Keats that Shelley elegized in *Adonais*, the winged spirit "killed by an article," is the mythologized version of publicly overlooked and undercompensated greatness. But mythologization should not blind one to the factual kernel of such stories, the truth that contemporary reading publics and critical establishments have often slighted or overlooked poets later recognized as important indeed.

Recent critical thinking concerning the processes of canon-formation and critical valuation has led us to be properly chary with unreflective statements about the discovery of previously unknown greatness, and even about the category of greatness itself. Literary evaluation no longer has the sense of positivistic truth that I. A. Richards sought to attribute to it. When we speak of the greatness of a given figure, it is clear, we reveal more about our own predilections, our own intellectual, aesthetic, and social agendas, than we do about any state of affairs obtaining in the real world—or so contemporary critical theory would hold. Both poetry itself and our various valuations of poems and poets are of course expressions of wider social truths of a given historical moment, as much cultural phenomena as a film, a television program, or a soft drink advertisement. But poetry is as well an art, a process of producing verbal constructions that most societies have traditionally considered among the higher pursuits available to the human race. Which is to say that in whatever diminished state we might find it, for at least the last two thousand years poetry has held center stage among the activities (among them philosophy, religion, and rational social order) that humans have used to distinguish themselves from other animal species. I do not mean to write a defense of poetry; if one, in Valéry's words, has no "appetite for poetry," then I am unlikely to convince that reader that any body of poetry—Zukofsky's or someone else's—ought to be considered "great." Yet, I cannot help but emphasize that on a certain level, poetry, as a social activity and as a tradition, wants no defense: it is too firmly embedded in human culture to need justification.

And poetry, in addition to its tremendous social importance as an art, is also a craft, a *technê* acquired, not solely through ecstatic inspiration, but through the poet's immersion in and study of the productions of precursor poets. It is in the degree to which a poet achieves an absolute mastery of the art of poetry itself, and the degree to which that poet becomes an example and school for younger practitioners of the art that an individual's poetic greatness lies, if it lies anywhere. I fear my definition is hopelessly old-fashioned, perhaps in the end no more objective than Emily Dickinson's observation, "If I feel physically as if the top of my head were taken off, I know *that* is poetry" (208); and my two considerations surely need modifying by some further description of the degree to which the poet represents her or his time, and the degree to which the poet surmounts, avoids, or transforms the clichés of her or his day. Nonetheless, one of the fundamental convictions underlying this book, and one of the conclusions to which I hope to draw readers, is that Louis Zukofsky is a great poet, perhaps the greatest American poet born in this century—perhaps even the greatest English-language poet *of* the century.

When Zukofsky died in 1978 he was largely unknown to most critics and readers of American poetry. Even those few who knew his work, or, more often, knew *of* it, too often dismissed it as the verse of a poet's poet—difficult, obscure, or worse, ornamental or trivial. Four years before Zukofsky's death, in a *Parnassus* magazine review of *"A"-24*, Guy Davenport named Zukofsky America's "greatest living poet" (*Geography* 107). Yet that encomium, coming at the end of an essay asserting that the difficulties of Zukofsky's poetry are "in the reader's mind, not in the poem" (106), could all too easily be dismissed as a potshot at the shortsightedness of the American publishing industry rather than taken as a seriously argued evaluation—a premise, that is, rather than a conclusion. At his death, even the *New York Times* seemed unintentionally to snub Zukofsky: the awkwardness of the header for his obituary—"Louis Zukofsky, 74, a Major Poet / Of Objectivist School and Novelist"—along with the flat-footed prose of the article itself—"Though Mr. Zukofsky's name was not too familiar to the public, he was well known among poets"—worked together to seem, in retrospect, scant praise indeed. The headline of that obituary foregrounded Zukofsky's perhaps most publicly prominent moment (his "leadership" back in the 1930s of the Objectivist "School"—a movement of which the *Poetry* issue mentioned earlier was a catalyzing moment), and the obituary itself stressed that his work had been "included in 'An Objectivist Anthology' " (in fact, Zukofsky had himself edited and contributed to *An "Objectivists" Anthology* in 1932). A quotation from the poet's wife, Celia, further served to stress his lack of recognition: " 'He felt his work was deserving of wider recognition but it was not his nature to complain or express envy about others,' Mrs. Zukofsky once said." All in all, while the obituary showered Zukofsky with secondhand praise, it gave, as is the way of obituaries, little firsthand evidence for its claim that this seventy-four-year-old native New Yorker had been one of this century's most fascinating, ambitious, and accomplished poets.

Physically and personally unprepossessing—an apparitionally thin, chain-smoking hypochondriac, in his later years Zukofsky saw visitors only with extreme reluctance, rarely spoke above a whisper, and seemed to live in perpetual fear of "drafts"—this child of Yiddish-speaking immigrants came to master the English language more thoroughly than any of his contemporaries and to create a large body of writings of unsurpassed intellectual rigor, emotional subtlety, and aural delicacy. Around 1950, in a much-quoted passage of the long poem *"A"*, his most expansive single work, Zukofsky would define his poetics in mathematical terms:

> I'll tell you.
> About my *poetics*—
>
> $$\int_{\text{speech}}^{\text{music}}$$
>
> An integral
> Lower limit speech
> Upper limit music
>
> No?
> ["A"-12, 138]

These lines' wry ending—not a lapel-grabbing "no?" but a sweetly Yiddish "*nu?*"—does not detract from their centrality to Zukofsky's conception of poetry. The essence of an integral's limits is that they are never reached, only approached—poetry is never quite music, never quite speech—but one should stress at the outset that Zukofsky's verse spends more time in the upper than the lower reaches of this integral; it proposes a species of pleasure that is more dependent on sound than on paraphrasable meaning. But this poetry is never meaningless, even at its most seemingly recondite: in Wallace Stevens's words, it "resist[s] the intelligence," not completely but "almost successfully" (*Opus Posthumous* 197).

It is characteristic that Zukofsky would define his poetry in terms borrowed from calculus, for he felt more in common with engineers and scientists than he did with most poets. The former's habits of concrete observation, careful measurement, and precise calculation, after all, accorded better with his notion of the poetic labor than did the latter's all too often unformed sentiment and personal outpourings. In the composer he most admired, Johann Sebastian Bach, Zukofsky saw a similar interest in precision and mathematical structure. But even with this emphasis on the structural, the formal, and the mathematical, Zukofsky never forgot the Horatian maxim of conjoined pleasure and instruction, the delight that his teaching anthology *A Test of Poetry* prescribes as the proper measure of verse: "The test of poetry is the range of pleasure it affords us as sight, sound, and intellection. This is its purpose as art" (*TP* n.p.). As Bruce Comens has rightly noted by italicizing the phrase *as art,* this formulation by no means prohibits poetry from having other functions, and indeed at various points in his career Zukofsky's poetry participates in processes of individual self-creation, in philosophical polemics, and even in political propagandizing (*Apocalypse and After* 169). But none of these uses to which Zukofsky puts his art obscures its recondite and careful, at times dazzling, attention to the visual image, the music of words in combination, and the precision of the "dance of the intellect among words." It is in these three aspects (a tripartite theoretical division fundamental to Zukofsky's poetics and thought, and not unvexed) that Zukofsky's poetry achieves the grace, density, and resonance that leads me to place it among the highest achievements of English-language writing in this century.

I have a number of things to say about Zukofsky, but the principal thesis of this book is fairly simple. In a century during which poetry saw itself losing most of the cultural prestige that it once enjoyed, saw itself rapidly losing cultural ground to the increasingly powerful physical and technological sciences, Louis Zukofsky, in both his poetry and his critical writings, advanced a vision of poetry as the human construction most capable of giving us reliable knowledge both of the world in which we live and of ourselves. That knowledge is for him bound up with poetry's formal essence, which is in turn bound up with the notion of music—an ideally formal art. The knowledge that his poetry imparts, then, can be described as a "musical" knowledge. While this thesis will be qualified and complicated in the pages to come, it remains the theme underlying all the variations and divagations of the book as a whole.

Unfortunately, it remains de rigueur to begin critical examinations of Zukofsky's work with a lament about the poet's lack of recognition, his status as the great undiscovered American modernist poet; Sandra Kumamoto Stanley describes such laments as "now almost a convention of Zukofsky criticism" (4)—and then begins her own book with one. The situation is in part less bleak than it once was, despite what one reviewer has noted as Zukofsky's continued "fashionably marginal" institutional status (Twitchell 186). While Zukofsky himself could not have been unaware of either his own public obscurity or the vacuum into which it seemed his works vanished as soon as they appeared, it has become apparent since his death that one's picture of twentieth-century American writing is incontestably impoverished if one has not come to terms with Zukofsky's writings and influence. One sign, evident since 1978, of the poet's increasing recognition is the remarkable and growing amount of critical attention paid to Zukofsky's work—at least three full-length studies, two collections of essays, and substantial sections of at least seven books (not to mention scores of fugitive essays and appreciations)—not enough perhaps to merit the announcement of a Zukofsky "industry" but certainly enough to signal that this is a poet whom the academy has begun (if only begun) to take seriously. More tellingly, in the years since Zukofsky's death poets and schools of poetics profoundly influenced by his example have emerged into public prominence, announcing their debt to Zukofsky as they attain the institutional pulpits from which to do so. And Zukofsky's name has begun to be heard in quarters where one least expected it. Some early lines of *"A"* appeared as the weekly "Book Bag" contest clue in an early-1995 *Washington Post Book World;* the implicit criterion for such inclusion—a writer must be neither *too* obscure nor a household name—suggests that Zukofsky's work has reached the stage of being among what an educated reader "ought to know."

The first critical shibboleth that such an educated reader must overcome says that Zukofsky is worthy only of peripheral attention, that he is little more than a disciple of Ezra Pound. It is true that Zukofsky and Pound enjoyed a decades-long (if at times sorely strained) friendship and that Zukofsky's poetics are to a large extent grounded in the imagistic, juxtapositional mode that Pound pioneered. In fact, I am convinced that the relationship with Pound is central to understanding Zukofsky's achievement—hence the attention I pay it here—but I am as well convinced that their relationship, while it may have begun in the mode of master and disciple, ultimately became a dialogue between equals, analogous perhaps to that of Emerson and Thoreau. Zukofsky maintained friendships with many of the major modernists besides Pound—Williams, Moore, Cummings—and would later in life assert a deep-seated kinship with Wallace Stevens, prominent representative of what many have seen as a poetic tradition diametrically opposed to Pound's. Zukofsky was also greatly influenced by the visual poetics and wordplay of French poet Guillaume Apollinaire, a major innovator whose work Pound for the most part offhandedly dismissed. While Pound was the poet to whom Zukofsky turned for practical advice on publishing and promoting his work, it could be argued that Gertrude Stein and James Joyce are just as important to Zukofsky's developing poetics. The young poets who came to learn from and pay homage to Zukofsky in the 1950s and 1960s, unlike his first critics—and many critics even now—were well aware that the writer they admired was no belated follower of Pound. While Zukofsky deeply admired Pound's poetry, the content, style, and formal invention of his own poems are not those of anyone's disciple; his poetics are inarguably his alone.

I stress this filiation with Pound at the outset, however, for I think it important in understanding both the nature of Zukofsky's art and the originality of his achievement—the manner in which he pushes beyond the example of even his closest immediate predecessors. Over his half-century writing career, Zukofsky pressed past the boundaries of the modernist poetics from which his works sprang, in the process laying the groundwork for a whole range of contemporary innovative writing practices that neither Pound, Williams, nor any other English-language poet of their generation could have foreseen. Zukofsky's writing career spans the century from Eliot's *The Waste Land* (1922) and Pound's *A Draft of XXX Cantos* (1930) to Robert Creeley's *Pieces* (1969), Michael Palmer's *Without Music* (1977), and Susan Howe's *Secret History of the Dividing Line* (1978). More important than simple chronological sweep, however, is the way Zukofsky's career seems both to inspire and to model a shift from the modernist to the postmodernist, from a post–Great War poetics of aesthetic rebellion to a post–Cold War poetics of linguistic and cultural experimentation and exploration.[2]

My approach to Zukofsky is both chronological and synchronic, both historical and abstract. To begin, and to provide a context for my approaches to Zukofsky, I open this study with a brief sketch of the poet's life and works—a narrative that I hope will provide a frame within which his texts, ideas, and developments can be contextualized and seen in mutual perspective. But at the outset of *Bottom: On Shakespeare,* Zukofsky's own study of the English poet he most admired, the poet announces quite emphatically that he is not interested in pursuing a reading of Shakespeare that tries to read into the canon of plays and poems the mental and emotional life progress of their author: "Guessing at the chronology of the forty-four items of [Shakespeare's] canon, the critics have been insistent on seeing his ideas grow, his feelings mature, his heart go through more exploits than a heart can, except as may be vaguely intimated from the beat and duration of any of the lines or works." Instead, Zukofsky asserts, he will "consider the forty-four items of the canon as one work, sometimes poor, sometimes good, sometimes great, always regardless of the time in which it was composed, and so, despite defects of quality, durable as one thing from 'itself never turning' " (*B* 13).

This is, in part, what I do in this book. At various moments—especially those chapters dealing with Zukofsky's poetics, his conception of poetic language, and his notion of the relationship between language and knowledge—I treat Zukofsky's entire body of poetic and critical writing as a synchronic whole—"one work." I do this not merely because of Zukofsky's critical approach to Shakespeare but because on certain matters Zukofsky came to convictions early in his writing career and held to them with little modification for the rest of his life. Carroll F. Terrell quotes Hugh Kenner on Zukofsky's early maturing: " 'One of the interesting things about Louis is that he came to complete maturity in poetry so quickly and so young.' Kenner suggests that by the time he was twenty-four, he had almost perfected his art, and by the time he was twenty-six, the rest of his life's work had been roughly laid out" (*LZMP* 145). Zukofsky's writings consistently demonstrate that the ideas expressed in his earliest critical articles, the "Objectivist" manifestos drafted when he was twenty-six or twenty-seven, would remain operative in his thought (with the inevitable terminological modifications) through *A Test of Poetry* (1935–40, published 1948), *Bottom: On Shakespeare* (1947–60, published 1963), and his very last critical work, the 1971 lecture "For Wallace Stevens."

At the same time, however, critical ideas that Zukofsky held throughout his lifetime produce a radically different poetic object in 1978's *80 Flowers* than in 1941's *55 Poems,* which was composed between 1923 and 1935. Certain assumptions about the function and importance of poetic form, many of them derived from such high modernist sources as his friend Ezra Pound, are fundamental to Zukofsky's work early and late. But the way in which Zukofsky explores a specific and central idea of poetic modernism, the notion of "musical" form, shifts and develops over the course of his career. These shifts and developments can be especially clearly gauged by looking at how Zukofsky develops his concept of fugal form in the early movements of *"A"* and by observing how that concept changes and evolves from that poem's inception in 1927 to its completion in 1974.

Separate and apart (however artificially) from my examination of the diachronic development of ideas and techniques over the course of Zukofsky's life is Zukofsky's own development as a poet and thinker within history, a writer whose works were influenced and shaped by the historical and cultural milieus in which he moved. In Chapters 5 and 6, as well as in various moments in the rest of this book, I try to give some sense of the backgrounds to Zukofsky's thought, not merely the literary influences, the writers he knew, read, and corresponded with, but the social and political positions in which he found himself. One of the great revelations of recent criticism of the Romantics has been a flood of studies situating Blake, Wordsworth, Coleridge, and the rest in their contemporary political contexts.[3] Such criticism has by no means impoverished the poetry, or limited our readings of it to the most vulgarly political, but instead has enriched our understanding of the various layers of signification of the poems and has (or ought to have) enhanced our appreciation of the poets' achievements. I have tried to do something similar in my readings of Zukofsky's political and social backgrounds, to place in even greater relief the extraordinary achievement of his writings.

I conceive of this book as an advanced introduction to Zukofsky's thought and writing. More detailed discussions of individual works can be found in Barry Ahearn's *Zukofsky's "A": An Introduction* and Michele J. Leggott's *Reading Zukofsky's 80 Flowers*, as well as in numerous individual essays. A more wide-ranging account of how other poets and thinkers have influenced Zukofsky's writing can be found in Sandra Kumamoto Stanley's *Louis Zukofsky and the Transformation of a Modern American Poetics*. I have aimed here, through an overview of Zukofsky's career and works and through intensive discussions of a number of salient ideas, clusters of ideas, and texts, to offer a reader three things: first and most important, a sense of the ideas and themes that motivate and are played out in Zukofsky's most important works, and an idea of how his poetry, formally and thematically, advances those ideas; second, a sense of Zukofsky's importance in twentieth-century American poetry and of his place as a peer within a constellation of modernists ranging from Pound and Eliot, on the transatlantic side, to Wallace Stevens, on the cisatlantic; and finally, an idea of the influence that Zukofsky has had on younger generations of American poets—poets now in their full maturity, producing works comparable in importance to Zukofsky's own.

My first chapter, as I have mentioned, is literary biography, a fairly detailed outline of Zukofsky's career and writings that aims, among other things, to show the relationship among his various and varied projects. Chapters 2 through 4 address the philosophical problem at the heart of Zukofsky's work: the epistemological uncertainty that manifests itself as skepticism. Although Zukofsky tends to dismiss the question of the reliability of human knowledge rather cavalierly when he addresses it directly, that problem remains implicit throughout his work. It is, I would venture, the heresy that both his poetry and prose exist to refute, and my readings of *Bottom: On Shakespeare* (a massive epistemological treatise disguised as a work of literary criticism) and "I's (pronounced *eyes*)" (an important mid-period poetic sequence) trace Zukofsky's critique of skepticism in many of its manifestations. *Bottom* advances a deceptively simple-seeming equation that seems to deny philosophical skepticism any validity whatsoever—a calculus of perception that places absolute trust in the evidence of the physical senses. Yet this rejection of epistemology is complicated both by *Bottom*'s quotational and juxtapositional form—which seems to argue that knowledge is grounded not in the individual's senses but in the community's agreement—and, what is more important, by Zukofsky's own poetry—which emphasizes both the communality of human knowledge and the extent to which knowledge is only transmissible through language, a shared human construct.

Chapters 5 and 6 examine Zukofsky as a poet within history, and at an almost uniquely illuminating location within the series of *Kulturkämpfen* that have characterized our century: on the one hand, the child of immigrant Jewish parents striving to force an entry into an overwhelmingly Gentile, implicitly and explicitly anti-Semitic high modernism; on the other, a hyperintellectual modernist trying to set down, in the dense parataxis and "fugal form" of his *"A"*, the manifestations of the class struggle that the Communist literary establishment preferred portrayed in the black-and-white images of hagiography and demonization. In Chapter 5 I argue that Zukofsky's conception of the poet's task, as that conception emerges into its full maturity in "A"-12, is dependent on the cultural influences of Zukofsky's own Jewish roots and is in part a reaction to the concept of "tradition" advanced by T. S. Eliot and to a more-or-less overtly anti-Semitic high modernist cultural agenda. In Chapter 6 I examine Zukofsky's identity as a Marxist modernist (a conjunction that has particularly interested many commentators committed simultaneously to left-wing political and avant-garde aesthetic causes) and look at the ways in which his modernist aesthetics worked to alienate him from the Communist Party literary establishment of the 1930s, especially as that conflict was played out in his relationship with the Party literary magazine, *New Masses.*

Chapters 7 through 9 examine the role of poetic form in Zukofsky's writing and discuss both his conception of language as a phenomenon that manifests itself in various physical states and his adoption and transformation of a Poundian notion of musical form in poetry. Chapter 7 looks at the relationship between music and poetry in the rhetoric of high modernism, at modernist theories of musical form in poetry, and most specifically at the Paterian-Poundian notions that seem to lie beneath the idea of fugal form that is played out in the movements of Zukofsky's epic poem *"A"*. Chapter 8 traces the poetic fugue in various sections of *"A"*, from its fairly straightforward structuring of "A"-1 to the almost numbingly drawn-out clusters of themes and images of "A"-12. Chapter 9 examines the metamorphosis the fugal form has undergone by the end of the poem—the sublimely dense "A"-22 and -23. These movements, along with *80 Flowers*, are the works that most perplex the casual reader; in their obscurity they seem to threaten the sort of uncommunicative solipsism that Zukofsky's theory of knowledge most fears. I argue that while "A"-22 and -23 are indeed difficult, they are difficult in ways for which the whole of "A"-1 through "A"-21 has been preparing a reader. "A"-22 and -23 represent not an incomprehensible poetic leap forward but the fruition of compositional and structural techniques Zukofsky had been developing throughout his career.

Chapters 10 and 11 aim to locate Zukofsky for the reader of contemporary American poetry. I begin by examining Zukofsky's own reading of Wallace Stevens—a reading that draws clearly the areas of difference and (perhaps surprising) commonality between the two figures. Zukofsky himself professed a radical closeness between his work and that of Stevens—a kinship spanning the half-century of life he shared with the poet of *Harmo-*

nium, closer even than that to the works of Pound or Williams. Zukofsky's reading of Stevens is not merely a fascinating conjunction of two ostensibly unlike poets, or an index of the former's idiosyncratic interpretive methods. That reading forecasts similar readings of Stevens, and similar strategies of appropriation, in the Language poets Charles Bernstein and Michael Palmer, participants in a movement that to some degree explicitly furthers Zukofsky's tradition of linguistic innovation.

In Chapter 11 I consider all too briefly the fruit of Zukofsky's achievements in two American poets of a generation contemporary with, or a bit older than, the Language poets: Ronald Johnson and John Taggart. As the end of this century nears, there is a growing consensus in the poetic community that Zukofsky is at the very least an important figure, and there are a large number of poets—ranging from such exponents of the "New American Poetry" as Allen Ginsberg and Robert Creeley to experimentalists like the Language poets Bernstein, Palmer, Bob Perelman, and Ron Silliman—who look to Zukofsky as a central (perhaps, along with Gertrude Stein, *the* central) figure of American modernism. Part of what I hope to do here is suggest some reasons for this centrality, and one of those reasons must necessarily be that Zukofsky has filled some need for the younger poets who have looked to him. The nature of that need will of course be reflected in the use that those writers have made of Zukofsky's work, the examples they have found in him. Accordingly, I have pursued my examination of Zukofsky's legacy in contemporary poetry by looking at radically different aspects of his influence upon, on the one hand, Bernstein and Palmer, and, on the other, Taggart and Johnson. There is already a struggle over Zukofsky's legacy, over which poets have most "truly" taken his lessons to heart and which are merely using the authority of his name to advance their own aesthetic agendas. Such arguments are perhaps the clearest evidence that Zukofsky's work remains alive and influential: its very status as a site for contestation demonstrates its power and suggestiveness.

Finally, in an admittedly polemical conclusion—a section no doubt more tediously theoretical than any of my earlier chapters—I discuss the implications of this book's governing metaphor, a "poetry of knowledge." Does poetry, in our own postmodern era, indeed give us knowledge? Is the knowledge it proffers identical to the positivistic knowledge offered by the sciences? How ought we to reconfigure our ideas of knowledge itself in order to accept what Zukofsky's poetry, in particular, offers us? My conclusions are no doubt far from definitive; but tenuousness is very much in the spirit of Zukofsky himself, a poet whose lectures, interview responses, and late poetic syntax all gesture toward an interpretive openness and a generative lack of closure.

I am well aware that this study is itself a critical intervention, that even as it proposes itself as a study *of* Zukofsky, or even at times an appreciation of his work, it is as well an exercise in canon-formation, in determining which poets and poems will be considered "standard" a century hence. I make no bones about the fact that I consider Zukofsky a major poet, an important artist of the American twentieth century. But neither my simply saying so, nor even the testimony of other critics and poets, will make his work either popular or canonical. When one aims, however, if not to make Zukofsky's a household name, then at least to advance his reputation among readers of American poetry, one must demonstrate, both through overviews of his work and career and through intensive examinations of individual poems and critical texts, the precise extent to which Zukofsky contributes to and advances the projects of twentieth-century American poetry and the extent to which his writing and career are articulated with the most pressing issues—political, philosophical, literary—of his and our day.

I hope this book suggests some of the pleasures Zukofsky makes available to his readers. Too often critical studies of figures as admittedly recondite as Zukofsky make the poetry of their subjects about as attractive as a root canal—a root canal, that is, which includes the moral payoff of having done something simultaneously difficult and virtuous. I believe that Zukofsky's work, even at its intellectually thorniest, offers a species of pleasure that is both profound and familiar: profound, in that it exercises our faculties to their utmost limits, along the way exhilarating and astonishing us with its ingenuity and variety of invention; familiar, in that it addresses, in a fresh and resonantly intelligent manner, the timeless themes of Western poetry, among them the beauty of the natural world, death and bereavement, the joys of creation, and above all, love, in all its guises. And that work makes peerless use of the instrument of language, modulating the denotations, connotations, etymologies, and sounds of words in patterns that are wonderfully consistent with any definition of poetic excellence that does not take as its primary criterion an immediate readerly transparency.

I cannot claim that Zukofsky will ever be a widely popular poet (leaving aside the question of whether such a creature even exists in the United States in the last years of this century). Some of his short poems, and some of the movements of *"A"*, have the openness and plainspoken, almost prosy guilelessness that often attracts readers to William Carlos Williams. Yet, for the most part, Zukofsky's poetry makes demands on his audience that Williams himself perhaps best formulated in "January Morning": "I wanted to write a poem / that you would understand. / For what good is it to me / if you can't understand it? / But you got to try hard—" (*Collected Earlier Poems* 165–66). "Trying hard" is of the essence in approaching Zukofsky; it is an effort that as often as not involves reeducating oneself in how one thinks about and reads poetry. I hope to suggest, however, that such trying in the end pays off richly in intellectual and musical pleasures—the very pleasures, perhaps, that the reader with a true taste for poetry values most highly.

1

"More than the words say"

Louis Zukofsky's Writing Life

Shakespeare led a life of Allegory: his works are the comments on it.
— John Keats (*Selected Letters* 229)

Anyone hoping to write the story of a poet's writing life is apt to receive that poet's autobiography with something like relief: here, at least, is a provisional template—a place to start. Louis Zukofsky's *Autobiography* of 1970, at first glance, frustrates such expectation. It is, to say the least, an odd book. The *Autobiography* consists of twenty-two musical settings by Zukofsky's wife, Celia, and eighteen of his shorter poems, interspersed with five brief prose paragraphs of autobiography and autobiographical reflection. Zukofsky's *Autobiography*, unlike works of the same title by W. B. Yeats or William Carlos Williams, declines to narrate its author's life at all conventionally. Nonetheless, it brings out a number of saliencies concerning Zukofsky. The fact that it consists of musical settings of his poems makes clear Zukofsky's conviction that the arts of music and poetry are closely entwined: as he quotes Dante, the poem is *"The completed action of one writing words to be set to music"* (*Auto* [7]). That the settings are by his wife, who, like his son, was a musician and composer, emphasizes the familial circle Zukofsky will so often celebrate. "My wife Celia and son Paul," he writes, "have been the only reason for the poet's persistence" (*Auto* 59). And as for the *Autobiography*'s form—a form that emphasizes the poetry *as* music while simultaneously failing to serve up the details of its subject's life—this form itself conforms to the book's two epigraphs. The first is from Zukofsky's novel *Little* and is spoken by the character Dala Baballo von Chulnt, a transparent stand-in for Zukofsky himself: "I too have been charged with obscurity, tho it's a case of listeners wanting to know too much about me, more than the words say"; the second simply clarifies the first: "As a poet I have always felt that the work says all that needs to be said of one's life" (*Auto* [5]).

That life, however, does bear pursuing, at least briefly. While Zukofsky's may not have been, as Keats says of Shakespeare's, a "life of allegory," it is certainly a life that is intimately entwined with his poetry and that sheds light upon it.[1] Zukofsky was born on Manhattan's Lower East Side in 1904, the same year the novelist Henry James revisited America for the last time. The poet would enjoy drawing attention to this coincidence, explaining in the *Autobiography*, "The contingency appeals to me as a forecast of the first-generation American infusion into twentieth-century literature" (*Auto* 13). "Infusion" is delicately put, with the hindsight of a man of sixty-six, but it serves to emphasize Zukofsky's awareness of his own anomalous position as a Jew in the midst of a modernist movement in literature whose heroes, such as James himself, would portray Western culture as fundamentally endangered by Jewish influences. Zukofsky's parents, Pinchos (ca. 1860–1950) and Chana Pruss Zukofsky (ca. 1862–1927), were born in the part of Russia that is now Lithuania; Pinchos immigrated to the United States in 1898, working as a pants-presser and night watchman until he could send for his wife and children in 1903. These immigrant parents are important presences in Zukofsky's work: the figure of his mother is central to his early "Poem beginning 'The' " (1926), and he mourns her 1927 death in the play *Arise, arise* (1936), in various early sections of *"A"*, and as late as 1945 in "A Song for the Year's End." Pinchos Zukofsky's Orthodox faith was a tradition against which his son reacted early—he would later claim that his own period of religious crisis lasted "from the age of 10 to 13 and no more" (*P* 29)—but the figure of Zukofsky's father would come to play an important role in the conception of the poet's task he developed in the process of composing *"A"*.

Zukofsky, the only one of his parent's children to be born in the New World, grew up in a Yiddish-speaking household in the midst of a Yiddish-speaking community. In *Autobiography* he is careful to distinguish between his "first exposure to letters"—the "Yiddish theaters, most memorably the Thalia on the Bowery" (33), to which his brother Morris took him, where "by the age of nine [he] had seen a good deal of Shakespeare, Ibsen, Strindberg and Tolstoy performed—all in Yiddish"—and his "first exposure to English," "to be exact, P.S. 7 on Chrystie and Hester Streets." As Zukofsky points out, he read both Longfellow's *Hiawatha* and Aeschylus's *Prometheus Bound* first in Yiddish. To approach *Hiawatha*, that paradigmatically American poem, in Yiddish; and to find Keats "rather difficult" beside the forceful syntax of Burns's "Scots, wha hae," reading the latter two poets with no sense of the institutional wisdom that the one represents a "dominant" tradition while the earthy vernacular of the other represents a "quaint" offshoot of the major stream of English letters—these must have been crucial experiences in forming the young Zukofsky's sense of language itself. By age eleven, Zukofsky had read all of Shakespeare (in English), a feat forecasting the wholesale consumption of texts that would mark his intellectual history, and forecasting as well his lifelong fascination with the poet who, on the Bowery as in the Raj, represented the apex of English letters.

The Jewish immigrant culture of turn-of-the-century New York was by no means either anti-intellectual or parochial, and to a boy as intelligent and curious as Zukofsky it afforded a wealth of cultural opportunities. Although he could have gone to City College for free, his parents sacrificed to send him to Columbia, where he studied philosophy and English, was a member of the student literary society, and saw his poems published in the student literary magazines. One of Zukofsky's closest friends in his first years at Columbia was Whittaker Chambers. At this point in his life, the future accuser of Alger Hiss and author of *Witness* (perhaps the most famous anti-Communist document of the century) was—to use Senator McCarthy's phrase—a card-carrying member of the Communist Party and could introduce the young Zukofsky both to radical modernist literature and to Party circles. In 1922 Chambers was expelled from Columbia for publishing an "atheistic" play in a student magazine; he remained an associate of Zukofsky: in 1931 he appeared among the poets of that new movement, the "Objectivists." Zukofsky's own writings of his Columbia period are not particularly political: they show a sensitive young man struggling to find his voice in poetry, with some success. One poem at least achieved publication in Harriet Monroe's *Poetry* (Chicago): "Of Dying Beauty," published in 1924, is moribundly conventional, if skillfully written, and shows little evidence of what would be the young poet's most striking talents—an at times whimsical lyricism combined with an almost astringent angularity of diction.[2]

By the time he left Columbia with his master's degree in English in 1926 (he never received the baccalaureate, having dropped out of the required physical education course), Zukofsky had studied with some of Columbia's most prominent scholars, including the poet Mark Van Doren, the philosopher John Dewey, and the novelist John Erskine, whose "Great Books" approach to literature Zukofsky would lampoon in "Poem beginning 'The.' " He had also written, as his M.A. thesis, the earliest version of his long essay "Henry Adams: A Criticism in Autobiography." Zukofsky's fascination with Adams—scion of perhaps the first family of Anglo-Saxon Boston, a self-proclaimed decadent representative of a heroic tradition, and like his contemporary Henry James a culture-hero for American modernism—was to persist through much of his career. Adams's late and rather recondite ideas about the progression of "phases" in history would greatly influence Zukofsky, and the form of his Adams essay, the vast majority of which is quotation from Adams's works, looks forward to Zukofsky's mature compositional methods in both criticism and poetry, where the magpie-like collaging of quotation lies at the heart of his writing.

Just as Pound, even before he introduced himself to London literary circles, had firmly decided that Yeats was the only living poet who mattered, the young Zukofsky had by the late 1920s clearly singled out Ezra Pound as his most important contemporary. Zukofsky first brought himself to Pound's attention in 1927 by sending the older poet (who by this time was comfortably self-exiled in Italy) his astonishingly precocious "Poem beginning 'The,' " which Pound published in 1928 in his short-lived periodical *Exile.* " 'The,' " in large part a response to T. S. Eliot's 1922 *The Waste Land,* rather caustically castigates the widespread modernist pessimism regarding what seemed the post–Great War disintegration of Western Culture. The poem looks forward to a new hopeful future both in literature, as stimulated by the "first generation . . . infusion" of new blood into the American body politic, and in politics itself, as demonstrated by the brave new experiment being carried forth in Soviet Russia, the homeland of the mother Zukofsky's poem also mourns. Pound was appropriately impressed, both by "Poem beginning 'The' " and by Zukofsky's critical sense, which he demonstrated in his 1929 essay on *The Cantos* (an essay that was among the first analyses of Pound's work-in-progress)—so impressed, in fact, that he persuaded the Chicago heiress and poetic impresario Harriet Monroe to allow Zukofsky to edit the February 1931 issue of her magazine *Poetry,* a journal for which Pound had long served as formal or informal overseas editor.

That issue, entitled " 'Objectivists' 1931," was the first appearance of what would later be seen as the Objectivist movement: a group of poets that included Zukofsky, George Oppen, Carl Rakosi, and one of Zukofsky's greatest influences, the New York poet Charles Reznikoff (1894–1976). The *Poetry* issue also included a number of writers whose associations with the movement ranged from commitment (William Carlos Williams) to bemused bewilderment (Kenneth Rexroth), among them John Wheelwright, Harry Roskolenkier, and Whittaker Chambers (who no doubt is, as Eliot Weinberger points out, "the most famous Objectivist" by far [*Works on Paper* 90]). In order to provide the *Poetry* issue with a manifesto of poetics, Zukofsky adapted an already-drafted essay on his friend Reznikoff, outfitting it with an elaborate theoretical apparatus. The resulting document, "Sincerity and Objectification: *With Special Reference to the Work of Charles Reznikoff,*" is more important as a description of how Zukofsky conceived of his own work than as a manifesto of an emergent movement, but it remains, in the truncated form in which it is published in *Prepositions,* a crucial text for understanding his poetics. Zukofsky would later be at some pains to insist that there never existed anything that could be called "Objectivism," insisting that the whole trappings of a poetic "school" had been reached at Monroe's insistence that his issue be structured around a "movement." Objectivist *doctrine,* however, was clearly not just an ad hoc construction for Zukofsky, and there is some tenuous evidence that he regarded the movement—at least for a short time—as more than an ex post facto umbrella under which to gather a number of more-or-less like-minded writers.

Whatever the ultimate truth about the Objectivist movement might be—and this remains a matter of somewhat divisive critical debate[3]—the " 'Objectivists' 1931" issue of *Poetry* was followed in 1932 by *An "Objectivists" Anthology,* edited by Zukofsky and published by TO Publishers, a loose consortium of Zukofsky, Reznikoff, and Oppen, the whole underwritten by Oppen, who was the only member of the group with any financial resources to speak of. While the number of poets in the *Anthology* was considerably diminished from the *Poetry* issue, there was little indication of any single aesthetic position shared among them. Zukofsky himself was at the time writing (along with a number of short poems) both the prose work *Thanks to the Dictionary,* a long short story of sorts that through its largely aleatoric compositional method hearkens forward to the works of John Cage and Jackson Mac Low,[4] and a critical study, *The Writing of Guillaume Apollinaire.* The bulk of this study, like the Henry Adams essay, consists of arranged and juxtaposed quotations from its subject's writings. This work was published in Paris in 1934 as *Le Style Apollinaire* in a translation by the French critic René Taupin, with both Taupin and Zukofsky listed as authors; most copies of the edition (save for the six copies Taupin brought back with him to the United States) were almost immediately destroyed in a warehouse fire, and it remains one of the rarest documents of American modernism.[5]

This "collaboration" with Taupin, himself author of the groundbreaking study *L'Influence du symbolisme française sur la poésie américaine de 1910 à 1920* and a friend of Zukofsky, was something of a ruse designed to help Taupin, a reluctant writer, along the tenure track of his academic position; he, in turn, funneled part of his salary to Zukofsky during the time of the book's writing. It was one of a number of exigencies to which Zukofsky was forced in order to support himself in the lean Depression years. Zukofsky translated a popular biography of Albert Einstein;

taught for an academic year at the University of Wisconsin, Madison (1930–31), where Kenneth Rexroth was his colleague; drew a stipend as the editor of TO Publishers for about a year; and from 1935 until the spring of 1942 worked, as did so many other writers, artists, and intellectuals of the day, for the Works Progress Administration. This work was not merely clock-punching for Zukofsky, although it did occupy time that he no doubt would have preferred to devote to poetry. From 1936 to 1940, Zukofsky wrote essays and radio scripts on various aspects of American craft and design for the *Index of American Design*, a large-scale project that aimed to record and catalogue the entire range of American handicrafts and design from colonial times through the end of the nineteenth century. He assiduously researched these pieces, in the process gaining an intimate knowledge of the history of American kitchenware, tinsmithing, friendship quilts, and other forms of material culture. This work strengthened his appreciation for the individual craftsman and cemented his own ideology of the poet as craftsman, rather than expressive vessel. The essays and scripts themselves, far more wide-ranging in content than their ostensible subjects might indicate, are documents of cultural criticism very much in the tradition of Henry Adams's *Mont Saint Michel and Chartres* or Williams Carlos Williams's *In the American Grain.*[6]

The 1930s were a busy and important decade for Zukofsky, both personally and artistically. The " 'Objectivists' 1931" *Poetry* issue and *An "Objectivists" Anthology* had made important connections for him, alerting both prominent and emerging poets to his existence and bringing down on him the scorn of such readers and reviewers as Morris Schappes and Yvor Winters.[7] Pound's continuing interest in Zukofsky's proper education brought him as a visitor to the "Ezuversity" at Rapallo in 1933, where he met Basil Bunting (1900–1985), a British poet included in both the *Poetry* issue and the anthology (Bunting is sometimes considered the sole English Objectivist). While Bunting's and Zukofsky's aesthetics and mental processes ultimately diverged—Bunting would fault Zukofsky especially on what he saw as the abstraction of his critical prose—there grew between the two poets a lasting friendship and mutual respect. They remained in close correspondence to the end of Zukofsky's life, and in the preface to his own collected poems Bunting would acknowledge Zukofsky as one of the two living poets (the other being Pound) who, "in his sterner, stonier way," had taught him something (*Complete Poems* 3). One inspired reader of the *Poetry* issue was Lorine Niedecker (1903–70), a young poet from Wisconsin. She initiated a correspondence with Zukofsky that continued for forty years, until her own death, and proved herself one of his earliest and most intelligent readers. Her own poetry is at times heavily reminiscent of Zukofsky's, but readers have in recent years come to recognize her as a major talent, one developed and shaped in large part by her personal association and intense correspondence with Zukofsky.[8]

Zukofsky began the 1930s by publishing the first installments of his long poem *"A"*. Much of "A"-1 through "A"-7, written between 1927 and 1930, had appeared in various small magazines, but the collective publication of these "movements" (as Zukofsky would call them) in *An "Objectivists" Anthology* signaled that a major project was clearly under way. *"A"*, which forms the centerpiece of Zukofsky's poetic achievement, is something of an anomaly among modern American long poems in that it is actually finished; part of that accomplishment is due to the fact that Zukofsky, at the very outset of his project, had decided it would consist of twenty-four sections. Barry Ahearn dates to 1927–28 Zukofsky's first overall schema, which specifies a twenty-four-movement length to the poem. The forms, themes, and subject matter of those movements were not clearly defined at the outset of the project—although there were rough titles, later abandoned, in the first schema: "A"-2 would be "The Dead"; "A"-18, "Coeur-de-Leon"; "A"-21, "Johann Sebastian" (*Zukofsky's "A"* 38). It seems clear that Zukofsky's conception of the poem, as is so often the case, shifted as the work progressed. While it would not be unfair to characterize the early movements of *"A"* as quite Poundian in their approach, in later movements Zukofsky effectively abandons (if he ever fully adopted) Pound's poetics of the ideogram—roughly speaking, a group of discrete images or ideas juxtaposed in order to yield a higher singular meaning—and opens his work to a whole range of formal experiments. But unlike Pound in *The Cantos*, Williams in *Paterson*, and Olson in *The*

Maximus Poems, Zukofsky projected a clear—if flexible—armature for his long poem and stuck to it.

The early sections of *"A"*—written in a juxtapositional style closely akin to that of *The Cantos* and informed throughout by the formal analogy of the musical fugue and the themes and lyrics of Bach's *St. Matthew Passion*—are in large part concerned with the political and economic situation of America in the late 1920s and early 1930s. The struggle between the captains of industry and the working masses dominates these early movements, but it is far from the only subject the poem treats. "A"-3, for instance, is in large part an elegy on the suicide of "Ricky," Whittaker Chambers's brother Richard, and finds Zukofsky positioning himself as Joseph of Arimathea to Ricky's Christ. The theme of death and resurrection, already implicit in the Passion itself, is firmly laid out in these first sections; Zukofsky deploys the image of "liveforever" (an evergreen plant of the *sedum* genus) as an emblem of immortality, whether a personal immortality for which one might hope or the vicarious immortality of artistic creation. In various guises, liveforever will recur up to the very end of Zukofsky's writing life. Like "Poem beginning 'The,' " "A"-4 addresses the subject of origins, "the courses we tide from" ("A"-4, 15), and plays out Zukofsky's status as the partially assimilated child of Orthodox parents, a Jewish poet able neither to accept his fathers' stringent religion and culture nor to claim as wholly his own a broader Western culture that regards him for the most part with hostility.

As I have mentioned, Zukofsky's contribution to *An "Objectivists" Anthology* included the first seven movements of *"A"*, a block comparable in cohesiveness to, if not nearly so long as, Pound's *A Draft of XXX Cantos* (1926). The seven movements culminated in "A"-7, a sequence of seven formally regular sonnets in which the poet contemplates a set of "street closed" wooden sawhorses—each of which, in shape, resembles a pair of capital *A*s—and then, through a series of dazzling puns and shifts of linguistic register, transforms them into imaginary "horses" and puts them through a breathtaking set of paces, culminating in their self-revelation: "words, words, we are words, horses, manes, / words" ("A"-7, 42). These seven sonnets fold in everything that has come before in the poem—the *St. Matthew Passion* with its themes of resurrection and judgment, the struggles of the working masses, Ricky's death, Zukofsky's own artistic and cultural identity—and they do so by taking as their primary objects of attention language itself, the literal forms and shapes of words, the relationships between the sounds and motions of words, and the concepts and objects to which they correspond. "A"-7, like a number of other moments in *"A"*, complicates any simple definition one might arrive at of precisely what Objectivist poetics might mean. While I believe the primary meaning of "objectivist" in Zukofsky's usage refers to his notion of the poem as a tangible object, "A"-7 demonstrates that Zukofsky's Objectivist poetics is as concerned with the *objective*, communal existence of language itself—the aural objects that constitute the social, human environment.

In the 1930s, Zukofsky also pursued the concerns of *"A"* in various shorter poems, most notably perhaps in "To my wash-stand" (1932) and " 'Mantis,' " along with its accompanying piece, " *'Mantis,' An Interpretation*" (1934). " 'Mantis' " is a crucial poem for understanding Zukofsky's conception of poetic form and its relation both to free verse innovation and to the history of formal poetry, and it merits discussion at length later in this book. "To my wash-stand" begins with a close physical examination of the poet's bathroom sink, in which the poet acknowledges that the "song / of water" he hears "is a song / entirely in my head" (*CSP* 52), and he moves from there into an imaginative re-creation of the morning ablutions of the poor,

> carefully attentive
> to what they have
> and to what they do not
> have
> [*CSP* 53]

The "flow of water" from the stand's two faucets "occasions invertible counterpoints," bringing forth in vivid detail the sordid realities and privations of a class for whom the morning washing-up is an occasion of attentiveness to the luxuries they lack.

Zukofsky's short poetry of the early 1930s, much of which has a distinctly political bent, was not collected until 1941's *55 Poems*, published by a small press in Prairie City, Illinois. He wrote steadily, publishing somewhat sporadically in the little magazines, but saw the widespread recognition promised by the Objectivist movement rapidly evaporating. Oppen and Rakosi, finding a literary life at odds with their social concerns, abandoned writing poetry altogether; Reznikoff continued as he always had, publishing his own work on his own hand-operated press; and the other Objectivists, finding the group with no organization or staying power comparable to that of, for instance, the Surrealists in France, simply drifted away.

Zukofsky's primary literary contacts during the latter part of the 1930s were with his close friend Williams, with his long-distance correspondent Niedecker, and in his transatlantic correspondence with Bunting and Pound; that latter correspondence, however, more and more swerved to the political, as Pound sought to impress his own views on fascism and social credit on a skeptical—and in fact quite outrightly Marxist—Zukofsky. From passionately "instigating" Zukofsky to form movements and schools at the beginning of the decade, Pound turned to berating his recalcitrant younger colleague for his misguided political views, even chastising him on a number of occasions for falling back into invidious "racial characteristics" (*P/Z* 163). In Pound's correspondence with Bunting, the extent to which Pound's anti-Semitism poisoned his opinion of Zukofsky is unfortunately evident: in 1935 Pound would write Bunting that Zukofsky "wants to argue about how good his defects are. and like every other god damn KIKE (this is not for transmission) he wants to put it over, and have others ADMIRE it." Bunting stood up to Pound on Zukofsky's behalf in ways that Zukofsky himself rarely would, commenting to Pound, "It makes me sick to see you covering yourself with that [anti-Semitic] filth. It is not an arguable question" (Makin, *Bunting* 78–79). Zukofsky, it seems, preferred to let pass all but the most outrageous manifestations of Pound's skewed worldview.

In 1933, working as supervisor on a WPA writing project, Zukofsky met the musician and composer Celia Thaew. Carroll F. Terrell's interview with Celia Thaew Zukofsky gives a charmingly businesslike account of their meeting, facilitated by Thaew's copy of *In the American Grain* and eventually leading to their first date—"Leonard Bernstein playing a piano piece of Aaron Copland's at Town Hall" (*LZMP* 56). After a protracted friendship and courtship, they were married in August 1939. Celia Zukofsky would become Zukofsky's devoted collaborator, typing his manuscripts and assisting with the elaborate research he carried out for every project he essayed. She would take a direct collaborative role in his translation of Catullus (1969), and the second volume of *Bottom: On Shakespeare* (1963) consisted of her spare operatic setting of Shakespeare's *Pericles, Prince of Tyre.* Her musical talents became an integral part of several of Zukofsky's later works: the *Autobiography,* of course, but also "A"-24, the concluding movement of *"A"*, which is "Celia's L.Z. Masque," an arrangement of a myriad of Zukofsky texts, both poetry and prose, in a four-voice counterpoint to some of Handel's harpsichord pieces.

Their only child, Paul (born 1943), was a young prodigy on the violin; he has gone on to become one of the world's foremost performers and conductors of twentieth-century music. In 1970 Zukofsky would publish a novel, *Little / for careenagers,* a roman à clef dealing with the upbringing of a young violin prodigy whose parents, not coincidentally, are a poet and a pianist. The novel—graceful, whimsical, and full of verbal wit—paints an exceedingly charming picture of the Zukofskys' domestic life; it includes pseudonymous portraits of a number of Zukofsky's acquaintances, including Ezra Pound ("R.Z. Draykup," "from his habit of 'draying' on one's kopf," as Paul Zukofsky explains [*CF* 309]), who during the period the novel describes was incarcerated in St. Elizabeths mental hospital in Washington, D.C. Despite their increasing differences through the course of the 1930s, the postwar Zukofsky still felt a strong bond to his older colleague. He felt Pound's confinement was an unfortunate outcome of a deep-seated desire to reform a demented society: "As [Draykup] put it, 'he hath spoken sooth'—and for Dala [Zukofsky] these archaic words completely expressed the sorrow of his friend's incarceration. In time he would be released, but not cleared of the charge of madness implying a sanity for which he had risked being executed" (*CF* 121). In 1954 Zukofsky, Celia, and Paul visited Pound at St. Elizabeths, where on the lawn of the ward Paul played Gerhard Münch's violin adaptation of Janequin's *Chant des Oiseaux*, Pound's Canto LXXV.

The turn of the 1930s was to mark the end of the period in which politics played a major role in Zukofsky's writings. From 1935 to 1940 he worked on compiling *A Test of Poetry* (published in 1948), a teaching anthology that bears a certain resemblance to Pound's *ABC of Reading*, though Zukofsky's anthology includes far less of its compiler's commentary than does the *ABC;* Zukofsky was, as always, inclined to let his material speak for itself. Significantly, *A Test of Poetry* followed directly on the heels of an aborted project, a *Workers' Anthology* that Zukofsky abandoned in 1935: the turn from the political to the more broadly aesthetic is indicative of an overall shift in Zukofsky's concerns. In the war years, with the birth of his son and the increasingly settled character of his domestic life, Zukofsky grew more inclined to pursue themes of domestic happiness, rather than wider social reformation, as an ideal state to be depicted in his poetry. And while he had both sincere Marxist convictions and very concrete ties to the Communist Party literary establishment through the 1930s, he was increasingly disillusioned at the Party literati's inability or unwillingness to publish, or to promote its causes through, such radically experimental works as his own "A"-8. The first half of "A"-9, which he published himself in 1940, was the last overtly leftist work he would write.

After "A"-8, the directions and forms of *"A"* grew more varied. The first half of "A"-9 was a translation of Cavalcanti's canzone "Donna mi priegha" (a text to which Pound often returned), a translation that not only preserves the elaborate rhyme scheme of the Italian original (a feat even Pound had claimed impossible) but does so by adapting phrases from Marx's *Capital.* Where Cavalcanti's poem had been a painstaking scholastic disquisition on the phenomenon of amorous love, Zukofsky's translation is a discussion of the economic roots of use-value and exchange-value. When Zukofsky returned to "A"-9 in 1948, he completed it by translating the same canzone again, this time using phrases from Spinoza's *Ethics*, making the poem (once again) into an analysis of love. Zukofsky had been fascinated with the ideas of this Jewish philosopher since "Poem beginning 'The,' " and Spinoza's categories of *natura naturans* and *natura naturata* ("nature naturing" and "nature natured"—creator and created, roughly, considered as moments of a single entity) are fundamental to his conception of poetics and recur throughout the early sections of *"A"*. But his turn from Marx to Spinoza at this crucial juncture of his poem is indicative of how the focus of *"A"* has shifted from the public sphere of economics and revolution to a more private one of familial love. "A"-10, a very public poem elegizing the 1940 fall of Paris to the Nazis, was written between the two halves of "A"-9. An argument can be made for "A"-10's importance as a "pivotal movement" of the poem (Comens 153), but I fear I am somehow blind to its achievement. For a poet whose great strength lies in his melodic mastery, this movement takes too literally its own words: "Let a better time say / The poet stopped singing to talk" ("A"-10, 120).

While *"A"*'s formal inventiveness had been evident even as the poem pursued what had at times threatened to become a didactic political dimension, after it turns aside from politics, *"A"*'s formal variety and experimentation become even more prominent. "A"-11 is a formal lyric, based on Cavalcanti's "Perch'io non spero" and addressed to Zukofsky's wife and child after his own death. "A"-12 is as long as the first eleven movements of the poem combined; it is a vast collage, incorporating themes from earlier sections of the poem, materials from the then-in-progress *Bottom: On Shakespeare,* and, perhaps most important, quotations and anecdotes that draw attention to the Zukofsky family. This movement takes familial happiness as a more fitting "epic" subject than class struggle. In contrast to "A"-12's expansive openness, "A"-13 announces itself as a "partita," and its five sections imitate, through their varied forms, the variations between the movements of one of Bach's violin partitas. Among the "subjects" of this movement is the daily life of the Zukofsky family, including a walk by Paul and Louis across the Brooklyn Bridge to the Duane Street Fire Museum and back to their Brooklyn Heights apartment.

It is easier to talk about formal structures, continuities, and discontinuities than about content when discussing Zukofsky's work, in large part because one has the distinct sense that he saw himself as planning structures, the materials of which were less crucial than the formal shapes and their engineering. As far as the later sections of *"A"* go, it is sufficient to note that Zukofsky winds all manner of personal and familial history, philosophy, literature, esoterica, and current events into these knotty but graceful poems: "A"-15, for instance, deals among much else with the death of John F. Kennedy, "A"-18 concerns itself off and on with the Vietnam War, and "A"-19 follows Paul Zukofsky to Genoa for his participation in the Paganini Competition, simultaneously cementing Zukofsky's conceptual bonds with Mallarmé, who is here quoted, paraphrased, and transliterated. "A"-14 announces itself as *"First of / eleven songs / beginning An"* ("A"-14, 315) and indeed each movement from "A"-14 through "A"-24 begins with the letters "an"—a tiny word that is itself a variation of "a." Similarly, the first phrase of each movement plays with and permutes a similar set of phonemes: "A"-14, "beginning" ("A"-14, 314); "A"-15, "An / hinny" ("A"-15, 359); "A"-16, "An / inequality" ("A"-16, 376); "A"-17, "Anemones" ("A"-17, 377); "A"-18, "An unearthing" ("A"-18, 389); "A"-19, "An other" ("A"-19, 408), and so forth. It is to such continuities and variations that we learn to attend in reading *"A"*, for the poem as a whole presents not a narrative or a continuously developed argument but a series of formal structures, interlinked one with another and proceeding out of a common "fugal" impulse—structures that Zukofsky has instantiated with materials from all realms of his life.

"A"-17 and "A"-20 are perhaps exemplary of Zukofsky's conception of what it means to *compose* a poem. "A"-17 is "a coronal for Floss" Williams, an homage to Zukofsky's recently deceased friend William Carlos Williams; it consists wholly of quotations: quotations from Williams's letters to Zukofsky, from all of Zukofsky's writings (prose and poetry) that bear on Williams's work, and, finally, a visual "quotation" of Williams's scrawled signature in Zukofsky's copy of *Pictures from Brueghel* ("A"-17, 388). "A"-20, a "Respond for P.Z.'s tone row / At twenty" ("A"-20, 436), consists simply of a list of the titles of twelve compositions that Paul had written up to the age of twenty, repeated four times in different orders, and a short poem that Paul had written at age nine in response to a poem of Henry VIII's included in *A Test of Poetry*. "Composition," for Zukofsky, is as much the arrangement of previously written texts as it is the wholesale invention of new ones.

The recombination of found materials, central to the Cubist and Surrealist arts of collage, is as well central to Zukofsky's working methods.

Clearly, the obvious parallels that can be drawn between Pound's *The Cantos* and the early movements of *"A"* tend to break down as the latter poem progresses, moving through a wider and wider range of forms and subject matters. A comparison of Pound's and Zukofsky's larger careers is also instructive. Once *The Cantos* were well under way, they became the center of Pound's poetic production; although he wrote large amounts of prose, except for translations (and there were many of those), Pound wrote no substantial poetry outside *The Cantos*. Zukofsky, on the other hand, was continually adding to his corpus of short poems. The collections *Anew* (1946) and *Some Time* (1956) include a number of delicate occasional pieces—birthday poems, wedding poems, valentines—and such important sequences as "Light" and "Chloride of Lime and Charcoal." These poems reflect the Zukofsky family's physical circumstances, their friendships, and the milieu of artists, musicians, and writers within which they (gingerly) moved. "4 Other Countries" and "Stratford-on-Avon," from the volume *Barely and Widely* (1958), record the family's 1957 vacation in Europe and show Zukofsky to be an assiduous literary tourist, seeking out the locales of Shakespeare's plays, classical poets' haunts, and the various "luminous details" of Italy and Provence that Pound presented so memorably in his poetry.

"Stratford-on-Avon," which records the family's visit to Shakespeare's birthplace, reflects Zukofsky's ongoing obsession with this English poet whose plays he had first seen performed in Yiddish. A much weightier, and earlier, evidence of that obsession, however, is Zukofsky's long prose work *Bottom: On Shakespeare*, which he wrote between 1947 and 1960. *Bottom*, as I shall argue, is central to understanding Zukofsky's work. This text is more than an almost unprecedentedly compendious act of homage by one poet to another: in effect it lays out Zukofsky's poetics and theory of knowledge on a grander scale than any other work except *"A"*. It is, however, decidedly heterodox as Shakespeare criticism: Guy Davenport—who compares it to Paul Valèry on Da Vinci, Søren Kierkegaard on Mozart's *Don Giovanni*, Martin

Heidegger on Hölderlin—describes it as "a critical activity happening between the poet and the philosopher; a professor teaching Hölderlin will not recommend it until the student proposes to write a doctoral dissertation" (*Every Force* 106). *Bottom* is large: not only did Zukofsky's own text run to 450 large pages, but it was only the first volume of two: the second volume of *Bottom: On Shakespeare* consists of Celia Zukofsky's setting of Shakespeare's *Pericles, Prince of Tyre*, a play in which Zukofsky saw Shakespeare rewriting the classic plots and tropes of the *Odyssey*. Both its oddness and its sheer bulk made *Bottom* a difficult book to sell. After Zukofsky had spent several years seeking a publisher, he made a deal with the University of Texas, whose Harry Ransom Humanities Research Center coveted his extensive correspondence with Pound and Williams. In lieu of payment for those letters, and for his own manuscript collection, they agreed to publish a limited edition of the complete work. It was finally issued in 1963.

Bottom, as I shall argue at some length, attempts to ground individual human knowledge on a recognition of the other, on the bases of human knowledge established by the community as a whole. A similar position is played out in the important mid-period sequence "I's (pronounced *eyes*)" (composed 1959–60). *I's (pronounced eyes)* (1963) and its "sequel," *After I's* (1964), are two slim volumes of typically angular, oblique poems, many of which are distinctly occasional. There are valentines here, a response to younger poets' recognition, and even a sequence celebrating the family's removal from their longtime abode, "The Old Poet Moves to a New Apartment 14 Times" (1962). Zukofsky, it should be emphasized, was a lifelong New Yorker; "At one time or another," as he notes in the *Autobiography*, "I have lived in all of the boroughs of New York City" (13). After his WPA work ended in 1942, he held a succession of jobs, including a couple of stints as a substitute teacher in the New York City high schools and technical editing jobs for several engineering firms.[9] In 1947 he became an instructor in the English department of the Polytechnic Institute of Brooklyn, where he would teach until 1966, when he retired at the rank of associate professor. It was not a particularly congenial atmosphere for a poet—he would make pointed remarks about the college and his department in *Little*—but Zukofsky made the best of it, teaching a wide range of literature courses and acting as faculty advisor to the poetry club. He was generous with his time and attention to those few students who showed an interest in literature, introducing them not merely to the classics but also to the then obscure works of his friends Niedecker and Reznikoff. At least one fledgling engineer, Hugh Seidman, went on to pursue poetry as a vocation; but in the main Zukofsky thought of his students (as he remarked to Charles Tomlinson) as "my plumbers" (*LZMP* 91).[10]

While Zukofsky was clearly a better teacher than that other poet-pedagogue Mallarmé (who seems to have inspired no poets among his own students and who by all accounts was a thorough failure in the classroom, his tenure marked by the paper dolls his students would pin to his coattails), Zukofsky was plagued by inattentive students—"chalk fights and 'kids of seventeen who cannot sit on their asses' " (*LZMP* 91)—and, like his French precursor, clearly would have preferred attending to his own writing over teaching English composition. In 1966, after Celia had carefully calculated his projected retirement income, Zukofsky retired from teaching to devote himself full-time to his poetry. The couple would eventually move to Port Jefferson, Long Island, where Zukofsky could plan and write his works and Celia could (among other pursuits) cultivate the plants on which Zukofsky would focus so intensely in *80 Flowers.*

It was not until 1965, when the first volume of *ALL* was published by W. W. Norton, that Zukofsky saw his poems printed by a major publisher. His career had begun auspiciously back in 1931, with his own issue of *Poetry* and his own anthology; but in the years since he had watched his elders and contemporaries, such poets as Cummings, Olson, and Oppen, go on to gain greater or lesser degrees of the fame Zukofsky himself coveted, while he himself remained in obscurity. Oppen, for instance, who had ceased writing poetry altogether for some twenty-five years, returned to print with *The Materials* from New Directions (1962) and went on to win the 1969 Pulitzer Prize for *Of Being Numerous.* Yet, despite the support New Directions' publisher James Laughlin had given Ezra Pound and William Carlos Williams, neither Zukofsky nor his friend Williams could interest Laughlin in a volume of Zukofsky's work.[11] Hence, in the years before

ALL—a volume that signaled a gradual opening up of medium and large presses to books by Zukofsky—the poet seemed to many to have become irremediably bitter, convinced that he had somehow been unreasonably passed over by the powers that conveyed poetic recognition. This bitterness, combined with increasingly debilitating illnesses and hypochondriac "aches," made Zukofsky more and more the recluse.[12] When Basil Bunting, among the very oldest of his friends, came to New York in 1967, he found Zukofsky "very bitter and, strangely, very jealous." Bunting was riding high on the success of his *Briggflatts,* but Zukofsky declined to attend his New York reading, complaining of "drafts" (Makin, *Bunting* 324).

Zukofsky, however, was by no means without friends nor, as the 1960s progressed, without admirers among younger poets. Edward Dahlberg, his contemporary, was his colleague at Brooklyn Polytechnic, and he and Zukofsky became close friends (there was to a be a break between them over, of all things, a canned ham).[13] A succession of young poets made their way to the Zukofskys' apartment in the 1950s and 1960s: Paul Blackburn, Jerome Rothenberg, Jonathan Williams, Denise Levertov, Gilbert Sorrentino, and Allen Ginsberg. The eclectic Robert Duncan, at the time writing a medievalist-cum-modernist verse, had added Zukofsky's influence to an aesthetic that counted Stein, Edith Sitwell, Williams, H.D., and St.-John Perse among its household gods. In "For A Muse Meant," Duncan described his poetics as a "Marianne Moore— / E.P.—Williams-H.D.—Stein— / Zukofsky—Stevens—Perse— / surrealist—dada—staind / pot" (*Selected Poems* 37). Ronald Johnson, whose early work was in the much "looser" paratactic vein of Charles Olson, would go on to write *ARK,* a long poem that made use of many of Zukofsky's compositional procedures. Indeed, during the heyday of Olson's reign at Black Mountain College, the poets there were well aware of Zukofsky's work—although Olson himself, it is said, was unable to read it. Cid Corman, who lived in Japan and edited the groundbreaking journal *Origin,* had published *"A" 1–12* in a limited edition in 1959 and was an indefatigable supporter of Zukofsky's work, as well as a close correspondent with both Zukofsky and Niedecker. Perhaps most influenced by Zukofsky was the young Robert Creeley, who marveled not merely at the older poet's craft but at the personal kindness he showed his impecunious young colleague.[14] As welcome as such recognition among poets was, in the end it failed, in Zukofsky's view, to compensate him for thirty years of public obscurity.

The two-volume *Bottom*, including Celia Zukofsky's setting of *Pericles*, published in 1963 by Ark Press of the University of Texas Press, attracted very little critical notice (especially among the Shakespeare criticism community). Zukofsky's next major project, begun in 1958 and completed in 1966, was also a collaboration with his wife. The Zukofskys' complete translation of Catullus, published in 1969, was a conceptual tour de force that baffled and angered classicists much as Pound's *Homage to Sextus Propertius* had a half-century earlier. Its purpose, Zukofsky writes, is "to breathe the 'literal' meaning" of the Latin original (*CSP* 243), adhering as closely as possible to the sounds and rhythms of Catullus, and letting the meaning take a distant back seat. The familiar "Odi et amo. Quare id faciam, fortasse requiris," for instance, which literally means "I hate and I love. Perhaps you want to know why I do this," becomes in Zukofsky's hands "O th'hate I move love. Quarry it fact I am, for that's so re queries" (*CSP* 310). (I speak here of Zukofsky alone: while the book is credited to both Louis and Celia Zukofsky, it was Celia who prepared the "trots"—literal paraphrases—and notated the sounds of the Latin; Louis alone was responsible for the final form of the translations.) Some readers have found this Catullus to be one long, tedious joke: M. L. Rosenthal, for instance, calls it "spiritless bilingual punning" (*LZMP* 228). And its most obvious precedents are in Jonathan Swift's light-hearted "Anglo-Latin" verses, scraps of poetry which are clearly little more than games: "Apud in is almi des ire / Mimis tres Ine ver re quir re" [A pudding is all my desire, my mistress I never require] (533). But *Catullus*, aside from its very real merits of wit and invention, is important in Zukofsky's work as a whole, exemplifying at least two central elements of his poetics. On the one hand, there is the notion of the word, as Zukofsky puts it in a 1968 interview, as a "physiological" thing, a tangible shaping of air and sound by an embodied person (*LZMP* 267); in that sense, the way to get closest to the historical Gaius Valerius Catullus would be to produce poems that shape sound and air as closely as possible to the ways in which he shaped them in his poetry some nineteen hundred years ago. When one reads the Zukofskys' *Catullus*, then, one experiences the Roman poet in a way that one cannot when reading a translation more faithful in literal "meaning."

On the other hand, there is the notion of phonetic transliteration as an active technique in poetry, of creating an English poetic text by following the sounds of a foreign language. By using as a template the sounds and rhythms of a non-English text, one can generate a new English text that may or may not bear a "meaningful" relationship to that template. In so doing, the poet is freed from the burden of formal originality in a way perhaps analogous to how the Provençal poet explored formal permutations, knowing that his absolutely conventional themes freed him from any need to dream up original subject matter. Zukofsky uses such transliteration often in his later work, drawing on texts in (among others) Greek, Hebrew, Latin, Ojibway, and Welsh: "A"-15 begins with passages from the *Book of Job*, "A"-22 and -23 include stretches of phonetically transliterated material, and large portions of *80 Flowers* (no one seems to know quite how much, although Guy Davenport claims *all* [*Every Force* 109]) are written over foreign templates.

In 1968 L. S. Dembo, author of *Conceptions of Reality in Modern American Poetry* and editor of the University of Wisconsin journal *Contemporary Literature*, invited the four principal Objectivist poets to Madison for a series of readings. Between April 14 and May 16 he conducted interviews with each of them, publishing these interviews as a series in *Contemporary Literature* as "The 'Objectivist' Poetry: Four Interviews." While the interviews revealed, unsurprisingly, that there was little consensus among the poets as to what they had been up to back in the early 1930s, one can date the *critical* construction of the Objectivist "school" from the publication of this series. This was a prolific period for Zukofsky in terms of publications: in addition to *Catullus*, he published the novella *Ferdinand* (1968) and *"A" 13–21* (1969), which was issued by Doubleday's Paris Review Editions in an edition uniform with its 1967 reissue of *"A" 1–12*. Rapp & Carroll in England and (somewhat later) the Horizon Press in the United States also issued Zukofsky's collected criticism, entitled *Prepositions* and organized around the headings "For," "With," and "About." Zukofsky had considerably revised most of the material that appeared in *Prepositions*, and as usual his revisionary practice consisted mostly of omission and cutting. The effect was to make what had at first appeared as ad hoc critical incursions, such as "Sincerity and Objectification: *With Special Reference to the Work of Charles Reznikoff*," take on the status of timeless and contextless critical dicta. The major statements of Objectivist poetics—"Sincerity and Objectification," "Program: 'Objectivists,' 1931," and " 'Recencies' in Poetry," the preface to *An "Objectivists" Anthology*—were pared of their specific readings (indeed, the whole of Zukofsky's lengthy discussions of Reznikoff went by the wayside) and combined into the single essay "An Objective."

Each of Zukofsky's volumes of the 1960s received a number of reviews, indicating the extent to which Zukofsky had begun to receive attention in literary circles. Much of that attention, however, remained baffled or aggressive. In a memorable inversion of Horace Gregory's description of the " 'Objectivists' 1931" issue of *Poetry* as "a Left Bank issue with office on lower Fifth Avenue, New York, where the *Menorah Journal* appears whenever it can raise enough money to ship copy to the printer," and as an issue characterized by "a curious strain of Jewish nationalism," Robert Conquest, in a review titled "The Abomination of Moab," grumbled at *Catullus*, "The Hun is at play—worse still, *at work*—among the ruins."

"A"-21 (1967) was a transliteration similar in procedure to Zukofsky's *Catullus*, in this case a full-length translation of Plautus's *Rudens* (*The Rope*), a play in which Zukofsky saw suggestive parallels to Shakespeare's *Pericles*. What makes the verse of "A"-21 even more knotted than mere transliteration would have it is the fact that Zukofsky here insists on translating line-for-line, one five-word English line for each line of Latin verse. Not merely is the sound of the verse alien, but the syntax, compressed to an absolute minimum, begins to fragment. At times the language seems to explore the further reaches of late-1960s countercultural hipness; at others, it seems almost unbearably oblique and hard to follow—an odd effect, particularly in a movement of his poem that seems particularly concerned with the values of the drama, an inherently *public* art. ("A"-21 is dedicated to the theater critic John Gassner and to Zukofsky's brother Morris

Ephraim, who had first taken the poet to the Thalia as a child.) Earlier sections of *"A"* had used three-word and even one-word lines, and "A"-21, -22, and -23 are all composed of five-word lines. Traditional English accentual-syllabic prosody, of course, takes no notice of the number of words to a line but counts the combinations of stressed and unstressed syllables. It had seemed odd when in the heyday of high modernism Marianne Moore deployed strict syllable-count prosodies—lines measured by the number of syllables, with no regard for accent—but Zukofsky's relentless pursuit of word-count forms seems an even more full-scale assault on the time-honored norms of what constitutes a "meter."

A problem Zukofsky no doubt found more pressing even than such questions of form was that of closure; in 1967, with "A"-21 finished and "A"-22 and -23 reasonably well planned out, Zukofsky needed to find the means to bring an end to his poem. How does one finish a long poem that is in large part a series of formal experiments, rather than a narrative or argument that might be brought to some sort of a logical close? What was to constitute "A"-24? Celia Zukofsky solved that problem when she presented him in 1968 with the gift of the "L.Z. Masque," a 240-page arrangement to music (Handel's "Harpsichord Pieces") of various of Zukofsky's texts. Zukofsky promptly named this work "A"-24 and designated it the closing movement of his "poem of a life." It is of course a characteristic gesture with which to end the poem; by naming Celia's composition the final movement of his own poem, Zukofsky carries out the ultimate destabilization of textual authority, rendering the attribution of authorship problematic in a way that even his wholesale quotation had not.[15]

"A"-22 and -23, the last-composed movements of *"A"*, are also perhaps the densest. Each is comprised of one thousand five-word lines, and each winds within it six thousand years of history: in "A"-22, that history is geological and botanical; in "A"-23, literary. There are passages of these two thousand lines that are readily apprehensible—perhaps most memorably, a 150-line stretch of "A"-23 that translates the Gilgamesh myth, renaming Gilgamesh "Strongest" and Enkidu "One Kid"—but for the most part the reader is hard-pressed to find the principle of continuity in these baffling but sonically exquisite lines. "History's best emptied of names' / impertinence" ("A"-22, 511), Zukofsky writes (or quotes, or transliterates) in "A"-22, and these movements indeed lack any proper names that might provide readerly signposts. Many of these lines are clearly transliterated or translated; most of them, one suspects, are quotations. Yet in the end, for all the evident care and labor that went into their composition—or perhaps because of it—they remain obdurately other, refusing to "mean" in conventionally circumscribed manners. They thereby might be seen, as I will suggest, to propose a new democracy of interpretation. We should not, that is, hunt after source texts or Poundian arcana, searching for a meaning *behind* the text, Zukofsky cautions, but should concentrate on the words themselves. As he says through his alter ego in *Little* and in the epigraph to the *Autobiography*, "I too have been charged with obscurity, tho it's a case of listeners wanting to know too much about me, more than the words say."

The poetics that produced "A"-22 and -23 is pretty much identical to that which generated *80 Flowers*, Zukofsky's last completed collection. This volume of eighty-one poems, each of eight five-word lines, takes to new extremes of density Zukofsky's methods of composition by quotation, transliteration, and compression. Each poem focuses on a particular flower (or class of flowers) and each aims to draw in and allude to as much knowledge as possible pertaining to that flower: botanical, commercial, historical, alchemical, literary, etymological, and personal knowledges are all compacted into these enormously resonant little poems. What they in the end suggest—and one wonders whether Zukofsky himself was wholly conscious of working toward such a goal—is the possibility of the word set free from meaning-determining context, liberated to interact with its neighbors in any or all of the combinations possible. The compression and foreshortening of syntax in *80 Flowers*, far from making the poems meaningless, open them up to a far broader range of potential meanings and connotations. Even an exhaustive ferreting out of the source texts and original contexts from which the words of *80 Flowers* are drawn, such as Michele J. Leggott has carried out in her *Reading Zukofsky's 80 Flowers*, does not pin the poems down to a determinate meaning or set of meanings but serves to enrich and expand our multidirectional, polysemous experience of the text.

80 Flowers (published in an extremely limited edition) and the University of California Press *"A"* (the first complete edition of what will no doubt be considered the poet's major work) were at the printer when Zukofsky died in 1978. He had planned the release of *80 Flowers* to coincide with his eightieth birthday in 1984; luckily, he had finished the work early and had begun taking notes for his next project, *Gamut: 90 Trees.* Of that volume, only the epigraph was drafted (*CSP* 355). This poem, brief as it is—five lines of five words apiece—seems to forecast a new turn in Zukofsky's poetics, a movement toward a barer, more stripped-down vocabulary, a language that hews to the koine even as it frustrates conventional syntactic expectations.

His very last written work was the index to the California *"A"*. He had originally indexed only the words "a," "an," and "the," reiterating a conviction he had first voiced in 1946: "a case can be made for the poet giving some of his life to the use of the words *the* and *a:* both of which are weighted with as much epos and historical destiny as one man can perhaps resolve. Those who do not believe this are too sure that the little words mean nothing among so many other words" (*P* 10). Celia Zukofsky persuaded him to let her index the book more fully, and he in turn revised her index to produce the final version. It is fitting that his last work was to be such a formal one—for what is more conventional in form than an index?—and it is also fitting that it was to be a collaboration with his partner of thirty-eight years.

Appropriately enough as well, the story of Zukofsky's life—unlike those of his friends Pound and Bunting, for instance—is more a chronicle of works than of events. In one of his early poems (and one of his mother's favorites), Pound had written, "I would rather have my sweet, / Though rose-leaves die of grieving, // Than do high deeds in Hungary / To pass all men's believing" (*Collected Early Poems* 192). Unfortunately, the "high deeds" of Pound's life would work for many to obscure from view his writings (leaving aside the still-vexed question of precisely the extent to which those writings themselves count as political and social interventions of a character quite unsavory indeed). In 1948 Zukofsky would write of his friend: "He may be condemned or forgiven. Biographers of the future [at least six of them, last time I looked] may find his character as charming a subject as that of Aaron Burr. It will matter very little against his finest work overshadowed in his lifetime by the hell of Belsen which he overlooked" (*P* 166). By his own effacement, both engineered through the relentlessly domestic and uncompromising turn of his later work, and imposed by a literary establishment unprepared for his innovations, Zukofsky ensured that his own writings, his own struggle with the twin problems of form and knowledge, rather than his biography, would dominate his readers' attention: perhaps "the work" does not say "*all* that needs to be said of one's life," but post-Shakespearean literary history offers few other examples of a life so subsumed in its words.

Zukofsky and Skepticism

The Evidence of the Eyes (pronounced *I's*)

2

Doing Away with Epistemology

Zukofsky and the Problem of Knowledge

It is assumed that epistemological problems do not affect existence.
—Louis Zukofsky, "An Objective" (*P* 13)

If one looks for a principle of continuity in Zukofsky's writings, an idea, theme, or motif that dominates his imaginative and critical productions, one quickly becomes aware of a constant rhythm of assertion against doubt, a rhythm whose locus is the question of human knowledge, of whether—or how reliably—we truly know the objects of our senses, the persons, places, and things that furnish our world and which we detest, abide, or love. The problem of philosophical skepticism—"that anxiety about our human capacities as knowers that can be taken to open modern philosophy in Descartes, interpreted by that philosophy as our human subjection to doubt" (Cavell, *Quest* 4)—is a constant subtext to Zukofsky's texts, whatever subjects they may ostensibly address. Zukofsky's concern with knowledge is evident as early as 1926's "Poem beginning 'The' " and as late as the last decade of his life: it is coeval with his writing life. Epistemology only occasionally rises to center stage of Zukofsky's work, but it constitutes a gnawing presence throughout the poet's writings—both his prose criticism and his poetry—and presents itself as perhaps the principal philosophical issue of his career.

In this book I argue that questions of epistemology are crucial to Zukofsky's writings and that those questions are intimately tied up with the formal concerns that ostensibly so dominate his poetry. I do not, however, begin by extolling Zukofsky's formal invention. One might almost mistake Zukofsky for Auden, given the amount of attention his formal devices have received from other critics. So many writers, for instance, have gone to the trouble of pointing out the astonishingly recondite formal system that underlies the canzone of "A"-9—in at least parts of that movement, the distribution of *n* and *r* sounds have been determined by the formula for a conic section—that Charles O. Hartman, in his study of free verse prosody, uses this very system as an example of precisely what a prosody is *not,* insofar as it is a formal agreement shared between the reader and the poet (*Free Verse* 20–21).

While I think a formalist reading of Zukofsky's work is eventually unavoidable, I would like to approach the question of epistemology at the very outset, because the manner in which Zukofsky deals with the problem of knowledge displays his fundamental cast of mind, his range of repeated concerns—what he calls, on any number of occasions, the "recurrences" of his thought. Furthermore, I want to approach the problem of knowledge initially not through Zukofsky's poetry but through his single largest work of prose criticism (although that classification itself will be put to the question): *Bottom: On Shakespeare. Bottom* lays out the concerns of Zukofsky's poetry and poetics more clearly and straightforwardly than almost any of his more conventionally poetic works. At the same time, it brings up questions of form and poetic composition that will prove crucial to a reading of Zukofsky's verse. *Bottom,* that is, proves an ideal entry to Zukofsky's corpus, not merely because it focuses explicitly on questions of knowledge but because, like so many of the poet's works, it presents itself initially as a work of daunting density, only to reveal underlying that density a structure of crystalline logic and surprisingly straightforward assumptions and preferences.

Even if we view with some skepticism the hypothesis that one of the central concerns of Zukofsky's writing career is the question of human knowledge—the status of our perceptions of the outside world—a careful examination of his writings will find evidence of those concerns at every turn. Zukofsky has provided us with a notably programmatic statement of the problem of knowledge, a tiny poem composed in 1942 and included in *Anew* as simply number 21 of forty-three lyrics:

> Can a mote of sunlight defeat its purpose
> When thought shows it to be deep or dark?
>
> See sun, and think shadow.
> [*CSP* 88]

As in so much of his work, Zukofsky is here addressing a scientific question, a problem squarely in the realm of the "non-poetic." (Reductive views that restrict poetry's realm to the purely aesthetic and emotional forget how deeply Newton's optics influenced eighteenth-century verse, or how Blake's and Shelley's poetry would repeatedly ponder questions of perception.) "Can a mote" works at some level with the irresolvable question of whether light is a wave or a particle, a scientific/perceptual problem that also appears at other moments in Zukofsky's work. In "A"-8 (composed 1935–37), for instance, he had written, "Light-wave and quantum, we have good proof both exist: / Our present effort is to see how this is: to / Perfect the composition of a two-point view" ("A"-8, 49) and "Light? / What is light? physicists failed" ("A"-8, 51). This physical dilemma is evident at the very beginning of "Can a mote," where the physical "mote" of sunlight metonymically substitutes for the expected "beam," playing on Christ's Sermon on the Mount injunction to "first cast out the beam out of thine own eye; and then shalt thou see clearly to cast out the mote out of thy brother's eye" (Matthew 7:5). Like the sunlight itself, both "mote" and "beam" partake of dual states. Since a mote is a solidly physical—if tiny—object, the word strikes one strangely in combination with "of sunlight"; at the same time "mote" has, according to the *OED*, a particular association with sunlight: "esp. one of the innumerable minute specks seen floating in the sun*beam*" (emphasis mine). While a "beam of light" and a "sunbeam" are common expressions, metaphors so conventional that they have lost their metaphoricity, "beam" itself has emphatically solid connotations, as an examination of the word's etymology suggests; nonphysical or immaterial uses of beam, such as "sunbeam," are historically posterior to the word's more concrete meanings, associated with trees, tree trunks, and so forth, and are thereby in a certain sense—a particularly Zukofskyan sense, as we shall see—secondary or metaphorical. A synchronic theory of linguistic meaning, such as Saussure's, would deny the significance of this derivation; Fredric Jameson, for instance, paraphrasing Jean Paulhan, calls the invocation of etymology "not so much a scientific fact as a rhetorical form, the illicit use of historical causality to support the drawing of logical consequences" (*Prison-House* 6). Zukofsky's investment in a diachronic or historical model of language, however, an investment that often manifests itself as an interest in the literal implications of etymological traces, clearly renders the metaphoricity of "beam" significant within the system of the poem, even as the word itself remains absent from the poem.

The term "mote of sunlight," then, can be read as a defamiliarized rendering of the more expected or conventional "beam of sunlight." The "purpose" of the mote, however, seems to be straightforward, identical to the purpose of any other quantum of sunlight: to illuminate. What might turn the sunlight against itself, causing it to "defeat" its own purpose, is the power of "thought" or analysis. "Can a mote of sunlight defeat its purpose / When thought shows it to be deep or dark?" asks whether the power of the questioning, skeptical intellect—the intellect that seeks a fundamental answer to the question of whether light is wave or particle, and in the process of seeking loses sight of the immediate sensuous qualities of light—makes any real difference in the objects of perception. No matter how "deep or dark"—complex, undecidable, un-"light-like"—scientific theory proves light "really" is, light makes the same impression on the clear physical eye. The eye, that is, that is not corrupted by the skepticism of the intellect: the person who can "See sun, and think shadow" is one who has let the mind overrule the senses to the extent that the very source of terrestrial light appears "dark" to him. His is, in Wallace Stevens's words, "an eye that studies its black lid" (*Collected Poems* 71).

A moral or ethical judgment is implied here, for seeing sun and thinking shadow is the hallmark, if not of a blind man, then of one whose disposition is unreasonably pessimistic: the person who sees the sun and thinks only of the shadow it casts would also, we suspect, see the proverbial glass as half empty. And a deep if unconscious misanthropy is involved in seeing the sunlight and thinking of it not in terms of its illuminating power—the way it facilitates one's seeing the objects of perception: the world around one, one's family, one's lover—but of its physical qualities as either particle or wave. In such a view, there is really no "light" as we know it but only various electromagnetic/physical movements taking place in a universe that is fundamentally dark, lightless. The notion of "light" necessarily implies a human observer, the intentionality of whose perception creates light from these blind movements of particles (or waves). Conceiving of light only in the terms of physics requires the necessary subtraction from the equation of the perceiving intentionality. To deny the sun its light, to "think shadow," is identical to the classical skeptical questioning of the senses and in effect denies the human consciousness that underwrites the evidence of the senses.[1]

The polemical point my reading has rather drastically spun from this poem's three lines is informed above all by the body of Zukofsky's critical writings, writings whose tenor suggests that the poet's abiding concern with questions of epistemology has more in common with thc apostle's rage to eliminate heresy than the philosopher's approach to a philosophical question. There is almost a vehemence to Zukofsky's indictments of traditional epistemology, a vehemence suggesting that the break with questions of knowledge represents more to him than a mere philosophical argument. For Zukofsky, to dismiss epistemology is clearly and aggressively to reject literary and cultural Romanticism and its idealization of the individual spirit and imagination confronting the world of phenomena. Like the pragmatist William James, whose *Varieties of Religious Experience* surveyed the psychology and sociology of religion, rather than the literal truth or falsity of its tenets, Zukofsky is uninterested in the specific questions classical skepticism raises—Does the world exist? Do other minds exist?—but passionately fascinated by the grounds of skepticism: What causes one to raise skeptical questions? What turns of thinking lead one to doubt the evidence of one's senses? For Zukofsky, even though the questions that the epistemologist poses may eventually prove (philosophically) trivial, the consequences of the rigid skeptical stance are almost inevitably tragic.

For Zukofsky, skepticism finds its most complete literary representation and exploration in the works of Shakespeare. As the philosopher Stanley Cavell suggests, (Shakespearean) tragedy "is the working out of skepticism," and conversely, "skepticism is the playing out of a tragedy . . . our ordinary lives partake of tragedy in partaking of skepticism" (*Quest* 8–9). Similarly, Zukofsky sees the deaths and disappointments of Shakespeare's tragedies as the end results of an epistemological misalignment in the outlooks of the principals: "all who are tragic in Shakespeare know the betrayal of the constant eyes [i.e., the reliable senses]; the villains are both scourged and dignified by this knowledge" (*B* 299). A concept of tragedy as the outcome of skepticism is important in understanding Zukofsky: for him, skepticism is malign or morbid not because it is wrong or incorrect but because of the wrong, harmful conclusions into which it leads us in our relationships with other people. As I argue in this chapter and the next, Zukofsky's continual attack on philosophical skepticism in *Bottom* and elsewhere is neither a wholly personal obsession nor (despite his protestations to the contrary) a conclusion arrived at inductively through a reading of the Shakespearean corpus. Rather, it is a philosophical corollary to, and justification of, his own Objectivist poetics, as well as the modernist theories of poetry and language underwriting that poetics. Zukofsky sees poetics as inextricably entwined with love, both as a relationship with other human beings and as an approach to a perceptible world.

In "Poem beginning 'The,' " the ex-philosophy student Zukofsky had spent a couple of lines scornfully dismissing the idealist epistemology of Plato, whose parable of the cave in the *Republic* had summarized a view of knowledge in which visible phenomena are merely the "shadows" of eternal ideas: "70 Not the old Greeks anymore,— / 71 the things themselves a shadow world scarce shifting the incessant thought" (*CSP* 11). In a footnote to "Sincerity and Objectification: *With Special Reference to the Work of Charles Reznikoff*" (a footnote later incorporated into the body of "An Objective" in *Prepositions*), he had simply dismissed out of hand objections about the epistemological status of perceived objects: "It is assumed that epistemological problems do not affect existence" (*P* 13). The work of the twenty-nine years between the " 'Objectivists' 1931" issue of *Poetry* and the completion of his massive prose work *Bottom: On Shakespeare* makes clear that for Zukofsky skepticism is less a valid philosophical position to be taken than a betrayal by the intellectualizing mind of the pragmatically serviceable physical senses. This is the explicit thesis of *Bottom*, a book Zukofsky describes in a brief 1961 note as a "long poem built on a theme for the variety of its recurrences. The theme is simply that Shakespeare's text throughout favors the clear physical eye against the erring brain, and that this theme has historical implications" (*P* 167).

As all of its readers have remarked, *Bottom* is far from a straightforward piece of Shakespeare exegesis. It is not surprising that, as Guy Davenport notes, "Shakespeare scholars have yet to discover" this text (*Every Force* 106–7), for *Bottom* represents a radical alternative to the traditionally conceived work of criticism or interpretation. It is not merely eccentric or iconoclastic, even when one takes into account its complete disdain of the conventions of scholarly prose and its apparent obliviousness to the traditions of Shakespeare scholarship: it is a generically indeterminate text, as one might gather from Zukofsky's description of it as a "long poem"; the difficulty its reader faces in deciding whether to consider it a work of criticism, imaginative prose, or poetry—in short, whether to take it as self-consciously "primary" text or self-conscious "commentary"—is mirrored in the position it assumes within Zukofsky's corpus of works. In terms of its form, *Bottom* is an extended exploration of the modernist poetics of collage that Zukofsky shares with Pound and Moore, poetics that give rise to *"A"* and much of Zukofsky's shorter poetry. In its overt argument, however, *Bottom* constitutes the most extended statement of the rejection of epistemology encapsulated in "Can a mote of sunlight." Its argument is an emphasis on the soundness of physical perception, an emphasis Zukofsky shares with other modernists.

Throughout *Bottom*, Zukofsky takes the "clear physical eye/erring brain" theme, which he claims emerges inductively from his examination of the whole of Shakespeare's works, and applies that theme to texts from the entire history of Western literature and philosophy, finding statements of, variations on, and inversions of it in the language of writers ranging from the pre-Socratic philosophers to William Carlos Williams. His method is that of "a reader who is inclined to feel that one book judges and is judged by all other books" (*B* 424), and for Zukofsky the "one book" par excellence is Shakespeare's *Works*. At least in part, *Bottom* is explicitly philosophical criticism, a reading of a text that advances a philosophical argument: "as 'philosophy of history' (taking in the arts and sciences) my book takes exception to all philosophies from Shakespeare's point of view" (*P* 167). ("Shakespeare" refers here to the *Works*, "Considered as an order of words and of drama" (*B* 20), rather than to any historical "bard of Avon.")

While it is of course debatable whether the argument *Bottom* claims to find in Shakespeare represents the "truth" of the Shakespearean text—and such is the case with *every* work of criticism or commentary—it is clear that the book's thesis continues and extends the polemic against epistemological speculation that is implicit throughout Zukofsky's own statements on poetics and throughout much of his poetry. In his 1968 interview with L. S. Dembo, Zukofsky claims that "the theory of knowledge" is "done away with in *Bottom*" (*LZMP* 276). Earlier in that interview he had claimed even more grandly that "*Bottom: on Shakespeare* was written to do away with all philosophy" (*LZMP* 265). If *Bottom* involves itself in philosophy, it is a "philosophy of suspecting philosophy" (*B* 325). Of course such suspicion might be considered itself skeptical, but it is important to note that Zukofsky describes his own book's method as "A *valid* skepticism" (*P* 166, emphasis mine). As he explains in his 1971 lecture on Wallace Stevens, Zukofsky considers the only valid skepticism to be a self-reflexive one that questions the grounds of its own doubting: "all [Stevens's] poems affect being involved in the old philosophical bugbear of a theory of knowledge, a question as to what (quotes) 'really' exists. To be sure, his most often gay, lovely skepticism doubts its own skepticism and becomes the only kind of skepticism true to itself" (*P* 27).

A reader is apt to hear a certain false bravado in Zukofsky's blithely calling traditional philosophical skepticism a "bugbear," for the threat of skepticism is of such prominence in Zukofsky's work, from that work's very beginnings, that it cannot be easily banished by a dismissive label. His 1931 assumption that "epistemological problems do not affect existence" was at least as blithe and offhand as the term "bugbear," but what underlies each statement is an ethical, almost religious, imperative to trust in the ultimate connection of word and world, a connection that is blurred by careless writing and wholly broken by skepticism: "The economy of presentation in writing is a reassertion of faith that the combined letters—the words—are absolute symbols for objects, states, acts, interrelations, thoughts about them. If not, why use words—new or old?" (*P* 14).

Consistent with the linguistic turn of twentieth-century philosophy, a shift of attention from questions of metaphysics to questions of language, Zukofsky's first response when confronting the question of why philosophers argue over questions of epistemology and "reality" is to figure their skepticism as a wrong turning in their use of language. While this stance is no doubt consistent with the American pragmatic philosophical tradition Zukofsky encountered at Columbia (personified in his teacher John Dewey), Zukofsky would find his assumption seconded in the work of Ludwig Wittgenstein. Wittgenstein, in the *Philosophical Investigations*, declares that "philosophical problems arise when language *goes on holiday*. . . . The confusions which occupy us arise when language is like an engine idling, not when it is doing work" (19e, 51e, emphasis in original). In the *Tractatus Logico-Philosophicus*, a text Zukofsky cites at length in *Bottom*, Wittgenstein describes philosophical skepticism as a matter of asking a question where there is no hope of an answer: "Scepticism is *not* irrefutable, but palpably senseless, if it would doubt where a question cannot be asked. For doubt can only exist where there is a question; a question only where there is an answer, and this only where something *can* be *said*" (187, emphasis in original).[2] It is crucial to recognize here that Wittgenstein's description of skepticism as an empty language act—asking a question where no answer can be given—is not merely a rhetorical turn but a description fundamental to his critique of metaphysical argument. That is, Wittgenstein's diagnosis of skepticism's groundlessness focuses less—or less explicitly—on its broader ethical or social implications—the stances skepticism causes the skeptic to take toward the world—than on the very language in which the skeptic must formulate his questions.

Like Wittgenstein, Zukofsky speaks of metaphysical problems as inherently linguistic. But where Wittgenstein implies that skepticism is an improper *use* of language, one in which language is "idling" rather than "doing work," Zukofsky prefers to explain the skeptical dilemma in terms of a particular *state* of language. In his impromptu talk "About the Gas Age" (1969), Zukofsky outlines what he sees as the three states of poetic language: "There is solid state, and there is liquid, and there is gas. It's the same with the materials of poetry, you make images—that's pretty solid—music, it's liquid; ultimately if something vaporizes, that's the intellect" (*P* 169).[3] These states correspond, as he points out a little further on, to "sight," "sound," and "intellection" (*P* 171), three critical terms he formalized earlier in "A Statement for Poetry" (1950) as "Image," "Sound," and "Interplay of Concepts" (*P* 21). These particular concepts largely repeat (although in an altered order) the critical categories that Pound lays out in his 1929 essay "How to Read":

> That is to say, there are three "kinds of poetry":
> MELOPŒIA, wherein the words are charged . . . with some musical property, which directs the bearing or trend of [their "ordinary"] meaning.
>
> PHANOPŒIA, which is a casting of images upon the visual imagination.
>
> LOGOPŒIA, 'the dance of the intellect among words.' . . . It holds the aesthetic content which is peculiarly the domain of verbal manifestation, and cannot possibly be contained in plastic or in music. It is the latest come, and perhaps most tricky and undependable mode. (*Literary Essays* 25)

Zukofsky was aware of these three terms as early as 1929, when he was drafting the ground-breaking essay on Pound in which he cites and discusses at length the version of the melopœia/phanopœia/logopœia distinction published in *Instigations* in 1920 (see *P* 77–83). What Pound theorizes in "How to Read" as three "kinds of poetry," Zukofsky will in 1950 (in "A Statement") distinguish as "components" of the poem. This repeated tripartite taxonomy, Zukofsky stresses, is by no means arbitrary: the components of the poem correspond directly to the sources of words, "The Means of Poetry":

> *Words*—consisting of *syllables*, in turn made up of *phones* that are denoted by *letters* that were once graphic symbols or pictures. Words grow out of affects of
>
> A. Sight, touch, taste, smell
>
> B. Hearing
>
> C. Thought with respect to other words, the interplay of concepts. (*P* 20–21)

It is significant that here the "interplay of concepts"—Pound's "logopœia"—is figured here as a derivative usage of language. As a component of poetry, logopœia is "judgments of other words either abstract or sensible, or both at once" (*P* 21). As Pound points out, its "aesthetic content" is "peculiarly the domain of verbal manifestation." Where Pound sees logopœia as manifesting itself in the poet's manipulation of the connotations of words and their expected contexts of usage—especially in works of satire or irony like his own *Homage to Sextus Propertius*—Zukofsky remains profoundly suspicious of "thought with respect to other words": a wide gulf separates the positive connotations of the "dance of the intellect among words" from the negative ones of "the gas age."

Zukofsky's view of this tripartite division among states of language seems to have been present from the very beginning of his writing career. In line with Kenner's remarks on Zukofsky's early maturing, I think it similarly reasonable to assert that Zukofsky's attitude toward epistemology, and his theory of linguistic states, were largely in place when he began writing in earnest in the second half of the 1920s. Such later formulations as occur in "The Gas Age" and his 1968 interview with Dembo represent not a newly arrived at position but the final theorization and crystallization of ideas that had been present, and were being worked out in his writings, from the beginning.

Zukofsky's conception of poetic language is almost certainly heavily influenced by the Fenollosa/Pound account of Chinese poetry, which emphasizes the basis of language in the objective processes of nature as apprehended through direct sensual experience. Ernest Fenollosa claims, "The sentence was forced upon primitive man by nature itself. It was not we who made it; it was a reflection of the temporal order in causation" (*Chinese Written Character* 12). Zukofsky's reliance on and interest in etymologies can as well be related to Fenollosa's essay, which views the bulk of language usage as a metaphorical, abstracted superstructure built on a foundation of concrete usage that can be recovered through an examination of a term's etymology: "The whole delicate substance of speech is built upon substrata of metaphor. Abstract terms, pressed by etymology, reveal their ancient roots still embedded in direct action. But the primitive metaphors do not spring from arbitrary subjective processes. They are possible only because they follow objective lines of relations in nature herself" (22).[4] The "interplay of concepts," itself the manifestation of the mind dealing with "other words either abstract or sensible," is at least once removed from the sensible sources of language.

Pound's own distrust of abstract language, of course, predates his discovery of Fenollosa's manuscripts by several years, and such distrust is indeed a general theme in the rhetoric of what Kenner calls "international Modernism." In *A Calculus of Ezra Pound,* Philip Kuberski argues persuasively that Pound's dislike of abstraction, as well as his attraction to the Chinese ideogram—which (at least in Pound's account) functions as a *visual* representation of its referent—is part of a larger American project to "motivate" what Saussure would show to be an essentially unmotivated, or arbitrary, signifier. Such an attempt seems a general theme in both American and British modernism. The cautions of Pound's 1912 Imagist manifesto, which urges the poet to "Go in fear of abstractions" (*Literary Essays* 5), can also be found in T. E. Hulme's "Notes on Language and Style"—an essay whose language strikingly anticipates Zukofsky's: in Hulme's words, "All emotion depends on real solid vision or sound" (*Further Speculations* 78).[5] The work of French psychologist Théodule Ribot, one of the major sources of Hulme's thought, suggested to

Hulme that "in moving away from the data of immediate experience one might ultimately lose touch with reality itself, as the abstractions with which one dealt became worthless counters with no practical basis" (Robinson, *Symbol to Vortex* 61).[6] Hulme's writings and conversation greatly influenced Pound, and Hulme is perhaps the most influential of the Imagists in terms of the movement's theoretical self-justifications. But Pound's own writings, far more accessible than those of his friend Hulme (who died in 1917, and whose essays were not collected until 1925), were the most immediate influence on Pound's younger colleague Zukofsky.

The three linguistic states Zukofsky derives from Pound's specifically poetic terms of *phanopœia, melopœia,* and *logopœia*—solid state, liquid, gaseous—are by no means confined to poetic language but can be used to describe all sorts of instances of the "handling of words." As Zukofsky explains in the Dembo interview,

> I said solid state, liquid, gas; as a matter of fact you can word it sense, essence, non-sense. As to the handling of words, there are the words of sense. Then, there are words that generalize and say "without this that thing can't be essence." So you have words like truth and reality. The "real" is bad enough, but at least it's a voice, a kid saying, "For real?" But then the philosopher adds the "i-t-y" and you start playing all kinds of word games and that's non-sense. (*LZMP* 277)

The questions of classical skepticism—questions about the relationship of knowledge and reality—are questions that are only raised when language reaches the "gaseous" state, when it has moved into the realm of the purely conceptual. Language in its gaseous form is "non-sense," mere "word games," because it has become disconnected from the bases of its meaningful power, the concrete physical senses that Zukofsky implies are at the root of language. "Words," after all, "grow out of affects of A. Sight, touch, taste, smell B. Hearing"; the fact that, according to Zukofsky, "*letters* . . . were once graphic symbols or pictures" serves to support a notion of language as founded in the evidence of the sensible

(*P* 20–21). "Solid state" language, then, not only makes "sense" (as opposed to "non-sense") but is directly related to the bodily senses. "So much of the word is a physiological thing," Zukofsky speculates in the same interview; "I know all of the linguists will say I'm crazy. In fact I think there's a close relationship between families of languages, in this physiological sense. Something must have led the Greeks to say *hudor* and for us to say *water*" (*LZMP* 267). The poet David Melnick perhaps best sums up the gist of Zukofsky's linguistic thought: "Sight, sound, and intellection are the solid, liquid, and gaseous states of language. Sight is best, and by the earliest times men had developed a language of definite reference (the logician's ideal). The liquidity of music, song, and fable gave way in our own time to pure air—discourse and thought" (61).

The extent to which Zukofsky takes seriously this Cratylic myth of language's origins is unclear. There is little indication, in his criticism of ancient poetry, that he believes classical or pre-classical writing is somehow inevitably closer to the sensible data of experience. But his remarks in "About the Gas Age" clearly imply that various ages are characterized by various states of language and thought. Responding to a questioner at a reading who observed (sensibly enough), "For one who *thinks* so much in his poetry, it seems rather strange to, in fact, *hear* you speak only of its music," Zukofsky says:

> I'd like to keep solid because I can't help myself, I was born in a gas age. . . .
>
> There is wonderful thinking, there are some thinkers as I imply at the end of the *partita* section of *"A"*. Actually I love Spinoza, but he is the gas stage and it really started for our time about then. You see it best in Shakespeare. He is just at the turning point. . . .
>
> You see what I am talking about—well actually I'm talking about *sight*, and *sound*, and then the third word has always bothered me but I've ended up with *intellection*. That is, Dante's *Paradiso* is a great intellect at work, not only an intelligence which is more involved with the senses, but it's when the senses vaporize and, the head floats, but sometimes it floats just beautifully. (*P* 169–71)

In referring to the present as a "gas age," Zukofsky adapts Henry Adams's posthumously published essay "The Rule of Phase Applied to History," in which Adams suggests (according to Zukofsky) "that Thought in time—like water or gas subject to certain forms—passes through a variety of phases, or changes, or states of equilibrium" (*P* 123). Adams's theory, based on the model of Willard Gibbs's physics, proposes that society passes through various phases, each one characterized by a particular "force" and a particular mode of thought. Here Zukofsky quotes Adams:

> According to the Phase Rule, [society] lived from remote times in terms of fetish force, and passed from that into terms of mechanical force, which again led to terms of electric force, without fairly realizing what had happened except in slow social and political revolutions. Thought in terms of ether means only Thought in terms of itself, or, in other words, pure Mathematics and Metaphysics, a stage often reached by individuals. (*P* 124)

What Adams calls "thought in terms of ether" is essentially similar to Zukofsky's "gas age." Adams's mathematical formulas specify only a very short time span for the ethereal phase—either 1900–1917 or 2000–2025 (*P* 124–25)—but it is clear that Zukofsky adopts his notion of successive phases, if not his actual calculations. For Zukofsky, the gas age had begun by the time of Spinoza, with Shakespeare standing "just at the turning point."

In *Bottom,* of course, Shakespeare occupies the central position in Zukofsky's exploration of epistemology and skepticism. The skeptical problematic that so absorbs Zukofsky is a product of the gas age; Shakespeare stands as the last and strongest exemplar of an anti-epistemological stance that belongs to an earlier, less gaseous state of language.[7] According to Zukofsky's reading of Wittgenstein in *Bottom,* the *Tractatus,* both in its overt statements and to the extent it stands as an exemplar of twentieth-century thought, implies a similar progression from "solid state" to "gaseous" thought, a progression that becomes increasingly abstracted from the concrete particulars perceived by the senses:

> Perhaps the chronological sequence implied in the comparison that has been made here between Shakespeare, Spinoza, and Wittgenstein suggests a convenient generic principle of "looking" at history—and that when all is said, in accordance with this principle, the thinking has spirited away the *singulars.* (*B* 81)

> Together, Wittgenstein and Shakespeare look back with longing almost two thousand years to "simple" (single) nature. (*B* 85)

Shakespeare stands at a turning point where language, though it has passed out of the solid state of pure image into the liquidity of music and fable, has not yet become invested in the abstractions of the gaseous state:

> Shakespeare's *Works* as they conceive history regret a great loss of physical looking. They recall with the abstracted "look" of a late time. The intellective propositions of their actions anticipate the present day's vanishing point, but unlike the present's propositions still sing an earthly underpinning.
>
> It follows that Shakespeare's *Works* say: seeing should be the object of speech (which in fabling time resolves into song), rather than that speech (which in late time often resolves into an unsingable "music of the spheres") should be the object of seeing. (*B* 88)

All of Zukofsky's analysis of Shakespeare bears the marks of his distinction among the three states of language, and all of *Bottom* asserts the primacy of solid state or imagistic language. For Zukofsky, the *Works* throughout present the drama of human love as "the tragic hero": "He is Amor, identified with the passion of the lover falling short of perfection—discernment, fitness, proportion—at those times when his imagination insufficient to itself is an aberration of the eyes" (*B* 15). Love, in short, finds its realization in Shakespeare's plays only when the character who loves relies implicitly on the evidence of her or his eyes; Zukofsky expresses this as a proportional analogy: *"love : reason :: eyes : mind"* (*B* 39). Although the specific values might change ("one play may act out 5 : 1 :: 5 : 1, another 1 : 5 :: 1 : 5" [*B* 266]), the proportion remains constant and implies that "from the desireable view of the perfection of character the characters are happy only when their eyes judge for equable equals. Then because they look with their eyes they love reasonably" (*B* 266).

As tragic hero, Love's progress is the subject of all of Shakespeare's works, and his success or failure is always linked to the degree to which Shakespeare's characters rely on the unmediated evidence of their eyes. In the proportion "love : reason :: eyes : mind," there cannot be a happy balance (a "comedic" ending) if the reason or mind outweighs the evidence of the senses: "Love needs no tongue of reason if love and the eyes are *1*—an identity. The good reasons of the mind's right judgment are but superfluities for saying: *Love sees*" (*B* 39). The proportion between love/eyes and reason/mind is played out in the psyches of Shakespeare's characters, and the balance of left-hand to right-hand terms determines those characters' fates. It also thereby determines the genre of each play, according to the conventional yardstick of "happy" or "unhappy" endings. When the mind overrides the evidence of the senses, it becomes not "reason" but "passion": "The formula of [Shakespeare's] dramatic writing is singular and simple: when the passions tend to constitute the least possible part of the mind of the characters, the result is 'comedy'; when the passions are irresoluble for them, the result is 'tragedy'; when either 'comedy' or 'tragedy' or blends of both involve the passions of historical characters, the result is 'history' " (*B* 24). Stephen Orgel, in his introduction to the Oxford *Tempest*, notes that we "have invented the category of romance because we believe that certain kinds of seriousness are inappropriate to comedy and because we are made uncomfortable by the late plays' commitment to non-realistic modes" (5). Zukofsky has as well disposed of that awkward generic category, presumably because it has no sanction from the First Folio publication of Shakespeare's plays—and of course it serves no useful purpose in the terms of his analysis.

By associating love with the unerring eye, Zukofsky in practice redefines love itself, removing it from the realm of the passions (which retain their Latin sense of "involuntary motions") and setting it up as a principle of absolute certainty.[8] Love is the access of the senses (the eyes) to the " 'simple' (single) nature" whose loss Wittgenstein and Shakespeare both regret:

> "Simple" loves like Shakespeare's Pericles and Wittgenstein somehow pair off. Fortune sees to it that the sight of the beloved is *their world.* Its uncluttered certainty that shows itself is the thing they love most. Tho they reason "better," they accept the sense of sight sooner than the other senses and the reason, because love depends most on sight for its being and origin (Aristotle, *Ethics, IX,12*). (*B* 73)

In Zukofsky's proportion the reason or the mind is variable, while love and the eye remain constant, perceiving objects and persons as they in reality are: "love's constant physical eye looks where all things exist to exist" (*B* 37). The trustworthy perceptions of "love's constant physical eye" are betrayed by the logically posterior meddling of the mind (whether passionate or intellective), and such meddling is responsible for the tragedies of Othello and Desdemona, Romeo and Juliet, Lear and Cordelia: "The eyes see—literally *see.* Don't blame the eyes for this fault of the mind, that of conceiving the nature of things (*Lucretius,IV,65*)" (*B* 89).

Zukofsky's equation of love and the eyes corresponds directly to his tripartite classification of the states of language. Physical vision, the direct evidence of the senses, is the basis of "solid-state language"; it is the only knowledge that one can hold to as assured and, indeed, solid. Solid-state language, based as it is on direct physical perceptions, is in an important way diffused and debased by the introduction of liquid and gaseous modes of language. "Liquid" language, which Zukofsky associates with song and "fable," is obviously an integral part of poetry and is not to be regarded as harshly as "gaseous" language; what crucially recommends liquid language for Zukofsky is the fact that it appeals directly to the senses by its fundamentally "musical" nature, even as it moves away from a simple positivist representativity, in a way that gaseous language does not.

Zukofsky associates the abstractions of gaseous language with the Renaissance conceit of the "music of the spheres," a purely conceptual music that can only be heard when one ignores the explicit evidence of the senses. As *Bottom* describes the progression of human thought through its various stages, the present gas age is a "late time" in which the human subject searches desperately for a firm "underpinning":

> In primitive time man looks around and into himself—his body and his cave to be decorated—then looks out and wonders how he first looked around and into himself; having reached fabling time he looks out by these means, above, underneath earth, its primitive life that once made him speak now rarifying his picturing sounds of earth into song like those of an Odyssey; in late time he conceives past a vanishing point, nowhere or everywhere projecting "objects" in signs and indices which may again let him look around, into, out, up, down for an underpinning of earth (like Prospero, looking into himself but mostly forgetting Caliban, or Pericles *listening* to "the music of the spheres" *before seeing* his wife and daughter to whom he is reunited). (*B* 87–88)

The questions of classical epistemology—questions about the relationship of knowledge and reality—are only raised when language has reached the gaseous state, when it has moved into the realm of the purely conceptual. Epistemological speculation (and the doubt that manifests itself as skepticism is the purest form of such speculation), as an expression of the mind's interference in the business of the senses, and as an instance of gaseous language encroaching on and complicating a realm of previously assured knowledge, is the epitome not of true reason but of a misguided betrayal of love, whose realm is the "constant physical eye": "*The object is simple (Tractatus)*—if logic is careful to make it so; the nature of the object is (quotes) 'simple' because there is no other way to *see* it with the eyes, except to philosophize on logic, like Wittgenstein, so as to see its avatar, as it were, as an event or incident in print" (*B* 49).

Epistemological speculation, in short, betrays love; love, which is only fulfilled through the lover's unquestioning trust in the evidence of his or her eyes, cannot withstand the corrosive doubt of skepticism. Pericles' blindness is like that of the skeptic: rather than perceiving, recognizing, and embracing his wife and daughter, he is distracted by the strains of a music that has no basis in the evidence of his ears but is a product solely of his mind.

Similarly, the skeptic, rather than embracing and acknowledging his fellow human beings and the world around him, pays heed to the doubts his intellect raises about the existence of the objective world.

The primary term of Zukofsky's epistemology, as seemingly commonplace yet as profound and complex as "sincerity," the primary term of his poetics, is "love." For Zukofsky, love implies not merely interpersonal affection but a trust in and reliance on the physical senses, especially the eye. It can be linked to an entire modernist ethos of perception, which invariably values personal, direct experience—"ocular proof"—over intellectual analysis and philosophizing. The Poundian doctrine of the ideogram, derived in part from Fenollosa's studies of Chinese poetry, is the most prominent modernist statement of the primacy of inductive experience in poetic composition.[9] Pound goes so far as to designate the ideogram "the method of science" (*ABC of Reading* 26); the basic method of his prose criticism, as well as of *The Cantos,* is the ideogrammic juxtaposition of particulars, whether individual perceptions or linguistic fragments, to create larger systems of relationship. Some version of the ideogrammic method, an explicitly inductive poetic, is also at the base of much of Zukofsky's work: the formal architecture of *Bottom* can be seen as a variation on the method, as can many sections of *"A"*. More generally, Pound's repeated emphasis on direct personal perception as the basis of critical and poetic evaluation can be seen as underwriting and echoing both the textbook method of Zukofsky's *A Test of Poetry* and the constant reliance on direct perception of Zukofsky's larger poetics.[10]

It would be misleading, however, to attribute solely to Pound an emphasis on particularized perception and a revulsion from abstract language and thought that is the general property of a whole tradition of American modernist writing practices. Williams's "no ideas but in things" encapsulates an ethos evident as well in Moore's "imaginary gardens with real toads in them." As Faulkner writes in Addie Bundren's bitter posthumous soliloquy in *As I Lay Dying:*

> That was when I learned that words are no good; that words dont ever fit even what they are trying to say at. . . . He had a word, too.

> Love, he called it. But I had been used to words for a long time. I knew that that word was like the others: just a shape to fill a lack; that when the right time came, you wouldn't need a word for that anymore than for pride or fear. . . . I would think how words go straight up in a thin line, quick and harmless, and how terribly doing goes along the earth, clinging to it, so that after a while the two lines are too far apart for the same person to straddle from one to the other; and that sin and love and fear are just sounds that people who never sinned nor loved nor feared have for what they never had and cannot have until they forget the words. (115–17)

Also relevant is Frederick Henry's impassioned denunciation of patriotic abstraction in Hemingway's *A Farewell to Arms:*

> I was always embarassed by the words sacred, glorious, and sacrifice and the expression in vain. . . . I had seen nothing sacred, and the things that were glorious had no glory and the sacrifices were like the stockyards at Chicago if nothing was done with the meat except to bury it. There were many words that you could not stand to hear and finally only the names of places had dignity. Certain numbers were the same way and certain dates and these with the names of places were all you could say and have them mean anything. Abstract words such as glory, honor, courage, or hallow were obscene beside the concrete names of villages, the numbers of roads, the names of rivers, the numbers of regiments and the dates. (184–85)

A final and striking statement of such a modernist reliance on immediate perception (and one with clear similarities to the Zukofskys' *Catullus*) can be found in H.D.'s translation of Euripides' *Ion* (1937), where the poet/translator asserts that the only way to grasp the essence of the Greek text is to "Parse the sun in heaven, distinguish between the taste of mountain air on different levels, feel with your bare foot a rock covered with sea-weed, one covered with sand, one washed and marbled by the tide. You can not learn Greek, only, with a dictionary. You can learn it with your hands and your feet and especially with your lungs" (16).

Zukofsky, by encapsulating his own doctrine of perception in the term "love," moves this modernist fascination with the particulars of perception from an epistemological to an ethical plane. "Love" signifies for Zukofsky an entire human stance toward experience, which he enunciates most memorably in the interview with Dembo: "Well, it's like my horses [an image that reappears throughout *"A"*]. If you're good enough to run or feel like running, you run. If you want to live, you love; if you don't want to live, you hate, that's all. It's as simple as that" (*LZMP* 278). In a moving passage of "A"-12 describing his dead father's remembrance of the Russian singing of his childhood, Zukofsky places "love" and "poetics" in direct apposition:

> A tear in an eye
> The quick hand wiped off—
> Casually:
> "I loved to hear them."
>
> As I love:
> My poetics.
> ["A"-12, 151]

"Love," as Zukofsky uses it to explain and underwrite his own poetic practice, has a compelling resemblance to the "love" described in *Bottom*—the tragic hero who is vindicated only through the immediate evidence of the eyes.

While the extent of Zukofsky's critical corpus is not at all comparable to that of Pound's, Zukofsky is unique among American modernist poets in the extent to which he tries to formalize and systematize his aesthetics and epistemology. This systematizing impulse has its roots, one might speculate, both in Zukofsky's situation of belatedness in relation to the major figures of American modernism (Pound, Williams, and Moore, in particular) and in the fundamentally philosophical bent of his thinking, an inclination that leads him to admire most strongly such systematic thinkers as Aristotle, Spinoza, Aquinas, and the early Wittgenstein, and to attempt to apply similarly systematized schemata to the poets he admires, Shakespeare in particular.[11] Zukofsky, it can be said, without being unnecessarily pejorative, *inherits* his poetics of direct perception from his modernist precursors, and his entire critical machinery of "sincerity" and "objectification" and solid/liquid/gaseous states of language is an a posteriori attempt to systematize the practice of his predecessors within an internally coherent philosophical framework, an attempt to make this poetic practice his own by putting it under the aegis of his own theoretical apparatus.

But his very systematizing impulse also works to make clear what Zukofsky would prefer remained obscure: the conceptual rift at the heart of his epistemology. If the individual perceiver is the basis of knowledge, and the soundness of that perceiver's physical senses are a guarantee against the danger of skepticism, how then does one theorize the interpersonal? How does one guard against the danger of solipsism, which is itself the most corrosive and ultimately damaging form of skepticism? Stanley Cavell, whose work on Shakespeare and skepticism is ostensibly similar to Zukofsky's, continually examines the connections between skepticism and solipsism. Cavell's work on *King Lear* provides a vantage point from which to uncover the self-contradictions in *Bottom*, self-contradictions most evident when one compares the book's overt argument to its formal structure. Beginning at this point and continuing through an examination of Zukofsky's writings on "practical" poetics and a reading of "I's (pronounced *eyes*)," one can come to see in what manner Zukofsky's poetry, rather than upholding the outright rejection of epistemology his prose advocates, seems to complicate and reject such a stance.

3

Bottom: On Shakespeare

"A philosophy of suspecting philosophy"

> And yet, to say the truth, reason and love keep little company together now-a-days. The more the pity that some honest neighbors will not make them friends.
> —*Midsummer Night's Dream* III.ii.143–46

The juxtaposition of Zukofsky's encapsulation of his poetic stance in the single word "love" with *Bottom*'s insistence on the importance of epistemological questions in Shakespeare might well bring to mind another examination of skepticism in the Shakespearean text: the American philosopher Stanley Cavell's "The Avoidance of Love: A Reading of *King Lear.*" By drawing Cavell into my discussion of *Bottom*, I hope to inject a marginally more "institutional" philosophical perspective on the issue of philosophical skepticism and to gesture toward a backdrop of history of philosophy against which one might assess Zukofsky's own assessment of skepticism in Western thought. There are certain clear continuities between these two writers. Cavell, like Zukofsky, repeatedly returns to the problem of skepticism as a fundamental moment in human thought; as with Zukofsky, Cavell's confrontation with skepticism finds one of its most profound expressions in his examination of Shakespeare; and like Zukofsky, Cavell sees a fundamental connection between skepticism and tragedy: "tragedy is the working out of a response to skepticism—as I now like to put the matter, . . . tragedy is an interpretation of what skepticism is itself an interpretation of" (*Disowning Knowledge* 5–6). Despite the deep differences between the two writers' approaches, and in part *because* of those differences, Cavell's work is useful in a discussion of Zukofsky insofar as it can suggest certain important questions and reservations that might be raised about the epistemological—and ethical—status of Zukofsky's method in *Bottom*.

The first and perhaps most obvious difference between the two writers' approaches is in the very form their interrogation of Shakespeare takes. Cavell's *Disowning Knowledge: In Six Plays of Shakespeare*, the volume in which "The Avoidance of Love" is most readily available, is a collection of six essays (one of them a lengthy introduction), each of which addresses a different aspect of skepticism in a different Shakespeare play, and each of which takes a different interpretive approach. As the essays in the collection become more recent, they increasingly address the problem of skepticism in terms of concepts of politics, gender, and psychoanalysis, thereby reflecting Cavell's expanding conception of that problem. In contrast to such a flexible, ad hoc, and clearly evolving critical practice, the reading of the Shakespearean canon Zukofsky advances in *Bottom* is a fundamentally unitary one that finds the same theme repeated, in a variety of keys and variations, throughout the *Works:* "All of Shakespeare's writing," Zukofsky argues, "embodies a definition, a continuing variant of it over so many years" (*B* 15). Shakespeare's *Works*, according to Zukofsky, "say one thing: love . . . moves all the leaves of his book to sound different degrees of 'love's mind' or its relative failures of judgment. For, by definition, only love looking with the eyes has perfect taste" (*B* 19). As Davenport describes, *Bottom: On Shakespeare* attempts to demonstrate a "unifying harmony" in all of Shakespeare (*Every Force* 106). For Zukofsky, Shakespeare's art is one "of a recurrence of images, like musical notes, that articulates the *definition of love* sounding precisely thru all the plays" (*B* 290). Those plays are "a vast musical work in singular and entire concord, so that all of it [makes] sense, even the frequently unsympathetic deviousness of its violent passage work and flourishes" (*B* 283).

As criticism (one text's attempt to describe or comment on another text), *Bottom* can been seen as fundamentally primitive, "single," or "simple"—to echo Zukofsky's description of the "nature" Shakespeare and Wittgenstein look back toward "with longing." David Melnick understandably finds "Nostalgia" a key term in describing Zukofsky's conclusions: "When we are torn away from the concrete seen particular by a generalizing, universalizing mind, what we feel is Nostalgia" (58). That nostalgia for concrete, "single" nature can be used to define *Bottom* itself, which then can be seen to stand as a large-scale working out of Zukofsky's own "nostalgia" for a concrete, "single" Shakespeare, whose works develop around a limited number of propositions in a manner analogous to that of Wittgenstein's *Tractatus* or, perhaps more germanely, Spinoza's *Ethics.* Zukofsky comments on the *Ethics*—with evident affection—in "About the Gas Age": "The wonderful thing about Spinoza's philosophy to me is that out of 8 definitions and 7 axioms he builds the whole system" (*P* 170).

Melnick's indictment of *Bottom: On Shakespeare* is respectful but unforgiving and focuses in part on the precise valence of the term *"On"* in the book's title. To what extent does Zukofsky's text function as a legitimate commentary on or explanation of the *Works?* Not surprisingly, Melnick finds *Bottom* wanting precisely to the extent that it pursues themes of love and physical seeing and sets aside questions of plot, character, and dramatic context: "After carefully putting away rhetoric, plot, local context, and the suggestive reach of single lines, there remain the special words of the definition. . . . 'Reason,' 'love,' 'mind,' etc., come under Zukofsky's rule for interpretation. The eyes themselves require it: Zukofsky seeks a reference to the generalized capacity of sight in every use Shakespeare made of the eyes as an image" (64). What this gives rise to, in Melnick's account, is a critical autism, a focus on seeing—and, in particular, on the language of seeing—that denies humanity to the person seen and that denies human multivalence and unpredictability to the texts at hand.

> The reader discovers at this point what he has suspected all along, that Zukofsky's world has no room for people in it: he will not deal with more than one pair of eyes at a time. At this point, the reader will rebel. He requires no context outside Zukofsky's [i.e., outside the passages of Shakespeare Zukofsky has quoted] to see the "definition" fall shy of the texts that are quoted as witnesses to it.

> . . . "Love, first learned in a lady's eyes," already entails a situation that Zukofsky's philosophical framework is insufficient to describe. (64)

Although Melnick acknowledges that *Bottom* is a bravura performance, his ultimate quarrel with *Bottom* remains irreconcilable and fundamental. For Melnick, the narrow, key-term-based antiskeptical rubric by which Zukofsky approaches Shakespeare's works both denies those works their broadly human valence and denies the possibility of interpersonal, truly reciprocal love.

It is clear that the focus of *Bottom*'s analysis of Shakespeare is on language and the imagistic and thematic structures of that language rather than on the plays' plots, the specific characters to which language is assigned, or the specific dramatic contexts in which the characters speak. As Zukofsky puts it in an exchange between the "son" and the "I" whose conversation makes up the seventy-five-page "Definition" chapter of "An Alphabet of Subjects":

> SON. Don't suggest the plots. I'm listening to the words.
>
> I. I'll try to remember not to. When I look at the text, the text looks back with so many episodes worked out of *see's, eyes, looks,* and their inevitable associations and contrasts, all urging something like, *Look, if you want to judge well.* (*B* 274)

Melnick notes, for instance, how the "faultless and beautifully achieved summary of his theory of love's and thought's dependence on sight" that occurs in the second chapter of Part II of *Bottom* and takes as its starting point the *Merchant of Venice* song "Tell me where is fancy bred" interprets that song in a manner expressly opposite to its significance within the narrative structure of the play: "the reader of *Bottom* understands precisely that Zukofsky knows all of this, and, knowing it, still prefers to read the song as if from an anthology or a Shakespeare garland. It is at this point that the reader readjusts his sights altogether, and accepts for the purpose a *dictum* that the context of the song is now (or *here*) not the play but *Bottom* itself" (63).

In Melnick's view, these sorts of interpretive and compositional strategies produce a reading of Shakespeare that reduces the whole of the canon to a single lyric poem to be analyzed in the familiar terms of critical discourse on the lyric—image, theme, and so forth—rather than in the more dynamic terms of dramatic or narrative criticism. By "reducing" Shakespeare's stories and characters to static linguistic structures, Zukofsky has denied the essence of human relations, which is their temporal character. This, according to Melnick, is the effect of Zukofsky's single-minded insistence on physical seeing in Shakespeare and, more broadly, of his approach to the Shakespearean text, which takes the word and the image, rather than the character or the fictive event, as its basic material for commentary.

Melnick finds Zukofsky's reading of Shakespeare troubling as well on the level of "explicit doctrine" (56). In Melnick's view, Zukofsky's staticizing approach to the Shakespearean text is crucially analogous to a doctrine of love and perception outlined in *Bottom*'s early sections and derived for the most part from Aristotle and Spinoza. The most important quote here, and one that Zukofsky returns to repeatedly, both for its "sense" and for its specific language, is from Spinoza's *Ethics:*

> Unhealthy states of mind and misfortunes owe their origin for the most part to excessive love for a thing that is liable to many variations, and of which we may never seize the mastery. For no one is anxious or cares about anything that he does towards a thing of which no one is truly master. From this we can easily conceive what a clear and distinct knowledge . . . can do with the emotions, namely that if it does not remove them entirely as they are passions . . . at least brings it about that they constitute the least possible part of the mind. . . . Moreover, it gives rise to a love towards a thing immutable and eternal . . . and of which we are in truth masters . . . and which cannot be polluted by any evils which are in common love, but which can become more and more powerful . . . and occupy the greatest part of the mind . . . and deeply affect it. And thus I have done with all that regards this present life. *Part V,Prop.XX,Note* (quoted in *B* 16, ellipses in original)

This passage would seem to be the source of Zukofsky's notion of "passions" that interfere with one's clear perception, as well as his rhetoric of "clear and distinct knowledge." In fact, Zukofsky quotes much of the Spinoza passage in his description of the role of Love as tragic hero:

> [Falstaff] owes his misfortune, only another aspect of Love's erring mind, to "excessive love for a thing that is liable to many variations [in Falstaff's case, Prince Hal], and of which we may never seize the mastery."
>
> There is but one cure for this lack of mastery: "a clear and distinct knowledge" that would have the "emotions," inasmuch as they are *passions*, "constitute the least possible part of the mind." (*B* 24)

The fundamental principle of the love that is underwritten by "clear and distinct knowledge"—insofar as it is derived from Spinoza—is that its object is timeless, not subject to temporal change. For Spinoza, this means that one's love should be directed toward God, who is the only unchanging, atemporal reality. Zukofsky does not of course import this divinely directed love into his analytical machinery unchanged, but Spinoza's description of love's object as something "immutable and eternal" appears in Zukofsky's prose both to figure the loved one and to describe the constancy of the physical eye. As Melnick reads *Bottom*, Zukofsky has thereby denied the power of time itself: "Zukofsky's choice of Spinoza and the early Wittgenstein as the coordinates of his argument reveals more than a critical interest in their 'abstracted look.' He shares with them, as with Shakespeare, fears of chance and change, i.e., of Time itself. Like them, but unlike Shakespeare, he deals with time by not dealing with it, by denying its reality, by making it into an unfortunate and self-deceptive quirk of the mind" (58).

A real human being exists in time and is thereby subject to alteration and fluctuation, unlike the ideal and permanent objects of love that Aristotle and Spinoza define. Othello, for instance, by murdering Desdemona, makes her into the "immutable and eternal" object of the loving gaze that she never could be as a living person. As Charles Bernstein puts it, "*Othello* plays out the insistence on lens-bound [i.e., physical] sight to its lethal end—to make a thing 'hold still you have to kill it.' . . . Othello's eyes make their object—Desdemona—into an 'objectification' at 'perfect rest', to use Zukofsky's terms for his poetics. . . . Desdemona, cast into stone, is a *solid* sight to look at, not mutable flesh to respond to" (*Content's Dream* 148). Melnick phrases this even more succinctly: "If Desdemona will not lie still, Othello will still her" (65). In a like manner, then, Zukofsky "murders" Shakespeare's text—purges it of all motion of character and plot—in order to find in it the timeless themes of "love" and "physical sight." Zukofsky's philosophical rubric, by its very terms, prevents him from dealing with the interpersonal involvements and entanglements that make up Shakespeare's plots: after all, the terms of *Bottom*'s ratio ("love : reason :: eyes : mind") allow no place for the *beloved*, the object of sight. The person loved is objectified, both as the object of love and as the object of perception; Zukofsky's calculus of affection at no point investigates the implications of a truly reciprocal love relationship.

Bottom's analysis of the Shakespearean text does not render the *Works* quite as static as one might gather from Melnick's polemic. This is obvious both from Zukofsky's characterization of Amor as the "tragic hero" (by definition involved in a temporally extended plot) and from his reliance on the traditional "happy/unhappy ending" yardstick to generically categorize the plays, arguing on that basis the extent to which those plays' characters have looked "with their eyes." But the thematic/imagistic element of Zukofsky's analysis is predominant and leads one to consider the questions of critical methodology Cavell raises in "The Avoidance of Love," where he begins with a few words on "the shift and conflict between character criticism and verbal analysis" (*Disowning Knowledge* 41) in Shakespeare studies:

> A common way to remember the history of writing about Shakespeare is to say that until Bradley's *Shakespearean Tragedy* appeared in 1904, and culminating there, its main tradition had concentrated on Shakespeare's characters, whereas in recent generations emphasis has fallen on general patterns of meaning, systems of image or metaphor or symbol now [Cavell writes in 1967] taking the brunt of significance. (39)

Cavell is careful to qualify this "intellectual map" as "crude" and overgeneralizing: it "fails worst in locating the figures one would like best to reach" (39). (Cavell refers here to Coleridge, Bradley, Empson, and G. Wilson Knight, but one might add Zukofsky's name to the list.) Nevertheless, using this chart, one could take *Bottom* as possibly the most extreme and fully realized instance of a reading of Shakespeare that concentrates significance on "general patterns of meaning, [or] systems of image or metaphor or symbol" while avoiding a view of the characters that would attribute to them the emotions, motivations, and overall autonomy that one attributes to real human beings. Denis Donoghue provides as appropriate a description of such readings as one could wish: "The scholar chooses certain images in, say, *Macbeth*, and establishes between them a metasyntax which is nearly independent of the *dramatis personae* and of the conflict they enact. It is then argued that this metasyntax, perhaps because it is unconscious, characterizes the play more intimately than any other description in terms of plot and character" (121).

The focus of Cavell's analysis of skepticism in *King Lear*, however, is more than a return to the character-centered criticism of Bradley. Cavell wants to show, within the context of the play, how intellectual and emotional forces that can be classified under the rubric of skepticism work to bring about Lear's personal tragedy. He wants as well to explore how similar "skeptical" movements on the part of Shakespeare's readers have led them to read the plays in mutually exclusive terms either of their characters or of their language. To this end, he begins with a discussion of various thematic readings of *Lear* that focus on imagery relating to "vision and the eyes." Cavell rejects these thematic interpretations and argues that Lear's figuration of sight must be interpreted within a firmer context of the play's plot: in particular, of the "traditional cruxes in this play for which any critic is likely to feel compelled to provide a solution" (*Disowning Knowledge* 43).

The skeptical problematic that Cavell traces in the text of *King Lear* is by no means identical to the garden-variety "outside world" skepticism that Zukofsky denies in his most explicit statements on epistemology. The skepticism that Zukofsky customarily attacks in his works seems a rather generalized one, a broadly defined doubting of one's knowledge. The classic example is Descartes's first Meditation, where Descartes realizes that the possibility that he is dreaming has undermined any certainty he might have had that what his senses tell him is true about the outside world. In his examination of skepticism in Shakespeare, Cavell focuses instead on failures in acknowledging other persons—what a philosopher would call "other minds" skepticism. As he takes "tragedy as the display of skepticism," Cavell also takes "skepticism with respect to other minds as allegorical of skepticism with respect to material objects" (*Disowning Knowledge* 8). Thus, the avoidance of other persons is for Cavell synecdochical and allegorical of the broader skepticism Zukofsky addresses.

Cavell's focus, then, is on the psychic forces that lead to the skeptical denial of the world and of others. Skepticism, in Cavell's account, is the human response to the realization of the human intellect's vulnerability to doubt; skepticism is the mind's nihilistic reaction to the recognition of the limits of its own knowledge: "Lear's 'avoidance' of Cordelia is an instance of the annihilation inherent in the skeptical problematic . . . skepticism's 'doubt' is motivated not by (not even when it is expressed as) a (misguided) intellectual scrupulousness but by a (displaced) denial, by a self-consuming disappointment that seeks world-consuming revenge" (*Disowning Knowledge* 6). In *Lear,* this "denial" takes the form of avoidance, the avoidance of acknowledging others and others' love. Cavell comes to this formulation through his examination of the familiar interpretive "cruxes" of the play, especially "How are we to understand Lear's motivation in his opening scene? How Cordelia's?" (*Disowning Knowledge* 43). In the tragedy, characters—especially Lear himself—play out the skeptical denial through the avoidance of responsibility (for love, or general responsibility to others), which most often becomes the avoidance of sight or being seen: "Lear's dominating motivation [up to the end of the fourth act] is to *avoid being recognized.* The isolation and avoidance of eyes is what the obsessive sight imagery of the play underlines" (*Disowning Knowledge* 46).

Lear's actions in the first scene of the play, Cavell contends, should not be interpreted as merely a far-fetched or fabulistic initiating moment for the wrenching tragedy that follows. Rather, they are explicable in terms of Lear's avoidance of the responsibility of love: when he divides his kingdom among his daughters,

"Lear knows it is a bribe he offers, and—part of him anyway—wants exactly what a bribe can buy: (1) false love and (2) a public expression of love" (*Disowning Knowledge* 61). Cordelia's refusal to speak, to dissemble as her sisters have, "threatens to expose both his plan for returning false love with no love, and expose the necessity for that plan—his terror of being loved, of needing love" (62). Simply to accept Cordelia's love is more than Lear can bear, for to accept her love is to confess himself powerless insofar as he is obligated to his daughter.

Lear's reaction to Cordelia, Cavell argues, is analogous to the skeptic's reaction to the world. Cavell concedes to the skeptic the classical arguments against knowledge of the world; when pursued to their logical ends, these argument are unanswerable (we have no way to *prove* to Descartes that he is not dreaming at the close of the first Meditation, for instance).[1] However, Cavell stresses, *knowledge* of the world's existence is not really the point; our relationship to the world is—or should be—a relationship more profound than simple knowing: "What skepticism suggests is that since we cannot know the world exists, its presentness to us cannot be a function of knowing. The world is to be *accepted;* as the presentness of other minds is not to be known, but acknowledged" (*Disowning Knowledge* 95). This acceptance, or "acknowledgment," is a relationship of a different intellectual form than knowledge. It has, in Cavell's account, elements in common with faith (in Luther's words, "we cannot know God but must have faith" [95]). Cavell describes this stance in his essay "Thinking of Emerson": "The [correct answer to skepticism] does not consist in denying the conclusion of skepticism but in reconceiving its truth. It is true that we do not know the existence of the world with certainty; our relation to its existence is deeper—one in which it is accepted, that is to say, received. My favorite way of putting this is to say that existence is to be acknowledged" (*Senses of Walden* 133).

The skeptic, however, must have more and demands certain intellectual knowledge of the existence of the world outside him. (Compare Zukofsky's Othello, "misconceiving" the notion of "ocular proof" [*B* 325].) When that knowledge is not forthcoming—or rather, when it becomes clear that the world's existence presents itself in a form that cannot be intellectually proven, or *known*—

the skeptic's reaction is to deny the existence of that which he is unable to prove. The skeptic rejects the world's existence because his relationship to the world proves the limits of his knowledge (which cannot with certainty *know* the world) and thereby convicts him as vulnerable, exposed. Lear casts out Cordelia because her sincere love requires him in acknowledging it to take on a similar vulnerability and exposure: although her sisters' declarations of love are false, they are part of a bargain that exposes Lear to no psychic risk.

Skepticism is for Cavell more than just a metaphysical or epistemological position; it is a position with profound social and (as with Zukofsky) ethical implications. Skepticism separates not only the thinker from the objects of knowledge but the individual from the larger community of human beings: "What skepticism threatens is precisely irretrievable outsideness, an uncrossable line, a position from which it is *obvious* (without argument) that the world is unknowable. . . . [Skepticism] is a power that all who possess language possess and may desire: to dissociate oneself, excommunicate oneself from the community in whose agreement, mutual attunement, words exist" (*Disowning Knowledge* 29). As the temptation and power to disavow acknowledgment in the absence of certain knowledge, to disavow one's place in the human universe of language, skepticism is an irreplaceable element of the "idea of the human"—an idea that emerges "no later than Descartes and Shakespeare" and that, Cavell speculates, may be disappearing, along with the skeptical problematic: "I assume that a further stage of this progress [of the Western problematic of knowledge] might be the loss of the problem altogether, which . . . will mean the loss of the idea of the human, hence of the human" (*Disowning Knowledge* 35–36).

For Cavell the "human" is a category that might be superseded at some point in the future, when the Cartesian problematic of knowledge finally loses all relevance. But for Zukofsky, skepticism is the product of a mode of thought peculiarly endemic to the modern (post-Shakespearean) period—namely, the gas age. He proposes no hypotheses about what (if anything) might follow an age that thinks in primarily "intellective," gaseous terms. In Zukofsky's account, one overcomes skepticism not by accepting its premises and working back to their roots and then forward through their implications—which is Cavell's way not of overcoming, but of coming to terms with, skepticism—but by reverting to an earlier, prelapsarian stage of thought and language: a solid or liquid state. While skepticism is the intellectual malady par excellence of our modern age, it is an ailment that the individual poet or philosopher, at her or his discretion, can set aside as pragmatically fruitless. One recalls that for Zukofsky, the only "valid" skepticism is self-reflexive, refusing to take its own premises too seriously (*P* 27), and one notes that among his intellectual heroes is the American Pragmatist philosopher Charles Sanders Peirce. Indeed, one might group the figures with whom Zukofsky claims the most affinity as, on the one hand, poets whose primary interest is in the evidence of the senses (Shakespeare, Pound, Williams) and, on the other, thinkers who, while unhappily marooned in the gas age, look back "with longing" to a "single simple nature" (Spinoza, Adams, Wittgenstein).

Much of "The Avoidance of Love" is concerned, as I have noted, with the question of why Shakespeare's critics have tended to approach his plays through the mutually exclusive rubrics of "character criticism" or "verbal analysis." A brief consideration of *Bottom*'s own treatment of *King Lear* is enough to assure one that Zukofsky's approach falls firmly into the latter camp. The most extended discussion of *Lear,* in the "Definition" chapter (*B* 310–12), consists of fifteen or so quotations from the play that bear directly on the theme of "eyes" and "sight," as well as brief discussions of the fool's song (III.ii.74–77), which reappears from *Twelfth Night,* and the incongruous French word *oeillades* (IV.v.25). The nearly twenty other references to *Lear* scattered throughout *Bottom* are more of the same: lines and phrases that work to bolster the "love : reason :: eyes : mind" proportion, or fragments in which Zukofsky finds echoes or foreshadowings of other significant writers (including a comparison of Homer's "Flensing [Spaying] an arrow and sprinkling antiseptic poisons, a surgeon's worth many another man" [*Illiad* XI.514] and Lear's "Let me have surgeons; / I am cut to the brains" [IV.vi.196] [*B* 380]).[2]

Zukofsky's reading of the plays is weakest when he attempts

to connect the mis-seeing of the characters to their tragic or comedic outcomes. Despite the conceptual elegance of Zukofsky's overall argument—or perhaps *because of* that very symmetry—the mind/eye dichotomy proves at best a clumsy instrument with which to interpret the plays' narratives, as Zukofsky's strained reading of Othello's "ocular proof" amply demonstrates. *Bottom* of course carefully enumerates the instances of "eyes," and so forth, in *Othello* but is notably vague about the precise connection between Othello's mis-seeing, his failure of vision, and the tragedy that befalls him and Desdemona. "Othello with eyes too strong or weak was moved to stare or pry into unreason" (175), Zukofsky claims, and "Pericles for all his wandering does not misconceive the ocular proof to the same degree as Othello, because his eyes never go that far wrong" (325). The implication is that Othello demands to see too much, to have an "ocular proof" of Desdemona's love that somehow, paradoxically, goes beyond the clear evidence of her love that the "physical eye" provides.

"Ocular proof" is, one assumes, a conceptualization, a rationalized version of the assurance of the senses that one ought to take for granted. But this assumption is an uncomfortable horse on which one must travel far, for Zukofsky never makes quite clear what it is Othello desires that constitutes a misprision of the trustworthy physical eye. The problem lies not only in Zukofsky's conceptual obscurity but in what he excludes from his analysis: the personhood of the beloved. Othello's actions in rendering Desdemona motionless and immune to alteration ("Love's not Time's fool . . . Love alters not with his brief hours and weeks" [Sonnet 116]), and his verbal figuring of her as a beautiful statue ("whiter skin of hers than snow, / And smooth as monumental alabaster" [V.ii.4–5]) implicate Othello within the same quest for an unchanging object of love that Zukofsky's heroes Aristotle and Spinoza repeatedly advocate. *Othello* can be read not as playing out the failure of the physical eye but as taking to its conclusion Zukofsky's own conception of the loving gaze.

In a reading such as Zukofsky's, Cavell sees an unwillingness to confront the "drama" of the play, an unwillingness separate from such intellectual "ghostly fashions" as the New Critical philosophy that the plays should be interpreted primarily as poetry.

The "failure to confront such drama as *King Lear* unearths . . . has to do with the mode of this drama itself. Indeed, if my reading of it is correct, the drama is exactly about this difficulty. The difficulty lies in a refusal, a refusal expressed as a failure to acknowledge" (*Disowning Knowledge* 84). The refusal of acknowledgment that the play presents can be seen as parallel to or allegorical of the reader's refusal to acknowledge the human drama of the play. For instance, traditional interpretations of the opening scene that characterize it as fabulistic or ritualistic work to avoid that scene's very implications: "The idea that the abdication scene strains belief suggests a careful ignorance of the quick routes taken in one's own rages and jealousies and brutalities" (87). The very mode of tragedy, and of *Lear* in particular, is one in which the reader is implicated in the same tragedy as the play's principals: "The medium is one which keeps significance continuously before our senses, so that when it comes over us that we have missed it, this discovery will reveal our ignorance to have been willful, complicitous, a refusal to see" (85). The play's characters "are, in a word, men and women; and our liabilities in responding to them are nothing other than our liabilities in responding to any person—rejection, brutality, sentimentality, indifference, the relief and terror in finding courage, the ironies of human wishes" (89).

Such a conception of the relationship between reader and play would convict Zukofsky, and on similar grounds to the critiques advanced by Melnick and Bernstein. In Cavell's view, *Bottom* would be guilty precisely of a skeptical misreading of Shakespeare, a failure to acknowledge the human drama the plays present. As Othello has murdered Desdemona to avoid responding to ("acknowledging") her, Zukofsky's reading of Shakespeare, in focusing exclusively on the plays' imagery and language, has refused to acknowledge the plays' intersubjective dimension and has retreated into a skeptical solipsism. In order to make the whole of this multivalent, self-contradictory Shakespearean corpus conform to the equation he has derived from it, Zukofsky must in effect murder it by reducing it to a set of static images and formulations. To what extent we can we then still regard *Bottom*, given its openness to such a potential Cavellian critique, as a useful text? Can we "rescue" Zukofsky from the skepticism to which, even as he continually repudiates it, he seems to have fallen prey?

It would be a mistake to consider the potential solipsism of *Bottom*'s calculus of perception and affection a problem that Zukofsky has simply ignored or overlooked. Such a position would imply on the part of the critic (whether Cavell, Melnick, or myself) a certain mastery that enables the reader to "correct" the blindness of Zukofsky's own reading of Shakespeare (a reading, one might note, that never claims such a commanding perspective for itself: "To say that [Shakespeare's] focus *was this* is presumptuous. All evaluations of him have been implicitly insolent" [*B* 10]). In the "Definition" chapter of Part III, the "I" (presumably the book's author) defends his method against the "Son," who questions the singlemindedness of *Bottom*'s conclusions: "Is your Shakespeare a cracked record playing over and over one point thru all the plays and poems?" (*B* 266). "Why," he asks, "do you cite endlessly, and presume to cover 'continents,' sidetracking to analogies which I've heard you say you have no taste for, you whom scholars and strays do not attract?" The "I" replies, "so the definition of love in Shakespeare may flourish" (*B* 267). Zukofsky is well aware that his reading of Shakespearean canon is a unitary, singular one, a reading that sees all of Shakespeare's works not merely as "one work, sometimes poor, sometimes good, sometimes great, always regardless of time in which it was composed" (13) but as "a vast musical work in singular and entire concord" (283).

One might begin approaching this problem by recalling the differences between Zukofsky's and Cavell's conceptions of the roots of skepticism and by pointing out some significant affinities between the two. For Cavell, skepticism historically arises concurrently with the "new science" of the seventeenth century:

> We will hardly say that it is *because* of the development of the new science and the establishing of epistemology as the monitor of philosophical inquiry that Shakespeare's mode of tragedy disappeared. But it may be that the loss of presentness—which is what

> the disappearance of that mode of tragedy means—is what works us into the idea that we can save our lives by knowing them. This seems to be the message both of the new epistemology and of Shakespeare's tragedy themselves. . . . [The skeptic] forgoes the world for just the reason that the world is important, that it is the scene and stage of connection with the present: he finds that it vanishes exactly with the effort to *make* it present. If this makes him unsuccessful, that is because the presentness achieved by *certainty* of the senses cannot compensate for the presentness which had been elaborated through our old absorption in the world. (*Disowning Knowledge* 94, last italics mine)

"Certainty," like other gaseous words such as "reality" (and indeed "epistemology"), would be for Zukofsky a prime example of a term that arises only from "intellective" thinking—a term that is "non-sense." In specifying a particular realm of language in which discourse is meaningless or nonsignificant, Zukofsky agrees with Wittgenstein, who in both his earlier and later work is concerned to demonstrate that certain uses of language are fundamentally futile. The *Tractatus,* which denounces skepticism as "palpably senseless, if it would doubt where a question cannot be asked" (187), argues at length that there are realms of discourse—particularly that of the ethical—where nothing meaningful can be said, for ethics can only be *shown,* not formulated: "Hence also there can be no ethical propositions. . . . It is clear that ethics cannot be expressed" (183). The *Philosophical Investigations* is to a great extent a diagnostic work, aimed at showing how certain uses of language, particularly metaphysical discourse—as attractive as they may seem to us—go against what Wittgenstein conceives of as the "grammar" or logic of language itself and are thereby meaningless: "Philosophy is a battle against the bewitchment of our intelligence by means of language. . . . The results of philosophy are the uncovering of one or another piece of plain nonsense and of bumps that the understanding has got by running its head up against the limits of language" (47e–48e).

This tendency to regard skeptical questions as nonsensical, fundamentally meaningless nonquestions—a tendency shared by

Wittgenstein, Zukofsky, and such Positivists as Rudolph Carnap (see Stroud 172)—might be read as symptomatic of a turn toward a postskeptical, "postmodern" way of thought that embodies the "loss of the idea of the human" that Cavell imagines (it of course might also, in Zukofsky's case, be regarded as an expression of a thoroughly American pragmatism). But for Zukofsky it is a salutary (re)turn, one that places language and thought on a firmer, more organic—and thus more solid—footing. At the same time, it is a return that Zukofsky himself can never fully make, for he is himself a thoroughgoing product of the gas age. And thought, even in gaseous terms, has its attractions: Zukofsky finds aesthetic virtue in Spinoza and Dante, both of whose work frequently "vaporizes": "Like mathematical formulae, that's pure abstract state, but who's not to say that that is as beautiful as some botanical convolvulae or something like that" (*P* 171). Although Zukofsky might regard philosophical skepticism as a "bugbear," a nonquestion that, in the end, only wastes the questioner's time and industry ("I don't see why Wallace Stevens ruined a great deal of his work by speaking vaguely about the imagination and reality and so on. He can be a wonderful poet, but so much of it is a bore, bad philosophy" [*LZMP* 277]), that dismissal cannot be taken to imply that he conceives perception itself to be an unproblematical process. Zukofsky's own poetry, I will show, nearly always involves a careful examination of the complex relationships among perception, ego, text, and communication.

In this light, *Bottom* appears as a lengthy attempt to diagnose and explore the "impediments" that obstruct the "marriage of true minds," the intellectual obstructions or skepticisms that prevent the lover from rightly perceiving the beloved—at least insofar as that problematic is thematized and dramatized in Shakespeare's *Works*. But the rubric under which Zukofsky undertakes this diagnosis, the "verbal analysis" by which he isolates his chosen themes in Shakespeare's text, and the conclusions he draws—all these seem guilty of a form of "other minds" skepticism akin to that which Cavell finds in *Lear* and in *Lear*'s critics. Zukofsky, however, is careful to stress that his reading of Shakespeare is neither "objective" nor totalizing, an encompassing explanation of the Shakespearean corpus:

> Anyone who *explains* William Shakespeare dreams in character, not with the wisdom of Bottom. . . . This approach must mean that the eyes of one person were fixed more on these lines [i.e., *Midsummer Night's Dream* III.ii.146–50 and I.i.232–39] than on all the others. Even a photographic eye—a lens—is placed by some human; when "shooting" at Shakespeare, at best perhaps by inevitable accident. To say that his focus *was this* is presumptuous. (*B* 9–10, first emphasis mine)

This disclaimer, which appears at the very outset of *Bottom*, is easily forgotten over the course of the book's more than four hundred pages of "eyes" and "seeing." Zukofsky's very reiteration of his terms makes them take on a totalizing, all-explanatory quality. But the disclaimer remains, as does the *On* of the title *Bottom: On Shakespeare*, a word that can be taken here, as so much in Zukofsky can, in a musical sense: *Bottom* can then be seen not as a (prescriptive) reading *of* Shakespeare but as a collection of variations and improvisations *on* a set of themes (among many other themes) implicit *in* Shakespeare.

Bottom appears as a staticizing, solipsistic misprision of Shakespeare only when viewed from a particular generic perspective, that which takes *On* as signaling a metatext, a work of explanation or commentary. Zukofsky's 1961 introduction to *Bottom*, however, offers two other descriptions of that book as something more—or at least something *other*—than a mere work of criticism or commentary: it is "A long poem built on a theme for the variety of its recurrences," and "A continuation of my work on prosody in my other writings" (*P* 167). If one is freed of the burden of regarding *Bottom*'s parade of citations and commentary as necessarily constituting an explanation of Shakespeare, totalizing or otherwise, then it becomes more apparent how Zukofsky's own description of *Bottom* as a "long poem" can help to situate our response to the epistemological doctrine that the book seems overtly to propose. As a long poem in prose, *Bottom* is a vast collage of quotations from Shakespeare and seemingly every other book Zukofsky has read, mortared together by longer or shorter passages of commentary. The seeds of its form are in Zukofsky's 1924 Henry Adams essay (over half of which consists of Adams's works), and the culmination of its method is the tightly packed five-word lines of quotation and translation that make up "A"-22, -23, and *80 Flowers*. Put in the context of these other works, *Bot tom* is a crucial analogue to the accomplishments of Zukofsky's more generically determinate "poetic" works. Bernstein sums up such a reading: "*Bottom* may be read more profitably as an *exemplary* poetics than as an antiepistemological tract; in this sense, it can be seen as a companion text to *'A'*, illustrating at a grosser level of collage the technique of finely milled textual citations that is central to Zukofsky's other work" (*Content's Dream* 151, emphasis mine). Even though *Bottom* may not describe or advocate, at least on the level of overt theorization, a particular mode of poetic composition, it nonetheless exemplifies a poetics closely related to the poetics that structure Zukofsky's explicitly "poetic" works.

Bottom's long stretches of carefully juxtaposed and arranged quotations—from Shakespeare and from a wide range of Western literature and philosophy—put one in mind of *"A"*, where similar masses of quotation appear in denser (and largely uncited) juxtaposition. The parallel is particularly clear when one compares the penultimate section of *"A"*—"A"-23, a cento anthology of six thousand years of poetic writing from Gilgamesh to Zukofsky himself—to *Bottom*'s "An Alphabet of Subjects," twenty-six alphabetically titled chapters that trace the eyes/mind dialectic through a number of bodies of works, including the entire Shakespeare corpus ("Definition"), classical Greek and Roman writing ("Greeks" and "Latine"), and canonical world literature as a whole ("Continents"). The method of *Bottom*, in the light of such a comparison, can be fairly represented as a larger-scale working out of the same compositional methods that produce *"A"*; in this sense, one can view *Bottom* as an exploration of Zukofsky's own brand of modernist poetics—a "prosody" of quotation and recontextualization in which a textual fragment's "original" context becomes secondary to the position it assumes in the composition at hand.

Two approaches to *Bottom* follow from a recognition that the work has far more in common with a modernist poem than with a traditional work of literary criticism. First, to read *Bottom* as a poem of sorts does not absolve one of the responsibility of confronting *Bottom*'s theory of love and perception qua theory, any more than a reader of *The Cantos* can ignore out of hand that poem's more than occasionally Fascist, authoritarian thrust simply because it is embodied in a poetic work. It does help, however, to see the question of what *Bottom* claims Shakespeare says as a problem of contexts rather than a problem of untenable beliefs asserted as extraliterary truth (as one *must* regard Pound's *Jefferson and/or Mussolini,* for instance). Melnick's quarrel with *Bottom* stems from his unwillingness to consider the immediate "poetic" context of Zukofsky's quotations from Shakespeare—their context, that is, within *Bottom*'s larger structure and argument—apart from their original context in the *Works.* Such unwillingness is by no means meretricious and may indeed be almost inevitable. But the possibility of overcoming (if only momentarily) that unwillingness, and thereby reading *Bottom* on Zukofsky's own recommended terms, as a long poem working musical variations on various themes of Shakespeare, or concurrently as an extended Burton-like meditation on how one *might* refute skepticism, using the language of the preeminent English poet—this possibility should continually discourage one from taking a too totalizing view of the themes *Bottom* proposes and from identifying those themes too closely as Zukofsky's or Shakespeare's own.

Second, when one regards *Bottom* as an exemplary prosody or as a long poem of sorts—two related viewpoints that have in common their emphasis on the *formal* aspects of the text—it becomes evident that *Bottom*'s very form works to undercut the thrust of its ostensible philosophical argument and to this extent models the double structure of Zukofsky's work as a whole. In general, Zukofsky's response to the problem of philosophical skepticism (at least in his prose writings) seems remarkably straightforward and dismissive, even to the point of appearing simplistic or nonphilosophical. For all of his erudition and education in the Western philosophical tradition, Zukofsky is content to dismiss the problem of knowledge in a characteristically American, pragmatic manner. As George Oppen, one of Zukofsky's colleagues in the 1930's Objectivist movement, puts it in a 1974 letter to John Taggart, "the philosophic background of Zuk[ofsky], Oppen, Rezi [Reznikoff] . . . is what the 'man in the street' . . . regards as common sense—'Realist' " (*Selected Letters* 288). Bernstein describes Zukofsky's poetics (though *not* his poetry) as "oddly in tune with American 'show me' pragmatism" (*Content's Dream* 157). And Zukofsky's only published comment on his philosophical education shows John Dewey in a decidedly unmetaphysical light: "sometimes . . . he sat on the radiator, and when it was hot of course he moved away. His educational philosophy did not interest me. The preoccupied man did" (*P* 30).

The explicit argument of *Bottom* assigns foundational validity to the evidence of the individual's senses, the "clear physical eye." According to this argument, knowledge is founded in the single Cartesian observer, and *Bottom* retains the subject/object dichotomy that persists through Kantian epistemology. Zukofsky has "done away with" epistemology, but only at the expense of risking a retreat into solipsism, the most radical form of the skepticism that is in itself the purest manifestation of the very epistemology *Bottom* has sought to escape. *Bottom*'s form, however, its radically heterogeneous weave of voices and texts, all refusing wholly to submit to the calculus of Zukofsky's argument, asserts the basis of knowledge, not in the Cartesian observer but in the ungrounded, communal "forms of life" to which Wittgenstein alludes in his *Philosophical Investigations*. As I have noted, *Bottom* quotes the *Tractatus Logico-Philosophicus* in order to bolster its own rejection of epistemological abstraction: "Skepticism is *not* irrefutable, but palpably senseless, if it would doubt where a question cannot be asked" (quoted in *B* 187). But while Wittgenstein's early work, along with Spinoza and Aristotle, is an important touchstone of Zukofsky's argument in *Bottom*, it is Wittgenstein's later writings on epistemology (writings of which, as Bernstein points out, Zukofsky "seems unaware" [150]) that provide a clearer picture of how *Bottom*'s form contradicts that argument. In the manuscript posthumously published as *On Certainty*, Wittgenstein delineates the boundaries between facts that can be reasonably questioned and grounds of belief that are simply accepted (or, as Cavell would say, acknowledged); his argument implies that the skeptical recital, which seeks to question the very grounds of knowledge, proves senseless exactly to the extent that it takes those grounds as questionable:

> But I did not get my picture of the world by satisfying myself of its correctness; nor do I have it because I am satisfied of its correctness. No: it is the inherited background against which I distinguish between true and false. (*On Certainty* 15e)

> Our knowledge forms an enormous system. And only within this system has a particular bit the value we give it. (52e)

> The existence of the earth is rather part of the whole *picture* which forms the starting-point of belief for me. (28e)

> As if giving grounds did not come to an end sometime. But the end is not an ungrounded presupposition: it is an ungrounded way of acting. (17e)

The existence of the world is part of our basic worldview. It is useless to expect it to be susceptible to—or in need of—the same principles of verification that we apply to our convictions. We do not believe (or know) that the world exists; rather the world's existence is a condition of our beliefs and knowledge.

When Wittgenstein asserts, "The difficulty is to realize the groundlessness of our believing" (*On Certainty* 24e), he strikes at the root of the skeptical dilemma, the refusal to let go of the desire for an intellectual grounding for our beliefs and our knowledge. Ultimately, Wittgenstein concludes, the process of questioning one's knowledge, of "giving grounds" for one's beliefs, must come to an end and reveal that knowledge and those beliefs to be based on something without grounds. It is crucial, however, to distinguish as Wittgenstein does between an "ungrounded presupposition" and an "ungrounded way of acting": the "ungrounded presupposition" would be a groundless intellectual assertion, a belief that, while logically capable of being tested and proved either false or true, has not been so tested and thereby stands without grounding. Our assumptions about the world's existence and about the general reliability of our knowledge do not have this form. Rather, they are part of an "ungrounded way of acting," what Wittgenstein would call in his *Philosophical Investigations* a "form of life."[3] What is crucial about a form of life is that it is not an individual's way of acting or knowing but, as philosopher of science David Bloor has best shown, a fundamentally *social* construction, a set of behaviors and beliefs held in common by a group of subjects.

It is to the extent that *Bottom* is a collage, a document constructed out of hundreds of fragments of others' voices ("Others['] letters," as one construction of "A"-22 has it [*A* 508]), that it allows the voices of a community of speakers to be heard and thereby transcends the Cartesian skepticism to which its explicit argument is vulnerable. Zukofsky's poetics of collage, as practiced in both *"A"* and *Bottom*, plays out in a strikingly foregrounded manner the properties of language and context that Derrida, in his "Signature Event Context," describes as the poetics of the "graft": "by virtue of its essential iterability, a written syntagm can always be detached from the chain in which it is inserted or given without causing it to lose all possibility of functioning, if not all possibility of 'communicating,' precisely. One can perhaps come to recognize other possibilities in it by inscribing it or *grafting* it onto other chains. No context can entirely enclose it" (*Limited Inc* 9). In his extended explorations of the grammatological nature of language, Derrida makes clear that such iterability is a property of all language use, not merely of the written word. But *Bottom*, a text composed to a striking extent of cited and re-cited fragments of others' writing, provides a clear example of how the cited text simultaneously signifies within its new context and refers back to its previous appearances. Derrida's remarks in *Dissemination* concerning his own quotations from Philippe Soller's *Numbers* are entirely germane to *Bottom*'s methods of quotation:

> Those textual samples provided by *Numbers* do not . . . serve as "quotations," "collages," or even "illustrations." They are not being applied upon the surface or in the interstices of a text that would already exist without them. And they themselves can only be read within the operation of their reinscription, within the graft. It is the sustained, discrete violence of an incision that is not apparent in the thickness of the text, a calculated insemination of the proliferating allogene through which the two texts are transformed, deform each other, or pass elliptically one into the other and become regenerated in the repetition, along the edge of an *overcast*

> *seam* [*un surjet*]. Each grafted text continues to radiate back toward the site of its removal, transforming that, too, as it affects the new territory. (*Dissemination* 355)

While the logic of *Bottom*'s anti-epistemological argument demands that Zukofsky's borrowed words support the evidence of the senses over the mind's rationalizations, those words carry within them the force of their original context—"radiate back toward the site of [their] removal"—constantly contradicting and subverting the single-minded argument of their Zukofskyan context.

When *Bottom*'s reader encounters Whitman's "I see Teheran . . ." (*B* 252), for instance, it is immediately evident, both by the ellipses and by the un-Whitmanesque brevity of the line, that the original context of the phrase might well involve something altogether other than simple physical sight. In Whitman, such a phrase could only be the beginning of a longer line and must in all probability be part of a catalogue of "I see"s. (Such is indeed the case in the line's original appearance in "Salut Au Monde"—"I see Teheran, I see Muscat and Medina and the intervening sands, I see the caravans toiling onward" [Whitman 294]—and of course the reference to Teheran makes clear that this is an instance of other than physical seeing for Whitman.) One could multiply similar examples, such as Zukofsky's citation of Mallarmé's "Prose (pour des Esseintes)"—

> Oui, dan une île que l'air charge
> De vue et non de visions
> Toute fleurs s'étalait plus large
> San que nous en devisions
> [*B* 231][4]

—in which Mallarmé's description of a visionary experience of such intensity that hallucinatory "visions" have the immediacy of sight itself (*vue*) is recontextualized to read as a simple valuing of *vue* over *visions*, the physical eye over the metaphysical mind.

It is useful to note how Zukofsky's three or four periods, the conventional signs of citational elision, function as the trace of originary context. That is, even as Zukofsky reinscribes his sources into his own logic of eyes and mind, the protocols of quotation (protocols ultimately overridden in *"A"* but adhered to fairly consistently in *Bottom*) mark and preserve what might argue against or mitigate that logic. Zukofsky quotes a famous passage of Emerson's "Self-Reliance":

> "quotes some saint or sage . . . ashamed before the . . . blowing rose. These roses under my window. . . . There is no time to them. There is simply the rose . . . its whole life acts . . . the full-blown flower . . . no more; . . . the leafless root . . . no less. . . . But man . . . does not live in the present . . . with reverted eye laments the past." (*B* 238, ellipses Zukofsky's)

The passage from which Zukofsky has extracted this reads in full:

> Man is timid and apologetic; he is no longer upright; he dares not say "I think," "I am," but quotes some saint or sage. He is ashamed before the blade of grass or the blowing rose. These roses under my window make no reference to former roses or to better ones; they are for what they are; they exist with God to-day. There is no time to them. There is simply the rose; it is perfect in every moment of its existence. Before a leaf-bud has burst, its whole life acts; in the full-blown flower there is no more; in the leafless root there is no less. Its nature is satisfied, and it satisfies nature, in all moments alike. But man postpones or remembers; he does not live in the present, but with reverted eye laments the past, or, heedless of the riches that surround him, stands on tiptoe to foresee the future. (*Essays and Lectures* 270)

On one level, what Zukofsky is up to here is a simple modernist paring down, a removal of excess connective passages like that of Pound's blue-penciling Eliot's drafts of *The Waste Land.* But Zukofsky's revision of Emerson, even as it preserves much of what is central to the transcendentalist's text, recasts that text so that it conforms more closely to the eyes/mind equation that governs *Bottom.* Whereas Emerson emphasizes the necessity for each person to achieve her or his own Cartesian breakthrough, to say " 'I think,' [therefore] 'I am,' " Zukofsky purges the text completely of this moment of discovery: *Bottom*'s epistemological certainty is based not on the subject's *thinking* but on the subject's *perceiving.* Emerson lauds the roses for their obliviousness to "former" or "better" roses: Zukofsky's text, built as it is on the citation of previous authority, effaces this emphasis on a present oblivious to the past. Emerson's final sentence, which bemoans the extent to which "man" fails to deal with the present in his concern with the past and the future, becomes in Zukofsky a restatement of the nostalgia for an age of "solid-state" language, a period in which the perceptions of the now "reverted" eye are not marred by the erring brain: "Together, Wittgenstein and Shakespeare look back with longing almost two thousand years to 'simple' (single) nature" (*B* 85).

Zukofsky's citation of Emerson here is typical of *Bottom*'s quotational strategies. Again and again, passages are chosen that contribute to the eyes-mind theme, then carefully pruned, weeded, and shaped by elision into what at times amount to soundbites endorsing Zukofsky's argument. Yet, as in this passage from "Self-Reliance," time and again Zukofsky's quotations signify beyond their immediate context and "radiate back" to their originary moments. They thereby form not a unitary chorus but a tenuous, momentary consensus, always liable to be shattered by the irruption of the voices of the irreducibly other.

On the level of philosophical argument, *Bottom* does not "do away with" epistemology but merely turns its back on the subject. Whereas Cavell concedes the skeptic his arguments and then proceeds to investigate the human causes that drive him to make those arguments in the first place, Zukofsky simply diagnoses skepticism as an intellectual malady, a product of the gas age, and a malady that one avoids by simply trusting one's senses. But even as *Bottom* repeats its formula of "eyes" and "mind" again and again in its parade of ostensibly illustrative quotations (quotations that stubbornly retain the traces of their originary contexts and speakers even in their recontextualization), the text brilliantly illustrates how knowledge is founded on a "form of life," a set of behaviors and "ways of acting" shared among a community of knowers. The same relationship exists between Zukofsky's works of poetics and his more recognizable "poetry," *"A"* especially. While Zukofsky's Objectivist manifestos argue that poetry is an almost positivistic art—"precise information on existence out of which it grows" (*P* 20)—and one founded on the perceptions of the individual poet, *"A"*, in its constant acknowledgment of the babel of voices that constitutes the background and the material of the poem's voice, makes a single "song" out of a host of subjectivities: "One song / Of many voices" ("A"-5, 18) and "Have your odyssey / How many voiced it be" ("A"-12, 128).

The contrast, almost contradiction, between *Bottom*'s dogma and its form is a contrast that emerges most clearly when one regards that text in light of Zukofsky's contrasting descriptions of it as both an imaginative work of poetics and a long poem in prose. While the polemics of *Bottom* as philosophical criticism remain grounded in the subject/object dichotomy of Cartesian and Kantian epistemology, Zukofsky's formal poetic practice performs the work of "do[ing] away with" epistemology by reimagining knowledge in post-Kantian, Wittgensteinian terms. *Bottom*, as generically indeterminate text, is indispensable to reading the double structure of Zukofsky's poetics. As critical treatise, it presents explicitly, and in its purest terms, Zukofsky's Objectivist valorization of subjective vision; simultaneously, as exemplary prosody, it plays out the dialogical conversation on which the epistemic certainty of Zukofsky's poetry *implicitly* founds itself. We shall see how this tension between the solipsist's rejection of epistemology and the Wittgensteinian's recognition of the interpersonal bases of knowledge are carried through and played out in Zukofsky's verse works, especially the crucial sequence "I's (pronounced *eyes*)."

4

"I's (pronounced *eyes*)"

Objectivist Epistemology; or, Seeing Things

When you look at a picture, you can always see
If a man of sense has painted he.
—William Blake, quoted in Zukofsky, *"Golgonoozà?"* (*P* 43)

Like many "critical" texts, *Bottom: On Shakespeare* reveals far more about its author than its ostensible subject, although it does so more explicitly and interestingly than most. It is perhaps useful to view this process in terms of Zukofsky's approach and expectations, recalling the proverb Emerson cites in "The American Scholar": "He that would bring home the wealth of the Indies, must carry out the wealth of the Indies." One might also recall the sentences that precede and follow the proverb: "One must be an inventor to read well. . . . There is then creative reading as well as creative writing" (*Essays and Lectures* 59). Zukofsky reads Shakespeare's *Works* more as poet than as critic; he examines them not as the inductive researcher (despite his protestations to the contrary) but to find support in the largest monument of Renaissance poetic tradition for an aesthetics and epistemology that are ultimately based in a specifically modernist approach to language. While Zukofsky's reading of Shakespeare—continually resolving as it does in the problematic of love, eyes, and the intellect—seems at times unrelentingly single-minded, almost obsessive, his fundamental concern with the question of perception and its mediations is evident throughout his own poetry, bearing fruit of far greater subtlety and complexity than the simple proportion "love : reason :: eyes : mind" might suggest.

"Can a mote of sunlight" is a clearly programmatic poem, and its lyric qualities are to a certain degree subordinated to its gnomic argument. In more complex and characteristic poetic statements, Zukofsky both reaffirms his commitment to the evidence of the senses and embodies in more nuanced forms the philosophy that in *Bottom* seems so frustratingly simple. By the time he published "I's (pronounced *eyes*)," the title sequence of his 1963 collection, Zukofsky was surveying the problem of knowledge in a complex manner no doubt enriched by his thirteen years' work on *Bottom.* But in order to approach Zukofsky's poetry, I think it useful to return to the critical terms introduced in the title of his most programmatic statement of poetics, the 1931 Objectivist "manifesto" "Sincerity and Objectification: *With Special Reference to the Work of Charles Reznikoff.*" There is a persuasive basis for viewing Zukofsky's entire written corpus on the model of Spinoza's *Ethics,* as an impressive and capacious set of developments out of a limited number of originary propositions. The 1930s doctrines of sincerity and objectification, which Zukofsky repeats with no signs of renunciation or revision in his 1968 interview with L. S. Dembo, remain central to him. These means of making a poet are at the heart of his practice, early and late.

"Sincerity," as the first term of Zukofsky's poetics, is an ascesis—an ethics—of composition: "In sincerity shapes appear concomitants of word combinations, precursors of (if there is continuance) completed sound or structure, melody or form. Writing occurs which is the detail, not mirage, of seeing, of thinking with the things as they exist, and of directing them along a line of melody" (*P* 12). John Taggart writes, in an analysis that remains among the closest and most sympathetic Zukofsky has received, that for Zukofsky, sincerity in composition is "the care for the detail . . . an attitude or ethics, one of whose enactments is the poet's focusing precisely upon details of the outside physical universe and upon details of the universe of language, words" (*Songs of Degrees* 85–86). Sincerity, then, is an attitude of absolute faithfulness both to one's perceptions and to one's language. When one writes with sincerity, writing is "the detail, not mirage, of seeing, of thinking with the things as they exist, and of directing them along a line of melody": writing does not aim to present a simulacrum ("mirage") of perception, cognition, or musical composition but rather itself embodies those processes. In a wholly pertinent passage, Pound claims that "technique is the only gauge and test of a man's lasting sincerity" (*Selected Prose* 34). In Zukofsky's critical vocabulary, sincerity is both the attitude and the technique by which it is manifested. One can describe the modernist movement in general as an attempt to reimagine poetry as a technique, to reject the perceived emotive bases of Romantic and Victorian poetry and concomitantly to value the poet as a master of a complex craft rather than as a sensitive observer. To Eliot, Pound is after all "il miglior *fabbro*" (the better maker). But Pound's and Zukofsky's notions of sincerity—of the poet as craftsperson rather than emotive vessel—do not really devalue the poet as person: rather, they work to shift emphasis from the poet's *public* character (which the Victorian era had either saluted or damned) to the poet's character as manifested in his pursuit of his craft—the only character that ought, to a reader of poems, to matter.

Zukofsky's sincerity not only implies absolute fidelity to one's materials—both experiences and words—but it demands in composing poetry the attitude, almost reverential, that the poem itself is the primary field of action and experience. What occurs in the poem is not the relation, suggestion, or approximation of events outside the poem—that would be the "mirage" rather than the "detail" of seeing. The text's mimesis of exterior events is displaced by the text itself as event. Although the poet must write in absolute truth to experience, her or his primary duty is to the poem itself, which must be as thoroughly realized an experience as anything outside it. (Something of a similar position, more extensively [and flamboyantly] developed, would be presented in Charles Olson's famous 1950 essay, "Projective Verse" [*Human Universe* 51–61]. According to Celia Zukofsky, Zukofsky "always felt the Olson's essay on Projective Verse was really a take-off on his own critical writings. . . . Really a restatement of what [Zukofsky] had said re the *Objectivists*" [*LZMP* 73].)[1]

Sincerity, then, can be taken as an attitude toward the poetic word as *sign*, in the Saussurean sense, and as such it can be analyzed into two separate spheres of attention: that to the signifier (*signifiant*), the word itself, and that to the signified (*signifié*), the mental concept to which the word corresponds (see Saussure 66–67).[2] These two focuses of compositional attention are by no means identical. Focus on the signified will ultimately lead to a poetics of mere notation of experience (and will lead beyond the realm of poetry itself, insofar as poetry necessarily involves a certain degree of formal self-consciousness), while focus on the signifier, if pursued to the exclusion of the other component of the sign, will lead to purely metonymic, linguistic wordplay. All poetic language is to a certain degree a foregrounding of the signifier (this is most evident in such traditional poetic markers as rhyme and meter), although the extent of that foregrounding varies from one poetics to another. Part of what makes Zukofsky's rendering of perception in his work interesting lies in the manner in which he balances the two separate demands of compositional sincerity. To write with sincerity, the poet must at all times pay the most scrupulous attention possible, not only to his perceptions but to all aspects of the words that she or he is manipulating: their primary and secondary meanings, their connotations, their idiomatic usages, their etymological roots, and their musical qualities, both alone and in combination with other words.

These musical qualities of separate words work together in combination and sequence to constitute the "line of melody" that is the poem's ongoing movement. As Taggart puts it,

> Melody is both the continuously moving line as it grows and defines itself in the concatenation of word sound detail and the completed structure or form that is the culmination and the memory of that motion. . . . All of the care-engendering movement that leads to and constitutes melody, attitude and composing act, occurs from and in a condition of sincerity. The completed structure of melody occurs in a separate condition of objectification, the second major term of Zukofsky's poetics, which he also calls rested totality, "the apprehension satisfied completely as to the appearance of the art form as an object." (*Songs of Degrees* 86–87)

While sincerity is a moment-by-moment compositional principle, objectification is in part the structural principle by which the poet's efforts of sincerity become the completed poem: objectification is "the arrangement, into one apprehended unit, of minor units of sincerity—in other words, the resolving of words and their ideation into structure" (*P* 13). Zukofsky's notion of objectification in poetry bears some resemblance to the New Critics' conception of the poem as a free-standing and self-sufficient object, a "well-wrought urn." Like the New Critics, Zukofsky is careful to distinguish the poem as object from other more rhetorical or journalistic uses of language: "distinct from print which records action and existence and incites the mind to further suggestion, there exists, though it may not be harbored as solidly in the crook of an elbow, writing (*audibility in two-dimensional print*) which is an object or affects the mind as such" (*P* 13, emphasis mine).[3] Where Zukofsky differs from the New Critics is in his emphasis on the phenomenological nature of objectification, on the fact that objectification is not so much a structural quality of the poem itself as the "rested totality" the mind obtains in apprehending the poem: "the *apprehension* satisfied completely as to the *appearance* of the art form as an object" (13, emphases mine). Objectification is as much a principle of readerly reception as it is a quality inherent to the text: the aim of writing is to produce the poem that "is an object or affects the mind as such," that enables the mind to achieve "the totality of perfect rest," "rested totality."

When Zukofsky's essay was published in the " 'Objectivists' 1931" issue of *Poetry*, it necessarily took on the (perhaps deceptive) appearance of a manifesto for a movement, such as Pound's earlier "A Few Don'ts by an Imagiste" (1913). In later statements, Zukofsky was eager to emphasize the ad hoc nature of the "Objectivist" label, which he claimed was arrived at on Harriet Monroe's insistence that " 'You must have a movement.' . . . Anyway, I told Harriet, 'All right, let's call it "Objectivists," ' and I wrote the essay on sincerity and objectification" (*LZMP* 266). This seems a trifle disingenuous, at least in its details, for much of the essay is precisely an analysis of his friend Reznikoff's poetry, an analysis that he had earlier submitted not to *Poetry* but to the *Menorah Journal* (where it had been rejected).

I will return later to the issue of precisely how much weight one ought to attach to the Objectivist "movement." What is clear is that Zukofsky's theory of sincerity and objectification is less important as an attempt at specifying what he finds vital in the poets he includes in his issue of *Poetry*—although it is that—than as a description of what he conceives as the poet's task during any period: "At any time, objectification in writing is rare. The poems or the prose structures of a generation are few. Properly no verse should be called a poem if it does not convey the totality of perfect rest" (*P* 13). As Zukofsky puts it later (and more simply) to Dembo, "The objectivist, then, is one person, not a group, and as I define him he is interested in living with things as they exist, and as a 'wordsman,' he is a craftsman who puts words together into an object" (*LZMP* 268). Although Zukofsky later expresses doubt about the terminology of his early essay—"I wouldn't do it today. (I've sworn off criticism after *Bottom*, after nineteen years of going through all that.) In any case I wouldn't use the same terminology anymore" (*LZMP* 266)—the compositional measures of sincerity and objectification remain operative throughout his work and provide useful critical paradigms for dealing with that work. They also provide a helpful framework for examining the interplay of Zukofsky's formal and epistemological concerns.

"I's (pronounced *eyes*)" was composed as eleven separate short poems, which were over a period of two years (1959–60) combined into a single sequence (Booth, "Zukofsky Papers," *LZMP* 395). These eleven brief poems seem slight, tossed-off, as do so many of Zukofsky's mid-period writings (compare the sequences "Light," or "The Old Poet Moves to a New Apartment 14 Times"), and can accordingly supply evidence for the slightness of Zukofsky's work or for the ludic element of sheer nonsensical play.[4] Obviously these poems seem on their face a trifle quaint, even "goofy," as one reader confided to me. I am convinced, however, that part of Zukofsky's strength and charm is in his ability to embody deeply considered philosophical ideas in seemingly casual verbal structures. The varied poems of "I's" might indeed be read as quick snapshots of perception, as a series of glimpses around. At the same time, however, they not only exemplify the variety of formal and musical shapes that objectification can take but also give clear evidence of Zukofsky's ongoing concern with the theory of knowledge. Zukofsky tells Dembo in 1968 that the first section (what one might call the "title" section) is "the short way" of the "getting rid of epistemology" that is *Bottom*'s task (*LZMP* 277–78):

> I's (pronounced *eyes*)
>
> Hi, Kuh,
>
> those
> gold'n bees
> are I's,
>
> eyes,
>
> skyscrapers.
> [*CSP* 214]

The poem works on several levels, but one might begin by observing how it serves as a record of perception. Zukofsky briefly glosses the poem in the interview with Dembo:

> As at the beginning of "I's (pronounced *eyes*) . . . " the *haiku*—everybody's writing *haiku*. You remember Elsie, Borden's cow? That's what I meant, and I greeted her up on the sign there: "Hi, Kuh." "Those / gold'n bees / are I's." Obviously some apparition or vision. She's up there anyway and the golden bees . . . I don't know, she makes honey. The bees are also "eyes." You were wondering which "eyes" see. On the other hand, suppose, without my glasses, I look out at the tower—"those / gold'n bees / are I's, / eyes, / skyscrapers": all I see is Christmas crystallography. It's wonderful, but absolutely astigmatic.
>
> All right, the epistemological question? I see this? Yes? The eyes see it? But there's also an object out there. All right, whichever way you want. (*LZMP* 278, ellipses in original)

The poet (in his own account) looks up at a billboard of Elsie, the Borden cow, and greets her, "Hi, Kuh" (*Kuh* is German for "cow"). He sees "gold'n bees" (the B's of the sign?), which also look like eyes and which taken together resemble skyscrapers. Or perhaps the billboard itself, towering over the poet, seems to scrape the sky. There is, as Zukofsky acknowledges, a somewhat hallucinatory quality to this perception: "Obviously some apparition or vision." But a second experience is fused here with the sight of the billboard: "On thc othcr hand, suppose, without my glasses, I look out at the tower." The lights of the city skyscrapers this New York poet would have seen every day and night, reduced by "absolute astigmatism" to "Christmas crystallography," look like golden bees or eyes. The poem is a conflation of two separate acts of perception, which have in common elements of metaphorical interpretation: the "gold'n bees," the eyes, the skyscraper-like scale.

It is through this metaphorical interpreting of perception that the poem "does away with" epistemology: "I see this? Yes. The eyes see it? But there's also an object out there. All right, whichever way you want." The golden bees seen by the poet are placed in apposition to both "I's" and "eyes." (The deictic "those" is crucial here, for it emphasizes that the "gold'n bees" are both specific and exterior to the perceiver.) There is an absolute continuity, then, between the perceiver (the I), the organs of perception (the eyes), and the objects of perception (the golden bees, whatever they might actually be). It is impossible, the poem implies, to separate the three. One might try to emphasize as primary any one of these elements ("All right, whichever way you want"), but one cannot deny the existence of any of them. No matter how hallucinatory or astigmatic the perceptions have been, the fact that they have occurred is sufficient reply to the skeptic.

When reading, of course, it is difficult to distinguish between what Zukofsky would consider individual instances of compositional sincerity, taking the form of minute attentions to the particulars of language, and what he would designate the objectification of the poem as a whole. One might perhaps note, as an instance of a "minor unit of sincerity," the initial pun of "Hi, Kuh"/*haiku*, which alerts readers to the fact that the poem might be some variation on the traditionally imagistic, perceptually based haiku. Like haiku (or the post-Imagist Western version of haiku—"everybody's writing *haiku*"), "I's (pronounced *eyes*)" presents an experience and a commentary on that experience in an extremely compacted space. Nevertheless, the overall melodic line of the poem is evident, especially in a careful reading aloud: the rhyming of "those"/"bees"/"I's"/"eyes," closed by the burst of *s*'s in "skyscrapers"; the assonance of "th**o**se," "g**o**ld'n," and "H**i**," "**I**'s," "**eye**s," "sk**y**"; the skyscraper-like, narrow-lined vertical reach of the poem as a whole. The short lines slow down the reading voice, making more apparent both the melodic integrity of the poem and its conceptual linkages. After the greeting to the cow (which doubles as a formal/generic marker) the deictic "those" immediately emphasizes the "objectiveness" of the bees, their exteriority to the speaker. The order of the equation (bees = I's = eyes = skyscrapers) seems counterintuitive; in a more straightforward, discursive analysis of perception, given the stated background experience of the poem, one might expect "bees = skyscrapers = eyes = I's." As the poem presents it, however, the equation is more akin to an algebraic equation, in which the variables might appear in a number of different orders, than to a progression in formal logic, in which each element of the argument builds on the one before. The poem asserts the integral nature of the elements of perception not by logical argument or progression but by a combination of repeated sounds and syntactic apposition.

The importance of syntax in Zukofsky's poetry cannot be overemphasized. And even when the word order of the poem does not differ significantly from some version of normative "prose" syntax, the formal arrangement of the lines serves to place emphasis on certain elements of the "sentence."[5] This is the case with the second section of "I's (pronounced *eyes*)," which seems at first glance somewhat more straightforward, simpler, and more polemical than the first:

> Red azaleas
>   make this
>   synagogue
> Not the
>   other way
>   round.
> [*CSP* 214]

The physical objects of perception are here, as in the first section, the focus of the poem: the deictic "this" (in the line-end point of emphasis) stresses their exteriority to the poet, and their freestanding, objective nature is emphasized by the fact that each object ("Red azaleas" and "synagogue") is isolated on a single line. The "subject" or "point" of the poem is the relationship of the flowers and the building, and it is clearly possible to take the poem as a broadly symbolic statement of the primacy of the natural over the man-made or artificial (or the religious, for that matter). It is the red azaleas that "make" the synagogue (make it beautiful, make it pleasing, make it into a satisfying sight—all of the connotations of the demotic "make"), rather than the synagogue, with all its cultural and religious resonance, lending importance to the flowers planted around it ("Not the / other way / round"). (Such a reading is of course inevitably complicated by the fact that the azaleas themselves, as an element of the synagogue's landscaping, are an instance of human artifice, "cultural" in the sense of "horticultural.")

Drawing such implications from the poem might be unavoidable, and for some readers is certainly fun. But one can find the poem effective and compelling simply as an objectified instance of perception, without necessarily straining to extract a discursive "statement." That is, Zukofsky has arranged his perceptions—the flowers, the building, their aesthetic/cultural relationship—into a formal unit that has about it the structural inevitability that, ideally, will give rise in the reader to the state of "rested totality." The poem, while nonmetrical, is clearly formally regular: two stanzas of three lines each; the first two lines of each stanza having two words and the third having one; the first line of each unit beginning with a capitalized letter; the latter two lines indented. The first stanza presents the objects of perception and their relationship as perceived by the poet, whereas the second, more rhetorical stanza emphatically rejects the converse of that relationship. The poem's single sentence comes to a resounding close on the word "round," which both implicitly acknowledges the circularity of the perceiving subject's constructions of relationships among exterior objects and closes off that circularity by fastening on and affirming this particular subject's conclusions. While it is possible for an observer in the world outside the poem to see the synagogue "making" the azaleas, in the context of the poem the poet's own perception of their relationship is the only version of reality that achieves objectification. Perception is in a certain way fundamentally subjective, dependent on a subject; at the same time, it can achieve a more universal, "objective" status through the objectification of the poem, thereby making itself available to readers.

The fourth section of the poem, "HARBOR," works in a similar, though more compressed manner to "Red azaleas." Its four lines—

> The winds
> agitating
> the
> waters
> [*CSP* 214]

—record a perception and a relation, and cast them into a formally objectified structure. The main thrust of the lines, which is to embody an instance of perception through a sincere compositional strategy into a form that achieves "rested totality" in the reader's mind, exists in a delicate balance with the symbolic resonances of the poem—here, the implied allusion to the Spirit of God moving on "the face of the waters" in the period before the Creation (Genesis 1:2). While the poem might spring out of an actual perception of the waters of a harbor, the symbolic resonances of the conjunction of "harbor"—both as noun (a place of refuge) and as verb (to give refuge to)—and the implied brooding (in the avian sense) of God's dovelike spirit are in fecund tension with the participle "agitating"—precisely what the winds (or the Spirit) ought *not* to do in a harbor.

In other sections of "I's," Zukofsky—as he is so often—is less the poker-faced philosopher than the high-spirited joker, less *A Portrait*'s Stephen Dedalus than *Finnegans Wake*'s Shem the Penman. Sections such as "Fiddler Age Nine" and "FOR" focus on language itself to the extent that they appear instances almost of mere wordplay (a measure of which is integral as well to "Hi, Kuh"). What is crucial to keep in mind is that these poems, for all their ostensible playfulness, evidence just as much sincerity in their composition and objectification in their structure as do the more "serious" statements "Red azaleas" and "HARBOR." Zukofsky imbues even the tiniest of his poems with an air of immense concentration. "Fiddler Age Nine," referring to a photograph of the poet's violin prodigy son, presents in its closing line a wry portrait of the violinist as a very young man "with brief-and violin-case": "Sir Attaché Détaché" (*CSP* 214). The boy, weighed down with double burdens, yet with a cavalier self-confidence and jauntiness, is both attached and detached; at the same time, "Attaché" and "détaché" refer directly back to the briefcase and the violin case. The French words attach to the objects in a firmly idiomatic way ("attaché" is of course a common term for a briefcase, while "détaché" is a technical term for a violin bowing) and are simultaneously turned back on the Fiddler to describe his carriage and attitude.[6] If one hoped clearly to distinguish two such evidently intertwined processes, one might cite the poet's awareness of the words' multivalences as an instance of sincerity, and the way by which the third line refers back to the two before, each time in a different register, as an index of the poem's objectification.

"FOR" is a tiny improvisation on sounds:

Four tubas
or
two-by-four's
[*CSP* 215]

The title "FOR" can be read as the "keynote" of the piece, which reappears in each line (fragmentarily or echoingly as "or" in the second), or it can be read as part of the poem's syntax—that is, this composition is "for" (meant to be played by) an ensemble of four tubas or four two-by-fours. The incongruity is immediately striking: four tubas make a beautiful (if ungainly) sound; four two-by-four's make only noise. Yet through a wry sonic shuffle, Zukofsky has rearranged his three syllables and drawn the musical out of the unmusical—and vice versa. It is no doubt significant that both "Fiddler Age Nine" and "FOR," two poem that draw attention to the sounds of their language, are on explicitly *musical* themes.

Following "FOR" are two sections, printed in the same center-justified lines as "Fiddler Age Nine" and "FOR," that present examples of working virtue, of conscientious labor:

Angelo

the Superintendent's
Porto Rican Helper—

See
I work
alread' start roof pla'form
ñ scratching floor
on
Eight

if
I
can do
you
good.

SEVEN DAYS A WEEK

A
good man
when everybody
is draping
the flag on a holiday
he's behind a box

or stamp or information
window in the
Post Office.

[*CSP* 215]

What ties these two poems together, in addition to their depictions of men in service positions who seem dedicated to helping those they serve, is the word "good." "Angelo" offers to do whatever his tenants need, "if / I / can do / you / good," while the postal worker, at his post seven days a week, is described as "A / good man." The compressed hagiography these two sections constitute is most notable for the precise notation of the "Porto Rican" helper's imperfect English and for the "Zukofskyan" quality of the syntax throughout. "Angelo" is unpunctuated, using line breaks to indicate speech pauses. The postman's location is both specified and rendered indeterminate in the last four lines of

"SEVEN DAYS A WEEK": "he's behind a box // or stamp or information / window in the / Post Office." Initially, it seems as if the man is behind a box, until it becomes clear that "box," like "stamp" and "information," specifies a particular window at the post office (a "box window," presumably, is where one drops off or picks up parcels). The indeterminacy of the man's position remains, however, and the amusing possibility arises that the poet is referring not to a particular person but to *the* postal worker in general. Since these windows are always "manned," and since the uniform of the postal service works to render its wearers identical in status, it is simpler to consider the various faces behind the counter aspects of a single person, and since this person is always present, he must inevitably be a "good man" to the postal customer.

"I's (pronounced *eyes*)," as the title indicates, is a set of variations on the theme of visual perception. That theme is kept before the reader in Angelo's offer of his own labor—"See / I work"—and in the "window" behind which the "good man" works. Visual perception becomes an overt leitmotif in the last four poems of the sequence, which play primarily linguistic, metonymic variations on the word "see." This is most evident in the titles: the "see" of "TREE—SEE?" becomes the "sea" of "A SEA"; reduced to their alphabetical equivalents, and with the logical addition of a "b," those two words become "A B C," and that alphabetic progression seems inevitably to lead to the "z" of "AZURE."

The humble sources from which Zukofsky drew his poems are well worth noting: "Fiddler Age Nine" is based on a snapshot; "Angelo" is most likely a direct quotation heard at the Zukofskys' 135 Willow Avenue or 160 Colonial Heights address. As Peter Quartermain notes in an essay on Zukofsky and Williams, "TREE—SEE?" is in effect a collaboration between Zukofsky and the poet Lorine Niedecker, playing on a 1959 exchange of letters. Zukofsky had written in a letter to Niedecker, "I see by your tree you draw." Niedecker, struck by the phrase, replied "What do you see?" "On 29 October, the day he completed the poem, Zukofsky wrote back to Niedecker saying she had given him the second (and final) stanza . . . ; the second stanza, he told her, is *yours*, but now, like Shakespeare's Plutarch, in the common domain" (Quartermain, *Disjunctive Poetics* 90). The final product, however, can be read without reference to either the correspondence or the two poets' friendship:

> TREE—SEE?
>
> —I see
>   by
>   your tree
>
> —What
>   do you
>   see
>
> [*CSP* 216]

This six-line poem is both a completed dialogue and an essay in miniature on perception and the problem of communicating perception between subjects. The first voice affirms an instance of its own perception: "I see / by / your tree." Although this affirmation is clear and straightforward—not "I think I see" or "I believe I see" but "I see"—the "by" renders the statement ambiguous. Has something been revealed to him by means of the second voice's tree—for instance, that the second person practices the art of bonsai cultivation, or that because of the way the second renders a tree in verse, she must also draw? Or does he see something in the vicinity of the second person's tree—for example, a person or a house standing "by" the tree? The second voice, echoing and rhyming the first, puts in stark relief the ambiguities of the affirmation: "What / do you / see[?]" The "What," isolated on its own line, is the core of the problem; although the first voice can easily and firmly state its act of perception, it has failed to communicate to the second the object of that perception. The poem does not put into question the act of perception (as does the questioning of the classical skeptic), but highlights the problematic nature of the interpersonal transmission of perceptions. The first person "sees" but finds it difficult to communicate *what* it sees to another.

While "I's (pronounced *eyes*)" at all points affirms the soundness of perception, one of its primary themes is the problem of communicating, in a linguistic medium, one's perceptions to others. Zukofsky's early doctrine of words as "absolute symbols for objects, states, interrelations, thoughts about them" (*P* 14), while remaining essential to his thought, has been somewhat modified in the years between "An Objective" and "I's." One index of that evolution is the extent to which the straightforward notation of perception has become interpenetrated and involved with the purely linguistic play of some of the poems. The title poem of "I's" is a good example in which the experience of seeing the billboard (or skyscraper) has become transmuted into the punning, melodic sound play of "bees / I's / eyes." The two aspects of sincerity—that which shows fidelity to the objects of perception and that which pays its most careful attention to the words of the poem themselves—combine here to both notate and dramatize how clear physical perceptions become problematized when they are embodied in a shared language. The pressures of language itself—its indeterminacy, its susceptibility to puns and wordplay, its continual slippage in the process of interpersonal transmission—are always working to hinder the easy communication of experience. This drama, so neatly encapsulated in "TREE—SEE?," is also played out in "A SEA":

A SEA

the
foam
claws

cloys
close
[*CSP* 216]

The threefold variation on the word "claws" produces a syntactic "duck-rabbit" effect (see Wittgenstein, *Philosophical Investigations* 194e): "foam" appears at first the subject of the verbs "claws" and "cloys," until "close" renders "claws" the subject of its sentence. Although the overall gist of the statement is fairly clear, the syntactic structure of the poem is ultimately undecidable. "[T]he foam claws [and] cloys" and "the foam claws close" are equally plausible but mutually exclusive constructions of the syntax. The figure can be either duck or rabbit, but not both at once. That the difficulty is based on a playfully logical movement of word sounds helps in some way to justify, but in no way to mitigate, this undecidability. What ought not be overlooked here, of course, is that despite that syntactic undecidability—or perhaps in some way *because* of it—the poem presents a remarkably vivid impression of the way foam behaves as it strikes the shore.

"A B C" is perhaps the most "difficult" of the poems of "I's":

A B C

He has wit—
but who has more—

who looks
some way more

withal

than
one eye

weeps, his voice
[*CSP* 216]

Despite the poem's tentative syntax, its general form seems to be that of a definition of "wit," not connoting humor but the earlier, more Shakespearean meaning of intelligence or canniness.[7] One can construe the poem's syntax in at least two ways:

> He has wit (but who has more?) who looks some way [i.e., somehow] more than one eye weeps [i.e., than with a single weeping eye]—his voice.

or:

> *He* has wit—but [he, i.e. another person] who has more . . . looks some way more than one eye weeps [than with a single weeping eye, which is the mode of looking/thinking of the first "he," or] *his* voice.

In either construction—and there are others—wit, the clear intellect, is contrasted to the seeing of a single eye that is obstructed by tears. Throughout *Bottom,* weeping is figured not as the immediate outward expression of emotion but as the access of the unseeing intellect that works to cloud the perception of the clear physical eye. Melnick rightly criticizes this figuration, seeing it as Zukofsky's sacrifice of the human in his single-minded pursuit of anti-epistemological theory: "Similarly, tears become inexcusable wanderings from the eyes' true function, not a witness to a man's obligations to others' grief" (64). But the equation of "wit" and clear perception is fundamental to Zukofsky's poetics, so important that its expression is as basic as an alphabetical primer, an "A B C." Where the Puritan alphabet book begins "In Adam's fall / We sinnèd all," Zukofsky dates the fall of "wit" from the moment when the eye's clear perception is clouded by the mind's emotion. Blake's dictum "a tear is an intellectual thing" (quoted in *B* 200) is completely germane here: for Zukofsky, a tear is evidence not of emotional immediacy but of the mind's interference in the business of the senses.

"AZURE" brings the sequence to a close on a note of renewed linguistic play and revived physical perception. It also includes the poet's signature, for the "z" of "AZURE" serves as a "signature" to the sequence as a whole, much like the "Z" section of *Bottom*'s "An Alphabet of Subjects," which is subtitled "(*signature*)" (*B* 442–43). Zukofsky is constantly aware of the happy accident of his own name beginning with the last letter of the alphabet, and this no doubt contributes to his fascination with the initial letters of works and their titles: *"A"*, which begins with the letter *A*, is only the most prominent example. (One also might note his quoting, with apparent approval, Stephen Dedalus's fantasy, in *Ulysses*' "Proteus" chapter, of writing books with letters as titles [*B* 214].)

AZURE

Azure
as ever
adz aver
[*CSP* 217]

The sky (or is it the sea, given the oceanic theme of "HARBOR" and "A SEA"?), the poet notes, is "Azure / as ever." But according to whom? "Azure," of course, is the stereotypically poetic term for the sky, both for the Romantics and the nineteenth-century French poets. Its most famous appearance is perhaps in Mallarmé's "L'Azur," where the sky becomes the symbol of infinity, poetic longing, and, most interestingly, the weight of poetic tradition that the poet is desperately trying to escape or surmount.[8] By calling the sky "azure," Zukofsky is not simply describing his perception but is invoking the entire mass of poetic usage that lies behind and mediates a poet's description of the heavens: "as ever" serves to emphasize the perduring nature of this poetic usage, as does, for that matter, the implied pun of the title—"Azure" = "as sure." But the sky is not merely azure by poetic convention; it remains azure because "adz aver" that it is so. The forces of the mass media have co-opted the term "azure," and advertisements—spelled here "adz," in imitation of vulgar business misspellings (such as the "Kwik Kar Wash" down the road from my house)—compete with poetic tradition in establishing the realms of usage from which our shared vocabulary is taken. (Of course, this is only one way of reading "adz": as Alison Rieke points out, adz is both a tool and a hieroglyph [*Senses of Nonsense* 163].)[9] The objectification of this tiny poem, as Zukofsky would analyze it, is high and grows out of one's perception of the degree of sincerity involved in constructing such an intellectually resonant utterance out of the transformed sounds of "azure." Although the poem's "voice" is unlocatable—that is, it does not emanate from a single identifiable lyric "speaker"—the three systems of immediate perception, poetic tradition, and mass media all come together in three variations on the phonemes æ and ∂r.

"AZURE," then, as it invokes both immediate perception and the linguistic systems in which that perception is embodied and by which it is communicated, brings "I's (pronounced *eyes*)" to a logical close, restating the sequence's overt theme of physical perception and its linguistic embodiment. What is striking, and strikingly canny, is the manner in which Zukofsky, while consistently hewing to his oft-stated faith in the evidence of the senses, recognizes and acknowledges the extent to which the poet, while possessing a body and eyes, dwells within language in his poetry and is only able to express what he feels and sees through language. While that language might serve, in a certain form of compositional sincerity, as a mere notation of experience, to bring the poem to a state of objectification the poet must acknowledge language per se: he must work with it as a set of sounds having musical values, a set of signs having graphic values, and a communally shared organism that brings with it not only a range of different spheres of usage but a continual process of miscommunication, (mis)interpretation, misprision, and—most important—the continual possibility of interpersonal communication.

One reading of *Bottom: On Shakespeare* convicts that text of a species of solipsism, an other-minds skepticism that subsumes the dialogic variety of the Shakespearean text (and all the other texts Zukofsky cites) under the monologic rubric of the single "love : reason :: eyes : mind" analogy. But whatever solipsism one might find in *Bottom*'s overt argument, and whatever solipsism one might extrapolate from Zukofsky's statements of Objectivist poetics, the poems give the lie to any reading that would characterize Zukofsky's notion of perception as simplistic or dogmatic. His only dogmatism (and one that is itself far from simplistic) is his constant rejection of skepticism, which is rarely presented as stridently and baldly in his poems as in his essays and interviews. This is merely to say, if the distinction makes any sense, that Zukofsky is more sophisticated as poet than as philosopher, that his most profound philosophizing occurs not in his prose but in his poems.

I think it evident that Zukofsky's corpus as a whole stands as a detailed exploration of the problem of knowledge. *Bottom* and Zukofsky's other prose statements can be said to affirm the individual's perceptions at the expense of the individual's recognition of other minds, or at least that is the conclusion to which one is led when one pursues Zukofsky's emphasis on the clear physical eye—an eye that by definition can be used by only one person. It would be incorrect, however, to take this as the whole of the Zukofskyan analysis of knowledge and the entire epistemological basis of Zukofsky's poetics. Where *Bottom* addresses that problem largely in terms of the possibility of a single subject knowing, the works of poetry—the shorter poems collected in *ALL*, *"A"*, *Catullus*, and *80 Flowers*—are concerned with knowledge as an intersubjective affair, and with all the filterings and complications that come about due to our knowledge's embodiment in a shared and exchanged language. This too is a very Wittgensteinian notion, and one that is continually implied throughout the *Philosophical Investigations* and Wittgenstein's other late writings.[10]

Bottom is a "poem" with an argument, and that argument is repeated in a variety of voices and keys over the length of the text. Despite the slippage of positions between various quoted voices, the arguments that seem inevitably to arise among disparate quotations, and above all the obdurately individual identities of the textual grafts Zukofsky has assembled in his book, the main thrust of *Bottom* remains an attempt to subsume all of its sources into the service of its overarching argument. The poems, on the other hand, while they often present ideas and views, rarely argue a single position for the reader's benefit. Where *Bottom* achieves a univocal (although tenuous) accord among its many voices, the poems achieve the equilibrium of discussion, in which a variety of tones and registers are sounded and allowed to be heard. The crucial distinction is that the poems have no voice outside their own voices, while the quoted material in *Bottom*, set apart and ghettoized by quotation marks, is always liable to be brought in line, corrected, by the author's voice. This, I believe, is why Zukofsky, having called his book a "long poem" in the 1960 note "Bottom, A Weaver," seems to regard it primarily as "criticism" in his 1968 interview with Dembo (see *LZMP* 266). In the poems, the integrity of the individual's perception is still taken as a given, but that perception is moved from a subjective, potentially solipsistic arena into the marketplace of interpersonal interpretation and exchange.

Section 3 of "All of December Toward New Year's," published in Zukofsky's 1956 collection *Some Time*, dates to 1953, six years before Zukofsky began composing the poems of "I's (pronounced *eyes*)."[11] This brief poem, which again seems deceptively slight, should be enough to assure one of the fundamentally nonsolipsistic, interpersonal nature of perception as Zukofsky's poetry presents it:

A WORLD ATLAS in a globe base:
Who turned the print to us?
We don't need to read it.

Turn it to the toile
That hangs on the wall,
The hand-blocked figures
Such blue shades
Should read it
And come to life,
The young sun.

The young son:
"If it's turned
from us, we
are the shades."
[*CSP* 144]

The "we" of the first stanza, one can be fairly well assured, is the ever-recurring family trio of Louis, Celia, and Paul; content in the security of the family circle, they have no need to read "the print" of the atlas and learn of other lands. Secure as well in their acknowledgment of the world's existence, they do not need the map's evidence as a bolster against skeptical doubt. Better to "Turn it to the toile / That hangs on the wall." ("A"-12 notes how this toile, described in *"It Was"* as a "white cotton print hand-blocked in blue with early American scenes of a naval battle, Indians, date palms, mules and elephants" [*CF* 184], has been "Re-cut / So often for the windows / Or different places we have lived in" [239]; it is as much a part of the permanent landscape of the Zukofskys' household as the sound of Paul's violin or Celia's piano.) As mere textual "blue shades," the "hand-blocked figures" there—Indians, mules, elephants—have more need of the intellectual proof that a mappemonde might provide. Indeed, just as the textual traces that constitute Shakespearean characters only "come to life" under the reading eye,[12] these blue shades "Should read it / And come to life, / The young sun": here one might imagine a representation of the sun on a page of the atlas, or a sun blazoned on the atlas's cover, under which the "hand-blocked figures" ("hand-blocked" as Adam was out of the clay) come to life in a species of spontaneous generation. The figures come to life through the (imaginative) perception of the poet and through their own perception of the atlas, a perception both textual and figural: they read the print, and they see the "young sun."

Yet, as Paul (the "young son" whose name duplicates the "young sun") reminds us, "If it's turned / from us, we / are the shades." The poem, which up to this point has been the meditation of a single mind, opens up to the wisdom of another voice, to the opening of epistemic perspective that accompanies interpersonal discourse. If we are deprived of the world, if it is "turned from us"—or, more significantly, if we turn it from ourselves—it is we who become the less-than-human "shades." The "print," which can be taken to represent the possibility of and traces of communication, can bring life even to the hand-blocked figures on the toile. When we, as human beings, are deprived of that "print," we become as lifeless as those figures.

The danger of skepticism is not merely in turning the world away, disavowing its existence, although that is always a danger in a gas age that has lost faith in the soundness of solid, sense-based language. Just as immediate is the danger of failing to acknowledge the existence and the speech of others. The son's voice, which the poet allows to enter the poem whole and unaltered, serves to remind him that skepticism is fundamentally bound up with solipsism, and that while the evidence of the senses may be enough to assure one writer of the existence of his own world, only acknowledgment of the voices of others—both their aural speech and the traces of that speech in print—can lay to rest the other-minds skepticism that leaves one alone in the world of one's own perception. Knowledge is not merely a matter of the single speaker's two "eyes"; it is just as importantly a property shared among a whole community of "I's," whose voices and "pronouncements" sound out in turn to create a collagistic, ideogrammic picture of a shared world dwelling. Although this is a lesson *Bottom* teaches only implicitly—in a fundamentally formal and *textual* manner, through the implication of its vast range of quotations—such a shared knowledge is a principle that receives explicit thematization in and lies at the heart of the body of Zukofsky's poetry.

The Poet in History

5

Bleistein Among the Nightingales

Zukofsky, the Jew as High Modernist

My father's precursors
Set masts in dinghies, chanted the Speech.
—Louis Zukofsky, "A"-4 (15)

While it is instructive to abstract an (anti-)epistemology from Zukofsky's writings, and to follow the fortunes of that stance toward the theory of knowledge as it develops and strengthens throughout his writing life, such an abstracting or abstraction puts us in peril. It endangers us precisely to the extent that it makes us lose sight of the poet behind the ideas, the passionate human being whose rejection of epistemology, whose philosophy of love, whose conception of culture and tradition, and whose poetics were shaped not in a philosophical vacuum but by his experience in a historical world. Before I address the complex subject of Zukofsky's formalism, which will occupy the third major section of this book, I think it appropriate to spend some time locating the poet in his particular historical milieu.

In an interpretive era when readerly focus has shifted from celebrations of textuality to a deeper attention to the historical and ideological contexts within which texts are produced and received, there are two aspects of Zukofsky's identity that seem to have seized the imagination of his readers: among a constellation of Gentile, politically reactionary modernist poets, Zukofsky was a modernist poet who was both Jewish and Marxist. I must confess at the outset that I am not sure precisely how one should go about determining the degree to which each of these identities shaped Zukofsky's work. I am quite certain, however, that neither constitutes an explanation of Zukofsky or a comprehensive description of him. Zukofsky became the poet he was not by embracing or rejecting ethnic or political identities but by navigating among them, by performing delicate negotiations between repudiation, fellow-traveling, and enthusiastic partisanship. I do not intend to offer a comprehensive account either of Zukofsky's relationship to his Jewish identity or of his left-wing politics during the 1920s and 1930s. Rather, I aim to introduce the subject of Zukofsky's modernist poetics as it relates to his two subject-positions: as a Jew, and as a Marxist. My account of each stance is necessarily brief, but the two together begin to situate Zukofsky's work in its proper historical and cultural context, casting light on the degree to which Zukofsky's mature views and mature sense of poetics were arrived at neither easily nor without struggle but as the outcome of vexing and incompatible claims and counterclaims on his allegiances.

According to Celia Zukofsky, her husband considered the seventeenth-century Dutch Jew Baruch Spinoza among the very few greatest philosophical minds, surpassed only by Aristotle, who so permeates *Bottom: On Shakespeare* (*LZMP* 67). In point of fact, it is actually easier to find evidence of Spinoza's influence in Zukofsky's work than Aristotle's. Such evidence ranges from the repeated citation of Spinoza's *"natura naturans / natura naturata"* (nature naturing / nature natured) distinction in *"A"*, to the great swatches of the *Ethics* in *Bottom*, to the very fact that when Zukofsky returns to finish the second half of "A"-9—the half dedicated not to economics but to love—he does so using phrases from the *Ethics*. Spinoza is important to Zukofsky partly because he was a philosopher whose ideas the poet found congenial and whose method dovetailed with his own. In "About the Gas Age," for instance, Zukofsky comments, "The wonderful thing about Spinoza's philosophy to me is that out of 8 definitions and 7 axioms he builds the whole system" (*P* 170), just as Zukofsky generates *Bottom* out of a single analogy. Yet I believe Spinoza's prominence in Zukofsky's thought and work can be traced as well to the fact that Spinoza was a specifically *Jewish* philosopher.

Such a statement requires some explanation. For the most part, a writer seizes on an earlier figure to admire not because of race or ethnicity but because that precursor offers the ephebe some technique, some mode of expression that is not otherwise available: note for instance Pound's decisive encounter with Chinese poetry and philosophy, or Aimé Césaire's wholesale adoption of the poetics of (white) French Surrealism. A great political example is Toussaint Louverture's reading of the Abbé Raynal's *Histoire des Deux Indes*, a thoroughly white text, typical of the Enlightenment, which led this black slave to lead the first (and only) successful slave revolt in the Western Hemisphere. There is a clear logic of conceptual affinity at work in these filiations. Pound's adoption of Chinese modes was a characteristic moment in the modernist extension of Western Orientalism—a discovery, in the philosophical and literary modes of an ostensibly alien civilization, of methods of thought that could both be reconciled with Western Enlightenment and could serve as weapons to break down the petrified procedures of post-Romantic English writing. Césaire found that the Surrealists, with their potent combination of Marx and Freud, preached a liberatory doctrine that dovetailed perfectly with the political needs of the Francophone Caribbean. And there is little mystery to the Encyclopedist's appeal to Toussaint: the Haitian leader responded precisely to Raynal's call for a West Indies slave rebellion.

Zukofsky, in contrast, was attracted to previous writers for reasons that often seem to have little to do with matters of style or content, reasons that might uncharitably be called odd or even frivolous. He had an almost superstitious regard for numerical symbolism, which led him to study and incorporate into *"A"* various Pythagorean ideas; a similar interest in aural coincidence seems to have drawn him to the sixteenth-century Spanish Jew Luis De Leon: "the parallels were uncanny: his first Luis like my first name; the patrilineal De Leon like my Hebrew surname. I don't feel like a lion, but for some reason in Hebrew the word lion repetitiously precedes the sense of my given name" (*P* 25). I would hazard that a like coincidence of shared first names contributed to Zukofsky's interest in *Ludwig* Wittgenstein's thought. Zukofsky, as can be seen from the very premises of the Catullus translation, was profoundly suspicious of the notion of an unmotivated signifier, a word whose shape and sound bears no meaningful relation to its referent. As he says to Dembo, "Something must have led the Greeks to say *hudor* and for us to say *water*" (*LZMP* 267).

The fact that Spinoza, like Zukofsky, lost his mother in youth—Spinoza's mother was named Hana; Zukofsky's, Chana—no doubt struck Zukofsky, enough probably to spur on or reinforce an already existing interest in the philosopher's ideas. And such an interest must inevitably have led Zukofsky to meditate on the parallels between his own social/ethnic position and that of Spinoza—who was, most probably, the only Jewish philosopher (apart from the obscure Philo Judaeus) on the Columbia philosophy curriculum. Zukofsky's position as the assimilating child of immigrant Orthodox parents—a fairly common generational divide, to be sure, repeated almost without exception in American immigrant families—was strikingly parallel to Spinoza' s experience, which Yirmiyahu Yovel describes so eloquently in the first volume of his *Spinoza and Other Heretics*. According to Yovel, not merely is Spinoza the inheritor of the Ibero-Judaic Marrano tradition of self-division and equivocation, but his own relentlessly rationalistic mind led him to proclaim "himself a heretic not only among the faithful, but also among representatives of the accepted heresies of his period, thus separating himself from all the major spiritual currents of his time" (Yovel 5). Spinoza cannot even, according to Yovel, be considered "the first secular Jew," since that category had yet to come into being: "Spinoza thus exemplifies and adumbrates the situation of the modern Jew—secular, assimilationist, or national—without himself falling neatly into any of these categories. . . . That the world regarded him as a Jew was one of the hallmarks of Spinoza's loneliness, which was not social, but existential" (172–73).

In Zukofsky's first major work, the 1925 "Poem beginning 'The,' " one of whose almost obsessive concerns is Jewish identity, Zukofsky cites Spinoza as both Jew and Jewish outsider, as one who has transgressed the laws both of the larger community and of his own enclave:

54 Let me be
55 Not by art have we lived,
56 Not by graven images forbidden to us
57 Not by letters I fancy,
58 Do we dare say
59 With Spinoza grinding lenses, Rabbaisi,
60 After living on Cathedral Parkway?
[*CSP* 11]

One suspects that the young Zukofsky, at least at times, fancied himself a contemporary New York Spinoza, "living on Cathedral Parkway." Although excommunicated by the elders of the Jewish community of Amsterdam, Spinoza went on to systematize, write, and publish his incomparable philosophy, achieving such status that Henri Bergson would say, "Every philosopher had two philosophies: his own and Spinoza's" (quoted in Yovel 5). Similarly, Zukofsky implies that once he himself is freed of his family's Orthodox faith, of the "Rabbaisi" and their prejudices against art, letters, and "graven images," he as well can achieve artistic immortality, even if it is at the price of becoming a "Shagetz" (someone altogether non-Jewish): "251 Assimilation is not hard, / 252 And once the Faith's askew / 253 I might as well look Shagetz just as much as Jew" (*CSP* 17).[1]

Zukofsky finds himself confronted with the invidious choice between maintaining his status as a Jew and pursuing his art in part because the Orthodox community in which he was born sees no value in his modernist poetry, and indeed—at its most hidebound—attempts to set aside modernity itself. The Orthodox elders of "A"-4 (1928) lament that their children have assimilated and dismiss the poetry of Yehoash (Solomon Bloomgarden, "the Yiddish Byron") as "a jargon":

Deafen us, God, deafen us to their music,
Our own children have passed over to the ostracized,
They assail us—
    'Religious, snarling monsters'—
And have mouthed a jargon:
    "Rain blows, light, on quiet water . . .
["A"-4, 13]

On a quite practical level, Zukofsky found his attempts to place material in the *Menorah Journal*, material which interestingly enough included the first version of "Sincerity and Objectification" (at that time a straight commentary on the then unknown and self-published Reznikoff), repeatedly repulsed. In a 1930 letter to Pound, he would bitingly refer to the editors of that magazine as "the Sanhedrin" (*P/Z* 32), a repressive and self-righteous—and worse, self-appointed—body of cultural dictators.[2]

I'm not primarily concerned here with Zukofsky's early gestures of rebellion against his Jewish heritage, although they do play some part in the tenuous narrative that I want to outline of the relationship between Zukofsky's poetics and his Jewishness. Nor do I care to speculate at length about what place Judaism held in his later life. The latter verges uncomfortably close to the delicious but unreliable genre of literary gossip. When Carroll F. Terrell asked Celia Zukofsky at what point her husband "became unorthodox," she replied, "Probably the moment he was aware; he always refused to wear the phylactaries. They did have a rabbi or biblical student . . . come and make an attempt to teach him to say his prayers in Hebrew and to read the Hebrew prayer book, but that didn't last long either. He refused to do that" (*LZMP* 39). Zukofsky's own bar mitzvah was a purely perfunctory affair, and Paul Zukofsky was himself never bar mitzvahed. One recalls as well that Edward Dahlberg fell out with the Zukofskys after they served him a canned ham (he cried poisoning)—clearly the Zukofsky family made no bones about keeping kosher. Guy Davenport recounts that on the occasion of the poet's early-1960s visit to Lexington, Kentucky, he and Zukofsky went for a walk. As they passed the Beth El synagogue, Zukofsky remarked, "I'm a Chinese Presbyterian Jew." That pins the mature Zukofsky down probably every bit as much as he would care to be pinned down. Yet, Celia Zukofsky's recollection that he was fired from a post office job in the 1920s for not coming to work on Yom Kippur—"He wasn't going to any synagogue, but he wasn't going to work on Yom Kippur either" (*LZMP* 52)—as well as the working contents page for *80 Flowers*, noting which poems were finished on particular Jewish holidays (Leggott 366–67), indicates that whatever sort of Jew Zukofsky considered himself, early and late he had some awareness of the High Holidays.

Aside from the pressures brought to bear on Zukofsky from the Jewish community and from his own internalization of that community's attitudes—what one might old-fashionedly call his conscience—I find more interesting the difficulties he faced from the larger community of non-Jewish modernism, difficulties he faced specifically as a young Jewish poet. Such difficulties were not those of access to publication venues nor even of outright discrimination but of psychological pressures brought to bear on him by the very ideologies expressed in the writings of the most prominent high modernists. My contention is that he navigated those pressures largely by ignoring their manifestations in his anti-Semitic friend and mentor Ezra Pound, simultaneously transferring them to and personifying them in the figure of T. S. Eliot, the most publicly visible and respectable representative of the new poetries.

By the late 1920s, Anglo-American modernism was already well on its way to becoming canonical, particularly with the establishment of such organs as the Eliot-edited *Criterion* in 1922. This is not to say that the modernist poets and writers were already household names, or that they were already enshrined in the standard anthologies (Yeats's snubbing of Pound's recent work in his introduction to the 1936 *Oxford Book of English Verse* makes that clear); nevertheless, they had gained a clear foothold among the younger generation, the undergraduates who would provide a model for *Brideshead Revisited*'s Anthony Blanche, reading *The Waste Land* through a megaphone from his Oxford balcony. The older poets who championed this movement were for the most part white, male, and all too often casually or pointedly anti-Semitic in their writings and self-presentation.

This was the literary-cultural milieu within which Zukofsky clearly essayed to be included, the context wherein he wanted his own poetry and criticism to be read. For Zukofsky, the first great Jewish-American poet born in this century—in the Hebrew poet Harold Schimmel's words, "The most American of Jewish poets [and] the most Jewish of American poets" (*LZMP* 235)—the immigrant child's crisis of assimilation led directly into and was bound up with a crisis of poetic vocation in which Zukofsky had to come to terms with the conflicting demands of the modernist literary culture he had chosen and the Jewish tradition into which he had been born. In the context of that crisis, Eliot comes to represent for Zukofsky not merely the Eurocentric and anti-nativist tendencies of the modernist project but the profoundly reactionary, even anti-Semitic, cultural agenda of poetic high modernism. For Zukofsky to arrive at his mature conception of both the poetic act and the poet's tradition, it is Eliot's conceptions both of tradition and of the individual talent that he must overcome.

What then does it mean to be "the Jew as high modernist," or the Jew among the high modernist nightingales—singing not among the *bloody* wood, as Eliot has it in "Sweeney Among the Nightingales," but, as I persist in misremembering, among that critic's own *sacred* wood? As we should note at the outset, the poetic modernism of Pound and Eliot is more than simply an arsenal of poetic techniques and discoveries. As Marcus Klein, among others, points out, what Eliot in particular advances is an assertive construction of "kulchur" or "tradition," a tradition purposefully erected to exclude the "barbarian" at the gates of Western culture (most obviously, the recent waves of Irish and Jewish immigrants to the United States). It is no coincidence that the targets of Eliot's early satire are named "Sweeney" and "Bleistein" (Klein 5–18). The title of this chapter is a conflation of the titles of two poems in Eliot's *Poems* (1920): "Burbank with a Baedeker, Bleistein with a Cigar" and "Sweeney Among the Nightingales." Pound would characterize the quatrains composed at this point in Eliot's career, like those of his own *Hugh Selwyn Mauberley,* as a gesture of formal reaction, a "counter-current" in the face of the "dilutation of vers libre, Amygism, Lee Masterism, [and] general floppiness" that followed the revolt of Imagism. Both *Mauberley* and *Poems,* that is, are strict lessons both in formalism and in morality. Eric Sigg has rightly described the poems of Eliot's volume as constituting something of a *Kulturkampf,* establishing "a poetic of cultural conflict" (153). Over and over in these obsessively crafted quatrains, Eliot contrasts the beauties and treasures of a fast-eroding (usually European) culture to the philistinism of the insurgent Irishman and Jew. The Bleistein of "Burbank with a Baedeker, Bleistein with a Cigar," most notably, is a Chaplinesque tourist whose "lustreless protrusive eye /

Stares from the protozoic slime" at the decay of Venice, itself the site of an earlier Jewish incursion into the culture of Renaissance Christendom (as dramatized in Shakespeare's *Merchant of Venice*):

> But this and such was Bleistein's way:
> A saggy bending of the knees
> And elbows, with the palms turned out,
> Chicago Semite Viennese.
> [*Complete Poems and Plays* 24]

Thirteen years before his bald assertion at the University of Virginia that "reasons of race and religion combine to make any large number of free-thinking Jews undesirable" (*After Strange Gods* 20), Eliot makes clear in these poems that the Jew is neither the creator nor the preserver of culture but is at best the spectator to its demise and at worst the "rat" tunneling beneath its "piles," undermining its very structure.

The twenty-one-year-old Zukofsky—one of four children of Yiddish-speaking Russian-Jewish immigrants, the honors student who had learned his own English at "P.S. 7 on Chrystie and Hester Streets" (*Auto* 33)—wrote "Poem beginning 'The' " in direct response to Eliot's *The Waste Land*, the 1922 "atom bomb" (in Williams's words [*Autobiography* 174]) that likewise provoked creative and reactive responses in both Williams and the Scottish poet Hugh MacDiarmid.[3] But where MacDiarmid, in his *A Drunk Man Looks at the Thistle*, directly confronts what he sees as Eliot's Anglocentric cultural agenda (and Eliot himself)—

> T. S. Eliot—it's a Scottish name—
> Afore he wrote 'The Waste Land' sud hae come
> To Scotland here. He wad hae written
> A better poem syne—like this, by gum!
> [*Selected Poetry* 21]

—Zukofsky pursues the strategies of Shylock, whose words he parodies in "Poem beginning 'The,' " subverting rather than confronting that agenda:

258 The villainy they teach me I will execute
259 And it shall go hard with them,
260 For I'll better the instruction,
261 Having learned, so to speak, in their colleges.
[*CSP* 18]

"Poem beginning 'The,' " written in 1925 and published in 1928, parodies *The Waste Land* from a specifically American and Jewish perspective. Even as it skillfully appropriates the high modernist techniques of fragmentation and collage, Zukofsky's poem gives pride of place to American and Yiddish, rather than British English, poetic monuments. " 'The' " is quite self-consciously aware that *The Waste Land* is its most important formal antecedent, as is evident from its far-from-subtle line-by-line multiplication of Eliot's line numbers and from its tongue-in-cheek dedication, which outscholasticizes Eliot's "Notes" by bunging all of the poem's references into a single dense paragraph (*CSP* 8). The poem cites Eliot's works themselves not with filial admiration but as symptoms of cultural decay—the productions of a dead-end cultural-aesthetic agenda:

24 Kerith is long dry, and the ravens that brought the prophet bread
25 Are dust in the waste land of a raven-winged evening.
26 And why if the waste land has been explored, traveled over, circumscribed,
27 Are there only wrathless skeletons exhumed new planted in its sacred wood?
[*CSP* 10]

Where Eliot quotes with comfortable approval Spenser, Goldsmith, Marvell, and Chaucer, Zukofsky cites similarly canonical figures but adds the Jewish Heine, the Yiddish poet Yehoash (Solomon Bloomgarden), and the Yiddish folk song "Raisins and Almonds." And where *The Waste Land* could be read as surveying with something like despair the decay of Western culture (or the decay of Eliot's marriage), " 'The' " elegiacally remembers Zukofsky's dead mother and looks hopefully toward the ongoing reorganization of society in Soviet Russia, a country that seems—or at least it did in 1925—to have overcome the anti-Semitism that had driven Zukofsky's parents to America.

I am not particularly concerned with the question of whether Eliot himself should be accused or convicted of anti-Semitism. Anthony Julius's recent *T.S. Eliot, Anti-Semitism, and Literary Form* makes the case against Eliot perhaps as strongly as it can be made, although Christopher Ricks's *T.S. Eliot and Prejudice* certainly remains more than a useful piece of apologetics. As is evident from Julius, there has been an impressive (if not oppressive) body of both scholarship and polemic devoted to the issue.[4] Of more immediate concern to the question of Eliot's influence on Zukofsky are the testimonies of other Jews in the academy, even those of a younger generation, such as Delmore Schwartz, Leslie Fiedler, or Harold Bloom. When Schwartz's plumbing broke down, he would parody Eliot's line in "Gerontion"—"the jew squats on the window sill, the owner" (*Complete Poems* 21)—by naming himself "Squatter Schwartz" (Julius 20). A genuinely troubled Fiedler, exiled to furthest Missoula, would question Eliot about the anti-Semitism evident not only in "Sweeney Among the Nightingales" and "Burbank with a Baedeker, Bleistein with a Cigar" but also in "Gerontion," and would receive little satisfaction: "he went on to write, in a cliché almost as offensive as spelling the name of my people without a capital letter, that some of his best friends were Jews" (*Fiedler on the Roof* 11). Bloom, entering the academy at the postwar height of Eliot's influence, recalls Yale as "An Anglo-Catholic nightmare. Everyone was on their knees to Mr. T.S. Eliot . . . God's vicar upon earth, the true custodian of Western tradition" (Interview 61). For the flamboyant (and perhaps overstating) Bloom, Eliot's "flair for demonstrating the authenticity of his Christianity by exhibiting a judicious anti-Semitism" made "an Academy that found its ideology in Eliot . . . not a place where one could teach comfortably, or where one could have remained, had the Age of Eliot not begun to wane" (*T.S. Eliot* 2).

Eliot's critical hegemony was by no means so well established when Zukofsky was reaching his majority, but it is perfectly reasonable to assume that this far-seeing young Jewish poet could read the anti-Semitic implications of Eliot's work with at least as much accuracy as he and his friend Williams saw its anti-nativist tendencies. And perhaps, on some level, it is not the anti-Semitism per se of Eliot's statements that is most significant for a Jewish poet starting out in the 1930s. As Peter Dale Scott notes, although Eliot would later privately retract *After Strange Gods*'s specific calumnies against Jews, "the problem lay not in the sentence about Jews, but in the construction of a positive Christian society built about religious unity, and threatened by the invasion of foreign races" (68). This cultural ideal, best summarized in 1940's *The Idea of a Christian Society*, was one Eliot never publicly renounced.

Odd as it may seem, given what literary history posits as the aesthetic/cultural closeness of Pound and Eliot in the 1920s, these two figures appear to occupy pretty much opposite positions in the young Zukofsky's personal pantheon. While Pound is manifestly his greatest influence in both poetics and aesthetics (one notes, for instance, the number of references to Pound in the introduction to the 1932 *An "Objectivists" Anthology*), Eliot is a powerfully negative figure in the early years of Zukofsky's writing, remaining something of an unspoken target for the younger poet's criticism throughout much of the rest of Zukofsky's career.[5] Although in his later writing, Zukofsky's close friend Williams would use *The Waste Land* as a focus for his own frustration, even before that poem was first published, the New Jersey poet recognized the implications for his own nativist work of Eliot's backward-looking, Anglocentric poetics: "Critically Eliot returned us to the classroom just at the moment when I felt that we were on the point of an escape to matters much closer to the essence of a new art for itself—rooted in the locality which should give it fruit" (*Autobiography* 174).[6] Zukofsky as well could see that Eliot's notion of modernism left little space in which a specifically American poetry might emerge—to say nothing of a *Jewish*-American poetry. As Zukofsky explains in a letter to Pound, one of his intentions in writing " 'The' " was "to tell [Eliot] why, spiritually speaking, a wimpus [as opposed, I suppose, to a bang] was still possible and might even bear fruit of another generation" (*P/Z* 79). While *The Waste Land* had sounded a note of despair regarding the future of English poetry, Zukofsky's task, along with Williams, was to lay the foundations of a new *American* poetry. Zukofsky's major editorial relationships in the early

1930s were with such American magazines as *Blues* and the nativist *Pagany* (named appropriately enough after a Williams novel), rather than with Eliot's increasingly influential *Criterion*, whose editor he dismisses in 1932 as "becoming more inelegant every day" (*An "Objectivists" Anthology* 11).

Eliot faults such poets as Blake for not basing their works on a solid enough foundation of myth and belief and conversely praises the mythological foundations of *The Divine Comedy* and Joyce's *Ulysses*—"The concentration resulting from a framework of mythology and theology and philosophy is one of the reasons why Dante is a classic, and Blake only a poet of genius" (*Sacred Wood* 158). In an influential review of Joyce's masterpiece, Eliot praises the Irish writer's skill at "manipulating a continuous parallel between contemporaneity and antiquity," finding in the achievement of that "mythical method" "a way of controlling, of ordering, of giving a shape and a significance to the immense panorama of futility and anarchy which is contemporary history" (*Selected Prose* 177). No doubt the Marxist Zukofsky of the mid-1920s saw contemporary history as far from merely futile and anarchic; yet throughout his career the poet Zukofsky would reject such prescriptive universalizations, asserting instead that the poet can find more than enough epic material from the most local of sources, his own language: "The poet wonders why so many today have raised up the word 'myth,' finding the lack of so-called 'myths' in our time a crisis the poet must overcome or die from . . . when instead a case can be made out for the poet giving some of his life to the use of the words *the* and *a:* both of which are weighted with as much epos and historical destiny as one man can perhaps resolve" (*P* 10). (It is worth noting that the little words Zukofsky singles out are English words: his commitment is to a poetry that, whether Jewish or not, is most definitely American. This matter of language, so crucial, sets him apart from New York modernists Jacob Glatshteyn and N. B. Minkov, whose periodical *In Zikh* published exclusively Yiddish verse.[7])

Zukofsky was well aware, even before the 1933 Charlottesville lectures published as *After Strange Gods*, of the hostility with which Eliot's construction of tradition viewed the "free-thinking Jew," and indeed was no doubt uncomfortably familiar with such hostility. Anti-Semitic rhetoric was by no means original to writers of the 1880s' generation; earlier aesthetic culture-heroes of the modernists had also bemoaned the imminent destruction of a hard-won and only barely emergent American culture by the waves of Eastern European immigration that ushered in the twentieth century. Henry James, for instance, who returned to the United States in the year of Zukofsky's birth and visited the very Lower East Side neighborhood where the infant poet lived with his Russian-born parents, confessed that traversing Hester Street was like walking about "at the bottom of some vast sallow aquarium in which innumerable fish, of over-developed proboscis, were to bump together, for ever, amid heaped spoils of the sea" (quoted in Conn 42). Henry Adams, whose writings would furnish the subject for Zukofsky's master's thesis at Columbia, noted in his *Education* the growing impotence of his own New England stock in contrast to the lively energy of the Jewish immigrants who were flooding the eastern seaboard: "His world was dead. Not a Polish Jew fresh from Warsaw or Cracow,—not a furtive Yacoob or Ysaac still reeking of the ghetto, snarling a weird Yiddish to the officers of the customs,—but had a keener instinct, an intenser energy, and a freer hand than he,—American of Americans, with Heaven knew how many Puritans and Patriots behind him, and an education that had cost a civil war" (938).[8]

But the extent to which Zukofsky ignores the very different anti-Semitism of these two modernist culture-heroes—one of whom (Adams) is inarguably central to his own thought—is surpassed only by his bland 1948 denial of his friend and mentor Pound's quite notorious anti-Semitism: "I never felt the least trace of anti-Semitism in his presence. . . . If we had occasion to use the words 'Jew' and 'Goy' they were no more or less ethnological in their sense than 'Chinese' and 'Italian' " (*P* 165). This is not a matter of ignorance but of willed refusal—perhaps even street loyalty—on Zukofsky's part, for Pound's anti-Semitism is reiterated with unsettling frequency in their published correspondence. In this correspondence one can see played out the familiar pattern of the assimilating child of immigrant parents. Zukofsky is eager to prove himself *echt* American: his very orthography—phonetic Brooklynese—approaches the American eccentricity of Pound's cracker-barrel backwoodsiness. He complains of American Jewish cultural backwardness, continually chastising the editorial board of *New Masses* for stupidity and literary near-sightedness and referring to the editors of *Menorah Journal* as a backward-looking, culturally retrograde "Sanhedrin" (*P/Z* 32). Throughout much of this correspondence, Zukofsky seems willing to let his own sense of himself as a Jew and as *Jewish* modernist take a back seat to his admiration for and desire to please Pound. In addition to representing himself as phallically masculine—"the Manhattan Mauler" (*P/Z* 166)—in a way that seems calculated to appeal to Pound's rather primitive notion of male (poetic) bonding, Zukofsky asserts his aggressive Americanness by flirting with the vocabulary of Pound's own anti-Semitism. One can read his description of himself as a "shagetz" in "Poem beginning 'The' " as patent and bitter irony, but it is less easy to reconcile or rationalize other statements to Pound—such as those found in a 1929 letter in which he writes of "the likes of an antisemite like myself" (*P/Z* 28), or the particularly unfortunate "I'd betray and immolate most of my people for 1 [Tibor] Serly" (*P/Z* 156).

But Zukofsky never quite sacrifices his Jewish heritage for his friendship with Pound, nor does he repudiate his hard-won cultural identity in favor of Pound's "kulchur." Although in a 1939 letter he denies being a "*very* Jewish Jew" (*P/Z* 198, emphasis mine), he is indeed—very consciously, and perhaps even proudly—a Jew. (One wonders whether Pound told Zukofsky of a letter he received from Eliot noting that Zukofsky's "verse is highly intelligent and honourably jewish [*sic*]" [quoted in Carpenter 482]; as Anthony Julius laconically notes, "by 'honourably,' Eliot means 'openly' " [91].) As his correspondence with Pound continues, Zukofsky begins to reply more and more pugnaciously to Pound's displays of anti-Semitism; the poet's own Jewish heritage, which had appeared in " 'The' " and the earliest sections of *"A"* as a source of considerable spiritual conflict, becomes more and more an inherited, accustomed, and even strengthening backdrop to Zukofsky's work. By the time Zukofsky comes to write "A"-12 (at around age 46), he has resolved some of the conflicts between the religion and nationality of his (literal) fathers and the poetics (cultural and literary) of his (Bloomian) forebears.

This resolution again involves Eliot, in this case in the form of his perhaps most influential essay, "Tradition and the Individual Talent." As early as "A"-1 (1928) Zukofsky attacks Eliot's notion of "tradition," as well as the younger poets who would take that term as talismanic:

> Mongers in mystic accretions;
> The stealers of "mélange adultère de tout,"
> Down East, Middle West, and West coast flaunters of the Clas-
> sics and of Tradition
> (A word to them of great contours)—
> Who sang of women raped by horses
> ["A"-1, 3][9]

What is wrong with these "immured holluschickies" is not that they are themselves provincial—"Down East, Middle West," etc.—but that they have forsaken the local (by implication here, the political) in the worship of a European canon: the Classics with a capital "C"; Tradition with a capital "T."

Much of what Zukofsky conveys in "A"-12 is the idea that a poet's tradition—the conception of tradition that Zukofsky himself has settled on—is not an "ideal order" of "monuments," as Eliot's essay would have it (*Sacred Wood* 50). It is rather a process, a motion in which the poet is only a moment on a continuum of poetic effort, a continuum marked not by extraordinary achievements that furnish the foundations upon which later writers can rear their own monuments (as in Eliot's quip that *of course* we know so much more than the dead writers, for "they are that which we know" [*Sacred Wood* 52])[10] but by a continual reworking of the same materials, a continual replowing of the same furrow. In "A"-12, Zukofsky writes,

> Literature, you remark
> Is in a way another's account
> Which if I can afford to carry
> May add up as my own.
> What culture there is, I chime in, is light
> From a persistent fire twitching
> Reflections of our momentary flames.
> ["A"-12, 238]

Invoking his favorite figure of the poet as horse, Zukofsky notes the persistence of culture, the reappearance of identical motifs over centuries and continents:

> The horse sees he is repeating
> All known cultures
> And suspects repeating
> Others unknown to him,
> Maybe he had better not
> Think of himself
> Hunting so to speak
> Sowing so to speak
> Composing always.
> The shape of his ground seems to have been
> A constant for all dead horses . . .
> ["A"-12, 175]

The tradition into which the poet enters is not an ideal order of monuments but a series of repetitions, a series of replowings by various writers of a single "ground," and an assurance that, even though the poet's work might echo in all particulars some text he has never before read, that work has not been in vain if performed in a spirit of dedication and "sincerity." Such creation in repetition goes forward, I would venture, in an authentically halakic spirit—a spirit that involves the continuous following of a given path rather than the burst of inspiration or divine afflatus that, however submerged, remains part of the ideology of Anglo-American poetic modernism. Eliot describes the poet, we recall, as a catalyst, the "filament of platinum" (*Sacred Wood* 54) that induces the instantaneous transmutation of his materials; Zukofsky's preferred figure for the poet, in contrast, is the horse, patiently plodding forward and only occasionally breaking into a canter. In his 1936 essay on Charlie Chaplin, Zukofsky writes, "There exists probably in the labors of any valid artist the sadness of the horse plodding with blinkers and his direction is for all we don't know filled with the difficulty of keeping a pace" (*P* 63), but "A"-12 will assert,

> To plod is not hobble.
> Each time has Love's way with music.

You keep up to date
On all fours
That canter sometimes
Before boughs that grace trees
["A"-12, 180]

Opposed as well to the Eliotian construction of the individual talent, and standing as the single most compelling index of the rapprochement Zukofsky has reached with his own Jewish heritage, is "A"-12's portrayal of his recently deceased father, Pinchos Zukofsky, whose moving goodness is embodied in the care with which he observes the responsibilities of his Orthodox faith. Pinchos works as a pants presser and night watchman in a men's shop, staying at times until midnight,

Except Fridays
When he left, enough time before sunset
Margolis begrudged.
My own business
My father told Margolis
Is to keep Sabbath
["A"-12, 152]

The street never wide enough for him,
Taking a diagonal to cross it,
To open and close the synagogue
For over six time ten years
Until three days before he died—
A longer journey than Odysseus'
["A"-12, 155]

That Zukofsky describes his own poetics in terms similar to those in which he describes his father's life, a life based on the humble and persistent repetition of necessary and proper tasks, indicates to what extent he finds the life lived within the path of Orthodoxy a more useful model of the poet's task than Eliot's impersonal catalyst of "impressions and experiences" (*Sacred Wood* 56). Zukofsky writes of his father:

Had he asked me to say Kadish
I believe I would have said it for him
["A"-12, 143]

In the text of "A"-12 as a whole, this "free-thinking Jew," while accepting the formal poetics of modernism, begs leave to reconsider the whole ideology of tradition and the individual talent that would banish his people from the republic of culture and return them, perhaps, to their native "protozoic slime."

6

"The Revolutionary Word"

Zukofsky, the Political Radical

> [*New Masses*] is just one more wailing place and the whole left now-a-days is a mob of wailers. I do very much believe in leftism in every direction, even in wailing. These people go about it in such a way that nobody listens to them except themselves; and that is a[t] least one reason why they get nowhere. They have the most magnificent cause in the world.
> —Wallace Stevens, 9 October 1935 (*Letters* 287)

> America when I was seven momma took me to Communist
> Cell meetings they sold us garbanzos a handful per ticket a ticket costs a nickel and the speeches were free everybody was angelic and sentimental about the workers it was all so sincere you have no idea what a good thing the party was . . .
> —Allen Ginsberg, "America" (147)

The line dividing responsible historiography from diverting anecdote is always a fine one, as is clearly seen when considering the work of recent historicist literary critics, and as Pound's doctrine of the "luminous detail" perhaps amply illustrates. "Luminous details," as Pound explains in *I Gather the Limbs of Osiris*, are "certain facts [which] give one a sudden insight into circumjacent conditions, into their causes, their effects, into sequence, and law. . . . A dozen facts of this nature give us intelligence of a period—a kind of intelligence not to be gathered from a great array of facts of the other sorts." While luminous details are "hard to find," they are happily "swift and easy of transmission" (*Selected Prose* 22–23). But when is a detail "luminous," and when is it merely amusing? When is the fascinating story introducing an essay evidence rather than ornament? And how often does the apocryphal attain the status of the historical merely through its conceptual rightness?[1] Anecdotes, of course, have an ambiguous status within the discipline of literary history, and their evidentiary value is certainly far less than that of the document. Nonetheless, the anecdote, particularly the anecdote that fulfills expectations one has perhaps already entertained, can have powerful imaginative resonance.

When it comes to discussions of the period in which political concerns dominated Zukofsky's writings—roughly speaking, the 1920s and 1930s—anecdotal reportage has, for the most part, far outstripped the presentation of hard data. Two diverting anecdotes concerning Zukofsky's political years seem neatly to sum up his political evolution. According to Hugh Kenner, sometime in the 1920s Columbia expellee Whittaker Chambers, who by that point had veered from being a "Calvin Coolidge admirer" (Celia Zukofsky's phrase) to joining the Communist Party, brought his friend Zukofsky to a meeting of his West Side Party cell and sponsored him for membership. "Mother" Bloor herself, presiding over the meeting, decided the young poet was a "bourgeois intellectual" and vetoed his induction ("Oppen, Zukofsky" 165).[2] (As Celia Zukofsky would later recall, "they suggested that he join someplace on the east side" [*LZMP* 50].) According to Kenner, this chilly reception set Zukofsky on a tangent away from the Communist Party: "debarred from membership, [he] soon cooled in fervor though he retained a lifelong respect for Marx's intelligence." Guy Davenport's account of Zukofsky's political disengagement, less Buster Keaton and more John Keats, derives from direct conversation with the poet and has a suspiciously neat literary symmetry: Zukofsky, "the friend of Whittaker Chambers at Columbia in its Reddest heyday . . . read Gibbon with an eye to seeing what Marx would have done about it all and thus bade farewell to Marx and all his host" (*Geography* 194).

I am no more prepared to write the history of Louis Zukofsky's political years than I am to summarize his relationship to Judaism, and I am reluctant to encapsulate and domesticate that history in a wry anecdote (despite the fact I have already offered two). Nor do I think it yet possible, pending extensive and painstaking examination of the relevant documentary evidence, to reach any unassailable conclusions concerning Zukofsky's relationship to American literary radicalism during the "committed" decade of the 1930s. More interesting at present, now that both the American and the Soviet Communist Parties have passed into history (at least under their old names), is determining the relationship between Zukofsky's Marxism—an undisputed biographical fact—and the poetry and statements of poetics he wrote during the period in which Marxist ideology was a central element of his mental landscape. Were Zukofsky's political and poetic radicalisms integrated, of a piece? Or was he, like so many of his contemporaries, unable to resolve the seeming contradictions between a progressive political stance and a poetic modernism that the Left coded, in Alan Wald's words, as "expressions of a reactionary ideology that reproduce[s] the fragmentation experienced in bourgeois society" (*Revolutionary Imagination* 3)?

Whatever the detailed answers to these questions might turn out to be, Zukofsky's relationship with the radical literary periodical *New Masses*, and with that magazine's editorship, is emblematic of his ultimate inability either to persuade a socialist-realism-minded Communist Party literary orthodoxy to accept his leftist poetic modernism or to force his own poetic productions into the realistic, hortatory mode that the Party, over the latter part of the 1930s, would increasingly favor. While this inability (or unwillingness) on Zukofsky's part to reach an accommodation with the established literary Left must at the time have seemed a signal failure, from the perspective of sixty years' history it appears an index of much of what contemporary readers value in Zukofsky's work. Its political anomalousness is representative of the larger obduracy of Zukofsky's poetry as a whole, and his refusal to fit his work into accepted party standards is of a piece with that work's refusal to fit comfortably any conventional measure of poetic ordinariness.

The relationship between Zukofsky's politics and poetics, of course, has been both explored and denied in the twenty years or so in which the academy has been seriously reading the poet. Davenport and Kenner, for instance, critics ranging from centrist to reactionary in their own political views, and decidedly conservative in cultural outlook, narrate the political curve of Zukofsky's work—which moves from a heavy emphasis on the class war in the 1920s and 1930s to an equally stressed investment in the domestic realm of familial affection from the 1940s onward—as reflecting the education of a young man realizing his youthful follies as he comes to maturity. (The favored emblem for such a reading might be the two halves of "A"-9: Marx's *Capital*, followed by Spinoza's *Ethics*.) Zukofsky's early leftism, far from being an integral element of his thought and poetic, is in this account merely an indiscretion of youth, the sort of folly that even the heroically Marxist John Reed would have outgrown, had he lived, and to which only the hardest-boiled of party hacks—men like Mike Gold or Joseph Freeman—would cling until death.

I believe that this narrative of Zukofsky's political career is to some degree an oversimplification—one that stems, at least in Kenner's case, not so much from a rejection of a political poetry per se as from Kenner's own rejection of Marxism, both as a viable political philosophy and as an intellectual framework capable of accommodating the radical experiments of modernism. For more "progressive" critics there are many attractions in taking seriously Zukofsky's political allegiances of the 1930s, not least of which is his usefulness as a counterexample—that is, a politically committed experimental poet who, as a leftist, stands in contrast to the reactionary giants of the first generation of modernism: the "fascist beasts" (Basil Bunting's term) Yeats, Pound, and Eliot. Zukofsky serves some critics as a progressive antidote to the canonical figures of high modernism, living proof that modernist poetics are not necessarily invested in fascism or reaction. As Burton Hatlen puts it, the first part of *"A"* "represents a sustained effort to write, within a poetic mode that derives from Pound, a democratic and socialist response to the elitist and fascist political epic that Pound himself was writing during the 1930s"—namely, *The Cantos*. According to Hatlen, Zukofsky overcomes the gulf between poetry and active politics by situating the poet's labor within an "explicitly Marxist conception of labor as the distinctively human act by which we collectively transform the world and make it our own" ("Art and/as Labor" 206). Edward Schelb ("Exaction of Song") and Michael Davidson ("Dismantling") have each explored the ways in which Zukofsky's formal experiments can be situated within a Marxist ideology. And with an argument reminiscent of the poetico-political statements of various Language poets, Peter Quartermain's *Disjunctive Poetics* rejects the political "content" of Zukofsky's poetics—in "A"-9, for instance, "it is irrelevant whether Zukofsky here is a Marxist or a Buddhist" (87)—but finds a liberatory potential precisely in the poetry's difficulty or obscurity.[3]

These critics explore how Zukofsky's poetry, especially the first third of *"A"*, can be read as an attempt to formulate a specifically Marxist modernism, a poetics in which the interplay of form and content works in a truly dialectical manner. In so doing, the critics amply demonstrate that political criticism of Zukofsky has long since passed the point of merely examining the poetry at those places where it explicitly addresses political subjects, and has itself moved to a more truly dialectical, formalist interpretive mode. But this criticism moves too much within an exclusively literary space; except for a few pages by Eric Homberger (163–86) and Linda Simon, there has been little attempt to read Zukofsky's literary Marxism (or Leninism) within the immediate literary-historical context of the American 1930s, a context in which, as the work of such critics as Cary Nelson (*Repression and Recovery*) and Walter Kalaidjian (*American Culture*) is increasingly demonstrating, various leftist literary movements loom every bit as large as the modernist avant-gardes: a context in which writers whom we now think of only as literary figures or stylistic innovators—Edward Dahlberg, Kenneth Rexroth, Stanley Burnshaw—were for a time passionately committed, verbal spokesmen for the revolutionary Left. Too often Zukofsky's work is read in the black-and-white categories of modernist poetics and Marxist-Leninist theory, as if those poetics and that theory could be considered outside their respective historical moments. When we hear that Zukofsky is a "poet of the Left," we too often overlook the reality pointedly conveyed through Wallace Stevens's bitter words in a 1935 letter to Ronald Lane Latimer, responding to Stanley Burnshaw's review (in *New Masses*) of *Ideas of Order*—a review that chastised Stevens for his unwillingness to take a firm political stand.[4] Stevens writes, "I hope I am headed left, but there are lefts and lefts, and certainly I am not headed for the ghastly left of masses" (*Letters* 286). It is easy to forget exactly how variegated the "Lefts" of the American 1930s could be; three weeks later Stevens would identify his own odd Left: "I am pro-Mussolini, personally" (289).

Zukofsky of course was no fan of Mussolini (his citation of the dictator in "Poem beginning 'The' " smacks of both revulsion and satire: "74 'Il Duce: I feel God deeply.' / 75 Black shirts—black shirts—some power is so funereal" [*CSP* 11]) although he was always something of an elitist in aesthetic matters. Zukofsky's elitism coexists uneasily with a Marxism that seems perfectly natural for a first-generation child of Russian-Jewish immigrants and 1920s-era Columbia graduate. In this uneasy marriage of ideologies lies the importance of his example, an importance beyond that of a mere counterweight to Eliot and Pound's conservatism. Zukofsky's career as a fellow-traveler, and the degree to which his very serious leftist commitments influenced the theories of poetics he propounded in the early 1930s, represent an early and important instance of an American poet trying to come to grips with the tension between the political and literary spheres, realms that the American pragmatist tradition—in so many ways Zukofsky's own—has tended to separate.

The relationship of poetry and politics has been an important issue at least since Plato's *Republic*. In the 1930s it became almost oppressively so for the politically committed poet writing in a culture where it seemed increasingly that, as Auden wrote in 1939, "poetry makes nothing happen." In this chapter I examine a pair of intertwined subjects. On the one hand, I want to consider Zukofsky's attitude toward and relationship with *New Masses*, the most prominent organ of American Marxist literary production in the 1930s and a magazine that would take a more hard-line pro-Stalinist bent as the decade proceeded. On the other, I want to unpack the political rhetoric and implications of some of Zukofsky's early published writings, viewing them in the light of the aesthetic increasingly promoted by the influential figures and important literary organs of the Left. These readings suggest that even as Zukofsky's works pioneer new ways of examining the political, the modes of those works make them incompatible with the aesthetic models that the leftist literary establishment of the 1930s, especially toward the end of the decade, set forward as orthodoxy. It would probably be impertinent to speculate on what made Zukofsky leave the Party's sphere of influence, but two points stand out. First, Zukofsky broke off his more-or-less serious flirtation with Communism at a time when millions were leaving the Party and the Left, when the gap between the rhetoric of American Communism and the practices of the Soviet government had grown too wide to be comfortably bridged. Second, Zukofsky's strongest allegiance was first and finally to his poetry. The refusal of the Left and its literary organs to accept his leftist modernism, combined with the disillusionments of the late 1930s, must have made further fellow-traveling a practically unendurable prospect.

The American 1930s was a time of copious, wide-ranging, and above all politically aware poetic production. The decade saw a number of leftist literary magazines—magazines with names like *Anvil, Dynamo, Liberator,* and various publications sponsored and run by local John Reed Clubs—but until the founding in 1934 of *Partisan Review,* a journal whose skeptical relationship to the Comintern would eventually lead it to outright Trotskyism, *New Masses* had unquestioned preeminence among them.[5] *New Masses* was founded in 1926 in large part to promote fine writing on the Left, and in its early years happily sacrificed Party orthodoxy for literary excellence, publishing pieces by Left-leaning writers of dubious political credentials and even by nonleftists like Ezra Pound whose names lent credibility to *New Masses*' attempt to establish itself as a serious literary journal. Editorial policy at *New Masses* was complex and variable, but it appears that over the course of the 1930s, the magazine shifted its focus more and more toward a rather amorphously defined proletarian aesthetic, based loosely on the "proletarian literature" then being explored in the Soviet Union. The most strenuous promoter of this aesthetic was *New Masses* editor Mike Gold, born Izhok Granich in 1893 in the Chrystie Street neighborhood of the Lower East Side, a few blocks from where Zukofsky himself would be born in 1904. In an editorial published in *New Masses* in 1926, Gold would describe his ideal proletarian litterateur in memorable, Whitmanesque words: "Send us a giant who can shame our writers back to their task of civilizing America. . . . Send a soldier who has studied history. Send a strong poet who loves the masses, and their future. . . . Send us a joker in overalls. Send no saint. Send an artist. Send a scientist. Send a Bolshevik. Send a man" (Gold 139). Gold himself, as Joseph Freeman describes him, set the fashion for this strapping Shakespeare-with-a-lunchbucket: "He affected dirty shirts, a big, black, uncleaned Stetson with the brim of a sombrero; smoked stinking, twisted, Italian three-cent cigars, and spat frequently and vigorously on the floor" (quoted in Aaron 86).[6]

While Mike Gold and his hypothetical proletarian bard might seem a radical contrast to the slim, effete, and above all, nattily dressed Zukofsky, the coincidence of his birth proximity to Gold—whom Edward Dahlberg would (with much hindsight) call "the barking Cerberus of pleb fiction" (286)—was not lost on Zukofsky. He mentioned it to Pound in a 1928 letter: "we were brought up together on Chrystie St., tho' I never met him down there and have seen him only once" (*P/Z* 17). Zukofsky claimed no close acquaintance with Gold. When Pound questioned him about the *New Masses* editor, the installments of whose novel *Jews Without Money* had aroused his interest, Zukofsky confessed, "I suppose Mike Gold is alright. . . . I don't think I've missed anything not seeing more of him in N.Y.—saw him once anyway. N. Masses a pretty bad best—I'd just as soon have H[ound] & H[orn]" (*P/Z* 62). Zukofsky's attitude toward *New Masses* in the late 1920s and early 1930s, it appears, was pretty much one of amused contempt. Part of this impression might be attributed to the fact that most of his published comments about *New Masses* occur in correspondence with Pound, from whom one could expect enthusiasm neither for Marxist theory nor for proletarian realism, at least in the crude form in which *New Masses* all too often dished it out. But Zukofsky's discomfort with the direction of *New Masses*' editorial policy goes beyond a desire to distance himself from the magazine in his letters to Pound. What separates Zukofsky, himself a committed Marxist, from the apparatus of the Communist literary establishment is his simultaneous commitment to a modernist poetics derived from the works of Apollinaire, Pound, Eliot, Williams, and Cummings. As he writes to Pound in 1933, "I am not here writing as a member of the U.S. Communist Party—I am sure that as far as they're concerned papa [Pound] & child [Zukofsky] & Unk Bill Walrus [Williams] are in the same galley" (*P/Z* 148).

And as far as Mike Gold would be concerned, Zukofsky is probably right. Gold's 1930 statement of the aesthetics of the new "Proletarian Realism" leaves little space for a poem such as "Poem beginning 'The,' " or even as overtly political a work as the early sections of *"A"*: "Swift action, clear form, the direct line, cinema in words; this seems to be one of the principles of proletarian realism" (Gold 207); "No straining or melodrama or other effects; life itself is the supreme melodrama. Feel this intensely, and everything becomes poetry—the new poetry of materials, of the so-called 'common man,' the Worker moulding his real world" (Gold 208). Most drastically, at least for a writer with as intensely verbal an imagination as Zukofsky's, the poet must use "As few words as possible" and must eschew "verbal acrobatics": "this is only another form for bourgeois idleness. The worker lives too close to reality to care about these literary show-offs, these verbalist heroes" (Gold 207). For Zukofsky, this aesthetic must have seemed severely limiting, not least because of the purely instrumental role it implicitly assigns literature: "Proletarian realism is never pointless. It does not believe in literature for its own sake, but in literature that is useful, has a social function. . . . Every poem, every novel and drama, must have a social theme, or it is merely confectionary" (Gold 207). And Zukofsky knew as well that his own advocacy of the formal innovators and innovations of poetic modernism set him apart from Gold and his collaborators: the *New Masses* editors, he writes in 1931, are a bunch of "New Asses" who "need continual tutoring" and who would "probably fire me out because my name has occasionally been associated with E.P. & W.C.W. and that *lump* Kewmangs [Cummings]" (*P/Z* 96). While the modernist movement had something to teach the Communists—just as Pound's "Bowmen of Shu," for instance, corrects Whittaker Chambers's story "You Have Seen the Heads" (see *P/Z* 96)—Zukofsky doubts that the writers of *New Masses* are likely to accept that tuition. Gold himself appears in *"A"*, neither as literary writer nor literary editor but as hack propagandist; he is "Carat" in "A"-1: "What's your next editorial about,

Carat, / We need propaganda, the thing's / becoming a mass movement" ("A"-1, 3).

Zukofsky's first two major publications, the " 'Objectivists' 1931" issue of *Poetry* and the 1932 *An "Objectivists" Anthology*, are editorial arrangements rather than acts of actual authorship, but it would be foolish to underestimate the ideological forces involved in anthology-making, then as now the primary weapon in various canon-making and -breaking strategies. Zukofsky's two collections are by no definition agitprop, but each of them shows his markedly leftist tendencies. The " 'Objectivists' 1931" *Poetry* issue contains work by a number of clearly left-wing poets—Norman MacLeod, Harry Roskolenkier, Whittaker Chambers, John Wheelwright—and mentions Herman Spector and Sherry Mangan as also-rans in its editor's notes. Zukofsky's explanatory manifesto, "Program: 'Objectivists' 1931," cites Lenin as "a great writer" (272) and mentions among other "particulars" "the Russian Revolution and the rise of metallurgical plants in Siberia" (268).[7] While the left-wing poets of *Poetry*'s " 'Objectivists' 1931" issue are largely absent from *An "Objectivists" Anthology*, much of the work in that volume is of a political nature: Zukofsky's "A"-1–7; Williams's "A Morning Imagination of Russia" and "The Pure Products of America," among others; and Frances Fletcher's "A Chair," a poem that almost certainly alludes to the 1927 executions of Sacco and Vanzetti, five years later still vivid in the minds of the Left.[8] And while that volume's preface, " 'Recencies' in Poetry," is for the most part an attack on the current critical establishment, and T. S. Eliot in particular, Zukofsky closes with a memorable image of the intersection of the "good poems of yesterday" and the progressive politics of today: "Stalin has been spending some of his time in his one or two rooms not destroying Shakespeare, but has been reading the not really predacious Englishm[a]n on his vacation" (25). Earlier in the essay Zukofsky has advocated a poetry free of "predatory intent" (18), the propagandistic advocacy so strongly prescribed by Gold and other cultural commissars of the Party. In this passage Zukofsky demonstrates that even Stalin, the current icon of Revolutionary values, is able to enjoy and learn from the works of Shakespeare—a dramatist "not really" political or "predacious."[9]

This chapter's title is itself a quotation from " 'Recencies' in

Poetry": "*Impossible* to communicate anything but particulars—historic and contemporary—things, human beings as things their instrumentalities of capillaries and vein binding up and bound up with events and contingencies. The revolutionary word if it must revolve cannot escape having a reference" (16). This, I think, is one of the few moments in which Zukofsky's writings on poetics assert a definite political dimension to poetic language itself. Other critics are right in finding political implications in Zukofsky's poetic forms and modes,[10] but at very few points does the poet himself *explicitly* theorize the political implications of his poetics. What Zukofsky implies in this passage of " 'Recencies' " is actually fairly straightforward: if one's language is to be "revolutionary," to have a political impact, it must have a "reference," must deal with "historic and contemporary" particulars rather than with abstractions. Here he has it both ways, hearkening back to both Pound's Imagist manifesto, which demands the poet "go in fear of abstractions" (*Literary Essays* 5), and the "scientific" proletarian realism of Gold and company, which demands above all the treatment of actual fact, "the *real conflicts* of men and women. . . . Away with all lies about human nature. We are scientists; we know what a man thinks and feels. . . . No straining or melodrama or other effects; life itself is the supreme melodrama" (Gold 208). By his treatment of "historic and contemporary particulars," Zukofsky simultaneously pursues the modernist poetics of his elders Pound and Williams, no matter how bourgeois or reactionary their politics, and fulfills at least the liminal requirements of a proletarian poetics, no matter how far his work might otherwise diverge from what Mike Gold or Joseph Freeman would recognize as proletarian realism.

The major divergences between Zukofsky's modernism and proletarian realism are clear: Zukofsky's poetry, despite its author's own emphasis on "clarity," is a difficult poetry, relying on tactics of juxtaposition and montage that, however easily apprehensible they may be in the cinema, pose formidable difficulties for the average reader. When Gold advocates "cinema in words," he means something exceedingly straightforward: "Swift action, clear form, the direct line" (Gold 207). Zukofsky, on the other hand, sees his own work "partak[ing] of the cinematic principle" (*P/Z* 112) to the extent its formal structures resemble those of Eisenstein's groundbreaking montage: as he writes Pound in 1931, "Advertising & montage, Mr. E.,—Eisenstein has nothing on us" (*P/Z* 121).[11] For such proponents of proletarian literature as the poet Herman Spector, modernist poetry is fundamentally decadent, the product of "sophisticated dilettante[s]" in an "age of the freak in matters esthetic" (quoted in Klein 74). Poetry, that is, ought to be readily apprehensible to the common reader; if it requires a second or even a third reading, this is a symptom of its political and social decadence. In contrast, Zukofsky's own response to misreadings and assaults is to chastise his readers for not paying enough attention. In " 'Recencies' " he grouses, "the absense of a habit of reading 4 or 5 times for a meaning—in certain readers is probably regrettable" (9).

Perhaps most important of all is the fact that no matter how profoundly Zukofsky's work may treat the class struggle, it almost wholly lacks the hortatory element essential to Gold's vision of proletarian writing. It analyzes, dramatizes, perhaps even (*avant la lettre*) deconstructs, but it does not inspire to action. The poem is, as Zukofsky puts it in " 'Recencies,' " an "object unrelated to palpable or predatory intent" (18). The poem supplies the information, the knowledge, that may make the mind "more temperate" (in Pound's phrase from *Mauberley*), but it only "records" "state and individual," it does not supply the necessary "application," the political action that must follow education (19). The very notion of "proletarian literature," it would seem, is for Zukofsky a problematic one: "By all means a literature of the proletariat—which will be only literature after all—if there are writers. They will never get across to the proletariat if they are not" (19).

Zukofsky's discomfort with proletarian realism is evident in the explicitly political selections of *55 Poems* (1923–35), the first major grouping in the *Complete Short Poetry*. "During the Passaic Strike of 1926"—a poem that ridicules the plight of the "rich parish of St. Mark's-on-the-Bouwerie," which has only two gravesites left for its wealthy parishioners—is perhaps the only one of these poems that would pass proletarian realist muster:

For Justice they are shrewdly killing the proletarian,
For Justice they are shrewdly shooting him dead,

Good Heavens, when the vaults are filled in St. Mark's-on-the-
Bouwerie,
How will the dead bury their dead!
[*CSP* 26]

"Memory of V. I. Ulianov" (Lenin) (*CSP* 21–22) is a lyric so lofty and abstract that one can imagine it addressed to Christ or Buddha rather than a political leader; "D. R." (Diego Rivera) (38–39), although addressed to "Comrade D.R." and using the leftist cant of "Executives of industry," "Workers," and "Heads over industry," is similarly abstract. More characteristic of Zukofsky's subtle treatment of political themes is the fourth poem of the section:

Buoy—no, how,
It is not a question: what
Is this freighter carrying?—
Did smoke blow?—That whistle?—
Of course, commerce will not complete
Anything, yet the harbor traffic is busy,
there shall be a complete fragment
Of—

Nothing, look! that gull
Streak the water!
Getting nearer are we,
Hear? count the dissonances,

Shoal? accost—cost
Cost accounting.
[*CSP* 23–24]

Much of the language of the poem can be taken in a political or economic sense: "commerce," the reference to "harbor traffic," the question of what the freighter is carrying. This craft is, perhaps, the capitalist ship of state, headed into dangerous waters. "[C]ount the dissonances," the poem advises: the freighter—the entire capitalist economy?—is headed for a "shoal," at which it will be "accosted" and called to "account" for what it has "cost" the ordinary worker. But the poem has little sense of urgency and none of the call-to-arms fury that a similar theme might have in the hands of a leftist poet such as Harry Roskolenkier or Max

Bodenheim. Rather, it mimes the "complete fragments" of interrupted or overheard conversation, breaking from a potentially damning critique of the harbor ("there shall be a complete fragment / Of—") to an immediate observation ("Look! that gull / streak the water!"). It arrives at its "accounting" not as the climax of an argued indictment of the capitalist system but as the result of a playful and sonically dense permutation of sounds: "Shoal? accost—cost / Cost accounting." Zukofsky's very joy in the sounds of his language, it seems, will rarely allow him to sit still long enough to deliver a definitive (and straightforward) political statement.

As significant as the actual words and form of a writer's work is its medium of dissemination, the material venue in which that work is presented to the public.[12] While Zukofsky's political sympathies might lie with the crowd at the *Daily Worker* or *Dynamo*, in the early 1930s, he—like his contemporaries John Wheelwright and Sherry Mangan, also modernist poets committed to leftist causes—generally published his poetry not in leftist journals like *New Masses* but in little magazines associated with the apolitical avant-garde: *Blues, Pagany, Contact,* and so forth.[13] (The three poems I have just cited, for instance—"Memory of V. I. Ulianov," "D. R.," and "Buoy—no, how"—were first published respectively in Pound's *Exile,* in *Morada,* an Italian magazine, and in *Pagany.*) Zukofsky's Marxism is no doubt as sincere as that of many a fellow-traveler published in a John Reed Club journal, and his theoretical stance is no doubt more subtly considered than that of many Party members. (Those who doubt Zukofsky's grasp of Marxian economic theory might consider the ease and the force with which he debates Pound in the latter stages of their correspondence, a correspondence that very nearly becomes what Paul Zukofsky [with no little irony] calls a "primer in economics" [*CF* 309].) Yet even taking these facts into consideration, no matter how evident the Marxist "argument" of Zukofsky's poems might be, their strident formal modernism pretty much forecloses the possibility of their publication in journals like *New Masses*, which is dominated by the aesthetic of proletarian realism. What results is the slightly odd spectacle of sections of *"A"*—a poem James Laughlin would in 1938 call an "epic of the class struggle" ("Notes")—appearing in such journals as the avant-garde *Pagany* and the grudgingly experimental but thoroughly bourgeois *Poetry: A Magazine of Verse.*[14]

What fueled much of the political radicalism of the 1930s, of course, was the spectacular collapse of the American capitalist economy that began in 1929. Even as the wrenching human tragedy of the Depression forced thousands of writers and intellectuals to what would have once seemed desperate conclusions—those of the Communist Party—and as Roosevelt's New Deal put into operation many of the very reforms the Left had long advocated, thereby validating programs that would have been considered extreme if implemented in the 1920s, the economic disaster also worked to destroy a large proportion of the network of little magazines that had sprung up during the 1920s to publish avant-garde and experimental writing. The Objectivist Press, edited by Zukofsky and underwritten by Oppen, was only one of many publishing ventures that went under in the mid-1930s. Just as the possibilities of publishing his work in the little avant-garde magazines seemed to be disappearing, over the course of the mid- to late 1930s, it seems that Zukofsky was becoming more personally involved in leftist literary organizations. Zukofsky was a member at least through 1938 of the League of American Writers, the United States affiliate of the International Union of Revolutionary Writers. Additionally, Eric Homberger has discovered a mention in a 1937 *Daily Worker* of one "Louis Zukonski" being elected by a division of that body to a committee organizing support for striking steelworkers (171). After the undignified petering out of the Objectivist Press, Zukofsky apparently became closely associated with *New Masses* itself, spending much time at the editorial offices and serving as an unpaid editorial advisor.[15] This association is an intriguing conjunction, especially when one considers that there is a substantial period in the late 1930s (beginning around late 1935 and continuing through 1941) where Zukofsky's only significant periodical publications appear in *New Masses,* that bastion of proletarian writing.

Mike Gold's aesthetic of "proletarian realism" dominated *New Masses* by the late 1930s, when Zukofsky published two sections of "A"-8 in the magazine. These years were a hard time for American Communists: slipping away were the heady days of the Popular Front and the Spanish Civil War, during which Communist Party organs for a short while became a forum for all who would support a common Loyalist cause, no matter how "suspect" their allegiances might have been a few years before. By 1939 the Hitler-Stalin pact, a joining of hands by the embodiment of fascism and the leader of the proletarian revolution, only served to drive away the remaining vacillators who had not been disillusioned by the Moscow show trials of 1936 and 1938. (These trials had driven loyalists like Gold into what Paul Buhle calls "a hard-nosed sectarianism" [180], an intense hard-line Stalinism.) Homberger characterizes what Zukofsky resorted to in the late 1930s as "writ[ing] for his desk drawer" (182), withholding his work from public examination. In part this is true, since "A"-8, which was composed between 1935 and 1938, only saw complete publication in 1958. But the sections of "A"-8 that Zukofsky *did* publish seem an interesting variation, rather than a repudiation, of Homberger's notion. I would submit as example the publication of a poem entitled "March Comrades" in the 3 May 1938 *New Masses* and, by way of contrast, the final appearance of that passage of verse in "A"-8, first published in 1958. These documents make clear, I believe, that Zukofsky had fully realized by 1938 that the only common ground between the aesthetic of Gold's *New Masses* and his own concatenation of "historic and contemporary particulars" was one in which the intellectual complexities and aural splendors of the ongoing *"A"* must yield to the merely hortatory.

A brief examination of both the contents and the contexts of these two passages is revealing. "March Comrades," as is evident from its refrain—"This is May Day! May!"—is something of a marching song, a May Day hymn "for a workers' chorus." Appropriately, it appears in the 1938 May Day issue of *New Masses*, under a small cartoon of a crowd of strikers with pickets:

"March Comrades"

(Words for a workers' chorus, from " 'A'-8")

Workers and farmers unite
You have nothing to lose

But your chains
The world is to win
This is May Day! May!
Your armies are veining the earth!

Railways and highways have tied
Blood of farmland and town
And the chains
Speed wheat to machine
This is May Day! May!
The poor's armies veining the earth!

Hirers once fed by the harried
Cannot feed them their hire
Nor can chains
Hold the hungry in
This is May Day! May!
The poor are veining the earth!

Light lights in air blossoms red
Like nothing on earth
Now the chains
Drag graves to lie in
This is May Day! May!
The poor's armies are veining the earth!

March comrades in revolution
From hirer unchained
Till your gain
Be the freedom of all
The World's May Day! May!
May of the Freed of All the Earth!

(The poem appears in the middle column of a three-column page, folded within an article on the American Federation of Labor; such a layout, in which poem, prose, and cartoon decoration are juxtaposed in uneasy hierarchy of text and decoration, reminds this reader of nothing so much as the presentation of poetry in that bastion of bourgeois respectability, the *New Yorker*.) There is elsewhere in this issue a brief column urging "Unity on May Day" and hailing, among other triumphs for democracy, "the swift progress of Socialism in the Soviet Union and the uprooting of Trotskyist wreckers and spies." The specter of the Moscow trials casts a long shadow over this *New Masses.* A column two pages further on reveals that Trotsky himself has "degenerate[d] into an accomplice of fascism": "Whatever it may mean to Trotsky subjectively, his 'revolution,' objectively, is nothing but counter-revolution and the triumph of fascism" ("His Main Enemy" 10). And finally, on page 19, there is a lengthy "Statement by American Progressives" on the Moscow trials, confidently citing the "clear presumption of the guilt of the defendants": "Drastic attack must be met by drastic defence: it is in this light that we regard the trials." This document is signed by well over a hundred writers, artists, and intellectuals, a group that exemplifies the reach of the CPUSA's soon-to-be-abandoned Popular Front strategy of welcoming left-leaning intellectuals of politically heterodox beliefs. Among the signators are Nelson Algren, Malcolm Cowley, Stuart Davis, Mike Gold, Dashiell Hammett, Langston Hughes, and Dorothy Parker. Zukofsky's name is conspicuous by its absence: one can only speculate whether he was asked to sign and refused or was never asked (the powers that be simply assuming his refusal). Present among the names, however, is that of Morris U. Schappes, who, five years before in *Poetry* itself, had attacked Zukofsky's *An "Objectivists" Anthology* as the work of "deracinated bourgeois poet[s]," who, piqued by capitalist society's devaluation of poetry itself, have withdrawn into "rootless esotericism." Zukofsky and company, Schappes advises, ought to model their work on Louis Aragon's *The Red Front* (343). Zukofsky bristles in reply, quoting Lenin and observing that Schappes "admires only those 'poets' who 'express' their 'service' to the revolutionary proletariat in the worst public-school honored manner of Milton" ("Objectivists Again" 117).

There is unintentional irony in this exchange, not merely because Zukofsky and Schappes will find themselves side by side five years later in an issue of *New Masses* but because "March Comrades" compares far more closely to Schappes's political aesthetic—the crowd-rousing, exhortative mode of Louis Aragon (or for that matter, Mike Gold's unesoteric, readily grasped proletarian aesthetic)—than to the principles of sincerity and objectification Zukofsky himself had put forward seven years earlier. "March Comrades" is, on its face, a concession to the poetry that *New Masses* would have. But it is not wholly a concession: Zukofsky frames his song, noting both that it is merely the "words" for a chorus and that it is only a section of "A"-8, a larger whole.

Zukofsky wrote "A"-8 between 1935 and 1937, and then re vised it in 1957 before its 1958 publication in Cid Corman's Origin Press *"A" 1–12.* The changes he made before the movement's final publication, in addition to demonstrating how Zukofsky's aesthetic was moving in more and more minimalist directions, reveal much about the distance between Zukofsky's own aesthetic and the aesthetic of the leftist establishment (even when one takes into account the hindsight that twenty years was to provide him).[16] Strictly speaking, nothing has been changed in the revision. Almost the whole of Zukofsky's revising, as one can also see comparing the *An "Objectivists" Anthology* versions of "A"-1 through "A"-7 to their final publications, consists of omission. Omitted here is the entire first stanza, with its heavy-handed restatement of the *Communist Manifesto.* Throughout the passage, the crowd-rousing "This is May Day! May!" becomes the barer but more suggestive "This is May," which invokes not an international worker's holiday but the cyclic change of seasons that so fascinated Vergil, Chaucer, Spenser, and Shakespeare. I set the last two stanzas of the two versions side by side, so that Zukofsky's omissions may be more evident:

[1938:]	[1957:]
Light lights in air blossoms red	Light lights in air blossoms red
Like nothing on earth	Like nothing on earth
Now the chains	Now the chains
Drag graves to lies in	Drag graves to lie in
This is May Day! May!	This is May
The poor's armies are veining the earth!	The poor's armies veining the earth!
March comrades in revolution	March
From hirer unchained	From hirer unchained
Till your gain	Till your gain
Be the freedom of all	Be the
The World's May Day! May!	World's
May of the Freed of All the Earth!	
	["A"-8, 48–49]

Apart from the complete omission of the first stanza, the final stanza shows the most drastic changes. "March Comrades" had ended on a crescendo in the form of a more than slightly bombastic iambic tetrameter line, punctuated embarrassingly with capitals. The passage from "A"-8 ends on a quiet, tentative note, not unhopeful but not at all bombastic or hortatory. The later version is no longer "words for a workers' chorus" but a calm, carefully modulated coda to such a marching song.

In the context of "A"-8 as a whole, this passage takes on an even more complex aspect, revealing itself as a lyrical interlude in a large-scale fugal structure of juxtaposed themes and subjects. "A"-8 is the longest of the first eight sections of *"A"*, as long as the first seven sections combined. It explores to the greatest degree yet the task Zukofsky sets himself in "A"-6 when he asks, "*Can* / The design / Of the fugue / Be transferred / To poetry?" (38). Preceding this passage are statements (in the musical sense) of the section's eight separate and interwoven themes, which Zukofsky enumerates in a 1935 letter to Lorine Niedecker:

> I—Labor as creator, as creature. [a pun on Spinoza's *natura naturans, natura naturata*]
>
> II—Burying Jesus, so connection with Bach's *Passion*, and what is to be said now is bridged and one can go on with what is to be said now. Also negative creating the positive . . . synthesized.
>
> III—Bach's life in relation to all this; and to rest of poem (1 - 7).
>
> IV—How others, not me, might look at it (beginning) "natural that Bach . . . and out of respect," which is Ezra, different mentalities, friends and writing, combination of Atheling theme, Kay etc., in earlier movement.
>
> V—IV as I synthesize it. Matters that relate, people, composition as action, ("How journeyed?")
>
> VI—V as Marx synthesized . . . a basis for right and wrong action, related to economic structure of society.
>
> VII—Reason for V and VI in general comprehension of the nature of things: matter thinking, bodily substance.
>
> VIII—Parallels to V, VI, VII in contemporary science: physics, mathematics ("Infinite is a meaningless word.")
>
> Each theme pumped on the organ as you say modulates or is heard

> against the other, then each one assumes phases of the others, appearing in different guises, but continuing to mean the same—till they'll all go together. (quoted in Ahearn, *Zukofsky's "A"* 75–76)

Ahearn boils the movement's eight themes down to "labor, Bach, economics, science, nominalism, personal history, literature and art, and the Adamses" (77). But even Zukofsky's own enumeration, which seems complex enough, does not indicate the variety of materials that make up "A"-8. There are quotations from various scientists and scholastic philosophers; passages chronicling the history of the labor movement; and a variety of perspectives on the philosophy of history, including those of Karl Marx, Brooks Adams, and Brooks's brother Henry. The "March" passage follows a series of meditations on the nature of thought and fact and on how capitalist advertising works to obscure the true relations of existents:

> Not enough to reject the falsely related,
> The mirrors of the facts must not be dis-
> simulated:
>
> In the advertisement
> One handle of a toothbrush lasts a lifetime,
> But brush your teeth of their tartar and
> Reenamel the handle.
> ["A"-8, 48]

Following the song is a three-page passage—consisting of nine 9-line stanzas—in which the distribution of *n* and *r* sounds is determined by the equation of a conic section. That passage is itself a concatenation of topics and quotations that range from Communist Party history, to quantum physics, to interwoven fragments of the poems—among them "Lollai, lollai," a Robin Hood ballad, Henry Clay Work's "Year of Jubilee," and Burns's "A Man's a Man"—Zukofsky was collecting for his *Workers Anthology*, some of which would later appear in his teaching anthology *A Test of Poetry* (see Ahearn, *Zukofsky's "A"* 231–39).

Despite whatever excisions Zukofsky made in 1957 when he was revising "A"-8 for its first complete publication, this complexity of structure and denseness of reference was already in place by 1938, as is clear from his correspondence with Niedecker and Pound. What this all suggests, in short, is that the twenty-three lines of poetry to which Zukofsky has reduced the bombast of "March Comrades" are far more resonant and complex in their context in "A"-8 than they are as "words for a workers' chorus" in a May Day issue of *New Masses*. Zukofsky's poetry could indeed serve the cause of the Revolution, or at the very least find a limited hearing in the Revolution's official publishing organs. However, to do so it must be both radically decontextualized, taken out of its place in the larger structures of his work, and padded out to grandiloquence and soapbox bluster, obscuring the careful music that Zukofsky, with hindsight and political levelheadedness, will excavate from its lines.

When Zukofsky finished "A"-8 in 1937, it was the most advanced and fully realized section to date of his "poem of a life," the most ambitious poetic fugue he had yet written, and one of the most achieved products in English of the modernist "revolution of the word." Yet he had nowhere to publish it, save for the two brief and relatively minor passages—two small and uncharacteristic ornaments, placed on exhibit without regard for their function within the structure of the cathedral as a whole—that appeared in *New Masses* in 1937 and 1938. It is perhaps useless to speculate about what might have happened had the Marxist literary establishment accepted and encouraged Zukofsky's own gropings toward a thoroughly materialist modernism, if *New Masses*, for instance, had been edited by a man like Zukofsky's friend Kenneth Burke rather than Michael Gold. Zukofsky's achievement in poetry would not have been greatly augmented, I think, but he might have had the opportunity to formalize and theorize what remains among the most interesting, and also the most problematic, bodies of political poetry of this century.

"*A*"

Musical Form and Musical Knowledge

7

Music and Poetic Form in the Pound/Zukofsky Era

I should like to say "What the picture tells me is itself." That is, its telling me something consists in its own structure, in *its* own lines and colours. (What would it mean to say "What this musical theme tells me is itself"?)
—Ludwig Wittgenstein, *Philosophical Investigations* (142e)

Flexible, unrepetitive line
to sing, not paint; sing, sing,
laying the tune on the air,
nimble and easy as a lizard,
still and sudden as a gecko . . .
—Basil Bunting, "Briggflatts" (*Complete Poems* 48–49)

In unwinding Zukofsky's theoretical distinctions among solid, liquid, and gaseous states of language, I have focused primarily on the poet's distrust of abstraction, or gaseous language. For Zukofsky, most philosophical writing—discussions of epistemology in particular—falls into this problematic category. In Zukofsky's linguistic universe, skepticism, the putting into question of the evidence of the senses, is gaseous language par excellence.

Skeptics, by talking about abstractions and using such words as "reality," have fallen prey to their own terminology; rather than "thinking with the things as they exist" (*P* 12), they are merely manipulating various counters of "non-sense." Zukofsky himself, however, a philosopher by training, is guilty of gaseous language with surprising frequency. *Bottom,* whose explicit aim is the destruction of epistemology, is rife with passages of daunting abstraction and philosophical complexity. Zukofsky explains this as an inevitable, if lamentable, consequence of "explaining a 'precise' metaphysics and a preference for eyes in Shakespeare, or hammering them . . . into a ring of history, as these notes have done" (*B* 91): "[one w]ho tries to tie Shakespeare's reiterations on *eyes* as *points* . . . to history, philosophizes by logical necessity" (*B* 90). But Zukofsky's other prose works, especially his early writings on poetics and his book on Apollinaire, *The Writing of Guillaume Apollinaire,* are distinguished stylistically not, as one might suppose, by their sinewy, concrete language but instead by their tense, clotted syntax and their overwhelming reliance on abstract terms and concepts.

Pound, commenting on the Apollinaire book in a letter of 6 December 1932, exhorts Zukofsky, "*you* MUST now at once start on study of technique of flow . . . you have to go out for the NEXT step/ which is clarity" (*P/Z* 137). Two years earlier he had chided Zukofsky for the convoluted prose of "Sincerity and Objectification," insisting that the telegraphic style of his own correspondence should not serve as a stylistic template for published criticism: "You must *stop* tangling yr. sentences. . . . AFTER you have abs. mastered simple (even to platichood) style you can start convolutin' = my letters done to save time are NOT model for print" (43). Zukofsky's friend Basil Bunting—master of a Swiftian plain style in his own prose—takes Zukofsky to task in a 1932 "Open Letter to Louis Zukofsky" concerning the latter's essay " 'Recencies' in Poetry" in *An "Objectivists" Anthology* of 1931: "these paragraphs about poetry look to me like flights into darkness, away from ascertained and reascertainable fact to speculative mysticism, to a region I think void of anything permanently valuable" ("Obiter Dicta" 58). And while Guy Davenport praises the "good sense and pure style" of Zukofsky's prose, he observes that Zukofsky "wrote prose as a race horse walks: nervous, skittery, itching for the bugle and the track" (*Geography* 108). There is, it would seem, a natural tendency toward abstraction in Zukofsky's critical writings; indeed, I myself wonder how much of Zukofsky's dislike of abstract or gaseous language springs from a consciousness of the failings of his own prose style.

If one takes Zukofsky at his word, however, and accepts that the abstraction and complexity of *Bottom*'s language are an unfortunate but unavoidable result of Zukofsky's attempt to write both philosophical criticism and literary history and to explore as thoroughly as possible the " 'precise' metaphysics" involved in Shakespeare's dramas, it becomes possible to see exactly where Zukofsky hopes to position *Bottom* as philosophical text. Zukofsky considers *Bottom* his confrontation with Western philosophy on that tradition's own grounds, an agonistic meeting in which traditional epistemology is in the end found wanting when weighed against the philosophical implications and poetic testimony of Shakespeare's works: "skepticism palpably makes no sense, if [the reader] continues to be affected by the seniority of eyes as the life of *his* Shakespeare" (*B* 91). *Bottom*'s is a "valid skepticism" to the extent that it skeptically questions the plausibility of the entire skeptical enterprise and to the extent that it sets against that enterprise a more compelling philosophy—one that Zukofsky derives from Shakespeare, Spinoza, Wittgenstein, and others—that speaks for the validity of physical perception.

The strategy of *Bottom*'s argument (though it at times incorporates dramatistic analysis) is one of exemplification, condensation, and abstraction rather than one of explanation or commentary. *Bottom* proposes itself as a "long poem" in prose (perhaps, in an odd way, one of the major American modernist long poems) whose primary theme is a philosophical one and whose primary aim is to destroy philosophy (epistemology in particular) from within. Shakespeare, the extraphilosophical "foreign agent" introduced into the history of Western epistemology, surpasses Plato's wildest anti-poetic fears, functioning as the *pharmakon* that both poisons and cures philosophical discourse (see Derrida, *Dissemination* 61–171). Zukofsky's own gaseous language, which expands and rarefies philosophical discourse to the point of explosion, at times traces a path analogous to Derrida's prose, opening the text of Western philosophy to the marginalized or suppressed nonphilosophical elements that expose, clarify, and bring to the fore the self-destructive contradictions internal to that text.[1]

But Zukofsky is far from a deconstructionist, or from being any sort of philosopher. He claims always to be ill at ease with abstraction and with the pure wordplay to which philosophy seems all too often to reduce itself. If he seems powerfully attracted to gaseous language in his prose, that is perhaps no more than an accident of chronology: "I was born in a gas age" (*P* 170). More germane to a discussion of Zukofsky's poetry per se than his attacks on gaseous language is his distinction between solid and liquid language, a distinction that presents a reader with a number of difficulties of definition and description.[2] In this section, I hope in some degree to clarify this distinction, showing how it contributes to and reflects Zukofsky's conception of poetry's music and of musical form in poetry, particularly the "fugal form" that shapes much of *"A"*. Zukofsky's ideas are by no means self-generated but arise out of a congeries of modernist attitudes toward music and poetry: they have their own genealogy, which warrants discussion.

Important to this discussion is the purely *instrumental* nature of Zukofsky's claims about the musicality of verse. Such claims, while they may have a certain degree of historical validity—that is, they do have some basis in the recorded development of the poetic arts—are largely arbitrary as a description of post-Renaissance verse in English. The fact that such poets as Williams and Apollinaire (two of Zukofsky's great influences), and even fellow Objectivist George Oppen, tend not to view poetry in musical terms—actually, these poets tend to view it more often in terms of painting or dance, if one must strain for extraliterary analogies—indicates that Zukofsky's emphasis on poetry as music is a product of the immediate tradition in which he situates himself—that of Pound—rather than a natural or inevitable conjunction. Zukofsky's sometime collaborator Williams rejects the analogy most bluntly in *Spring and All* (1923). "I do not believe that writing is music," Williams writes; "I do not believe writing would gain in quality or force by seeking to attain to the conditions of music" (*Imaginations* 150). But whereas his old friend might clearly realize that the equation of music and poetry is only metaphorical, Zukofsky unrelentingly pursues the analogy, both in his criticism and his poetic composition. The analogy of music, then, remains an important critical tool for assessing the structures of and presuppositions behind Zukofsky's poetry, and beyond that, for assessing the precise project that results in *"A"* and the position of that project within American modernist writing.

Zukofsky's later poetry has a well-earned reputation for formidable obscurity, much of it a result of his adoption of a Poundian poetics of composition through compression and condensation. *"Dichten = condensare"* (*ABC of Reading* 36), a familiar dictum of Pound's, is clearly crucial to Zukofsky's poetics. An important concern of any critical examination of *"A"* should be to ascertain in what way the dense, texturally heteroglot verse of Zukofsky's later years—what Ron Silliman describes as "an opaque music of hollowed-out signifiers" (*New Sentence* 142) and Eliot Weinberger calls a "black hole" of "impossible density" (*Works on Paper* 118)—can be said to fulfill the aims of Zukofsky's criteria that poetry should "show . . . that order that of itself can speak to all men" (*P* 8) and should be "precise information on existence out of which it grows, and information of its own existence, that is, the movement (and tone) of words" (*P* 20). How, that is, can one reconcile the communicative and the musical in Zukofsky's later work? As in the works of Mallarmé, Stein, Stevens, and indeed, all overtly obscure poetries, the specter of solipsism reemerges with this question. I have argued that poems such as "I's (pronounced *eyes*)," through their emphasis on the interpersonal nature of knowledge, present a socially grounded epistemology far more nuanced than Zukofsky's blunt prose denials of skepticism. I now need to show how his later poetry, which at times seems to define new ranges of the unreadable, might be recuperated into a social ethic of reception—although perhaps never of *interpretation*—that transcends the solipsism of the hermetic. At the heart of such a recuperation will be Zukofsky's conception of poetry's music as an integral element of its informational, communicative import—a conception that in effect reimagines both the sort of knowledge that poetry can provide and the epistemological community that poetry creates and cements among its writers and readers.

Before approaching Zukofsky's distinction between solid and liquid language and his notion of musical form in poetry it is necessary to give some account of the modernist (specifically, Poundian) conceptions of music in poetry that inform those ideas. Much has been written about the importance of Impressionist and post-Impressionist painting as a model for modernist American poets.[3] Equally important, at least in the case of Pound, is the status of music as an art form that instigates various fruitful analogies with poetry. Pound's most straightforward statement of his conception of the interrelationship between music and poetry comes in the first part of the *ABC of Reading*. "The author's conviction on this day of New Year," Pound writes, "is that music begins to atrophy when it departs too far from the dance; that poetry begins to atrophy when it gets too far from music; but this must not be taken as implying that all good music is dance music or all poetry lyric" (14). Earlier, in the opening of the essay "Vers Libre and Arnold Dolmetsch" (1918), Pound wrote,

> Poetry is a composition of words set to music. Most other definitions of it are indefensible, or metaphysical. The proportion or quality of the music may, and does, vary; but poetry withers and "dries out" when it leaves music, or at least an imagined music, too far behind it. The horrors of modern "readings of poetry" are due to oratorical recitation. Poetry must be read *as music* and not as oratory. (*Literary Essays* 437, emphasis added)

There is a familiar story being told here. Poetry (and here, despite Pound's cautions in the first quote cited, there is no clear distinction between "poetry" and "lyric") was originally a branch of the musical arts; lyric developed and reached its highest perfection as the writing of texts to be sung or set to music. When the poem becomes a primarily spoken or silently read entity, it loses a certain vitality.

It is certainly no coincidence that in Canto LXXXI, a climax of the *Pisan Cantos*—itself an emotional watershed for Pound's entire epic sequence—Pound finds it to his compositional advantage to introduce one of his most striking lyrical moments under the rubric of "libretto":

> Yet
> Ere the season died a-cold
> Borne upon a zephyr's shoulder
> I rose through the aureate sky
>   *Lawes and Jenkyns guard thy rest*
>   *Dolmetsch ever be thy guest,*
> Has he tempered the viol's wood
> To enforce both the grave and the acute?
> Has he curved us the bowl of the lute?
>   *Lawes and Jenkyns guard thy rest*
>   *Dolmetsch ever be thy guest*
> [*The Cantos* 519–20]

The significance of this moment as an index of the Poundian aesthetic can scarcely be underestimated: in the midst of a vast collage-poem, which incorporates literally scores of different voices, registers, and modes of discourse, and at the point of the greatest emotional and ideological stress for that poem's Odysseus-narrator, calm and respite comes in the form of a utopian moment that visualizes the perfect reunification of music and lyric. Arnold Dolmetsch's instrument making becomes an emblem of the potential (re)marriage of song and setting (as his instruments themselves, precursors of the more recent interest in "authentic" early music, represent to Pound the Renaissance union of lyric and music).[4]

Pound himself locates the period English poetry becomes irrevocably separate from a musical score sometime in the Renaissance. Zukofsky's friend Basil Bunting, one of Pound's more thoughtful followers, argues that Edmund Spenser is the first English poet to try to generate a poetic music using the words themselves rather than an extraverbal musical accompaniment: "Sidney's slightly older contemporary, Spenser, invented a new thing which has given a complexion to English verse ever since. . . . Spenser made the words produce their own music, instead of depending on the musician to do it" (quoted in Terrell, "Basil

Bunting" 37).[5] Or as the critic John Hollander puts it, "since the fundamental separation between the lyric poem and the actual text for music early in the seventeenth century, the expressive rhythms of language have come to permit the lyric poem to sing its own song" ("Romantic Verse Form" 182).

But how precisely can we speak of poetry's music when the lyric is no longer necessarily complemented by an actual musical setting? How can there be music without notes? Hollander cogently argues that any identification of music and poetry (aside from verse explicitly written to be sung) in modern (post–ancient Greek) writing is necessarily metaphorical: "The perfect identification of music and poetry in antiquity that has always been prized by Neoclassicisms of various sorts has already, by the time of the writing of this passage [i.e., of the Pseudo-Longinus], been sundered. The bridge of an analogy has already been built" (*Vision and Resonance* 8). For Pound and those poets who follow him (Zukofsky included), this "analogical" or metaphorical identification of poetry and music takes two separate (although often confused) forms. On the one hand, there is the notion of the sound of words themselves forming a kind of music. This is what Bunting refers to in his remarks on Spenser and what Zukofsky means when he claims, "The music of verse carries an emotional quality; when the music slackens, emotion dissipates, and the poetry is poor" (*TP* 50). This "music," the actual tonal qualities of words, is Pound's "melopœia." But melopœia is not identical to what we commonly mean by "music"; while the Greek μέλοσ and μονσικὴ commonly refer to lyric poetry, which in Helladic and Hellenic Greece was clearly inseparable from music, the English words *melody* and *music* can apply to poetry only through analogy. While words have the same general mode of existence as musical notes—like a musical tone, a word is a sonic event occurring over time—words do not (at least in English) share music's qualities of pitch, timbre, and so on. More important, perhaps, the words of a poem follow one another one at a time; the harmonizing (or discord) of simultaneous tones, the basis of modern Western musical composition, is a technique not available to the composer who works with words.[6] English poets have traditionally considered vowel sounds more musical than consonants, as Hollander points out, but such a distinction is again fundamentally metaphorical, one that reflects nothing more than "English poetic language's mythology about itself" (*Vision and Resonance* 4).

Beyond Poundian melopœia, or the literal sounds of words interpreted as music, is the notion of music as a formal model for poetry. One can speak of a poem in terms that draw an analogy between its form and the form of a piece of music; conversely, one can compose a poem in a form that is reminiscent of a given musical form. Eliot's *Four Quartets* is the most widely known modernist example of a poem's form referring to a musical form, although Bunting's "sonatas" are surely more fully realized examples of the procedure. Pound refers to *The Cantos* on several occasions as being composed in a "fugal" form, and the model of the fugue, as we shall see, is crucial to Zukofsky's *"A"*. The formal analogy between music and poetry is, I would argue, every bit as central to Zukofsky's musical poetics as the melopœia he so often emphasizes.

Zukofsky is, I think, well aware of the analogical nature of any claims about the inherent "musicality" of poetic language. Yet his rhetoric, like Pound's, tends to stress the origins of poetry as a sung art and to claim that music-libretto relationship as an implied subtext to any discussion of a poem's music. In giving his comprehensive "scientific definition of poetry," Zukofsky quotes Dante:

> Matters worthy of the "highest common speech—all that flows from the head of illustrious poets down to their lips"—properly embrace the whole art of poetry which is "nothing else but the completed action of writing words to be set to music"—music being the one art that more than the others aims in its reach to speak to all men. Beside this definition of poetry, all other definitions of poetry would appear niggardly. (*P* 9)

(This entire passage seems a reworking of Pound's "Poetry is a composition of words set to music" statement, quoted above.) While Zukofsky's definition reaches beyond Dante, it includes the notion of "writing words to be set to music" as one of its integral elements. Like Pound, Zukofsky sees a process of atrophy and abstraction taking hold of English poetry once it becomes separate from literal music. In *A Test of Poetry*, he discusses poems written expressly to be sung:

> Simplicity of utterance and song go together. The fitting of words to musical composition seems to have reached its maximum development in English poetry as early as the 14th century. The complications of rhetorical ornament (similes, metaphors, conceits) in later times seem to have erected a printed (and worse, a *bookish*) poetry written to be read silently rather than to be spoken or sung. (*TP* 65)

Even when poetry is no longer written specifically for musical setting, an "implied musical accompaniment" lurks behind the arras (as it were) and gives it vitality. Such an implied music is at the root of Zukofsky's comparison of Browning's *Pippa Passes* and Swinburne's *Atalanta in Calydon:* "There is verse movement which directs matter and sense and implied musical accompaniment to a fitting end: A [Browning]. There is verse movement which rolls in one place so that sense, matter, etc. seem to have no beginning or end: B [Swinburne]. A is preferable to B" (*TP* 96). One notes how Zukofsky here rejects the traditionally asserted musicality of Swinburne's verse—musicality expressed in complex rhythms, abundant alliteration, and satisfying rhymes and off-rhymes—claiming instead that a true poetic music is necessarily directed less toward such local effects than toward a "fitting end," a formal "objectification."

In Zukofsky's "scientific definition of poetry," music is the "universal language," "an order that aims in its reach to speak to all men," and the goal of the poet's sincerity in composition is to achieve an objectification that is as universally comprehensible as music:

> With respect to such action [i.e., poetic composition] the specialized concern to the poet will be, first, its proper conduct—a concern to avoid clutter no matter how many details outside and in the head are ordered. This does not presume that the style will be the man, but rather that the order of his syllables will define his awareness of order. For his second and major aim is not to show himself but that order that of itself can speak to all men. (*P* 8)

The state of music, then, as a universally comprehensible form is the aim of the poet's composing.[7] Zukofsky figures this aim in his own poetics as a mathematical integral in which the upper and lower terms are limits that, while they may be asymptotically approached, can never be fully reached: "An integral / Lower limit speech / Upper limit music" ("A"-12, 138). In more "straightforward" prose, Zukofsky defines poetry as "an order of words that as movement and tone (rhythm and pitch) approaches in varying degrees the wordless art of music as a kind of mathematical limit" (*P* 19). "It is possible in imagination," he writes, "to divorce speech of all graphic elements, to let it become a movement of sounds. It is this musical horizon of poetry (which incidentally poems perhaps never reach) that permits anybody who does not know Greek to listen and get something out of the poetry of Homer" (*P* 20).

The influence of Walter Pater's famous remark in the seventh chapter of *The Renaissance* is unmistakable here. "All art," Pater writes, "constantly aspires to the condition of music" (106). Pater's claim occurs in the course of his discussion of *Anders-streben* (the striving of one art form to achieve the state of another):

> Thus, again, sculpture aspires out of the hard limitations of pure form towards colour, or its equivalent; poetry also, in many ways, finding guidance from the other arts, the analogy between a Greek tragedy and a work of Greek sculpture, between a sonnet and a relief, of French poetry generally with the art of engraving, being more than mere figures of speech; and all the arts in common aspiring towards the principle of music; music being the typical, or ideally consummate art, the object of the great *Anders-streben* of all art. (105–6)

Music is the "typical, or ideally consummate" art because music is purely formal; it makes no mimetic demands on the listener and appeals directly to the senses without the mediation of a palpable language, whether verbal or visual. Music, simply put, is the least representational of the arts, and therefore Pater identifies it as the one that appeals most directly to the receptive portion of the listener's soul, spirit, or mind. Whatever its conceptual difficulties, Pater's dictum regarding the "condition of music" is certainly crucial to Pound, who (mis)quotes it at least twice in his memorial volume for the French sculptor Henri Gaudier-Brzeska.

Zukofsky's claim is that the musical or aural aspect of poetry is as important to poetry's impact on a reader or listener as the literal meaning of the words: one with no previous knowledge of classical Greek can hear Homer and "get something out of" the verse. (Hugh MacDiarmid, in his "Gairmscoile" [poet's school], will similarly claim, "It's soon', no' sense, that faddoms the herts o' men" [*Selected Poetry* 21].) This is certainly a familiar claim, and one only need recall the emphasis on sound values of such a Romantic as Shelley (who would trace out the vowel sounds of a poem, then fill in the words around them) to see that Zukofsky only repeats widely held tenets about the role of sound in poetry. His and Celia Zukofsky's version of Catullus, which aims to "breathe the 'literal' meaning" (*CSP* 243) of the Latin by following its sounds as closely as possible, is one (perhaps extreme) outcome of these tenets.

At least as interesting is Zukofsky's notion of the "wordless art of music" as a "kind of mathematical limit" that poetry approaches. For Zukofsky, the condition of music, while it persists as an ideal toward which the poet should strive—a "horizon" "poems perhaps never reach"—remains a limit that the poem, as verbal artifact, can never achieve. The reasons for this are twofold. On the one hand is the very metaphorical nature of the association of words and music; although they are indeed both "sound forms in time,"[8] words (unless they are literally sung) are *not* musical events. More important, words, through their status as signifiers in a system of linguistic signs, have a referential function totally beyond that of even the most overtly programmatic music (which must itself often rely on the verbal support of titles and program notes to assert its referential function): while the poem is "a context associated with 'musical' shape," it is a music not of notes but of words inseparable from their "communicative reference" (*P* 16).

Zukofsky's poetry presents itself as music in three ways, all of which are implicit in Pound: (1) a literal melopœia, (2) a thematization of the poem as song, and (3) a reliance on musical compositions as formal models. The first way involves the actual melodious sound of the words as they are spoken, a music analogous to that which Pound praises in the verse of the troubadours, or the "music" that allows one to enjoy the *Iliad* with no knowledge of Greek. Such music is evident, for example, in Zukofsky's adaptation of Cavalcanti's canzone "Donna mi priegha," "A"-9:

> Virtue flames value, merriment love—any
> Compassed perfection a projection solely
> Power, the lowly do not tune the senses;
> More apt, more salutary body moves many
> Minds whose direction makes defection wholly
> Vague.
> ["A"-9, 109]

The effect of such foregrounding of the aural value of words, as Barry Ahearn notes of "A"-22 and -23 ("no matter how hard we try to stick to 'thinking' about these puzzling passages, the music eventually carries us away" [*Zukofsky's "A"* 180]), is initially to draw a reader's attention away from the words' communicative meanings and to force it to linger on their aural qualities. Such an emphasis reaches its highest pitch in Zukofsky's phonetic "translations" of foreign texts, among them his and Celia Zukofsky's *Catullus* and the opening of "A"-15, which is a transliteration of passages from *Job:*

> Wind: Yahweh at Iyyob
> Mien his roar 'Why yammer
> Measly make short hates oh
> By milling bleat doubt?
> Eye sore gnaw key heaver haul its core
> Weigh as I lug where hide any?'
> ["A"-15, 359]

This music is implicit to the order of the words of the poem as sounded and does not require commentary or direction to be made evident. Poetry's music, in this sense, is part of what Jakobson calls the "poetic function" of language, that which involves the foregrounding of the signifier itself (see Culler 55–74). One cannot help noting, as well, the extent to which Zukofsky's verbal "music" differs from the Romantic musicality of Shelley and Keats, or the later lushnesses of Tennyson or Swinburne. Zukofsky's music is less dependent on the lulling effects of open vowels and metrical cadences and more attuned to the contrasts and discords of clusters of consonants. In Zukofsky's music, Brahms gives way to Webern.

The second way that Zukofsky's poetry presents itself as music is through an almost omnipresent rhetoric of music and song, similar to that which W. R. Johnson finds in Horace. According to Johnson, Horace's response to the lack of actual music in the lyric is not the creation of a verbal music (at least in Pound's sense) but the creation of "an overwhelmingly persuasive illusion of music" through constant reference to music in "settings, themes, and images" and a delicate balance of "stillness" and "dynamism" that mimes the motion of music even though embodied in an essentially static verbal art (*Idea of Lyric* 126–29). Like Horace's, Zukofsky's poetry continually presents itself as song. Zukofsky's shorter poems, with greater frequency than the work of any other modern poet (except perhaps the Pound of *Lustra*), are explicitly referred to as "songs." A section of the *55 Poems* collection (1923–35) is designated "29 Songs" (*CSP* 40–65), and throughout the rest of the body of Zukofsky's shorter poetry are poems and sequences that bear "song" in their titles: "A Marriage Song for Florence and Henry" (*CSP* 93), "A Song for the Year's End" (*CSP* 111–14), "Songs of Degrees" (*CSP* 145–52), "Song Theme" (*CSP* 33). "A"-14 through "A"-24, each section of which begins with the word "an," are designated "songs" at their outset: "A"-14 advertises itself as *"First of / eleven songs / beginning An"* (*A* 315). "A"-9, based on Cavalcanti's song-form canzone, begins and ends with an explicit statement of musical intent: "An impulse to action *sings* of a semblance / Of things related as equated values" ("A"-9, 106, emphasis mine), and

> now
> Weep, love's heir, rhyme now how *song's* exaction
> Is your distraction—related is equated
> How else is love's distance approximated.
> ["A"-9, 111, emphasis mine]

"A"-11, formally based on another Cavalcanti work, the "Perch'io non spero," is an envoi by the poet to his work, another "song": "Song, my song, raise grief to music / Light as my loves' thought" (*A* 124).[9] And early in *"A"*, when the poet/speaker is still embroiled in the task of justifying his poetics to the skeptical "Kay," the overall method of the poem is revealed to be "One song / Of many voices" ("A"-5, 18). It seems almost pointless to multiply examples, although one could easily cite a number more; suffice it to say that Zukofsky's poetry, insofar as it projects a self-reflexive awareness of its own mode of existence, tends almost invariably to refer to itself not as poem but as musical text, promoting a rhetorical illusion of itself not as spoken or read text but as song.

This rhetoric of song is inextricably bound up with a third form of poetic "music," that in which music appears primarily as a formal model. As I have mentioned, Eliot's *Four Quartets* are perhaps the most famous twentieth-century instance of such a model. But Eliot's critical remarks linking the *Quartets* with such musical compositions as Bartók's or Beethoven's string quartets seem remarkably tentative, and in fact the formal movement of the *Quartets* bears only a tenuous connection to these works (the more relevant formal analogy clearly is to Eliot's own *Waste Land*). In contrast, Zukofsky labors hard to make explicit connections between his works and specific musical models. This is evident in a number of cases in the shorter poems: the "Song Theme" is *"To the last movement of Beethoven's Quartet in C Sharp Minor";* the "Imitation" is footnoted "Imitation: *Mus.* The repetition of a phrase or subject in another voice-part or in a different key" (*CSP* 50); an amusing pastiche of Marx is titled "Song—3/4 time (*pleasantly drunk*)" and is written in descending stanzas (like those of Williams's late work) of alternating three and four lines (*CSP* 58–61); poem 27 of *Anew* is "A madrigal for 3 voices" (*CSP* 92); "Spook's Sabbath, Five Bowings"'s five sections are each subtitled with the name of a particular violin bowing: *"spiccato," "martelé,"* and so forth (*CSP* 135–38). *"A"* as well contains sections explicitly modeled on musical forms: "A"-13 calls itself a partita, and the forms of its five sections are loosely based on the movements of the Baroque partita, a dance form;[10] "A"-20, a "Respond for P.Z.'s tone row / At twenty" ("A"-20, 435), alludes to twentieth-century twelve-tone composition, presenting the twelve titles of Paul Zukofsky's compositions in three varying orders.

More or less useful critical commentary has been written on the extent to which these "imitations" of musical form actually model the forms on which they are ostensibly based. Among the most provocative is Kenneth Cox's essay on "A"-19, which Cox argues can be seen as a composition for solo violin, in part revolving around the Paganini Prize for which the young Paul Zukofsky competed in Genoa and settling into "a chaconne, possibly the chaconne set for the competition and called in *Little* '*the* chaconne' " ("Zukofsky and Mallarmé" 3). Cox speculates that "under one of [the poem's] aspects," the poem's stanzaic form (each stanza consisting of thirteen lines; two words to the line, except for the final line, which has three), which seems almost reminiscent of compressed and "stretched" Spenserian stanzas, mimes the back-and-forth bowing of the violinist:

> the two words are produced by the down-stroke and the up-stroke of the bow, with an extra down-stroke at the end of each strophe. In a line which exceptionally is one word short it is therefore to be supposed that the bow is lifted for the duration of a rest, in a line which has its two words separated by a space there are two down-strokes, in a line which exceptionally has three words . . . there is a sinking, an extra down-stroke in mid-strophe, in
>
> *The wistaria 's*
> *blessing*
>
> a grace-note on down-bow. (1–2)

The bulk of Cox's essay, in which he discusses the allusions to Mallarmé in "A"-19, strikes me as highly intelligent and useful, but this particular passage seems to take a musical analogy altogether too literally. Zukofsky's grasp of the technicalities of music was shaky at best. In a 1931 letter to Pound, he explains that "as far as notes are concerned I can see or hear when they go up or down, & linger or proceed" (*P/Z* 111), and Celia Zukofsky recalls that "Paul would get furious when Louis would get mixed up thinking he was playing one thing when he was really playing something else" (Ahearn, "Two Conversations" 126). In other words, Zukofsky as poet is attracted not to the technical specificities of a given musical form or composition but to its potential as a productive analogy for his own verbal composing. To find the details of a violin bowing in the forms of his lines is to pursue his musical allegory far beyond its useful bounds.[11]

While Zukofsky never clarifies exactly what he intends by his remarks on "liquid" language, I associate that state of "the handling of words" with the first and third of these uses of music that I have just laid out: the melopœia of individual passage, and the musical structures used to determine the work's form. The second use, the rhetoric of music and song, is the conceptual framework that continually forces these more integral uses of the musical analogy before the reader's attention. Zukofsky's constant reminders of the role that music plays in his compositional methods continually foreground the musical aspects of his work, impressing that musicality on a readership that may or may not recognize his verbal structures as intentionally musical. What Zukofsky fundamentally means by "liquid" language is identical to what Pound means by melopœia—that is, the aspect of poetry that concerns the sounds of the words: "I'm talking about *sight*, and *sound*, and then the third word has always bothered me but I've ended up with *intellection*" (*P* 171). As detailed in this volume's first section, "Zukofsky and Skepticism," these three states represent for Zukofsky descending degrees of faithfulness to the trustworthy senses, like the "recurring interest of all of Shakespeare's works. . . . Ranging and circling abstractly from an ironic 'victory' of the *spirit* to the *audible* necessary confidence that runs on of 'music do I hear,' and last to what should be the certain good of staying *eyes*" (*B* 70–71, emphases mine). But while sight is the "purest organ of sense" (*B* 61), the mode of poetry—by its nature sound forms in time—can never be wholly visual. Zukofsky clearly believes that poetry's nature is an aural one and that while a poem's attention should be on the objects of direct visual perception rather than the objects of abstract ratiocination ("Shakespeare's *Works* say: seeing should be the object of speech [which in fabling time resolves into song], rather than that speech . . . should be the object of seeing" [*B* 88]), a certain degree of abstraction from the visual objects of sight is inescapable. As Zukofsky says, (playfully) glossing Stevens's "It Must Be Abstract," "yes, all words are abstract, post-*solids* or other *actual states*—things *after the* things, only relatively that one word is 'concrete,' another 'conceptual' " (*P* 35).

What distinguishes Zukofsky's Objectivist stance from that of the earlier Imagists (although such a distinction was not immediately apparent to the readers of *Poetry*'s " 'Objectivists' 1931" issue) is Zukofsky's realization that the imagistic epiphany contained in the poem must be subordinated to the poem's musical structuring: "Writing occurs which is the detail, not mirage, of seeing, of thinking with the things as they exist, and of directing them *along a line of melody*" (*P* 12, emphasis mine). It is this "line of melody" that constitutes the objectification of the poem, for the poem is a tangible object precisely through its musical form: "This rested totality may be called objectification—the apprehension satisfied completely as to the appearance of the art form as an object . . . writing (*audibility in two-dimensional print*) which is an object or affects the mind as such" (*P* 13, emphasis mine). While the Imagist poem may be thought of as a linguistic equivalent for a given vision or experience, the Objectivist poem (at least in Zukofsky's practice) is a set of imagistic perceptions resolved into an objectlike, musical structure. The decline of Imagism as a vital movement, and its metamorphosis into the diluted movement led by Amy Lowell that Pound dubbed "Amygism," could have been foreseen by an acute observer. The doctrines of Imagism, that is, lack two vital conceptions. On the one hand, the notion of the single arrested image makes no provision for motion, progression, or profluence in the poem: this particular shortcoming would lead Pound to the doctrines of Vorticism, a more dynamic and more ostentatiously technologized version of Imagism. On the other hand, the doctrine of *dos* and *don'ts* put forward by Pound fails to provide a formal principle or rationale for the Imagist poem. It is this latter need that Zukofsky's conception of formal objectification supplies.

The Imagist poem most often juxtaposes a concrete, visual image with an implied emotional or intellectual state: within the poem's context, the former image would suggest the latter state. Pound's dicta provide only this principle of juxtaposition and various protocols of compression. Without a notion of what might constitute a finished form for the poem, too often Imagism degenerates into the mere presentation of striking and suggestive pictures. Zukofsky's Objectivist manifestos, in contrast, specify a shape, a structure into which moments of perception are formed. This "objective" structure is independent of the degree of concreteness of the poem's contents: although Zukofsky firmly believes that poetry should hew as closely as possible to direct visual experience, objectification can be achieved even with the most abstract, gaseous subject: "Dante's *Paradiso* is a great intellect at work, not only an intelligence which is more involved with the senses, but it's when the senses vaporize and, the head floats, but sometimes it floats beautifully. All these gases are very nice if you know what you're talking about" (*P* 171). The tangibility or objectification of the artwork is for Zukofsky a universal aesthetic principle: "That is the interest of the arts—and even the convolvuli of mathematics (and why may they not be called so) partake of it—the feeling that even the most intellective of them are *tangible*" (*B* 423). For Zukofsky, it is poetry's particular telos to achieve its tangibility through a musical, or musiclike, objectification.

Cox, in a keenly critical discussion of the "musicality" of Zukofsky's poetry, draws a careful distinction between Zukofsky as "librettist" and as "composer." Zukofsky's poetry, according to him,

> does not depend on mellifluous sequences of sound, exhilarating rhythms or the *innumerable bees* effect. It is concerned for the pitch of vowel and duration of syllable which fit verse to be sung and it distinguishes song from declamation and declamation from recitative. . . . He seeks not so much expressive word or rhythm as what he calls "melody," phrasing, such shaping of syllables as carries conviction without fuss and such changes of tone and pace as, with repetition and crossing of themes, augmentation, imitation, and all the other devices of musicians, construct a composition of English words. Zukofsky may be said to have the intellect of a composer and the ear of a librettist. ("Poetry of Louis Zukofsky" 82–83)

The poet's "ear of a librettist" is what enables him to work with the melopœia of individual words and phrases, though this melopœia does not result in Tennysonian "mellifluous sequences of sound" but in phrases "fit . . . to be sung," as are the phrases of Wyatt or Dante (for whom, one is reminded, poetry is "words to be set to music"). Zukofsky's "intellect of a composer" allows him to use "repetition and crossing of themes, augmentation, imitation and all the other devices of musicians" to combine these single particles of melody into a "composition of English words" that approaches the tangible objecthood of a musical composition.

While the aim of writing poetry as if it were to be set to music constitutes a direct (if perhaps tenuous) connection between Zukofsky's poetic praxis and the parallel realm of musical composition, the relationship between his musiclike structuring of poetry and the actual structure of the music he proposes as model remains a relationship easily grasped but purely analogical. Musical structure is one of the necessary fictions of Zukofsky's poetics, and while approaching *"A"* with Zukofsky's claims in mind can yield valuable insight into the work's complex makeup, one must continually remind oneself of the instrumentality of Zukofsky's characterizations of his own art, and one must continually question the presuppositions on the poet's part that make him present his musical analogies as self-evident or natural. Musical form, in Bob Perelman's words, is for Zukofsky only "an extended metaphor, that is, an allegory" (*Trouble With Genius* 186), but that allegory is the most powerful and compelling of the formal frames within which his work is constituted.

8

Zukofsky as Formalist

Fugue and Form in *"A"*

> The order of all poetry is to approach a state of music wherein the ideas present themselves sensuously and intelligently and are of no predatory intention. A hard job, as poets have found reconciling contrasting principles of facts. In poetry the poet is continually encountering the facts which in the making seem to want to disturb the music and yet the movement cannot exist without the facts, without its facts.
> —Louis Zukofsky, "An Objective" (*P* 18)

Music is most important to Zukofsky insofar as it provides a formal model for his poetry, though it is important to stress that such modeling is primarily metaphorical—wishful thinking, if you will, rather than direct imitation. On a more fundamental level, however, it is difficult to overestimate the importance of the notion of form itself to Zukofsky's poetics. As he explains in *A Test of Poetry*, "Poetry convinces not by argument but by the *form* it creates to carry its content" (*TP* 52). For Zukofsky, poetic form is always associated with music. "A poem," he writes, is "a context associated with 'musical' shape, musical with quotation marks since it is not of notes as music, but of words more variable than variables, and used outside as well as within the context with communicative reference" (*P* 16). The tension Zukofsky defines in the passage from "An Objective" quoted as epigraph to this chapter (and one ought not overlook the Paterian echo in "a state of music") is between the formal and the communicative aspects of poetry. As this passage assumes, poetry is essentially informative: "Good poetry is the barest—most essentially complete—form of presenting a subject" (*TP* 89). "A"-12 puts it succinctly: "A poetics is informed and informs— / Just *informs* maybe—the rest a risk" ("A"-12, 168). But part of what it in*forms* one of is its own *form:* "Good poetry is definite information on the subject dealt with, on the movement of the lines of verse, and on the emotion of verbal construction." While the formal objectification of a well-constructed poem ought to be immediately evident to a competent reader, the poet must always take care that the poem's musical form does not obscure the "precise information on existence" that the poem exists to embody and transmit. At the same time, and perhaps more important for Zukofsky, the poet must learn to work with "the facts which in the making seem to want to disturb the music." Neither form nor content, in short, can exist independently in the poem: "the movement cannot exist without the facts" (*P* 18).

This interdependence of "music" and "information" might strike one as a somewhat banal insight, but only, I must emphasize, if it is confused with the old bugbear of "form and content." The poem's music and the information it conveys are two inextricably entwined moments of the poetic process for Zukofsky: the former exists to serve the latter, but the latter would have no existence at all without the former. Two short poems that explicitly thematize this interdependence can serve as an introduction to my larger discussion of musical form in *"A"*. The first, "It's a gay li - ife," invokes once again the image of the horse, which throughout Zukofsky's work, and especially in *"A"*, stands for the poet:

It's a gay li - ife

There's naw—thing
  lak po—ee try
it's a delicacy
  for   a horse:

Dere's na—thing
  lak pea-   nut-brittle
it's a delicacy
  for   the molars.
[*CSP* 43]

This is Zukofsky at his most playful, celebrating with rare élan both the pleasures of the senses (the sensation of peanut brittle between the molars) and the occasional pleasures of the poetic craft. The poem, while it does not conform to any traditional formal model, is rigidly formal in an immediately recognizable way: the two stanzas are metrically identical in their first and third lines (indeed, they share a common third line) and syntactically parallel in their second and fourth; the pattern of continuity and discontinuity in those latter lines is emphasized by the near-rhymes of "po—ee" / "pea-" and "horse" / "molars." Thematically, the poem stresses the objectification of its own form as it draws a parallel between the experience of "po—ee try" and "pea-   nut-brittle." The candy, as sticky, crunchy, and ultimately material an object as one could ask for, is compared to the objectification of the poem, which must similarly be experienced as a freestanding, sensual object (perhaps a crisp apple for the "horse"). While the poem may also be read as a satire of poetic pretension, in which poetry, for a latter-day Bentham, is "as good as peanut brittle," it also argues for and stands as an exemplar of a conception of poetry in which the poem takes its place as another object in a world of objects, among which are horses, the reader's molars, and peanut brittle. The typographical distension of the spaces between syllables and the phonetic Brooklynese spellings both mime the experience of eating the simultaneously crunchy and sticky peanut brittle and, by a species of unsubtle defamiliarization, force a reader to sound the words of the poem slowly and carefully. Peanut brittle is a candy that asks to be eaten with deliberation, crisply breaking between the incisors and tenaciously adhering to the molars. Poetry, similarly, demands to be read in a careful and systematic manner, yielding a range of intellectual and sensual pleasures that parallels the juxtaposition of tastes and textures that the candy presents.

Number 20 of *Anew* takes a perhaps more sober approach to the question of poetic form:

> The lines of this new song are nothing
> But a tune making the nothing full
> Stonelike become more hard than silent
> The tune's image holding in the line.
> [*CSP* 88]

In this poem, as he remarks in an earlier lyric, Zukofsky has "emptied the meaning / Leaving the song" (*CSP* 81). "The lines of this new song" is perhaps as close as one can get to a purely self-reflexive poem, a poem about nothing but its own "tune" or form.[1] Like "It's a gay li - ife," the poem is rigidly formal: its four lines recall the traditional ballad quatrain, and while there is no metrical continuity between lines, each line has exactly nine syllables.[2] The lines are "nothing"—that is, they convey no positivistic information about the world outside the poem—but at the same time they constitute a "tune" that "mak[es] the nothing full." Together they form an object, "stonelike," that occupies a space where before there was emptiness. As they are laid down in their four parallel lines, like rows of stones one upon another in a wall, they become palpable, "more hard than silent"—as objective as a stone wall, but by no means as mute: the poem, even as it stands as an object, is "audibility in two-dimensional print" (*P* 13).[3]

These two short poems emphasize the extent to which the poetic, for Zukofsky, is identified with the formal, while the fact that the second of them refers to itself as a "new song" implies that the formal is implicated with the musical. The questions raised by the poet embarking on a work of the scale of *"A"* should be evident: How should such a poem be formally organized? In what way should that form relate to music? The formal problem of the long poem, of course, is central to American modernist poetic thought. Whether or not he is a direct influence, many American modernist poets seem to take to heart some version of Poe's dictum that "a long poem does not exist" (*Essays and Reviews* 71). To judge by the number of long modernist poems written, however, it would seem that Pound, Williams, and others accept as impossible not a "poem of some length," per se, but a long *narrative poem.* Poe's own attack on the long poem centers on *Paradise Lost,* the canonical English poem most closely modeled on the classical narrative epic. (Interestingly enough, Poe describes his own long prose work *Eureka* as a "poem.") Perhaps the most striking formal development of modernist and postmodernist poetry in the United States has been the reconception of the "epic" poem ("epic" in length, breadth, and historical resonance) as a nonnarrative form.[4] Whether in "open-ended" or "closed" form, "series" or "sequence," such poems as *The Cantos, Paterson,*

Melvin Tolson's *Harlem Gallery*, Charles Olson's *Maximus*, Robert Duncan's *Passages*, and Ronald Johnson's *ARK* all seek to recover the possibility of an epic-length poem within a nonnarrative, modernist idiom.[5]

All of these poems (except, to some degree, Tolson's) take as their basic formal method some version of Pound's "ideogrammic method," the juxtaposition of particular linguistic units (images, concepts, quotations) without direct connectives. The classic example of this method in its simplest form is Pound's "In a Station of the Metro," in which the "faces in the crowd" are juxtaposed with the image of the petals on the bough. When Pound embarks on the larger project of *The Cantos*, however, he feels a need to supplement the ideogrammic method with other structuring devices. As broadly useful as he finds the method, he seems unwilling to trust it as the ultimate structural principle of his magnum opus, a long poem that seeks to rival the scale of Dante's *Divine Comedy*. Among the various large-scale structural models he proposes for his emerging work is a specifically musical one, that of the fugue. In a 1927 letter to his father, he seeks to clear up some of the structural "obscurity" of the Cantos he has published up to that point:

> Dear Dad:-/-/ Afraid the whole damn poem is rather obscure, especially in fragments. Have I given you outline of main scheme : : : or whatever it is?
>
> I. Rather like, or unlike subject and response and counter subject in fugue.
> A. A. Live man goes down into world of Dead
> C. B. The "repeat in history"
> B. C. The "magic moment" or moment of metamorphosis, bust thru from quotidien into "divine or permanent world." Gods, etc. (*Selected Letters* 210)

While Pound felt that Yeats's 1929 characterization of *The Cantos* as fugal in *A Packet for Ezra Pound* proved more obfuscatory than useful for his readers,[6] Pound repeats the fugal analogy in a 1939 letter, invoking Zukofsky's *"A"* (under way since at least 1928) as well: "Take a fugue: theme, response, contrasujet. *Not* that I mean to make an exact analogy of structure. Vide, incidentally, Zukofsky's experiment, possibly suggested by my having stated the Cantos are in a way fugal" (*Selected Letters* 294). One should not overestimate the usefulness of the analogy of the fugue in describing or explaining the structure of *The Cantos*. Peter Makin, discussing the fugue in Pound, dismisses the notion of an overall form for *The Cantos*, fugal or otherwise, and instead finds "a bundle of principles of organization; of local ordering of the relations of elements with one another" (*Pound's Cantos* 65). Philip Kuberski goes a bit further, describing the fugal model as a compensatory device on Pound's part, an attempt to avoid the implications of his own evolvingly transgeneric work: "Such severe and alien models as the fugue . . . reveal Pound's need for a recognized esthetic organization—however distant from poetry—to govern and metaphorize his own form 'of no known category' " (*Calculus* 108).

While these strictures are just, it remains indisputable that Pound and Zukofsky view the fugue as the crowning achievement of Baroque musical composition and come to it as a formal analogy for their poetry in large part because of their long-standing and often repeated admiration for the music of the eighteenth century.[7] A consistent theme of the music reviews Pound wrote while he was in London from 1917 to 1921 (published in the *New Age* under the pseudonym "William Atheling") is his rejection of contemporary "impressionist" or "emotional" music, such as the chromatic music of Wagner or Debussy, in favor of "pattern music," which Pound sees best exemplified in the early music popularized and performed by Arnold Dolmetsch and his family on their replicas of seventeenth- and eighteenth-century instruments (*Pound and Music* 38). This is not solely a matter of personal preference, or of Pound's invariably iconoclastic public tastes, which tend always to promote the overlooked at the expense of the conventionally accepted. As one music critic points out, Pound's rejection of musical Romanticism is clearly in tune with a broader intellectual trend among the avant-garde of his day:

> At the time Pound began to write about music there was a widespread feeling among the musical avant-garde and their support-

> ers, in tune with wider intellectual trends, that it was time to liquidate the massive and suffocating presence of the nineteenth century. . . . The key to destroying its hegemony was to attack in the name both of the old and the new, of the music before Beethoven and after Wagner and his followers. Among composers no better example of this phenomenon can be found than Stravinsky, with his barbaric and shocking *Rite of Spring* (1911–13) and his shift several years later to neoclassicism. (Lipman 202–3)

But apart from the "intellectual trends" in which he participated, Pound's enthusiasm for the highly formalized music of the eighteenth century and before is fundamentally related to his conception of art—whether musical, verbal, or plastic—as above all *structure*. His clearest statement of this credo is in his memoir of Gaudier-Brzeska:

> The pine-tree in mist upon the far hill looks like a fragment of Japanese armour.
>
> The beauty of this pine-tree in the mist is not caused by its resemblance to the plates of the armour.
>
> The armour, if it be beautiful at all, is not beautiful *because* of its resemblance to the pine in the mist.
>
> In either case the beauty, in so far as it is beauty of form, is the result of "planes in relation" . . .
>
> This is the common ground of the arts, this combat of arrangement or "harmony." The musician, the writer, the sculptor, the higher mathematician have here their common sanctuary. (*Gaudier-Brzeska* 120–21)

The music of the Romantic period is for Pound "romance and sentiment and description" (*Gaudier-Brzeska* 93). Its impressionism, emotivism, and above all, its malleable tempos (particularly at the hands of its more "sensitive" interpreters) seem to him directly analogous to the rhetoricity and vagueness of the Romantic and post-Romantic poetry against which he is revolting. In contrast to this rhetoricity he proposes the clear-cut structural relationships of medieval and Provençal troubadour poetry, whose complex formal patterns evoke for him a historically past *clari-*

tas, what he describes in "Cavalcanti" as a "radiant world where one thought cuts through another with clean edge, a world of moving energies *'mezzo oscuro rade'* " (*Literary Essays* 154).

Pound is then inevitably attracted to the notion of music "as a structure" (*Pound and Music* 187)—a structure one is more likely to find, for instance, in Mozart's operas than in Wagner's: "one can sit through these Mozart, or musically formed, operas time after time, whereas in a dramatically formed opera, as in the Wagnerian, which has an emotional rather than musical structure, the effect of the piece diminishes the more often one hears it" (*Pound and Music* 65). Pattern music, according to Pound, is infinitely superior to chromatic music, since it is a full realization of music's essence as formally patterned sound rather than a mere approximation of an emotional impression:

> I do not mean that Bach is not emotional, but the early music starts with the mystery of pattern; if you like, with the vortex of pattern; with something which is, first of all, music, and which is capable of being, after that, many things. What I call emotional, or impressionistic music, starts with being emotion or impression and then becomes only approximately music. It is, that is to say, something in the terms of something else. (*Pound and Music* 38)

(While Pound will return repeatedly to Pater's "condition of music" dictum, here he shows his deep suspicion of the *Anders-streben* that Pater describes in the "School of Giorgione" chapter of *The Renaissance*, the striving of one art form literally to *be* another.) What Pound finds attractive in pattern music, insofar as it can be related to the composition of poetry, is the fact that it is music whose primary attribute is a clear and defined structure; such music suggests analogies to the writing of poetry, in which (for a formalist) the patterning or structuring of words is the main concern. Pound makes such an analogy clear in his review of a concert of Moroccan music:

> In especial one notes the "extraordinary" length of the rhythm pattern units, comparable to the mediæval rhyme-scheme of Provençal canzos, where, for example, one finds a rhyme pattern which begins its six-ply repeat after the seventeenth different ter-

> minal sound. In this Arabian music, as in the Provençal metrical scheme, the effect of the subtler repetitions only becomes apparent in the third or fourth strophe, and then culminates in the fifth or sixth, as a sort of horizontal instead of perpendicular chord. One might call it a "sort of" counterpoint; if one can conceive a counterpoint which plays not against a sound newly struck, but against the residuum and residua of sound which hangs in the auditory memory. (*Pound and Music* 224)

The notion of "counterpoint" that Pound outlines here, a counterpoint that works horizontally between repeated rhyme words rather than vertically, as between two lines of music played simultaneously, is an important element in understanding how Zukofsky makes use of fugal form in *"A"*. But we are already deep in allegory: in strict musical terminology, a "horizontal" counterpoint is sheer nonsense.

That Zukofsky thought of the formal structure of *"A"* as in some manner fugal, and that he came to this conception before encountering Yeats's essay on *The Cantos*, is evident from his correspondence with Pound.[8] Pound's first reaction, on receiving "A"-1 through "A"-7 in 1930, is to identify them as somehow fugal and to note their formal resemblance to his own published *Cantos:* "recd. one development or fugue or fuagal etc. produced by Ludwig von Zuk und Sohn, on not always digested meat of his forebears" (*P/Z* 75). But Zukofsky is quick to deny the charge of having imperfectly repeated Pound's own work. "You remember," he writes Pound, "that I had read *Cantos* 4, 5 and 6 as separate poems, or poems dealing with the histories of several periods." In "late 1927 or early 1928," when Zukofsky started *"A"*, he "still had no inkling of the main intention of *The Cantos*. . . . I had started <without knowing it,> something in 1928 which you had started in 1908 (?)—the dangers of being young and too poor to get hold of the books that matter" (*P/Z* 79). In a 1931 letter that discusses *"A"* at length, Zukofsky makes clear that he has regarded his poem as fugal for some time and that while his work and *The Cantos* share a similar technique, *"A"* is more clearly fugal than Pound's poem (while *The Cantos* are perhaps more "cinematic" than *"A"*):

> The difference between Cantos & "A" aside from diction <& quality of line> in the matter of musical approximation—The difference between polyphony (many voices of angels, if you will permit it) and one human voice thematically split in two—but so far the fugal principle is more obvious in the last [i.e., "A"]. We both partake of the cinematic principle, you to a greater & more progressive degree, tho' it wd. be pretty hard to distinguish in either case where montage leaves off & narration begins & vice versa. (*P/Z* 112)

It needs to be shown, however, exactly on what basis *"A"*, even as it develops and furthers the methods of Pound's early *Cantos*, can be called "fugal": what, that is, is the basis of the analogy Zukofsky draws between musical fugues and his own poem?

At the outset, one cannot emphasize too strongly that the fugal form of *"A"*—whatever it might be—is not an aural structure or sound patterning. It is a "counterpointing" of linguistic, thematic, and conceptual units rather than a counterpointing of particular sounds or rhymes. As Zukofsky explains in a 1935 letter to Lorine Niedecker, understanding *"A"*'s musical structure "must involve its reader's learning to interpret juxtaposed concepts and statements as music" (Ahearn, *Zukofsky's "A"* 75). To discern in *"A"* a form analogous to that of the fugue, then, the reader must perform the crucial work of analogizing, of discerning a music in the juxtaposition of statements and verbal constructions.

Alerted by Zukofsky's own announced machinery of fuguelike poetic form, his readers in the academy have found fugal patterns most easily traced in the very early movements of *"A"*, especially "A"-1.[9] The *Harvard Dictionary of Music* defines the basic elements of fugal composition:

> [The fugue] is based on a short melody, called *subject* or *theme*, which is stated at the beginning of the fugue by one voice alone, being taken up ("imitated") by the other voices. . . . In each voice the space between one statement and the next is filled in by a freely invented counterpoint, which, however, is usually unified by the use of recurrent motifs. These motifs are derived either from the subject itself, or, more usually, from its continuation, which forms the counterpoint to the first imitation (second statement) of the subject, near the beginning of the fugue. Frequently, but not al-

> ways, this continuation takes on a rather definite form. . . . In such cases it is called *countersubject* and reappears throughout the fugue in a manner similar to the main subject. . . . A section of the fugue that does not include a statement of the subject is called an *episode*. (Apel 335)[10]

"A"-1, commentators have been anxious to show, is written with these elements in mind, although the musical fugue provides at best only a loose analogy for Zukofsky's verbal construction. As in the "Sirens" episode of *Ulysses*—a chapter Joyce claimed was written on the model of a *fuga per canonem*—here "the relationship of music and writing can be most fruitfully regarded not as an airtight analogy but as a kind of experimental premise" (Lawrence 91). It is not a constraining set of rules but a suggestive allegory.

"A"-1 begins with the "subject" or "theme" of Bach's *St. Matthew Passion*, as presented in a 1928 Carnegie Hall performance at which it appears Zukofsky himself was present:

> A
> Round of fiddles playing Bach.
> *Come, ye daughters, share my anguish—*
> Bare arms, black dresses
> *See Him! Whom?*
> Bediamond the passion of our Lord,
> *See Him! How?*
> His legs blue, tendons bleeding,
> *O Lamb of God most holy!*
> Black full dress of the audience.
> Dead century, where are your motley
> Country people in Leipzig,
> Easter,
> Matronly flounces, starched, heaving,
> Cheeks of the patrons of Leipzig—
> "Going to Church? Where's the baby?"
> "Ah, there's the Kapellmeister
> in a terrible hurry—
> Johann Sebastian, twenty-two
> children!"

The Passion According to Matthew,
Composed seventeen twenty-nine,
Rendered at Carnegie Hall,
Nineteen twenty-eight
Thursday evening, the fifth of April.
The autos parked, honking.
["A"-1, 1]

The italicized phrases are of course from the *Passion*'s libretto, in particular the majestic opening chorus. The "Bare arms" and "Black full dress of the audience" signal that this is twentieth-century America—more specifically, that it is the 5 April 1928 performance, since the conductor, Ossip Gabrilowitsch, "had requested plain black dress and a silent reception of the masterpiece" (according to the *New York Times*' April 6 review of the concert). Such somber garments are in sharp contrast to those of the *Passion*'s first auditors in 1729: "motley / Country people" in definite motion ("Matronly flounces, starched, heaving"), whose interest in the Kapellmeister Bach's twenty-two children presents a refreshingly earthy contrast to the funereal seriousness expected of the New York concertgoer. If we take the *St. Matthew Passion* as the "subject" of "A"-1, its first statement is in the form of its 1928 performance, black audience dress and all. That subject is immediately "imitated," or restated in a different "voice," when the poem invokes the 1729 Leipzig premiere of the work. The two performances of the composition, as Zukofsky has juxtaposed them, both "rhyme" with one another and display telling contrasts.

The "subject" of the *St. Matthew Passion* is repeated throughout "A"-1 in the form of direct reference to the two performances and their social contexts, or quotation of the work's libretto. On pages 2 and 3 we are given the immediate aftermath of the 1928 concert, Zukofsky himself hearing about him "the voices of those who had been at the concert, / Feet stopping everywhere in the streets" ("A"-1, 2–3). Their chatter is predictably inane: "Poor Thomas Hardy he had to go so soon" (Hardy was eighty-seven when he died in January 1928); "Lovely soprano" ("A"-1, 3). And punctuating the poet's late-night writing vigil, as he sits and tries to record the feelings the performance has given rise to, are the words of the *Passion:*

Cold stone above Thy head.
Weary, broken bodies.
Sleeping: their eyes were full of sleep.
["A"-1, 4]

Interspersed with the theme of the *St. Matthew Passion* and entangled with one another, are two countersubjects. On the one hand is the economic struggle that dominates and colors even the pre-Depression society in which the poet/narrator finds himself, a struggle embodied first in the "tramp" he confronts as he leaves the concert hall—"Greasy, solicitous . . . / Hips looking out of ripped trousers" ("A"-1, 2)—and later, more globally, in the struggles of labor and management that dominate the news:

And on one side near an elevated,
Lamenting,
Foreheads wrinkled with injunctions:
"The Pennsylvania miners are again on the lockout,
We must send relief to the wives and children—
What's your next editorial about, Carat,
We need propaganda, the thing's
becoming a mass movement."
["A"-1, 3][11]

In sharp contrast to this is another countersubject, the poet/narrator's own struggle to arrive at an aesthetic that can encompass both the sublimity of Bach's music, "Desire longing for perfection" ("A"-1, 2), and the brutal realities of the class struggle. How to write all this, how to bring it into the poem as music, is the dilemma that confronts the poet. Even as he contemplates the organic perfection of the music, he must also acknowledge the society that denies that perfection, both by its economic inequities and its debasement of poetry itself:

Patrons of poetry, business devotees of arts and letters,
Cornerstones of waste paper,—

"Such lyric weather"—
Chirping quatrain on quatrain;
And the sonneteers—when I consider
again and over again—
["A"-1, 3]

While the poet seeks to achieve the atemporal beauty of music ("liveforever"), he is repeatedly brought back to an awareness of harsh immediacy and privation:[12]

The next day the reverses
As if the music were only a taunt:
As if it had not kept, flower-cell, liveforever,
before the eyes, perfecting.
—I thought that was finished:
Existence not even subsistence,
Worm eating the bark of the street tree,
Smoke sooting skyscraper chimneys,
That which looked for substitutes, tired,
Ready to give up the ghost in a cellar—
Remembering love in a taxi:
A country of state roads and automobiles,
But great numbers idle, shiftless, disguised on streets—
The excuse of the experts
'Production exceeds demand so we curtail employment';
And the Wobblies hollering reply,
Yeh, but why don't you give us more than a meal
to increase the consumption!
["A"-1, 4–5]

"A"-1 as a whole is brought to a close by a doubled statement of one of the countersubjects (the business executive's memories of his "management techniques" and a brief urban vignette) and a restatement of the subject, here in the form of a quotation from the *Passion:*

"We ran 'em in chain gangs, down in the Argentine,
Executive 's not the word, use *engineer,*
Single handed, ran 'em like soldiers,
Seventy-four yesterday, and could run 'em today,

Been fishin' all Easter
Nothin' like nature for hell-fire!"

Dogs cuddling to lamp-posts,
Maybe broken forged iron,
"Ye lightnings, ye thunders
In clouds are ye vanished?

Open, O fierce flaming pit!"
["A"-1, 5][13]

Perhaps the most significant difference between the fugue in music and in poetry is that in a musical fugue more than one voice can sound simultaneously, while in a poem only one voice can be heard at once (see Davis 72). Simply put, music is a polyphonic form, while a poem is inherently monophonic.[14] Zukofsky is well aware of this: in "A"-8 he writes, "Voice a voice blown: print / Must not overlap, but the notes of the voices would" ("A"-8, 52–53). In a Bach fugue, for instance, the countersubject is sounded at the same time as the first imitation (i.e., the repetition of the subject in a different voice). It is an effect impossible to duplicate in words. Zukofsky responds to this lack of fit between his formal model and his medium in two ways. First, he takes the obvious course of sounding his themes in sequence rather than (as he obviously cannot) simultaneously: his evocation of the 1729 *Passion* follows that of the 1928 *Passion* and is followed in turn by his portrait of the poet as an aesthetically indecisive young man. More subtly, he is able to a certain degree linguistically to superimpose his thematic units. The "Bare arms, black dresses" of his opening description of the *Passion*, for instance, must belong to a 1928 New York performance, in contrast to the "Matronly flounces" of the 1729 Leipzig premiere, though the "round of fiddles playing Bach" could belong to either era. "The blood's tide like the music. / A round of fiddles playing / Without effort" ("A"-1, 4) describes both the musical performance and the mind of the poet on which it has made its impact. And the "executive/engineer"'s "Been fishin' all Easter / Nothin' like nature for hell-fire!" brings together in a single statement both the holiday celebrated by the *Passion*, the language of the religious libretto, and the unthinking rapacity of the economic order.

The first six movements of *"A"* form something of an overture to the work as a whole, a finding out and testing of "what will suffice," what aesthetics and poetics will serve in writing an epic-length poem in twentieth-century America. The struggle between a "desire longing for perfection"—a utopian-aesthetic longing—and the political and economic realities of contemporary life remains at the fore and is played out in the debate on poetics with "Kay" in "A"-2 and "A"-5. Also at issue is the problem of influence and origins, particularly acute for the son of Russian-Jewish immigrants aspiring to write a modernist poetry whose primary exemplars, Pound and Eliot, are vociferous advocates of a cultural hegemony in which Jewish influences play no part. Like Stevens's Canon Aspirin, however, whose choice is "not a choice / Between, but of," Zukofsky's poetics opts to include all of its surroundings rather than exclude anything as nonpoetic or inherently inappropriate. Even "Kay," the vociferous advocate of a pure poetry, "Clear music" ("A"-2, 6), has his say and takes his place in the poem: "The song—omits? / No, includes Kay, Anybody" ("A"-6, 23).

Like "A"-1, the first five movements are all fugally structured, although not until "A"-6 is the fugue explicitly mentioned. "A"-6, while it includes many of the themes and characters that have entered the first five movements, seems to be structured more on geographical and historical than musical principles. The poem invokes Lenin, Bach, Beethoven, Whittaker Chambers's dead brother Ricky, and the sententious economic and literary criticisms of Henry Ford; it moves from the New York docks, to Riverside Drive, to the Midwest, and even to Reno, Nevada, and San Francisco before returning

> Three thousand miles over rails,
> To adequate distribution of "Camels";
> New York—Staten Island—
> ["A"-6, 35–36]

Almost as an afterthought, after "Connie's Hot Chocolates" have reminded him of Bach's Kaffee Cantata ("A"-6, 37), Zukofsky reinvokes the *Passion* ("Schweigt still—plaudert nicht" ["A"-6, 38]) and closes the movement with a clear statement of intent:

Forgetting
I said:
Can
The design
Of the fugue
Be transferred
To poetry? . . .

With all this material
To what distinction—
["A"-6, 38]

The analogy between poetic composition and fugal composition, at least at the early stages of *"A"*, is a crucial element of the poet's struggle toward a sufficient aesthetic—"Desire longing for perfection" (*A* 2)—as Zukofsky's contributor's note for the " 'Objectivists' 1931" issue of *Poetry* clearly indicates:

> His poem *"A"*—in process—includes two themes: I—desire for the potentially perfect finding its direction inextricably the direction of historic and contemporary particulars; and II—approximate attainment of this perfection in the feeling of the contrapuntal design of the [fugue] transferred to poetry; both themes related to the text of Bach's *St. Matthew Passion.* ("Contributors' Notes")

(In this crucial passage, "design of the fugue" is incorrectly printed as "design of the figure," a mistranscription perfectly understandable to anyone who has encountered Zukofsky's crabbed handwriting. I will say more about this textual moment shortly.) The fugue, then, as a formal design, to some degree works to satisfy the desire for the poetically perfect that the speaker of "A"-1 expresses. While the poet takes account of the political imperative that he finds placed on him—"historic and contemporary particulars"—these demands find a fundamentally formal resolution, rather than a polemical or argumentative one. As I argued in Chapter 6, it is a complicated question of how and to what degree Zukofsky's early work is truly political, or in what way it might be committed to the same Marxist cause Zukofsky the man espouses. Zukofsky's aesthetic formalism, however, leaves little opportunity for the writing of poems as overtly and polemically political as those of Kenneth Fearing or Edwin Rolfe.

Just as he avoids a doctrinaire stance that would elevate politics over aesthetics, Zukofsky chooses the analogy of fugal composition not for its constraint but for its freedom. Rather than a set *form*, the fugue is a formal *process:* "The fugue a music heap, / only by the name's grace music" ("A"-6, 22). As Taggart elaborates, "fugue is not a form . . . [but] a process of continual expansion or growth, the many from the one, based on the principle of imitation" (*Songs of Degrees* 193). Unlike such closed poetic forms as the sonnet or the canzone, "fugal structure . . . is endless, that is, new material can always be brought in to complement and carry further the interplay of subject, response, and countersubject" (Géfin 55). *Grove's Dictionary of Music* strongly suggests that the very term "*a* fugue" is misguided: "we should rather speak of a composition as being written 'in fugue,' just as we speak of a poem as being written in hexameters" (513). F. Murray Schafer's remarks on the fugue in the context of *The Cantos* are also relevant:

> Strictly speaking, the fugue is not a form at all, but rather a procedure. Unlike the sonata, where the length and shape of the exposition determines the development and recapitulation sections, the fugue regenerates itself constantly from its own motivic material, according to the invention of the composer. And it is judged by the craftsmanship of its texture rather than the boldness of its form. (*Pound and Music* 22)[15]

What the fugue offers Zukofsky, then, is a fundamentally musical structuring principle that can organize the diverse materials of his poem without excluding, on formal or aesthetic grounds, any subject he desires to treat. While a high modernist parataxis remains his basic compositional method, the overall model of fugal composition allows him to introduce into his poem as much heterogeneous material as he cares to, whether in the form of multiple repeated countersubjects or of nonrepeating episodes.

Let me return for a moment to the *Poetry* magazine misprinting of "figure" for "fugue" in the Contributors' Notes to Zukofsky's " 'Objectivists' 1931" issue. While this is no doubt a simple typographical error, a misreading of a notoriously misreadable hand, I find this error oddly proleptic. For although Zukofsky begins *"A"* by constructing poetic "fugues" that are finished, clear-cut formal objects, as his project progresses the notion of the fugue becomes less a formal model and more a principle of concatenation, less a hard and fast shape to be imitated and more a trope for form, a "figure." We can trace this shift in Zukofsky's conception of the poetic fugue by looking at how fugal form balloons out of all reasonable proportion in "A"-12, and then seems—perhaps deceptively—to disappear altogether in "A"-22 and -23.

Zukofsky's fugal form reaches its most expansive moment in "A"-12, the culmination of the poem's first half and a movement fully as long as the preceding eleven movements put together. But "A"-12 also represents a sort of limit case for the analogy of fugal form: that is, while the fugue is by definition an infinite formal principle and can take in an indefinite amount of new material, there comes a certain point at which the form reaches a saturation level, when the amount of information to be enfolded in the poem becomes so great that fugal organization loses its immediacy as a structuring device. This can be seen in part when one compares "A"-12 on the basis of size alone to the earlier fugues of *"A"*. The first five movements of the poem are openly fugal, and all are shorter than six pages. "A"-8 is an upping of the ante similar to that of "A"-12, for its sixty-three pages make it longer than "A"-1 through -7 combined. "A"-8 is fugal, however, in a way that can be straightforwardly diagrammed: it consists of (unsurprisingly) eight primary themes, all of which are presented in the first seven pages of the poem (*A* 43–49). "A"-7, -9, -10, and -11 are nonfugal—a pause before the grand fugue of "A"-12. "A"-7 is a sonnet sequence; "A"-9 is a double canzone modeled on Cavalcanti's "Donna mi priegha"; "A"-10 is an inverted mass on the fall of Paris; and "A"-11 is an adaptation of Cavalcanti's "Perch'io non spero." When Zukofsky returns to his analogy of fugal form in "A"-12, he does so for the last time explicitly, and he does it on a massive scale.

"A"-12 can be read as a companion text to *Bottom: On Shakespeare*. In the "Definition" section of *Bottom*, the "I" specifically invokes the fugue: "Shakespeare's art is simple, with its eyeing subject love. Without love's eyes art sees no sensible life. 'Life is like a fugue,' you remember, 'everything must grow out of the subject and there must be nothing new' " (*B* 266).[16] "A"-12 works in a similar, though more condensed, manner to *Bottom*'s "graph of culture," treating the same Shakespearean problematic of eye and mind and making use of many of the same quotations and borrowings. Zukofsky is well aware of the ungainly dimensions of this movement when compared to the three- and five-page early movements of "*A*". Toward the end of "A"-12 he implies that the 135 pages of the movement are a single summer's work, put together after "12 summers" of collecting:

A kind of childlike
Play this division
Into 24,
Enough perhaps for
12 books in this one
All done in a summer
After a gathering of 12 summers.
["A"-12, 258]

The very extent of "A"-12's materials and quotations—twelve years in the amassing—seems to promise that the movement will be of a complexity far surpassing that of any given movement of the first eleven sections of the poem. While adhering to the basic principles of "fugal" composition as played out comparatively simply in "A"-1 and with more variety in "A"-8, "A"-12 introduces a range of complications and variations on the subject/imitation/countersubject form that stretch the fugal analogy to a limit beyond which it no longer bears any resemblance to what Zukofsky has previously presented as "fugal" form in poetry. "A"-12 also makes greater use of peripherally related "episodic" material than do any of the earlier movements, much of it appearing in an extended passage—an "episode"—preceding the closing recapitulation of the original subject/theme. "A"-12 has some claim to be considered the heart of Zukofsky's oeuvre, both in its physical placement and in its concerns, and it represents the summing-up of both the poetics and the "argument" of the first half of "*A*".

But if "A"-12 approaches the "ragbag" of Pound's *Cantos* more closely than anything Zukofsky had previously written, it clearly aims to invoke the fuguelike procedures that lie behind the first half of *"A"*, and it does so in a manner that pays specific tribute to the master of fugal composition, Johann Sebastian Bach. The first lines recall the title of one of Bach's choral preludes and announce the theme of the movement as that of Bach's own name:

> *Out of deep need*
> Four trombones and the organ in the nave
> A torch surged—
> Timed the theme Bach's name
> ["A"-12, 126]

In their interplay, the letters B, A, C, H represent "harmony / certain in concord with reason" ("A"-12, 127), just as, in Bach's own formulation in the *Art of the Fugue,* "The parts of a fugue should behave like reasonable men / in an orderly discussion."[17] The letters, taken individually, represent the tutelary spirits of that harmony:

> Blest
> Ardent good
> Celia, speak simply, rarely scarce, seldom—
> Happy, immeasurable love
> heart or head's greater part unhurt and happy,
> things that bear harmony
> certain in concord with reason.
> ["A"-12, 127]

"Blest" stands for Spinoza, whose first name, Baruch (Latin "Benedictus"), means "blest"; "Ardent" is for Aristotle, who is "ardent" in pursuit of knowledge; "Happy" is for Paracelsus, whose real name, Philippus Aureolus Theophrastus Bombastus Hohenheim, begins with H; and "C" stands simply and without translation for Celia, the source of that domestic harmony that becomes a recurrent theme in the movement (Ahearn, *Zukofsky's "A"* 125–26).

The inherently multiple nature of his primary theme (B-A-C-H) enables Zukofsky to achieve a striking measure of immediately recognizable fugal coherence in this movement. The notes B-A-C-H form a tune that Zukofsky can evoke by citing any one of the individual notes: while one might call "harmony" the overall theme of "A"-12, the fact that "harmony" is itself embodied in the signature B-A-C-H enables Zukofsky to manipulate four separate subthemes revolving around the lives and writings of Spinoza, Aristotle, and Paracelsus, and the conversation and events of his own household, of which Celia is the reigning spirit of harmony. Intertwined with these four themes are a number of countersubjects. Most important is the eyes/mind theme of *Bottom*, which appears here as a capsule précis of *Bottom*'s most crucial quotations from Shakespeare, particularly those from *A Midsummer Night's Dream* (see especially "A"-12, 132–34). The right alignment of the eyes and the mind is important here (and throughout Zukofsky) because it brings about the only love that can be called truly harmonious: as Zukofsky restates his own epistemology, "Voice without scurf or gray matter, / For the eyes of the mind are proofs" ("A"-12, 130).

Another countersubject is Zukofsky's relationship to his own Jewish heritage and the tradition of rabbinical thought, embodied most clearly in his pious father, Pinchos Zukofsky, for whom Paul was named. In "A"-12, as I have implied in Chapter 5, Zukofsky lovingly embraces and accepts the tradition that had posed such a vexing obstacle in "Poem beginning 'The' " and the genealogical wanderings of "A"-4 ("The courses we tide from" [*A* 15]), in which the Orthodox elders lament the loss of the young:

> We had a Speech, our children have
> evolved a jargon.
> . . . .
> Deafen us, God, deafen us to their music,
> Our own children have passed over to the ostracized
> ["A"-4, 12–13]

With his father's death, Zukofsky has come to an understanding of his own ethnicity and inheritance, leaving behind his earlier pose as the intellectual "Shagetz": "Had he asked me to say Kadish / I believe I would have said it for him" ("A"-12, 143). Like Spinoza, Zukofsky's father, Pinchos, is "blest," a quiet man ("Who had taught himself to be simple" ["A"-12, 143]) whose piety and perseverance point to a harmony that is peculiarly Jewish, like that exemplified in the Talmudic commentaries Zukofsky condenses in pages 158–61 of *"A":*

> Rabbi Leib:
> What is the worth of their
> Expounding the Torah:
> All a man's actions
> Should make him a Torah—
> So to light up
> Whether he moves or is still.
> [*A* 158–59][18]

The elegiac remembering of Zukofsky's father is responsible for some of the most emotionally immediate moments of "A"-12 and is tied in closely with the speech and actions of Pinchos's grandson and namesake, born in 1943:

> The street never wide enough for him,
> Taking a diagonal to cross it,
> To open and close the synagogue
> For over six times ten years
> Until three days before he died—
> A longer journey than Odysseus'.
> Now his namesake says:
> "If it's not my kind of words
>   I don't want to hear them."
> he died certain—
> With such the angel of death does not wrestle—
> And alone,
> Not to let me see death:
> "Isn't visiting over?
> Go home,
> Celia must be anxious,
> Kiss Paul."
> ["A"-12, 155–56]

Where the primary scene of the earlier sections of the poem up through "A"-10 (excepting the mourning of "A"-3, the second half of "A"-9, and the farewell song of "A"-11) has been political, "A"-12 finalizes the poem's decisive shift of focus and attention to the domestic. The dominant locus of the harmony that Zukofsky delineates here is the family: the world at large becomes not the world of the newspapers and the class struggle but the world as seen by the three Zukofskys, and the world of Zukofsky's library. Citing the twelve Vivaldi concerti collectively titled "The Trial of Harmony and Invention" (see Ahearn, *Zukofsky's "A"* 212),[19] Zukofsky summarizes the overall movement of "A"-12:

From Battle of
Discord and Harmony
Come home beloved
["A"-12, 136]

Indeed, the shape of the movement as a whole is that of a homecoming whose archetypal literary precursor is the *Odyssey:* "Have your odyssey / How many voiced it be" ("A"-12, 128). Just as "A"-5 announced the poem as "One song / Of many voices" ("A"-5, 18), "A"-12 becomes a "many-voiced" "odyssey" in which the figure of the poet, after a 140-page sojourn, returns to his "true Penelope" (Celia), his son Telemachos (Paul), and the initial theme of his poem ("Bach's name"):

Tell me of that man who got around
After sacred Troy fell,
He knew men and cities
His heart riled in the sea
As he strove for himself and his friends:
He did not save them.
Tell us about it, my Light,
Start where you please.

It's so simple,
Telemachos rose from his bed
And dressed

Blest
Ardent
Celia
    unhurt and
Happy.
["A"-12, 261]

The first two of these stanzas directly paraphrase passages from the *Odyssey*. The first is from the invocation to the muse at the beginning of Book I:

> The hero of the tale which I beg the Muse to help me tell is that resourceful man who roamed the wide world after he had sacked the holy citadel of Troy. He saw the cities of many peoples and he learnt their ways. He suffered many hardships on the high seas in his struggles to preserve his life and bring his comrades home. But he failed to save those comrades, in spite of all his efforts. . . . This is the tale I pray the divine Muse to unfold to us. Begin it, goddess, at whatever point you will. (Homer 26)

The second is from the beginning of Book II: "As soon as dawn with her rose-tinted hands had lit the East, Odysseus' son put on his clothes and got up from his bed" (37).

An integral part of the Odyssean curve of the poem is the very real odyssey of Jackie, the soldier whose orthographically irregular letters Zukofsky reproduces from page 216 to page 223. Jackie's posting to Japan (and after that, to Korea) is an echo of Odysseus's descent into hell, the *Nekuia* of Book XI of the *Odyssey*, an account that Pound believed predated the rest of that poem and which, in a significantly transmogrified form, becomes the first Canto. Beginning on page 215 of "A"-12 ("For hell we launched / And trimmed the gear despite our tears"), and interleaved between Jackie's letters, is Zukofsky's own version of the passage from Homer that Pound uses in Canto I.[20] Odysseus's crew comes to the land

> where the Cimmerii live:
> In cloud and fog no sun ever
> Broke, or a star. Beached in pitch-dark
> ["A"-12, 218]

In parallel, Jackie's ship reaches Japan, and he disembarks in "pitch-dark":

> Friday, April 13, we derk at the port of Yokahama 5,263 miles from San Francisco. We derk about 1 o'clock in the afternoon and stay on the ship until midnight. (What for I don't now [*sic*]) ("A"-12, 219)

Just as Odysseus and his men "[follow] / The shore to wet hell" ("A"-12, 221), Jackie's unit proceeds to a landing in Korea: "Right now we are on a ship heading down the coast of Japan. We are to make a landing tomorrow morning" ("A"-12, 222).

But while Jackie, the "poor pay pfc," appears as an important Odysseus figure, the poet himself—

> [paying his] respects in hell:
> Forgetting none,
> Praying over and over
> Vowing that home—
> ["A"-12, 223]

—as in Canto I, is the most crucial pursuer of the Odyssean quest. In the first Canto, Pound delineates the method of his poem as bringing life to forgotten and silenced voices—giving "blood" to the "ghosts" just as Odysseus gives blood to the ghost of Tiresias—in order to hear his "soothsay" (*Cantos* 4).[21] Zukofsky's odyssey is one of memory, in which he returns home with the spirit of his father intact within him through the power of filial love:

> Living, you love
> So I love
> With the dead
> In me
> Thru wet and dry
> For the living
> ["A"-12, 261]

(The "wet and dry" here evokes the earlier "shore to wet hell.") This love is a profoundly domestic love, but it is also the "love" that gives rise to compositional sincerity, and the love that drives all of the poet's actions: "If you want to live, you love; if you don't want to live, you hate, that's all. It's as simple as that" (*LZMP* 278).

The rhetoric of such love is central to Zukofsky's poetics, another important countersubject of the movement. "Love" is the groundspring of sincerity, the fineness of perception that allows the poet to perceive the differences and similarities in what he sees, feels, and reads. While experience in general is common to all, like the weather and the seasons in Paracelsus's example, human responses to experience differ according to the variable of love:

> Paracelsus' *Book of Bad and Good Fortune:*
> The sun shines upon all of us equally
> With its luck. The summer comes
> To all of us equally
> With its luck. Our love is unequal.
> ["A"-12, 134][22]

Only through love can the poet's eye (in the broadest sense) be keen enough to distinguish the degrees of difference that constitute the total reality of culture and life. Citing Plato's parable of the cave, Zukofsky observes,

> the instrument of knowledge
> Plays only when the beloved's head
> Turns from Passing to Being
> So learns by degrees . . .
> ["A"-12, 177]

The notion of "degrees" (of "perceived differences") is central to Zukofsky's work; it is a notion that informs and is informed by both his epistemology of direct perception and his persistent tracing of a "graph of culture." According to John Taggart, the poet begins "with delight in knowing things through their perceived differences, and end[s] with an inwreathed (co-ordinate) image (poem) that makes those things flourish, light up; and thus they may give even more delight, be even more loved, because they have been apprehended with a greater intensity of perception" (*Songs of Degrees* 99). Ultimately, "It is the acknowledgment of difference which offers evidence that eyes have looked without haste, with sincerity, and it is by means of—'through'—such an acknowledgment that an image of the beloved object may be constructed" (*Songs of Degrees* 199).

Zukofsky's concern with a "graph of culture," which leads in *Bottom* to a painstaking trek through all of Western literature and philosophy, takes the form in "A"-12 of a set of extended meditations on the relationship between the poet and "tradition." Zukofsky is also interested in the sense of history in general, and in the sense of the tradition established in a single writer's work. In a letter to Lorine Niedecker that Zukofsky reproduces in "A"-12, the poet outlines his notion of a writer's personal tradition:

> . . . Each writer writes
> one long work whose beat he cannot
> entirely be aware of. Recurrences
> follow him, crib and drink from a
> well that's his cadence—after
> he's gone . . .
>
> Like the sea fishing
> Constantly fishing
>   Its own waters.
>
> The continuity—
> Its pulse.
> ["A"-12, 214–15, first ellipsis in original]

Bottom is the uncovering of such a set of "recurrences" in the writing of Shakespeare—whose plays and poems Zukofsky similarly sees as "one work, sometimes poor, sometimes good, sometimes great" (*B* 14)—and it involves the act of placing Shakespeare within a larger "tradition" of Western literature and thought, one that extends both into the past and up to the present, as embodied in contemporary writers. The sense of historical simultaneity governing *Bottom*'s logic of quotation—where Wittgenstein, Pound, Williams, and Mallarmé (among many others), as well as Firdosi, Scotus Erigina, and Aristotle are cited in order to site Shakespeare's work within a "universal" tradition—is also evident in "A"-12. Paul's childlike sense of history, Zukofsky claims, is "clearer" than that of contemporary political leaders, insofar as Paul recognizes the conceptual presentness of what is traditionally considered past, historical, or merely "literary":

> Paul's sense of the present is clearer.
> —Does Lars come from Troy
> Where all those men fell?
> (He had misheard:
> *Troy* for *Detroit.*)
> ["A"-12, 205]

The countersubject of Zukofsky's poetics, which reappears throughout the movement with unmistakable iteration, continually emphasizes this conception of history as a simultaneously present whole. For the horse that is Zukofsky's poet, an important aspect of love is the immediate presence of whatever manifestation of experience, no matter how far removed in time, that the horse finds worthy of attention: "Can love rouse a thing of the past / And not see it as present?" ("A"-12, 199). The graph of culture, like a physical time line, is a spatial construct, all of whose moments are simultaneously present to the reader/poet. This conception, of course, does away with the notion of "originality," already suspect in a poetics that relies as heavily on principles of quotation and collage as Zukofsky's. As Paul laconically puts it,

> Wait till they find out
> Where you took most of "your" poetry.
> ["A"-12, 214]

As I argued earlier, the poet's efforts are not a creation ex nihilo but a repetition of the cultural acts of all previous shapers of culture:

> The horse sees he is repeating
> All known cultures
> And suspects repeating
> Others unknown to him,
> Maybe he had better not
> Think of himself
> Hunting so to speak

> Sowing so to speak
> Composing always.
> ["A"-12, 175]

In the poet's activity—a "composing" that involves hunting and gathering more than it does Romantic "inspiration"—the poet is better off viewing himself in impersonal terms, subsuming his personality to his activity. This particular horse's experience of the simultaneity of culture is by no means exceptional (although he may be exceptional in his consciousness thereof) but merely a repetition of the "constant" cultural ground of poetic creation:

> The shape of his ground seems to have been
> A constant for all dead horses
> His neigh cultural constant
> Also his sniff—
> Is it some such constant when a culture
> Seems to revert a hundred years
> Or some thousands?
> And instances from "different" cultures, surprisingly inwreathed,
> Seem to look back at one another,
> Aristotle at Shakespeare (both so fond of blind heroes)
> And blest Spinoza at Shakespeare—
> How?
> Or for that matter uninwreathed
> As Rig-Veda to me,
> Because none has read the
>   other yet it happens.
> ["A"-12, 175–76]

That each writer's work manifests "instances from 'different' cultures, surprisingly / inwreathed," is fundamental to Zukofsky's poetics and can be seen as the basic premise behind the entire project of both *Bottom* and of *"A"*. It is certainly fundamental to *"A"*'s analogy of fugal form, in which the play of subject, imitation, and countersubject most often takes the form of a counterpointing of textual material from different historical, cultural, and linguistic spheres. This is a matter of recontextualization, as Bruce Comens points out ("Soundings" 96–101), of lifting material from an "original" context and placing it in a new relationship that, if treated with love's sincerity, can become a tangible, objectified artifact in its own right:

> Literature, you remark
> Is in a way another's account
> Which if I can afford to carry
> May add up as my own.
> ["A"-12, 238]

Taggart, expanding on Zukofsky's own terminology, sees his method as that of weaving: "The analogous motion for the process of fugue, this bringing together, is conceived of as a weaving in both 'A' and 'Bottom' " (*Songs of Degrees* 194).[23] Like Shakespeare's Nick Bottom, Zukofsky is a weaver, plaiting the warp and woof of his textual material—here, the etymological pun of "textual" is wholly significant—into a new creation, "Weaving, instead of unweaving, / A fiddle— / Or Penelope's web" ("A"-12, 162). The horse as weaver creates (improbably) a "fiddle" (a musical instrument) as well as a mimetic tapestry ("Penelope's web," which is unlike Penelope herself, who each night "unweaves" the day's work). (Penelope's nightly unweaving may be Zukofsky's way of poking fun at his own revision methods, which consisted far more often of excision than outright change: page after page of the manuscripts now at the University of Texas are struck through and discarded.)

As weaver, the poet is always aware of his position within culture, his identity as both cultural producer and cultural product—or, as Spinoza puts it, *natura naturans* (nature as creator) and *natura naturata* (nature as creation):[24]

> What culture there is, I chime in, is light
> From a persistent fire twitching
> Reflection of our momentary flames.
> ["A"-12, 238]

I have already noted how Zukofsky's conception of the poetic act, and his attitude toward the "monuments" of the past, distinguish him from the view laid out in Eliot's "Tradition and the Individual Talent." Perhaps the most striking single element that distinguishes Zukofsky's practice from Eliot's is the inclusiveness of Zukofsky's poetics, the heterogeneous nature of the materials that go into the poetic "fugue." Where fragments of popular song ("O O O O that Shakespeherian Rag—") and popular speech ("When Lil's husband got demobbed, I said—") enter Eliot's *Waste Land* primarily as ironic indices of the debasement of the high cultural "fragments" that the poem seeks to "shore" against the "ruin" of Western civilization (or of the poet's psyche, or of the sexual relationship, and so on), similar material appears in "A"-12 on an equal footing with the poem's more overtly philosophical or literary material. Jackie's letters appear not as an object of ridicule or critique, however shaky their grasp of spelling and grammar, but as an altogether serious contemporary analogue to Homer's *Nekuia.*[25] The "Trust and honor" Zukofsky pays to these letters is the same as that he pays to Jackie himself, who, on his first meeting with Zukofsky, is "Surprised when I addressed him as Mister" ("A"-12, 223).

The primary source in "A"-12 of such nonliterary material is the conversation of Zukofsky's young son, and Zukofsky repeatedly demonstrates that his child's utterances have in them as much "poetry" as anyone could wish for in a more "composed" text:

> "My eyes are bloodshy"
> (Clear, I see, clear)
> Said my son
> After practicing
> An hour on his fiddle . . .
> Of a dream he dreamed
> Paganini playing
> Mozart's Turkish Concerto.
> —What did he look like, Paul?
> —A river!
> ["A"-12, 146–47]

The valentine Paul sends his father, which Zukofsky includes graphically in his own text, is perhaps the most striking instance in "A"-12 of such incorporation, comparable to the moment in

Canto IX when Pound directly transcribes the contents of Sigismundo Malatesta's mailbag (*Cantos* 34–41):[26]

> I would like to
> have a happy
>
> Paul Louis
> from
> his
> nice best best
> friend of Louis
>
> Valentine's day because
> there are no hearts. There
> will be a heart because
> we will send you a letter
> that was from me to
> divide it in half.
>
> ["A"-12, 128–29]

This moment, like the incorporation of Jackie's letters, represents both a continuance and a furthering of Pound's poetics; as Marjorie Perloff argues, "Zukofsky thus carries further Pound's program for a poem including history, a poem that no longer privileges the lyric over, say, the found object (actual letter received, newspaper passage, document)" (*Poetic License* 137). The crucial difference between the two poets' practice, however, is the difference between ideogram and fugue. The ideogram, which seeks to build higher meanings out of smaller constituent units, is an inherently totalizing, perhaps even totalitarian form: "totalitarian" particularly in the context of Pound's practice, where the poem is so often represented as merely providing the raw evidence from which the reader may draw a conclusion. The conclusion at which Pound would have one arrive, as one sees so often in his early commentators, is invariably in line with Pound's own economic/political/cultural polemics. Pound's own work transcends this totalitarian imperative to the degree that the materials he has constellated in *The Cantos* refuse to stay fixed to single, predetermined significances. In contrast, Zukofsky's poetics of parataxis, with all of its radical openness to the nonliterary and subliterary, is involved with a formal principle that is less form than texture. The principle of "fugal" composition, as constantly self-generating and regenerating "weave," escapes the totalizing tendencies of the ideogram; it is, as Zukofsky writes of the poem in "An Objective," "of no predatory intention" (*P* 18).

While the very size of "A"-12, as I have earlier argued, works to make its formal principles less than evident, the movement ends in a manner that is plainly meant to invoke the fugue. This begins with a restatement of the B-A-C-H theme in which each of the first three letters are reproduced in large, bold type:

> **B**lest
> Infinite things
> So many
> Which confuse imagination
> Thru its weakness
> ["A"-12, 231]

(These lines are a version of a passage from the appendix to Part I of Spinoza's *Ethics.*) Five pages later, Zukofsky writes,

> **A**rdent
>   good
> Nichomachus, the physician, had a son
> Aristotle who had a son Nichomachus—
> Aristotle's sun?
> ["A"-12, 236]

(That Aristotle's own father was named Nichomachus, as well as his son, for whom the *Nichomachean Ethics* is named, is a clear parallel to the Pinchos/Louis/Paul relationship, for Paul was named after his grandfather.) And on the next page, we find

> **C**elia
>
>   Over coffee.
> ["A"-12, 237]

The "H" does not appear at this point; its appearance—completing a restatement of the original B-A-C-H theme—would, by the definition of the form, bring the fugue to a close. Instead there follows an extended episode, a twenty-page passage of fragments of the themes, interspersed with various heterogeneous material, much of which is a simple cataloguing of Zukofsky's immediate surroundings and the contents of his desk. This is Zukofsky's method at its most naked; in a comment of striking self-reflexiveness, the poem presents the materials of its own construction as nothing more than one poet's random accumulations:

> All that follows here
> You may see as
>   my object
> And your record.
>
> Notes of things
> That may please you . . .
>
>   I clear my desk of clippings . . .
>
>   Files and head
>   Of twenty years notes
>   To make life easier to
>   handle . . .
>
> Enough for a book
> ["A"-12, 244–45]

What follows is in some sense a clearing of the decks, a sweeping clean of the poet's accumulated notes in recognition of the fact that "A"-12 closes the first half of the poem and that "A"-13 might well mark a significant shift, both in method and subject matter. I believe that "A"-12, to a greater degree than any earlier section of *"A"*, marks the explicit entrance of textuality into the poem. This section of the poem consists of a series of textual traces that reflect, not the poet's personality or inspiration, but his identity as a textual construct, the locus of convergence of a number of written documents.[27] Nowhere is this more evident than in the closing pages of "A"-12, which present a list of Paul's titles for his own paintings—

West East In The Old Days
Paul Lying Down Scribbling
A Harpsichord
Long Long Ago When It Was Raining
    When Bach Lived
["A"-12, 243]

—a list of group names for birds—

A sege of herons
A spring of teals
A bevy of quails
A gaggle of geese
["A"-12, 245]

—a variation of a passage of "A"-11—

River, since a song does not turn back
        to speak to
Everyone of its order, but will run on
In the words after the sun on
The singer stops shining
["A"-12, 247][28]

—and a quotation from Schoenberg that seems to bear on Zukofsky's own compositional methods:

"Adversaries have
called me a constructor,
an engineer, an architect,
a mathematician . . .
I have often wondered
why (Beethoven) called himself
brain-owner, when the
possession of a brain
spells a danger to
the naivete of an artist
for many pseudo-historians?"
["A"-12, 248]

The materials here defy categorization by any Aristotelian means, though perhaps a Borgesian taxonomy might capture them all. Their only point of commonality is that they have caught the eye of the composing poet, who has at one time or another thought to make use of them:

> These are some things I wanted
> To get into a poem,
> Some unfinished work
> I may never finish,
> Some that will never be used anywhere
> ["A"-12, 251]

In their parataxis these textual fragments differ from Pound's ideogram, where the guiding principle is to fashion a textual construct that will draw a higher meaning out of the sum of its parts. Zukofsky's passage, in contrast, has as its object merely to "clear [his] desk of clippings," to signal an end of the first half of his long poem by acknowledging what *might* have made it into the text but did not. Paradoxically, what has been set aside as supplement or excess does finally find a place in the structure of the poem, through that very act of being set aside.

Of course there is more to this extended passage than simply discarded materials for *"A":* there are two items that "Could have gone into *A Test of Poetry*"—a poem by "one John Soowthern or Soothern" and "Elizabeth's *Princess of Espinoy*"—both of which are reproduced in full ("A"-12, 252, 259). And there is an annotated list of works in several genres that Zukofsky planned and never finished, never began, or never published:

> Notes for different plays
> I'd have done in my twenties
> At the slightest encouragement . . .
> *Lights Festival:* a musicale . . .
> *The Windows:* the drama of a textile plant . . .
>
> Two operas:
> *The Ghost Dance* (Wovoka),

Ovid's *Metamorphoses*
That would sing Golding.

A historical drama: *Edward VIII* . . .

A spy story: *The Lifesaver Antenna*
["A"-12, 253–54]

There are also novels (*The Little Girl* and *That People the Sunbeams* ["A"-12, 254–55]), short stories ("It Was," "Rutgers St.," and "The Hounds" ["A"-12, 256]), and various nonfiction prose works: *A Life of William Byrd, How Jefferson Used Words, A History of American Design,* and *Graph: Of Culture* ("A"-12, 256–57).[29] By acknowledging these works, Zukofsky puts them behind him, letting them go: "Anybody's welcome to it. / Take: a raft of stuff" ("A"-12, 257). And by releasing all of these plans, enough projects to keep any three poets busy for a lifetime, Zukofsky can turn back to his primary theme, the domestic harmony represented by B-A-C-H and located in the familial triangle of Louis, Celia, and Paul. He prepares for this closing point, the restatement of his original theme, in a quiet and tender manner, addressing his typist Celia: "Why bother more. Give some thoughts to a performance / Of your *Pericles*, Celia" ("A"-12, 257).[30] The Zukofskys have found their own way of doing what they want to do, and there is no need to write an essay explaining the historical "calculus" of their "poetics":

Why write an essay
Saying Bach took from the folk
Their church for a calculus,
And Mozart from the folk
Their stage for his calculus,
And some of us
Folk as we are from
Two wars what calculus.

Everyone
Will explain to us
How to do

The wrong things
The right way
["A"-12, 258]

The Odyssean homecoming to which the poet returns from his textual wanderings takes the form of a moment of gentle reminder—

—Still awake, still pothering?
—What, goddess?

—This is your house,
Your wife's here
And your boy
["A"-12, 260],

—and the harmony that B-A-C-H signifies is emblematized in a moment of the mother's deferral to the son:

When Paul tunes his fiddle
The piano needs tuning
He says "I was right,
The note was right
As I played it the first time,"
You say "his ear
Is better than mine"—
That is love.
["A"-12, 261]

The unfinished restatement of the "fugal" subject begun thirty pages before is completed with "Blest / Ardent / Celia / unhurt and / Happy," and the structure of "A"-12 is brought to a close, the "deep need" of its opening line ("*Out of deep need*" ["A"-12, 126]) satisfied in the warmth of the domestic bond.

This ending, however, raises some critical questions. At the outset, one is tempted to associate the references to and the close thematic tracking of the *Odyssey* with Eliot's "mythical method," a compositional device that Zukofsky himself had firmly rejected, preferring instead a poetics that seeks its epos in such tiny linguistic moments as "*the* and *a*." Has Zukofsky gone over to the enemy camp, following *Ulysses, The Cocktail Party,* and *Mourning Becomes Electra* down the path of "manipulating a close parallel between contemporaneity and antiquity"? I think not. The Odyssean parallels of "A"-12 are only one of that movement's host of structural devices. The fugue, most obviously, is far more crucial for Zukofsky, and the masses of catalogued information toward the movement's end resist assimilation into *any* structuring scheme less welcoming than the fugue's elastic texture. "A"-12 resists any totalizing structure whatsoever, and the appearance of Homeric motifs serves, not to shut down the movement's (theoretical) endlessness but to lay emphasis on the manner in which the poet (awares or unawares) continually repeats the achievements and experiences of those who have come before him.

Where Eliot's conception of tradition is an ultimately unfriendly one, placing an enormous burden of awareness and responsibility on the young poet, Zukofsky's is liberating. If one knows in advance that one's work will consist essentially of plowing furrows that others have already plowed, rehearsing themes that others have broached, then one is freed to take joy in the repetitions, the moments when one writer seems to be reading the poems or the mind of another, although the two may be separated by languages, continents, and centuries. One is freed to see one's own work within the same nexus, as repeating and repeated in the writings of every writer one happens to read. There is every evidence that Zukofsky read the poetry of others, and his own poetry, precisely in this way.

But the ending, as beautiful a chord as it strikes, may impress one as perhaps a bit *too* harmonious. A reader is all too apt to find the domestic scene at the close of "A"-12 as idealized and even sentimentalized, given the urban unrest, capitalist exploitation, and overt class struggle presented in earlier movements. The disappearance from the poem of this political sphere is felt as a distinct loss, particularly since Zukofsky, unlike his older contemporary Stevens, began his career deeply interested in embodying history in his poetry in an analytic but emotionally immediate form. The historiographical systems that Zukofsky deploys in the early movements of *"A"*, derived from his careful readings of Henry Adams and Marx, are far superior both to "the farrago of American rural populism, Douglasite economics, and Fascist propaganda that we find in Pound" (Hatlen, "From Modernism" 215) and to the Romantic mythologizing through which Stevens confronts contemporary history in *Owl's Clover* (1937). One can of course regard Zukofsky's shift as one from an idealized representation of history (idealized because of its thoroughly theorized nature, filtered already through the equations of Adams and Marx) to an idealized representation of the family, one that has its avatars in the trio of Odysseus, Penelope, and Telemachus, and perhaps even the holy family of Joseph, Mary, and Jesus. Nonetheless, what is clear is that Zukofsky's formalist poetics, despite his rhetoric of "historic and contemporary particulars," is not in any essential way bound to the political sphere, as his early writings on poetics might seem to imply.

"A" begins as a political poem and midway through becomes a domestic poem. I am not certain what the implications of this are for an assessment of modernist poetics in general, but I believe it indicates quite unequivocally that Zukofsky's allegory of fugal composition, like his Objectivist poetics, is a purely formal principle, without any direct or necessary connection to the political realm. If one is to seek a politics in Zukofsky's poetry, apart from the overtly Marxist poems he wrote up through the end of the 1930s, one must seek to derive ideological significance not from his forms per se but from the social relationships within which the poems locate themselves, in particular the relationship of the reader to the poem. In this light, the communicative aspect of poetry, what Zukofsky calls its "informational" aspect, would seem to be the most direct avenue of interpersonal connection, the most promising area in which to find a liberating potential, or at the very least a potential to "give delight and hurt not," like the music of Prospero's isle.

9

Obscurity, Solipsism, and Community in "A"-23

But you got to try hard—
—William Carlos Williams, "January Morning" (*Collected Earlier Poems* 166)

While the fugue of "A"-12 is the single most expansive example of musiclike structuring in *"A"*, Zukofsky by no means abandons formal musical analogies in the second half of his long poem. Musical analogies (some of which I have already mentioned) proliferate in "A"-13 through -24, many in far subtler manifestations than the self-proclaimed fugues of the first twelve sections. "A"-22 and -23, the last-written movements of the poem, however, are not explicitly based on musical models: they do not invoke the partita or fugue, for instance, nor are they modeled on a song form such as the canzone. Nonetheless, the two thousand lines of these painstakingly compacted sections bring to a high pitch the musical counterpointing of thematic, aural, and textual repetitions that structures "A"-1 and "A"-12. It is as if Zukofsky, at the close of his life's work, has become comfortable enough with the musical foundations and implications of his poetics to dispense with the scaffolding of explicit analogy, to leave behind the whole more or less intrusive machinery of announced "fugal form." The formal ideal posed as a question in "A"-6—"*Can* / The design / Of the fugue / Be transferred / To poetry?" ("A"-6, 38)—and repeated as an explicit goal in the contributor's note in the 1931 *Poetry*—"the poetically perfect . . . in the feeling of the contrapuntal design of the [fugue] transferred to poetry" (294)—has now become an integral, and implicit, formal principle of the long poem as a whole. The "fugue" has become, as I intimated earlier, not a formal model but a "figure" of form in general, a generative device.

As one approaches these latter sections of *"A"*, the problem of skepticism once again confronts the reader. *Bottom* was written as a refutation of epistemological speculation and serves as a large-scale argument for the reliability of the physical senses, as thematized in Shakespeare and much of the rest of the tradition of Western writing. "I's (pronounced *eyes*)" is also invested in this argument, although that sequence makes clear that an epistemic stance based on the evidence of the individual's eyes must be tempered by a recognition of the discourse-based, interpersonal nature of knowledge. Dealing with Zukofsky's notion of poetry's music as played out in "A"-22 and -23, however, gives the issue of knowledge a certain turn: the primary question here is not the sources of one's knowledge but the degree to which that knowledge is transmissible as embodied in an objectlike, musical form. Williams perhaps summarizes the problem best in his "Asphodel, That Greeny Flower": "It is difficult / to get the news from poems" (*Pictures from Brueghel* 161). As Mallarmé was well aware, the poem cannot serve the function of the newspaper; but what manner of news *can* it give the reader?

According to Cavell, a crucial element of the skeptical rejection of the world is a rejection of other people, a refusal to acknowledge one's responsibility to others. The immediate danger in a poetry as "difficult" as Zukofsky's is the always-present specter of solipsism, the sort of other-minds skepticism represented by a private language, a poetics that produces poetry that no one other than the poet can comprehend. Abstraction and difficulty, of course, are more than casually related, and if Zukofsky's prose is more than occasionally abstract, his poetry can be unrelentingly obscure. As Williams writes, reviewing Zukofsky's *55 Po-*

ems, "[Zukofsky's] method is wholly justified. But as I say, it is difficult for the writer and the reader, and always dangerous, for to bore by an unsolvable obscurity is the worst of all writing. And when sense, even if ploddingly, cannot solve a sentence because of an over-absence of its parts—the fault cannot be said to lie with the reader" (*Something to Say* 130–31). He had earlier written Zukofsky and commented on his poetry's difficulty in a somewhat more positive vein: "It is thoughtful poetry, but actual word stuff, not thoughts for thoughts. It escapes me in its analysis (thank God) and strikes against me a thing (thank God)" (*Selected Letters* 94).[1]

It is unclear why Zukofsky should write such obscure poetry when his friend Reznikoff, for instance, a poet for whom Zukofsky's admiration is clear, writes such lucid, immediately graspable work. The density of Zukofsky's work—early, middle, but especially late—would seem to actively discourage communication, and to discourage a reader who hopes to gain some useful information from the verse. A casual reading might find this sort of rejection of communication at any point in "A"-22 and -23. Consider the following lines (selected pretty much at random):

> Hush seeking oath now go
> brightness pass you, high hill
> lifted hand water anointed rush—
> *the labour of the olive*
> horses walk thru, the sun
> moon stood, singer stringed instrument.
> ["A"-23, 547]

How is one to read this poetry? What sort of interpretive approach can deliver up the "meaning" of these lines? Or, alternatively, how does this poetry reconceive the very notion of "meaning," too often represented as a prose statement that can somehow (if only imperfectly) sum up the import of the verse? What "information" (Zukofsky's own term) does this poetics deliver?

It is easy to say that the two thousand lines of "A"-22 and -23 represent perhaps the most obscure poetry written in English in this century, and it might seem attractive to concur with Eliot Weinberger in labeling Zukofsky's last work a "black hole" of impenetrability. Such an approach, however, ignores Zukofsky's own statements regarding his supposed obscurity. In *Little,* the character Dala (who stands in for Zukofsky) comments, "I too have been charged with obscurity, tho it's a case of listeners wanting to know too much about me, more than the words say" (*CF* 119–20). But what complicates the issue is the very nature of Zukofsky's late poetics—an exponential compounding and compression of the collagist, quotational method in evidence from the very earliest sections of *"A"*—and the existence, in the Harry Ransom Humanities Research Center at the University of Texas, of essentially complete drafts and compositional notes for the last sections of *"A"*.[2] "A"-22 and -23 are made up largely (if not completely) of altered, compressed, transliterated, and cross-referenced quotations from Zukofsky's readings. In "A"-22, Zukofsky describes his own method, using his favored image of the poet as horse:

> old in
> a greenhouse the stabled horse
> sings sometimes, thoughts' template
> somehow furthers a cento reading
> ["A"-22, 535]

The *Century* dictionary (Zukofsky's habitual source) defines "cento" as "1. A patchwork[;] 2. In *music* and *literature* a composition made up of selections from the works of various authors or composers; a pasticcio; a medley" (quoted in Ahearn, *Zukofsky's "A"* 188). The text of these sections, then, is a painstakingly compounded patchwork of five years of Zukofsky's reading. The nature of Zukofsky's method—as we have earlier seen in "A"-12—renders indeterminate the very notions of quotation and originality and makes the question of whether a given phrase is Zukofsky's own or a borrowing practically meaningless.[3] Zukofsky himself characterizes his method as a "rewriting" of an already overwritten text and contrasts it with the ex nihilo creation for which the naive young poet strives: "A / child learns on blank paper, / an old man rewrites palimpsest" ("A"-22, 524–25).

The preservation of Zukofsky's manuscripts at the University of Texas, and the example of the exegetical industries built on the works of Pound and Joyce (two of Zukofsky's acknowledged masters), have led some critics to the conclusion that Zukofsky's later work can only be profitably approached through the documentation of his sources and borrowings, and to the further conclusion that Zukofsky himself would sanction such an approach. Michele J. Leggott states this position most completely:

> Conventional wisdom would have it that notes and draft materials are unnecessary to the reading of a poem, and in most cases wisdom has its way—Zukofsky said often enough that paying sufficient attention elucidates a work. But what happens when that work is a radical departure not only from current modes but also from the very work that has preceded it? Zukofsky was ready to concede that the shape of *"A"* fell into three parts: *"A" 1–21*, *"A" 22 & 23*, and *"A"-24*. The difficulty of the last-written movements was of an order to baffle and eventually alienate all but the most persistent of readers. The condescension of explanations was as distasteful as ever to Zukofsky, but just the same there was a real risk of losing his audience altogether. The solution, as Zukofskian as those quiet indexes that critique the poet's work without seeming to do anything more than give page numbers, was to legitimize use of the draft material by housing it in a public collection. (31–32)

Alison Rieke echoes this position in her "Quotation and Originality" essay:

> Will future readers catch Zukofsky's sense? They will if they seek the information Zukofsky has so generously made available. . . . It stands to reason that anyone looking for a complete *"A"* must also seek its notes. Like a good pun, *"A"* is doubled, section after section, by its notebooks. They are as much a part of the complete *"A"* as its cover and its index. (104)[4]

Leggott's own critical approach is in line with these manifestos. She examines in detail thirty-six of the eighty-one poems of *80 Flowers*, exhaustively delineating the translations, transliterations, quotations, allusions, and cross-references that Zukofsky has woven into them. This method, painstaking, careful, and sometimes revelatory, gives one a clear picture of the breathtaking range of materials out of which Zukofsky has made his poems (see, in particular, her "unpackings" of the opening passages of "A"-22 and the "Epigraph" to *80 Flowers* [34–70, 73–90]).[5]

The rhetoric by which Leggott supports her readings, however, leaves one with a sense of disquiet concerning Zukofsky's earlier statements about the "informational" aspect of his poetry, especially the assertion in *A Test of Poetry* that "Good poetry is the barest—most essentially complete—form of presenting a subject" (*TP* 89). The picture that Leggott and Rieke paint of Zukofsky's later works is that of an irredeemably hermetic poetics, one whose obscurity is a direct function of a reader's lack of necessary information: a poetry restricted to a tiny coterie of initiates whose interest is compelling enough to send them to the University of Texas in a quest for the keys that will unlock the enigma of the work. There are two ways to reply to this picture. On the one hand, one can argue that clear biographical contingencies, considerations having little to do with matters of poetics, were in large part responsible for Zukofsky's decision to deposit his worksheets at the University of Texas. While such considerations cannot of course rule out the possibility that Zukofsky placed his manuscripts in a library with the readerly reception of his work specifically in mind, they suggest that his actions may have had other, more immediate motives; at the very least, they make problematic any claim that the existence of Zukofsky's notes, however enlightening they may be, is by authorial dictate the determining element in a critical approach to his work. Zukofsky's own statements, as well, put into question the degree to which the poet considered his sources a useful object of study. In a 1960 letter to Cid Corman, Zukofsky explains that *"A"*'s "references" are usually not singular quotations but verbal constructions in which several references are simultaneously combined. They must be explained not by source hunting or reference books but by their context within the poem itself: the reader who pursues a precise identification of a reference is neither hearing the music of the text nor truly reading its words.[6]

George Steiner, in his essay "On Difficulty," lays out another, more theoretical basis for this discussion. Steiner outlines a schema of four broadly defined types of "difficulty" one is likely to encounter in literary texts: *contingent difficulty*, where the text presents "something that 'we need to look up,' " a difficulty that can be resolved by consulting the proper reference work; *modal difficulty,* "the failure of the reader to coerce his sensibilities into the relevant frame of reference"; *tactical difficulty,* where a poet is difficult out of a conscious impulse, whether aesthetic, political, or personal; and *ontological difficulty:*

> Difficulties of this category cannot be looked up; they cannot be resolved by genuine readjustment or artifice of sensibility; they are not an intentional technique of retardation and creative uncertainty (though these may be their immediate effect). *Ontological* difficulties confront us with blank questions about the nature of human speech, about the status of significance, about the necessity and purpose of the construct which we have, with more or less rough and ready consensus, come to perceive as a poem. (*On Difficulty* 19, 33, 41).

The sort of difficulty that can be cleared up by Terrell's *Companion to The Cantos* or Butterick's *Guide to The Maximus Poems*—two exemplary reference works—is clearly a contingent difficulty, one which results from, as Leggott puts it, the reader not "holding as many cards as [the poet] does" (52).

The whole of Leggott's passage is instructive, for she acknowledges that even the existence of the notebooks does not guarantee access to Zukofsky's "idiosyncratic" syntax:

> Then comes *"A" 22 & 23* . . . and the problem of impermeability seems to have compounded itself tenfold. Syntax is now totally idiosyncratic; readers grab at what they can. . . . To "make sense" of syntax this difficult is really a matter of holding as many cards as Zukofsky holds. Failing that (and who does not, notebooks at Texas regardless), all we can do is listen hard and puzzle connections with what is available. (52)

And the problem of Zukofsky's syntax is clearly at the heart of his later work's difficulty. Even if one is fully aware that the following passage is a transformation of lines 86–100 of *Beowulf* (as Leggott shows in detail [59–60]), that knowledge will not untangle the syntax:

Dragged thole
load—sea-dark bided, day urged
merriment harp-swag Almighty earthen worth,
sea-water bowed, sun and moon,
lumine lighted land beings' hum
tree-limb, leaf, all-welcome shape quick
so that men life don
heartily
["A"-23, 556]

Peter Quartermain, like Leggott, stresses the role of syntax in the difficulty of Zukofsky's later work, contrasting it with Joyce's *Finnegans Wake:*

> Zukofsky's insistence that "the story must exist in each word" leads him to formulate a writing that relies heavily on syntactic distortion and pun to achieve a simultaneity of effects and multiplicity of meaning—a polysemousness akin to Joyce's. (*Disjunctive Poetics* 114)

> Zukofsky, in his syntax, characteristically plays with parts of speech, leaving the role of words essentially ambiguous. He foregrounds semantic play through fooling with syntax: Joyce, foregrounding through puns, tends to leave his syntax pretty straightforward. (108)

Such characterizations of Zukofsky's later work emphasize that there is more to its obscurity than a mere contingent difficulty, a denseness of uncited references. This is a poetry that involves Steiner's "ontological" difficulty, a difficulty in which the "contract of ultimate or preponderant intelligibility between poet and reader, between text and meaning . . . is itself wholly or in part broken" (40). Both Quartermain and Comens stress that the density of the late work, its impenetrability to the hermeneutic act, is an integral part of Zukofsky's poetics. "Both Zukofsky and Joyce," Quartermain writes, "wind in as many meanings as possible: both consequently cultivate an opacity of text—for if the text is to contain the world, then it must, like the world, in its quiddity stubbornly resist the hermeneutic act" (*Disjunctive Poetics* 108). In contrast to a poetics that achieves "depth" through "symbolism or mythology," Comens argues, "Zukofsky's method results in a multiplicity of meanings having no central 'point,' so that, while the poem itself is remarkably assured, the reader is likely to feel considerable insecurity among the rapidly shifting perspectives available in reading any given line" ("Soundings" 97). Such dense, multivalent writing, what Quartermain calls "this nonlinear, unhierarchic writing, this generative incoherence" (*Disjunctive Poetics* 113), is a clear example of Steiner's "ontological" difficulty and must be approached as such: in other words, the degree to which the text resists conventional interpretation is part of a reconception of the very meaning-bearing stance of the poem.

Comens is correct in tracing much of the polysemous nature of Zukofsky's work to "the removal of context, for it is context that limits meaning and thereby determines it" ("Soundings" 96). By removing textual material from its original context and recontextualizing it within his own poem, and by rendering that new context indeterminate through a radical ambiguity of syntax, Zukofsky achieves a "multiplicity of meanings": "Rather than excluding meaning, Zukofsky's increasing suppression of context in *'A'*—to the point where words are scarcely limited by syntax at all—*expands* meaning" (Comens, "Soundings" 97). Here again it is useful, as with *Bottom,* to regard Zukofsky's borrowings and quotations in the context of Derrida's notion of the "graft," in which one comes to "recognize other possibilities" of meaning by detaching "a written syntagm . . . from the chain in which it is inserted or given" and "inscribing it or *grafting*" it into another (*Limited Inc* 9). Here, of course, the graft is at once more subtle and more radical than the fairly straightforward quotations of *Bottom,* which are regularized both by quotation marks and references to their originary contexts. In Zukofsky's later works, one must take quotation or borrowing as a continual given: the very texture of the verse is a tissue of quotations, translations, and transliterations, only a minimal proportion of which are acknowledged as such through quotation marks or italics. Such a texture does not of course necessarily lead to readerly obscurity, as one can see from an earlier experiment like the young William Empson's "Two Centos" (*Royal Beasts* 104). But Zukofsky weaves his borrowings into a texture where individual words and phrases are set free from larger contexts of discourse, where the construction of meaning becomes a word-by-word, phrase-by-phrase process rather than the usual, almost automatic proccss by which a reader proceeds confidently down a syntagmatic string. Syntax has not been destroyed in later Zukofsky, but it has been largely disrupted, rendered tenuous, ambiguous, and continuously provisional.

The difficulty of later Zukofsky, then, is much more than a matter of hidden references or withheld knowledge. Taggart, repeating his figure of the Zukofskyan text as a woven tapestry, cautions against a single-minded tracking down of Zukofsky's sources: "It is tempting . . . to try to locate specific sources, other texts used for the weaving of these texts. Zukofsky's way of working renders such a temptation difficult and even misleading." For Taggart, Zukofsky's borrowings work "more as a grid of resonating individual words and phrases—the way we remember Bach and Shakespeare—than as a group of discrete texts which will read the rewoven text for us. Locating sources has value only as it calls our attention to the skill of the poet's weaving, as it calls attention to how objectification has been brought about" (*Songs of Degrees* 207–8).[7] It is abundantly clear than both Leggott and Rieke realize that Zukofsky's obscurity is something much more complex than the difficulty that confronts a novice reader of, for instance, *Sordello*—a reader who knows nothing of the history Browning treats but who has access to the reference works that will eventually clear up all but the most obdurate cruxes. Nevertheless, I take issue with Leggott and Rieke's emphasis on the unearthing of Zukofsky's sources as a *necessary* (although not necessarily *sufficient*) step in approaching "A"-22 and -23. Aside from the shaky theoretical foundations on which such an activity rests, too often "sourcing" a text becomes an end in itself, and the documentation of sources completely displaces any active *reading* on the critic's part. For Zukofsky, the act of reading is an act of perceiving structures, rather than one of demonstrating one's erudition or spadework. Compare his statement from his lecture on Wallace Stevens:

> I try not to read into things, I try to read, which means that if the page doesn't have it any imagination on my part as to what I might

read into it has no significance. I hope everybody would read me the same way—that is, not wonder whether I was afraid of a draft as I am at the moment, but just read the words. This activity is a kind of mathematics but more sensuous, and *it has little to do with learning, it has something to do with structure.* (*P* 24, emphasis mine)

(This passage on "structure" dovetails interestingly with Leggott's scorn for readers who opt not to pursue Zukofsky's sources: "There is nothing wrong with staying on the surface and admiring the configurations, just as there is nothing wrong with being an appreciative, fluent speaker of one's own language" [90]. One reader's "structure," I suppose, is another's "configuration.") What Rieke is interested in demonstrating through her own sourcing activity is the presence in Zukofsky's later work of submerged structures—scaffoldings that determine the placement of the ostensibly randomly deployed "minute bits and scraps of language" (*Senses of Nonsense* 191). For Rieke, the indeterminacy of the poem's syntax renders the poem's words dismayingly "mobile": since their combinations are devoid of conventional "sense," it seems they might just as well appear in alternate orders. Nonetheless, according to Rieke, "Zukofsky's interest in the chronological arrangement of quotations in both 'A'-22 and 'A'-23 undermines surface appearances of mobility. After the quotations have been identified, they resonate with meanings which simply cannot be fathomed in the text's surface randomness" (*Senses of Nonsense* 195). Rieke is right, at least in part: the conversations among source texts that she uncovers are certainly present, and certainly illuminating. Yet I believe she has been too hasty in dismissing as nonsensical or random the surface of the poem, the meaning of the words as *read*, rather than as traced.

Such a reading is of course an understandable response to a text as obdurately alien to conventional interpretive procedures as "A"-23. If, as Comens argues, Zukofsky's later work, through its "increasing suppression of context" and its increasingly ambiguous syntax, becomes "more or less constantly ironic," thereby achieving the "valid skepticism" Zukofsky admires in Stevens, what implications does such an ironical stance have for the relationship of poet and reader, the interpersonal ground on which knowledge itself, the epistemic certainty that drives Zukofsky's poetics, rests? It is the quandary raised at the outset of this chapter: how can a poetry as "difficult" as Zukofsky's later work avoid the condition of solipsism, the denial of the existence of other minds (or what is the same thing, the denial of access to other minds)? Has Zukofsky, in his later poetics, abandoned the informational aspect of "good poetry," "definite information on the subject dealt with, on the movement of the lines of verse, and on the emotion of verbal construction" (*TP* 89)? Is his later poetry, as Leggott and Rieke argue, merely a surface of nonsense, screening a set of submerged structures, buried treasures to reward the dedicated hierophant?

An approach to "A"-23 that would recuperate this work into an ethics of readerly reception—and I believe an attempt at such a recuperation is essential, if only to determine to what degree the work escapes a self-consuming solipsism—must begin by again returning to Zukofsky's statements on the "music" of poetry. Such an approach, I believe, will reveal that one of the achievements of Zukofsky's later poetics is to rethink the relationship of text and reader, and simultaneously to reconceive the sort of knowledge the poem conveys, the information by which it is "informed" and which it "informs." While this poetics does not present us quite with the "blank questions about the nature of human speech [and] about the status of signification" that Steiner finds, for instance, in Celan, it does work to reconceive the basis of such questions: a related reconception begins in the works of Stein and Joyce and is being further explored and expanded by writers of the Language movement.[8]

"A"-22 and -23 are companion movements, as is evident both from their original publication in a single volume and their formal similarities. Each movement has exactly one thousand lines, and those lines—each of five words—are formed from the simple word-count prosody that, from "A"-14 forward, Zukofsky increasingly favors. The two movements are of epic breadth, aiming to fold in both the universal and the personal, as plotted along a six-thousand-year time line.[9] Ahearn characterizes "A"-22 as "nothing less than Zukofsky's attempt to translate nature into English" (*Zukofsky's "A"* 189). "A"-22 is a natural history that moves from the first emergence of a volcanic island—

> surge sea erupts boiling molten
> lava island from ice, land
> seen into color thru day
> and night
> ["A"-22, 511]

—to a vacation on a similarly formed island, where a hurricane echoes the eruptive force of the first island's birth:

> Idlers of extinct volcanic island
> thinking quincunx when a flash
> hurricane bid early tea
> ["A"-22, 533]

It is also an exploration of human culture in its relationship to nature, in particular the development of the most fundamentally enabling of human traits: language. "A"-22 traces, through fragments, quotations, and piths, the history of human natural philosophy, considered above all as the linguistic systems by which people strive to make sense of and find ways of living in the natural world. And while this history makes use of the words of many prominent thinkers—Pythagoras, Lucretius, Aristotle, Spinoza, and Sir Thomas Browne among those immediately recognizable—it does so for the most part without naming them.

This is an essential element of Zukofsky's method in "A"-22 and -23, the tracing of history without the "impertinence" of specific naming: "History's best emptied of names' / impertinence met on the ways" ("A"-22, 511). So while both "A"-22 and -23 trace, in their own ways, specific "histories," they do so for the most part without the specification of particular names. At the same time, however, Zukofsky (the poet as horse) is impatient with historiographical theorization and generalizing:

>   No knowledge but
> intimate pleasure, tho a trained

horse's no stone, takes trouble—
historic abstraction riffles his mane—
["A"-22, 517]

These histories are histories traced through specific linguistic moments—moments that have given or give the horse/poet/reader "intimate pleasure"—rather than overarching theories or narratives. What this amounts to, then, is that "A"-22 and -23 are chronologically plotted assemblages of linguistic material ("centos"), each of which traces the history of a given aspect of language: "A"-22, the language of natural philosophy; and "A"-23, the language of poetry.

Although it is possible to go through these sections and restore the "names," to identify the sources of Zukofsky's material, such a reading merely reasserts the "impertinence" of the names that Zukofsky has carefully "emptied" out of his text and reasserts the egos of the authors—himself among them—that Zukofsky wishes to condense to their textual traces. The "key" to "A"-23 is not source hunting but concentrated reading:

why deny what you've not
tried: read, not into, it:
desire until all be bright
["A"-22, 528]

Approaching "A"-23 with an awareness of the corpus of Zukofsky's previous work, an ear sensitive to the sounds and movements of his words, and an openness to the multiple readings that his syntax continually demands, one should be able to tease out and untangle many of the musical and conceptual structures that constitute the movement. Such an approach is most definitely not, in Leggott's words, merely "staying on the surface and admiring the configurations" (90) but is an attempt to engage the Zukofskyan text on its own terms, to put Zukofsky's poetry to the "test" of communicability that his own attacks on philosophical skepticism demand.

"A"-23 begins by invoking once again the musiclike structures of earlier sections of *"A"*, clearly signaling Zukofsky's intention that this, the last movement of his long poem, will function to bring together the most crucial themes of the earlier sections, just as Celia's "A"-24 constitutes a recapitulation of the themes of his work as a whole:[10]

> An unforeseen delight a round
> beginning ardent: to end blest
> presence less than nothing thrives:
> a world worn in whose
> happiest reins preempt their histories
>
> which cannot help or hurt
> a foreseen curve where many
> loci would dispose and *and's*
> compound creature and creature together.
> ["A"-23, 536]

The poem, which began with the words "A round" ("A"-1, 1), written by a young poet "ardent" for creation ("Desire longing for perfection" ["A"-1, 2]), is being brought to its conclusion, a conclusion "unforeseen" by the twenty-four-year-old of "A"-1. While the poem began "ardent," it is "to end blest" in a spirit of domestic harmony. By the device of *apo koinou,*[11] "blest" attaches itself both to the "round," the song-form of the poem, and to the "presence"—Celia, one assumes, the "blest presence" who has presided over the bulk of the poem. The "reins" of the horse/poet, here driven by the "world worn" rather than master of his own destiny, "preempt" "their histories," the unnamed sources whose presences neither "help [n]or hurt" the body of the poem, "a foreseen curve." While the specific shapes of the individual sections of *"A"* were "unforeseen" to the young Zukofsky, its overall twenty-four-section structure was clear to him early on: according to Ahearn, the oldest surviving outline for *"A"*, proposing little more than a long poem of twenty-four sections, dates back to 1927 or 1928 (*Zukofsky's "A"* 38). That "curve" is a shape on which Zukofsky has "disposed" the "many loci" of his quotations and borrowings, stringing together the various textual manifestations of *natura naturata* through the implied "and" of parataxis: "and *and's* / compound creature and creature together" (such "and's," merely implied in Zukofsky's method, are one of the most striking elements of *The Cantos:* "And then went down to the ship").

These first lines of "A"-23, in addition to announcing the theme and status of the movement, also invoke the fugue of "A"-12. As Ahearn notes, three of the four elements of the B-A-C-H theme are present here: "ardent," "blest," and "happiest" (*Zukofsky's "A"* 191). All that remains to make the equation complete is C, Celia, who appears two pages later (in anagrammatical form) as "what / submerged name in coldénia" ("A"-23, 538). Zukofsky implies here—in a manner analogous to that in the unfinished restatement of the B-A-C-H theme which begins on page 231 of "A"-12—that what follows, however far afield it may seem to go from its starting point, will constitute a structurally fuguelike resolution to the work at hand. In the case of "A"-23, that work at hand is the whole of *"A"*. This is driven home by the passages of the movement that deal directly with the harmonious resolution of apparent dissonance:

> by *heart-strings* 13 frets
> propound a law of 'all'
> and each fret tuned singly
> salves fret or singularly frets
> to salve thing to End
> dissonance harmonized:
> ["A"-23, 558]

The "13 frets" are the markers on a fingerboard that represent the ideal of equal temperament, or "propound a law of 'all.' " They suggest as well the thirteen sections of *"A"*, from "A"-11 to "A"-23, written in the period when the Zukofsky family had reached its full number of three (Paul Zukofsky was born in 1943)—the "13 frets" to which Zukofsky subjected his wife and son, whose luck was to find his own voice on the violin, a "fretless" instrument. The poet himself, in the hoariest of Romantic clichés, plays on his own "heart-strings," and those of his readers. Each section, "tuned singly," works to "salve fret," as Zukofsky celebrates his domestic happiness, and each of the thirteen, culminating in the present movement, struggles ("frets") to bring about a harmonious conclusion: "to salve thing to End / dissonance harmonized."

The dissonances that the horse/poet seeks to harmonize are

not primarily within his own family, at least in this movement of the poem, but between the various "voices" that make up the history he is assembling. His method of harmonizing them is at the base of "A"-23's poetics. The first step is the "emptying" of "names' impertinence" and the reduction of authorial egos (Zukofsky's included) to unnamed voices. What the method of "A"-23 allows Zukofsky to glimpse is the possibility of real dialogue among the voices of his source materials; without their names, names which immediately situate them within a hierarchical, chronological, and hegemonical construction of "literary history," these voices are able to breathe in their original measures (as does Zukofsky's Catullus) and thereby to sound their original music—in a history that takes the form of a "persistent noise" rather than a chronicle of names—achieving a true measure of community:

> tongues commonly inaccurate talk viable
> one to one, ear to
> eye loving song greater than
>
> anything
> ["A"-23, 537]

Paradoxically perhaps, the "lov[e of] song" Zukofsky manifests in combining all these voices into a one-thousand-line extended "song" is precisely what allows the voices to emerge individually and talk one to another.

On one level, of course, this community takes the form of an unspoken, invisible dialogue among Zukofsky's sources, similar to the compressed dialogue among fragments that makes up so much of Pound's later Cantos.[12] For instance, the following short passage—

> An art of honor, laud—
> 'pleasures do' wit's joy accord:
> so on hand-vowed integrities, unaltered
> syllables, the tended wrist, fires'
> light rest
> ["A"-23, 560–61]

—constitutes a conversation among Rabelais, Wyatt, and the sixteenth-century Spanish writer Luis de Leon, whom Zukofsky cites in his lecture on Wallace Stevens (see Leggott 138–39). It is abundantly clear, both from Leggott's and Rieke's careful and revealing work and from the radically patchwork, "crazed" surface of the text that such a conversation is going on, invisible to our ears (as Nick Bottom might say) at every point of the movement.[13] What is more important to this nameless history is the fact that all of the voices have been incorporated into a single text "sounding" one piece of music—a piece that, while every individual element is borrowed, is identifiably Zukofsky's:

> the saving history
> not to deny the gifts
> of time where those who
> never met together may hear
> this other time sound *one*.
> sn["A"-23, 539]

This oneness among particulars, a principle that in its broadest form underlies the entire doctrine of the Poundian ideogram, is also the underpinning of all the notions of music and poetry that Zukofsky holds dear: the fugue, with its overall form achieved through the sounding of various individual themes; the objectlike poem, "Inextricably the direct of historic and contemporary particulars" ("A"-6, 24); and the grand construction of *"A"*, made out of a more disparate collection of materials and forms than any other poetic work of its scale.

But this use of the many to create the one—the "A"—is neither a totalitarian strategy, as some have argued of the poetics of *The Cantos,* nor a heroic effort to make it all "cohere." As Don Byrd points out, "the design of *'A'* is not deductive but accretional" ("Getting Ready" 302), or as Leggott phrases it (in a somewhat different context), *"A"* is "multiplicity unbowed by homogeneity" (51). This accretionary aspect of Zukofsky's poetics, the continual openness to contingency and the absence of an overarching, totalizing structure, "den[ies] the instrumentality of language . . . [and thereby] opens the millenni[um] of language" (Byrd, "Getting Ready" 293). Byrd argues that the millennial aspect of Zukofsky's poetics (at least as manifested in *"A"*) lies in his realization that the human being's language is not merely a tool but the constitutive element of human reality, a reality that is radically contingent: "For Zukofsky, Human beings do not stand in relation to the absolute or an absolute but to the structure of the merely possible. . . . Public reality exists in the intervals which create multiplicity. Zukofsky has a kabbalistic sense of the letters of the alphabet as the constituents of public reality" (296).

It is in the light of the "millennial agitation" Byrd points out in Zukofsky's work, the concern with contingency and "the minute intervals in which linguistic decisions are made" (293), that one should view Zukofsky's decision, at the very outset of his project, to compose *"A"* in twenty-four sections. While that decision might seem on its surface a denial of contingency, a fixing of form that binds the poet from the very beginning, it functions in a precisely opposite manner. The twenty-four books are an analogue to a number of things—twenty-four books in the *Odyssey,* twenty-four hours in a day, twenty-four letters in the Greek alphabet—but are fixed to no one model. *"A"* becomes a "poem of a life"[14] in a manner far different from *The Cantos,* where only the catastrophe of the war and the Detention Training Center at Pisa could thrust Pound—wholly against his will—to center stage of his own epic. In contrast, Zukofsky projects the barest possible scaffolding—a finite number of movements into which his poem will be divided—and proceeds to live the life that will provide the materials and forms for those movements. Silliman is correct in noting that the 1927 or 1928 outline of *"A"*, proposing little more than a poem of twenty-four sections, "is not the declaration of an autobiography yet to be lived, but the mapping out of a structure: a poem to be composed in 24 parts" (*New Sentence* 144); the twenty-four-section scaffolding is the frame for an artifact rather than a life. The life to be lived, a parade of unforeseeable contingencies—"An unforeseen delight"—will provide materials to be disposed on the "foreseen curve" of the poem's twenty-four movements. The curve does not deny contingency, forcing history into a given form, but provides a context that welcomes contingency, accepting the unexpected into the ongoing whole of the poem.

Similarly, the voices of "A"-23, while they "sound one" melody over the course of the movement's one thousand lines, remain identifiably themselves, whether through the stubbornly non-English sounds of phonetic transliteration (the Arapaho of "io we hay we see / hay io we see knee" [539] or the Old English of "day urged / merriment harp-swag Almighty earthen worth" [556]), the un-American orthography and diction of direct—though "ventilated"—quotation (*"Tuning / to sounding stringe . . . Won by / his song: O framar of / the starry circle"* [555][15] or " 'We cannot meet so the / false Spirit flee, leave thee / thy integrity' " [559]), or the punning evocations of names, recalling the "dream of named history" that emerges at the end of "A"-22 (535) ("word's earth—the saving history" ["Wordsworth," "A"-23, 539], "Guide, o were / a star seem us one" ["Guido" Cavalcanti, "A"-23, 559], "two centuries teaching cold-ridge inventoried" ["Coleridge," "A"-23, 562], or "Praise! gill. . gam. . mesh" ["A"-23, 540]). Even here, one is careful to stress, it is a traduction of the text merely to reduce the pun to its aural equivalent. Even though this last phrase introduces a 150-line redaction of the Gilgamesh story (in which Endiku becomes "One Kid"), one cannot overlook the playful connotations of the words of the text—a "gilled" siren, perhaps, her Brooklynese "gams" in fishnet stockings.

Leggott suggests that Zukofsky's motive in "emptying" history of "names' impertinence" is to tell a history only of things he loves, avoiding the "hated things taking / more space than their worth / 'politic reasons whore' " ("A"-23, 562) (Leggott 57–58). Even so, Zukofsky preserves a "dream of named history" that leads him to find Celia (*"there / she's hid"*) in *The Tempest*'s "*still-vext Bermoothes*" ("A"-22, 535). This "dream"—a vision of naming that would simultaneously remain innocent of the "Histories [which] dye the streets" ("A"-23, 563)—reappears as well at the end of "A"-23. These twenty-six lines, the last purely verbal passage of *"A"*, consist of the most substantial burst of naming of either "A"-22 or "A"-23:

A living calendar, names inwreath'd
Bach's innocence longing Handel's untouched.
Cue in new-old quantities—'Don't
bother me'—Bach quieted bothered;
since Eden gardens labor, For
series distributes harmonies, attraction Governs

destinies. Histories dye the streets:
intimate whispers magnanimity flourishes: doubts'
passionate Judgment, passion the task.
Kalenderes enlumined 21-2-3, *nigher . . fire*—
Land or—sea, air—gathered.
Most art, object-the-mentor, donn'd one—
smiles ray *immaterial Nimbus . . Oes*
sun-pinned to red threads—thrice-urged
posato (poised) 'support from the
source'—horn-note out of a
string (Quest returns answer—'to
rethink the Caprices') *sawhorses silver*
all these fruit-tree tops: consonances
and dissonances only of degree, never-
Unfinished hairlike water of notes
vital free as Itself—impossible's
sort-of think-cramp work x: moonwort:
music, thought, drama, story, poem
parks' sunburst—animals, grace notes—
z-sited path are but us.
["A"-23, 562–63]

These twenty-six lines are "A living calendar, names inwreath'd," and their immediate model is Chaucer's "An A.B.C.," the "K" stanza of which begins "*K*alenderes enlumined ben they."[16] Among the persons named, punned on, or alluded to, are Bach and Handel ("Bach's innocence longing Handel's untouched" ["A"-23, 562]); Richard Eden, author of *History of Travaile* (1577) ("Eden gardens labor"); Charles-Marie Fourier, inventor of the *gamme,* or Fourier series ("For / series distributes harmonies, attraction Governs / destinies"); Walter Savage Landor ("Land or—sea, air"); Mozart ("Most art, object-the-mentor"); John Donne ("donn'd one"); Paul Zukofsky, whose aim in recording Paganini is "to / rethink the Caprices";[17] and Celia Zukofsky, the five voices of whose *L.Z. Masque* ("A"-24) are "music, thought, drama, story, poem" ("A"-23, 563).[18]

These names in themselves constitute a musical close to the poem, summing up the texts, figures, and ideas that have inspired, informed, and motivated the poet. But while the passage seems to invite us to read it as a series of namings, an Easter egg hunt of finding the figures in the carpet, a mere enumeration of the personages concealed in the passage might cause one to overlook what the language is actually signifying, and signifying in a multivalent manner that is obscured when one views this "calendar" as a simple parade of *lares penatesque*. One cannot ignore the "naming" aspect of these twenty-six lines—that much is announced irrefutably in the first line, "A living calendar, *names* inwreath'd." Yet these lines constitute a "fugal" close to the poem—a close, like that of "A"-12, recapitulating ideas and themes introduced earlier in the poem—that exists on a semantic, as well as a hermetic, level. When one reads the lines straight through, paying close attention to what they signify as syntactic strings, it becomes clear that they recapitulate both the nameless "histories" of "A"-22 and -23 and the poetics of "A" as a whole.

The "calendar" begins with a series of statements on creation, labor, and the labor of the poet and continues "A"'s long-standing theme of the nature of poetic creation. "Bach's innocence longing Handel's untouched": Bach, whose music is both the scaffolding and the focus of so much of "A", is "innocent," but with an innocence that desires, or "longs"—"Desire longing for perfection" ("A"-1, 2). Handel's own innocence is "untouched"—that composer is known (perhaps wrongly) for a certain stolidity in comparison to Bach, his contemporary—or perhaps Handel himself is "untouched," for Celia has left Handel's "Harpsichord Pieces" unchanged in her "A"-24. The poet's own method, and the method of any poet ("The shape of his ground seems to have been / A constant for all dead horses" ["A"-12, 175]), is to "Cue in new-old quantities," to make the new out of the "constant" "grounds" of poetic composition and to insert, as one "cues" up a record, the textual "grafts" that make up his poem, at once "old" and "new" in their renewed context.[19] The artist's petulant cry, " 'Don't / bother me,' " is a necessary accompaniment to the privacy of composition, the "bothering" that both Bach and Zukofsky engage in: "Bach quieted bothered."[20] The necessity for such labor, as Milton and other Puritans were fond of pointing out, stems from the Adamic fall—"since Eden gardens labor" (taking "since" in a chronological sense and "gardens" as a metonym for those who labor therein); however, "labor" itself, both poetic and physical, is informed by a millennial vision, is "gardened"—

cultivated, nurtured—by a hope for a new paradise, a second Eden (perhaps the "second paradise"—Paracelsus's term for "the striving for wisdom"—that first appears in "A"-11 ["A"-11, 125; see Ahearn, *Zukofsky's "A"* 123]). That same "gardening" is evident in the organization of the world, both harmonic and passional: "series distributes harmonies, attraction Governs / destinies." As Zukofsky phrases it in "A"-12,

> The order that rules music, the same
>   controls the placing of the stars and the feathers
>   in a bird's wing.
> In the middle of harmony
> Most heavenly music
> For the universe is true enough.
> ["A"-12, 128]

History, however, is a chronicle of bloody events—"Histories dye the streets"—and "magnanimity" cheapens intimacy by "flourishing" "intimate whispers." Alternatively, when true intimacy exists between subjects, when one can "whisper" to another in an "intimate" setting, "magnanimity flourishes." The poet's "task" as a subject in history is "passion," a passion that arises out of "doubts"—discriminations, the perceptions of "degrees" of difference—and gives rise to the "passionate Judgment" that enables him both to compose his artifact and to live as a responsible citizen of the world. The poet is never outside history, even when he chooses to represent that history as a nameless textual "noise," and while Zukofsky may have abandoned the overtly political stance of early sections of *"A"*, the "horse"'s responsibility to his fellow humans is reiterated here, even though that responsibility may take the ostensibly attenuated form of making "passionate Judgments" about the world in which he lives.

"Kalenderes enlumined 21-2-3, *nigher"*—these twenty-six lines are obviously a calendar, and so is the entirety of "A"-21, -22, and -23: while "A"-22 and -23 constitute broad historical "calendars," "A"-21, a translation of Plautus's *Rudens*, is a bringing together of Plautus, Shakespeare's *Pericles*, and the immediately contemporary, in the form of the poet and his family. These three movements stand apart from "A"-1 through -20 and consti-

tute an approach *"nigher"* to the grand summation of "A"-24, a work in which all the elements (*"fire—* / Land or—sea, air") are "gathered." Empedocles' four constitutive elements are of course crucial to the "natural history" of "A"-22 and have earlier served, as Ahearn points out, as one of the organizing principles of "A"-12 (*Zukofsky's "A"* 126, 212–14). The next line seems to be an address, a series of vocative appositives. Something of "Most art" is addressed, an entity of which the "object" is the "mentor": this is, perhaps, the Objectivist poem, "the resolving of words and their ideation into structure" (*P* 13), a structure inextricably associated with sound—"donn'd." (According to the *OED*, "donne" is an obsolete form of "dun," one of whose meanings is "to sound, ring with sound, resound.") And the emotional bonds and interactions represented by "smiles" are crucial to the poet's work; they "ray *immaterial Nimbus*," giving out a cloud of goodwill, a context in which the poet might work. He composes in a phenomenal, physical world: "*Oes* / sun-pinned to red threads." The *"Oes,"* perhaps the eyes of his family, certainly the *o*es of his lines of verse—as in "Most art, object-the-mentor, donn'd one," a line in which *o* takes at least four phonetic shapes—are "pinned" to the "red threads" of the sunlight, an echo of the "rays" that emanate from "smiles." The poet is "poised" (as the violinist is *Posato*) because of his rootedness, the "support from a source" on which he can depend.

The poet's "Quest," the forty-six-year labor of *"A"*, has returned an "answer," a formulation of what the poet-horse has been up to all along: "to / rethink the Caprices," to reconceive the "capricious" poetics of his occasional lyrics, to "rethink" a context in which the "Caprices" of the events of his life and his reading can be contained and presented. With this clear conception of his aim, and with a strong assurance of the "support" that is behind him, the poet can produce (as can the violinist) a "horn-note out of a / string": *"sawhorses silver / all these fruit-tree tops."*[21] The "sawhorses" of "A"-7 reappear here. In their first appearance, they were "Street Closed" barriers that the poet's verbal imagination could transform into live horses: "Horses: who will do it? out of manes? Words / Will do it, out of manes, out of airs"; "No horse is here, no horse is there? / Says you! Than I—fellow me, airs! we'll make / Wood horse, and recognize it with our words"

("A"-7, 39).[22] While the seven sonnets of "A"-7 put these horses through dazzling imaginative paces, the most striking aspect of that movement is its steady self reflexiveness, the poet's explicit acknowledgment that this alchemy is solely a verbal matter: "horses seven . . . trot—trot— / Spoke: words, words, we are words, horses, manes, words" ("A"-7, 42). (The verbal existence of the poem is no new discovery. The classic statement of it is of course Mallarmé's, who is said to have told Degas—who despaired of turning his sublime ideas into poems—that poems are made not of ideas but of *words*. Or, as Osbert Sitwell once remarked, "may I ask of what else should Miss Sitwell's poems consist but 'words, words, words'—dead larks, tea cozies, antimacassars, and fragments of a stage elephant?" [quoted in Jonathan Williams, *In the Azure* 11].) The sawhorses stand as emblem of the power of the poet's art, and the magic of his accomplishment is reflected in his perception of the physical world "silvered" by the combinatory metamorphosis of words: *"sawhorses silver / all these fruit-tree tops."* (Such a vision works backward, as well, as the wood of the trees may itself one day go to form humble sawhorses.) One is unable to resist hearing an outburst of punning enthusiasm here, the poet crying "Hi ho Silver, away!" to his "sawhorses."

The remaining lines of "A"-23 can be seen as proposing a description of the poem itself, and of the poetics that has produced the poem:

> consonances
> and dissonances only of degree, never-
> Unfinished hairlike water of notes
> vital free as Itself—impossible's
> sort-of think-cramp work x: moonwort:
> music, thought, drama, story, poem
> parks' sunburst—animals, grace notes—
> z-sited path are but us.

As a "poem of a life," the work is necessarily "Unfinished" as long as the poet lives, although as a fully realized, objectlike "context," it remains "vital free as Itself"—"never- / Unfinished." The music of themes and of melopœia, systems of perceived differences—

"consonances /and dissonances only of degree"—makes up a tapestry of intertextually woven threads, "hairlike water of notes." The work as a whole, "impossible's / sort-of think-cramp work x," or in a more organicist metaphor, "moonwort"—appropriately, the plant Honesty—is described in the final summary:

> music, thought, drama, story, poem
> parks' sunburst—animals, grace notes—
> z-sited path are but us.

It is all here: the constitutive elements of the work, "music, thought, drama, story, poem" (which are also, looking forward, the five constituent "voices" of "A"-24); the immediate natural context of the poet's life, the "parks' sunburst"; and the elements of chance contingency—"animals"—that have entered the poem as "grace notes," bringing to mind in particular the horse (Zukofsky's preeminent symbol of "grace," in a theological as well as an aesthetic sense), a textual marker that functions both as literary allusion and as metaphorical cipher—Bottom's "as true as truest horse" and the poet as "bent dray-horse" ("A"-12, 560), who, "A"-12 reminds us, "has large eyes [the better, no doubt, to see with] / Man's virtue his feeling" ("A"-12, 181). Together they constitute the "z-sited path"—the poet's signature again—that is a shared dwelling place for the poet, his family, and his readers—"are but us."

Nowhere is the "multiplicity of meaning" Comens invokes or the reader's "active performance" that Byrd describes as evident as in the experience of reading "A"-23. At almost every point, one is confronted with a range of possible readings and interpretations, no one of which can claim absolute or exclusive validity. This makes my reading of the final passage of "A"-23—and any such reading—profoundly provisional, incomplete. As Byrd points out, Zukofsky works not toward an "absolute" but toward "the structure of possibilities . . . the instituting concrete multiplicity, the crystalline logic of language itself" ("Getting Ready" 299). "We are accustomed," Byrd writes, "to reading poetry as listening to a ghost. Our eyes follow the line of words, but, in our minds' eyes, we see airy sprites rise and speak, act, witness to a world we do not see. In *'A'*, we are asked to read words—to perform, to fill the space where words have their full-bodied and disruptive existence and where the moving human body finds its proper sphere" (307). Whatever else might be the merits of "sourcing" Zukofsky's text, it is clear that such activity—viewed as an end in itself—works to immediately short-circuit the "performative," creative aspect of reading *"A"*—or as Byrd suggests, following the poet Jed Rasula, "wreading" *"A"* ("Getting Ready" 291). While these textual grafts are never completely separable from their original context—as Derrida points out when speaking of "textual samples," which "are not being applied upon the surface or in the interstices of a text that would already exist without them," "Each grafted text continues to radiate back toward the site of its removal" (*Dissemination* 33)—their meaningful potential is expanded and complicated by the most immediate and important context in which they appear to a reader: that of Zukofsky's own text, a poem that arises out of a "desire to place everything—everything aptly, perfectly, belonging within, one with, a context" (*P* 15).

The "participatory" reading that *"A"* demands, in Byrd's account (also Comens's and Quartermain's), is in itself a sufficient refutation of the charges of solipsism that might be brought against "A"-23. Far from being a private or hermetic text, accessible only to initiates or family members, "A"-23 stands as a fundamentally democratic text, one that solicits a proactive participation on the part of its readers, thereby working to dismantle any model of the poem's meaning as verbal commodity passed from poet/producer to reader/consumer. The reader, that is, is no longer a passive consumer of the text but an equal participant in the construction of its meaning. In their engagement with this text, readers are implicated in a community that includes not only the reader and the poet but the whole range of voices that have gone into the "weaving" of the textual "web." Zukofsky implies something of this community in "A Statement for Poetry" when he writes, "The best way to find out about poetry is to read the poems. That way the reader becomes something of a poet himself: not because he 'contributes' to the poetry, but because he finds himself subject of its energy" (*P* 23). This participation in the poem's "energy," which Zukofsky proposes as a necessary part of any reading of poetry, is an element that takes center stage in the last sections of *"A"*. As reader, one is thrown back upon one's own resources in the navigation of the verse's diction, syntax, and unfamiliar/familiar syntactic "content," and one becomes a determining force in the direction of the "energy" that in "A"-23 pushes, often in the space of a single line, in various divergent and sometimes self-contradictory directions.

One might speak of "A"-23 as approaching the asymptotic limit of the "writerly" text that Roland Barthes defines in *S/Z:* "the writerly text is *ourselves writing,* before the infinite play of the world (the world as function) is traversed, intersected, stopped, plasticized by some singular system (Ideology, Genus, Criticism) which reduces the plurality of entrances, the opening of networks, the infinity of languages" (5). But Barthes is clear in asserting that the absolutely writerly text does not actually exist; it is merely a limit that can be more or less closely approached: "There may be nothing to say about writerly texts. First of all, where can we find them? Certainly not in reading (or at least very rarely: by accident, fleetingly, obliquely in certain limit-works): the writerly text is not a thing, we would have a hard time finding it in a bookstore" (5). A reading of "A"-23, then, should not be confused with a process of simple free association or improvisation, although those processes certainly have their place in one's approach to the poem. The movement is not a Rorschach blot or a space for infinite readerly free play, for the reader's progress is at all points bounded and guided by the contingencies of the poem's structure, the musical crossing of reference and theme that Zukofsky has spent the whole of *"A"* refining and complicating. Reading the movement straight through, for instance, one is always confronted by the noise of reference, quotation, and transliteration. The extent of one's acquaintance with Western literature, and of one's acquaintance with Zukofsky's habitual sources and themes, will to a great degree determine to what extent such passages as the one beginning "Rose spume's disarmed enamored readiness" ("A"-23, 555) will appear as textual paraphrase, as naggingly familiar but unidentifiable static, or as simple improvisation, to be read solely in terms of its own syntax and semantic value. The text itself enforces no single one of these levels, and richly rewards readerly participation on each, as long as the reader retains the openness to ambiguity and indirection that the work's texture enforces. What binds the text together is not a semantic resolution, an overarching narrative or story (such as the multiple narratives of economics, sexuality, and so on, that structure *The Cantos*), but, on the one hand, a continual textual contingency in which the reader is at all points drawn into an extraordinarily active role in constituting the text's meaning, and, on the other hand, a musiclike structuring, a counterpointing of language and themes that extends and rarifies the "fugal" texture of the earliest sections of *"A"*.

Any poem exists as a source of "knowledge" or "information," as Zukofsky points out in "A Statement": "[good poetry] is precise information on existence out of which it grows, and information of its own existence, that is, the movement (and tone) of words" (*P* 20). What "A"-22 and -23 reveal is that this conception of "information" has never depended on a simplistic commodity model of information in which the reader simply receives what the poem has to offer. The knowledge bound up with the poem's form and structure, qua poem, is a musical knowledge, and the poem, inviting the reader to distinguish among the multiple horizons of meaning present in its own language, constitutes the experience of reading as analogous to that of listening. (One of those horizons of meaning lies in the melopœia of words themselves, of course; Zukofsky notes that "the sound and pitch emphasis of a word are never apart from its meaning" [*P* 17].) Listening to a piece of music, or reading a poem, is a matter of perceiving differences: degrees of tonality, harmony, timbre; of diction, vocabulary, syntax. The poem itself, like music—and language as a whole, in Saussure's model—is a system of such distinctions: "consonances / and dissonances only of degree" ("A"-23, 563).

Zukofsky's epistemology and his poetics are based on this awareness of differences and distinctions: "[The poet's] ear is sincere, if his words convey his awareness of the range of differences and subtleties of duration" (*P* 23), and "Good verse is determined by the poet's susceptibilities involving a precise awareness of the differences, forms and possibilities of existence—words with their own attractions included" (*P* 7). One might argue, wholly apart from any question of "musical" structure or form, that this poetics grows out of the same fundamental perceptions of distinctions that makes music itself possible and to that extent can represent itself as "musical" in a sense that transcends analogy. The perceiving of differences that the reader actively carries out in reading "A"-23, then, is a "musical" activity. Comens, explicating the last lines of the "An-song" that begins "A"-22, describes this experience:

> As an object in process, the musical chord that ends the poem is neither means nor end, but both at once, for music is an activity that necessitates participation, and which moves toward an end while simultaneously being the end. Music, however, does not replace argument: rather, the two coexist as necessary complements throughout the poem. Just as the world is both an object of thought and an event involving each of us, words, once sounded, are both physical events and signs. ("Soundings" 105–6)

Even as one might regard a reading of the poem, as Comens does, as an experience of the tension between words as music ("physical events") and words as "argument" ("signs"), it is also clear that the musical structure Zukofsky has cultivated throughout his long poem is a major force in "A"-22 and -23. The "information" that "A"-23 conveys is "information of its own existence," a musical knowledge that involves both the melopœic "movement (and tone) of words" and the analogically musical counterpointing of themes, voices, and textual fragments. Whereas such information might seem to bear little resemblance to poetry's other responsibility ("precise information on existence out of which it grows"), the exact opposite is true, although admittedly "A"-23 might seem to have nothing in common with the realist, purely recording aesthetic that such a phrase suggests. The poem is "Inextricably the result of historic and contemporary particulars," but this does not imply that it must constitute a simple presentation of those particulars; the poet's "major aim is not to show himself but that order that of itself can speak to all men" (*P* 8), and that universally communicable order, in Zukofsky's poetics, is always a musical one. As Hatlen notes, for Zukofsky "To 'make sense' is to make a pattern that the sense can apprehend with delight" (*LZMP* 348): a pattern, a musical shape, by no means *non*sensical.

The "particulars" with which Zukofsky works are not events, speeches, and personages—as presented, say, in the works of his fellow Objectivist Charles Reznikoff—but textual moments, fragments of language that Zukofsky has concatenated into a seamless, but "crazed," musical structure. The principle of this structure—an "order that of itself can speak to all men"—is present from the very beginning of *"A"* and stands as Zukofsky's single strongest repudiation of the solipsism of hermeticism. In addition, the radically "writerly," participatory nature of the texture "A"-23 presents to the reader implicates that reader as coproducer of the text, "subject of [the poem's] energy" to a greater degree than in any of Zukofsky's earlier works. When one approaches "A"-23 as reader, one makes oneself a willing participant in the perception of differences that lies at the base of Zukofsky's poetics, and one is received into an epistemological community that revolves around a shared epistemic commitment to the sensed degrees of difference among words, vocabularies, realms of discourse, and speaking human subjects. The "music, thought, drama, story, poem . . . z-sited path" of Zukofsky's poem, indeed, "are but us."

Zukofsky Among the Poets

10

"A Sense of Duration"

Zukofsky, Stevens, and "Language"

I care for neither fugues nor feathers.
—Wallace Stevens, "Lytton Strachey, Also, Enters into Heaven" (*Opus Posthumous* 71)

Zukofsky's last published piece of literary criticism, like his first, is an homage to an older poet: the essay "For Wallace Stevens," first delivered on 29 April 1971, "on the occasion of the Eighth Annual Wallace Stevens Memorial Program and Awards to young poets, sponsored by the Department of English of the University of Connecticut at Storrs and the Hartford Insurance Group" (*P* 24). His presence at this seemingly unlikely occasion had been arranged by, among others, Marcella Booth (formerly Spann), a faculty member at the University of Connecticut and erstwhile associate of Ezra Pound (she coedited with him the anthology *Confucius to Cummings*), at work at the time on a catalogue of the University of Texas's Zukofsky holdings. The fulsome praise Zukofsky accords Stevens in his talk, then, *could* be read as part of the language of the visiting lecturer, as much homage to the event as to the subject thereof. But some of the lecture's statements speak to the heart of Zukofsky's poetic career: "Reading [Stevens] for the last three months," Zukofsky notes, "I felt that my own writing, without my being aware of it, was closer to his than to that of any of my contemporaries in the last half century of life we shared together" (*P* 27). What can Zukofsky mean by this confession of "closeness"? The "last half century of life" the two poets shared was from 1904 (Zukofsky's birth) to 1956 (Stevens's death). How are we meant to compare "Notes Toward a Supreme Fiction" and "A"-12, or "Owl's Clover" and " 'Mantis' "? Stevens certainly never shared Zukofsky's closeness with Pound or his post-Poundian poetics of quotation and juxtaposition, nor did Zukofsky share Stevens's taste for airy, Shelleyan speculations on the relationship between the "reality" outside the human consciousness and the "imagination" that shapes it into form.

Perhaps the intellectual concern with consciousness and the world outside, despite Zukofsky's very different approach to the question, is indeed the deepest point of coincidence between Zukofsky and Stevens—deeper even than the investment in tangible, melopœic language that Alan Golding finds they share, or the ludic, clownlike humor P. Michael Campbell traces in their works. As disparate as their generational positions, social milieus, and poetics may be, both poets are heavily invested in questions of epistemology. Stevens's formulation of and investment in the problem of knowledge is most succinctly summarized in the subtitle of *The Necessary Angel:* "Essays on Reality and the Imagination." But this very formulation is as well an index of the differences between the two writers. Whereas Zukofsky invariably refers to epistemological questions in the specifically philosophical vocabulary of "knowledge" and "epistemology," Stevens casts the dialectic that informs his works in fundamentally Romantic terms: the "imagination" he invokes always bears some reference to Coleridge's "imagination," "the living power and prime agent of all human perception . . . a repetition in the finite mind of the eternal act of creation in the infinite I AM" (*Biographia Literaria* 167). Joseph Riddel stresses the degree to which Stevens's conception of the poetic task diverges from that of the Romantics; his particular modernism "makes claims for the imagination in terms which reflect the degeneration, from Coleridge to the present, of the romantic vision. . . . Whatever else one can say of Stevens' debt to Coleridge, the fact that he finds the source of imaginative light . . . to be wholly human is a signal difference" (30). However, to argue that Stevens's work reflects the "degeneration . . . of the romantic vision" emphasizes both the degree to which that poet is initially invested in that

Romantic vision and his work's clear continuity with the Romanticism of Keats, Shelley, Wordsworth, and Coleridge. That Stevens's most important poetic influences are the English Romantic poets is a critical commonplace, and this genealogical and thematic continuity allows many readers to place Stevens centrally in a Romantic tradition and to read the tropes and movements of his poems as revisions of those of his English forebears.

Zukofsky, in contrast, implicitly participates in the large-scale critical devaluation of Romanticism that Pound instigated and Eliot sought to make orthodoxy. Pound's "text-book" of poetry, the *ABC of Reading*, for instance, does not include a single poem by a major Romantic poet (unless that assessment is stretched to include Landor). Eliot, famously, works to disestablish the reputation of Milton, the most important influence on the Romantics, and to supplant him (presumably) with Dryden. Eliot's famous 1936 essay on Milton concludes, and not wryly, that "although [Milton's] work realizes superbly an important element in poetry, he may still be considered as having done damage to the English language from which it has not wholly recovered" (*On Poetry and Poets* 164). In general, the high modernism of Pound and Eliot represents itself as a breaking away from the models of Romanticism, and Zukofsky's readers, many of whom come to him from Pound, tend therefore to place him in a context of poets for whom Romanticism is literary history rather than an active influence and environment.

Stevens was born twenty-five years before Zukofsky, and his reading habits were honed principally on the Romantics and their Victorian epigones. When *Harmonium* appeared in 1923, showing the insurance executive "thawing out so beautifully at forty" (in Williams's cutting phrase [*Imaginations* 27]), Zukofsky was a precocious nineteen-year-old at Columbia and had written only two of the poems that would survive into his mature collections. That crucial quarter-century difference in age accounts for much of the disparity between the two poets; in many respects, Stevens remains a child of the Victorian era, while Zukofsky is thoroughly twentieth century. (Edward Mendelson is, I believe, presumptuous when he calls Auden rather than Zukofsky "The first poet writing in English who felt at home in the twentieth century" [Auden, *Selected Poems* ix].) The cultural milieu in which Zukofsky came of age was not that of Stephen Foster, Bliss Carman, and Sarah Bernhardt, as it was for Stevens, but that of Krazy Kat, E. E. Cummings, Charlie Chaplin, and the frenetic cultural ferment of the American 1920s.

Zukofsky was also nineteen years younger than Pound, with whom he is so often associated, and twenty-one years younger than Williams, a close friend and sometime collaborator. The "rightness" we feel in identifying Zukofsky with those two figures, and conversely the initial strangeness of coupling him with Stevens, are largely the result of canon-constructing forces within the American academy rather than a dispassionate analysis of the field of modern American poetry. These forces are responsible for the "split" in twentieth-century American poetic camps that Marjorie Perloff has emphasized so polemically in her essay "Pound/Stevens: Whose Era?" (*Dance of the Intellect* 1–32). This rift, it seems to me, is only an apparent one: it should be regarded not as an actual division within the communities of practicing poets but as an ex post facto critical formulation in which opposing camps of critics construct mutually exclusive canons of modernism (Helen Vendler and Harold Bloom, say, versus Hugh Kenner and Donald Davie). As Norman Finkelstein notes, "the 'tradition' of Stevens or the 'tradition' of Pound are . . . critical fictions, to which active poets rarely subordinate themselves" (*Utopian Moment* 142). Nonetheless, it is difficult to deny how often Zukofsky is still identified, both biographically and stylistically, as a "disciple of Pound." (One can be pleased at least that the era of criticism has passed in which Zukofsky's name appeared in print primarily as ammunition for those who wished to disprove Pound's anti-Semitism: one of his best friends, after all, was a Jew.)

Zukofsky's association with Pound is part of what makes his 1971 statement of admiration for Stevens's work so unexpected. It is difficult to imagine a bond of kinship among two poets whose poetics are more ostensibly dissimilar: on the one hand Stevens, for whom poetry is "an interdependence of the imagination and reality as equals" (*Necessary Angel* 27); on the other, Zukofsky, who defines poetry on occasion in the strikingly positivistic terms we have seen, "precise information on existence out of which it grows, and information of its own existence, that is, the movement (and tone) of words" (*P* 20). When Zukofsky turns his mature attention to Stevens's work, the meditation that results—the lecture "For Wallace Stevens"—provides us not only with an introduction to Zukofsky's own conception of poetic influence but a significant index of the shifts in poets' readerly practice that have accompanied American poetry's postmodern turn toward "language." These shifts are most evident in such writers as the members of the roughly defined "Language" school, poets heavily influenced by Zukofsky himself. In their own revisions of the Stevensian text, Charles Bernstein and Michael Palmer participate, unconsciously or (probably) consciously, in a movement that owes much of its instigation to Zukofsky.

In his lecture at the University of Connecticut, Zukofsky recalled that, although he had read *Harmonium* "constantly" after its first appearance in 1923, around 1936, "impatient with [Stevens's] and most anybody's use of the words *reality* and *imagination*," he "deferred" reading Stevens's further work (*P* 30, 27). Given his enduring impatience with language of the gas age, this deferral can be forgiven. Only in the three months before the lecture, when he went back and read all of Stevens's published writings, did Zukofsky realize the closeness of that work to his own.[1] That closeness, however, is not one of conceptual structure and by no means involves the interchange of "reality" and "imagination" that originally deterred him from further exploring Stevens's poetry. Zukofsky's Objectivist poetics leaves little space for the epistemological speculations to which Stevens's version of Romanticism leads. And Zukofsky's polemical rejection of epistemology, evident from the 1931 Objectivist "manifesto" to the 1968 interview with L. S. Dembo, would seem to leave him no common ground with Stevens's constant reshiftings of the balance between the "bare board" of nature's sounds and "the sweeping meanings that we add to them" (*Collected Poems* 384).

But Zukofsky's early "impatience" with the skeptical dialectics of Stevens's work gives way in his later reading to an interpretation of Stevens in which the interplay of "reality" and "imagination" becomes a merely superficial, rather than an integral, part of the poetry. In Zukofsky's reading, philosophical questions have been moved to the periphery of Stevens's work: "all his poems *affect* being involved in the old philosophical bugbear of a theory of knowledge, a question as to what (quotes) 'really' exists. To be sure his most often gay, lovely skepticism doubts its own skepticism and becomes the only kind of skepticism true to itself. . . . philosophy is not [Stevens's poems'] end, tho they *seem* to be philosophizing" (*P* 27, emphases mine). Zukofsky is unwilling to allow a "theory of knowledge" to be the center of Stevens's poetry. For him what saves that poetry from becoming pure "philosophizing"—language in its most gaseous state—is the self-reflexiveness of its skepticism. For Zukofsky, the "only kind of skepticism true to itself," or useful to the poet in his practice, is an ironical, self-conscious one that escapes dogmatism by turning its foundational questioning upon its own premises.

Stevens criticism in general, like Zukofsky, has in the last decades sought to shift attention from the intellectual content or argument of Stevens's poems—first to the poems' own linguistic mode of existence, as analyzed by various forms of rhetorical and deconstructive criticism, and then to the complex biographical, social, historical, and ideological matrices within which the poems were composed and received. The most recent group of studies has sought to remove Stevens's work from the rarefied realms of epistemology and the theory of language by focusing on the social and political contexts within which that work was produced, the specific "pressures of reality" that led to the shaping of the poems (Stevens, *Necessary Angel* 20–23).[2] Like Stevens's most recent critics, Zukofsky reads Stevens willfully, against the grain of the readings that the poems and the essays seem consciously to solicit. Reading primarily as a *poet,* however, Zukofsky locates a common ground between his own work and Stevens's by finding Stevens's work most vital in the moments where it proposes a model of reading and interpretation that dovetails with Zukofsky's own conception of the event of one poet reading another.

In the course of his lecture Zukofsky quotes two Stevens poems, "The House Was Quiet and the World Was Calm" and "The Lack of Repose," in each of which the act of reading is figured as an epiphanic moment in which the reader loses consciousness of both time and identity—"The access of perfection to the page" (*P* 26, *Collected Poems* 358).

The truth in a calm world,
In which there is no other meaning, itself

Is calm, itself is summer and night, itself
Is the reader leaning late and reading there.
[*Collected Poems* 359]

This atemporal, calm, absorbed moment is what Zukofsky calls "duration," citing Spinoza's definition of duration as "an indefinite continuation of existence" (*P* 25). In Zukofsky's usage, duration is the experience of timelessness that one undergoes when reading the poem: "It is not a temporal thing, may be felt only an instant, but that instant call it love, eternity, infinity: whatever you *want*—that's it. Stevens describes that feeling" (*P* 25).[3] In the moment of "duration," then, the reader and the text become interchangeable: "in effect," in Zukofsky's words, "when the sense of duration is felt the legend on the page literally reads the reader, makes his existence while he reads the legend's existence" (*P* 25). "Duration" proposes a scene of communion that is wholly removed from actual physical and temporal coincidence, that is in Zukofsky's words wholly "contingency": "what *dures* or endures as impersonal friendship when one poet reads another is a reading removed from yet out of time, without actual influence or conscious awareness of tradition, literary handbooks, or chronometers. Both poets may not be contemporaries, only one of them actually alive—the other, legend like Shakespeare or Homer" (*P* 25). Duration involves "an instant certainty of the words of a poem bringing at least two persons and then maybe many persons, even peoples together. . . . it does not matter whether the reader is the book or the book is the reader. . . . The instant certainty of the words is all that exists for one become two" (*P* 26–27).

Zukofsky intends his remarks on duration to illuminate his own interest in Stevens's poetry and to justify his perhaps surprising avowal of kinship to a poet whose works he has scarcely mentioned for a third of a century.[4] But for Zukofsky, kinship or influence is more significantly a matter of moments of "duration" in one poet's reading of another than of membership in literary "schools" or actual firsthand, acknowledged influence. In an early statement on poetic influence, Zukofsky argues that the "conscious choice or rejection of a literary tradition" is less important than a generalized influence "in the air" or the "coincidence of the temperament affected and the temperament only apparently, not actually affecting"—a coincidence between "two similar individuals, different as to locale, and contemporary or anachronistic as to their birth and mortuary dates" (*P* 135). The places and times in which the two poets live are irrelevant to the experience of duration, since poetic values, in Zukofsky's account, are historical constants: "Naturally the values poets deal with are alike for all of them" (*P* 136). Like Eliot and especially like Pound, whose constant demands for poetic renovation are grounded in an ostensibly comprehensive conception of the literary tradition, Zukofsky conceives the body of past poetic production, to some degree, as a simultaneous whole: the contemporary poet "secretly measures himself against each word of poetry ever written" (*P* 3).

This account of influence, of course, is intimately related to Zukofsky's thoroughgoing sense of "simultaneity" (derived in part from Apollinaire). As I argued in my earlier discussions of *"A"* and *Bottom*, that simultaneity is an integral element of the collage poetic that allows him such extraordinary freedom and range in quotation and concatenation. But while Zukofsky's readings of other poets are certainly predatory and appropriative, the actual manner of his appropriations—as is clear from an examination of *"A"*—is far different from Harold Bloom's model in which a poet adapts or reverses his predecessor's tropes and movements. Zukofsky, that is to say, reads the tradition in a distinctively twentieth-century—one might venture, "postmodern"—way. Like Derrida, whose drawn-out examinations of key words and phrases of texts go against the grain of a philosophical tradition whose hallmark is the examination of arguments rather than terminology, Zukofsky reads other poets in a way that systematically subordinates their tropes, scenes, and "arguments" to the specific details of their language. This is perhaps most evident in *Bottom*, whose great masses of quotations, taken in their original contexts, by no means argue for Zukofsky's conclusion that "Shakespeare's text throughout favors the clear physical eye against the erring brain." All of these quotations, however, in some detail of their language, refer to the problematic with which

Zukofsky is dealing, and he thereby feels free to recontextualize them into the argument he is mounting. Practically any passage of Western literature or philosophy that contains one of Zukofsky's key words or concepts—"eye," "seeing," "blind," and so forth—is fair game to be appropriated for the machine of his argument, regardless of the extent to which that passage endorses—or even pertains to—*Bottom*'s thesis.

The evidence that Zukofsky brings forward to validate the "closeness" he feels between Stevens's writing and his own is characterized as well by such moments of linguistic coincidence. While "For Wallace Stevens" does not mount a single argument on anything like the monolithic scale of *Bottom*, Zukofsky's quotations from Stevens are freely recontextualized within Zukofsky's own favored spheres of thought, recontextualized according to a logic in which theme and trope are subordinated to small-scale linguistic details. At the end of his lecture, Zukofsky reads a passage of six Stevens poems, followed by an "antiphonal sequence" of six passages of his own work (*P* 37); the texts of the first group are related to those of the second by an imagistic and thematic continuity that emerges not overtly but through coincidences of linguistic detail. This relationship is evident in the parallel Zukofsky implies between a passage from *Bottom* and Stevens's "The Planet on the Table":

> Ariel was glad he had written his poems.
> They were of a remembered time
> Or of something seen that he liked.
>
> Other makings of the sun
> Were waste and welter
> And the ripe shrub writhed.
>
> His self and the sun were one
> And his poems, although makings of his self,
> Were no less makings of the sun.
>
> It was not important that they should survive.
> What mattered was that they should bear
> Some lineament or character,
>
> Some affluence, if only half-perceived,

In the poverty of their words,
Of the planet of which they were part.
[*Collected Poems* 532–33]

The next passage, from the "Continents" section of *Bottom*'s "Alphabet of Subjects," is a concatenation of quotations from More's *Utopia* and Isaiah 29:

> Οὐ Τόποσ, meaning *not place, New Atlantis,* its Governor say has "this: that by means of our solitary situation, and of the laws of secrecy . . . for our travelers . . . our rare admission of strangers, we know well most of the habitable world, and . . . are ourselves unknown." The scene of *The Tempest,* in contrast, is known: "an un-inhabited island" (Folio), "Names of the Actors" include "Ariell, an ayrie spirit."
>
> "Woe to Ariel, to Ariel, the city where David dwelt! Add ye year to year; let them kill sacrifices.
>
> Yet I will distress Ariel, and there shall be heaviness and sorrow: and it shall be unto me as Ariel. . .
>
> And thou shalt be brought down, and shalt speak out of the ground, and thy speech shall be low out of the dust, and thy voice shall be as of one that hath a familiar spirit, out of the ground, and thy speech shall whisper out of the dust.
>
> Moreover the multitude of thy strangers shall be like small dust, and the multitude of the terrible ones shall be as chaff that passeth away: yea, it shall be at an instant suddenly." (*B* 155–56, ellipses in original)

The immediate link between these two passages is the name "Ariel," for Stevens the figure of the poet, for Zukofsky the "ayrie spirit" of *The Tempest* and the name of Jerusalem, the city of David. Stevens's Ariel creates poems that "bear / Some lineament or character . . . Of the planet of which they were part" and that share the passing nature of other "makings of the sun," which are now "waste and welter." The poems' survival is far from assured—indeed, the implication is that they too shall perish. The important thing is that they, at least for the moment, should (in Zukofsky's words) "keep the life that has gone" (*P* 3). The *Bottom* passage, in contrast, focuses on the "waste and welter" of the city of David, where the forces of necessity have brought the human voice to its lowest ebb: "thy speech shall be low out of the dust, and thy voice shall be as of one that hath a familiar spirit, out of the ground, and thy speech shall whisper out of the dust." Ariel, *The Tempest*'s "ayrie spirit," is here reduced to the demonic "familiar spirit" that animates the voice of the downtrodden inhabitant of Zion.

By juxtaposing "The Planet on the Table" and his own passage, Zukofsky *necessarily* proposes a thematic continuity between the two texts. This is, of course, a very Poundian operation, like the scientist's juxtaposition of specimens Pound cites as a model for his method in the *ABC of Reading* (17). The passage from *Bottom*, when read immediately after "The Planet on the Table," takes on the character of a pessimistic, apocalyptic counterpoint to Stevens's poem. Where "The Planet" offers a vision of the poem as "what will suffice," a "making of the sun" that, while perishing with other makings of the sun, nonetheless serves the human function of embodying "Some lineament or character, / Some affluence" of the human world from which it springs, the passage from *Bottom* vividly dramatizes the "waste and welter" to which the poetic voice will succumb. Where Stevens's Ariel can rest satisfied with the fruits of his poetic production, Zukofsky's Ariel must struggle to "whisper out of the dust."

Significant here is the method by which Zukofsky juxtaposes these passages. A more "conventional" approach—one that Stevens himself might take, as evidenced by his (in)famous form/content distinction between poetry "that is modern in respect to what it says" and poetry "that is modern in respect to form" (*Necessary Angel* 168)—would be to place "The Planet on the Table" next to a Zukofsky poem on a similar theme (such as one of the several envois scattered throughout *"A"*, or the long passage toward the end of "A"-12 in which Zukofsky enumerates the contents of his desk—not a "planet," certainly, but a similar stocktaking), a poem that "says" something similar to what "The Planet on the Table" "says." In contrast, Zukofsky relates his two specimens by a purely paradigmatic similarity, the word "Ariel," and lets their implicit thematic continuities emerge in the process of one's reading them in juxtaposition. While Pound provides the model for this "ideogrammic" composition, what is unique to

Zukofsky is his overt reliance on a single word to provide the germ of the combination. The word "Ariel" is the key word that, as Robert Duncan would have it, "rimes" these two ostensibly dissimilar passages.

Zukofsky's further justifications of the kinship he perceives between himself and Stevens, which take up the better part of the lecture, have a similarly contingent, paradigmatic logic. He presents what amounts to a condensed autobiography, centered around his own "incidents—or shall I spell it i-n-c-i-d-e-n-c-e of . . . reading Stevens, referring as the geometers do to partial coincidence or community of elements between two figures" (*P* 33–34). In addition to a number of purely biographical coincidences between himself and Stevens—they may have, unknown to each other, walked the same streets in New York City; Zukofsky once applied for a job at the Hartford; and so on—Zukofsky mentions his admiration for Stevens's "care for particulars," the "grass roots or local, often barbaric" American voice of Stevens's poems, and the predilection he and Stevens share for images of "horses and donkeys." The moments of imagistic or linguistic correspondence in their poetry, such as that between Zukofsky's "A"-7 (1928–30) and Stevens's "Primordia - 4" (1916), or between Zukofsky's "Poem 14" (1926) and "Song 18" (1932) and Stevens's "The Sick Man" (1950), Zukofsky prefers to ascribe to an influence "in the air": "with respect to vapors I prefer to settle for *this most excellent canopy, the air, look you.*" Even though his own lines "We sing who were many in the South, / At each live river mouth / Sparse-lighted, carried along!" (*CSP* 29) predate Stevens's "Bands of black men seem to be drifting in the air, / In the south . . . Here in the North, late, late, there are voices of men, / Voices in chorus, singing without words" (*Opus Posthumous* 118) by twenty-four years, Zukofsky does not want to be taken (seriously) as implying that he has directly influenced Stevens; what is important is that there are moments in which he feels that Stevens's oeuvre and his own are "reading" one another, moments in which the experience of "duration" is taking place.

In one of his few moments of actually "interpreting" Stevens, Zukofsky "glosses" the three section headings of "Notes Toward a Supreme Fiction"—(1) *It Must Be Abstract,* (2) *It Must Change,* (3) *It Must Give Pleasure*—in a manner that fits them snugly among his own concerns: "(1) yes, all words are abstract, post-*solids* or other actual states—things *after the* things, only relatively that one word is 'concrete,' another 'conceptual'; (2) whatever is written changes, in the way Stevens and I are transmuted in my reading—what is constant, as he says toward the end of the poem, *Pleased that the irrational is rational;* (3) how fine, it does" (*P* 35). This "gloss," although it may seem willful in comparison to "conventional" readings of "Notes," is fully in keeping with the process of reading as Zukofsky has described it. Zukofsky's claim that Stevens's "It Must Change" describes the way both reader and text are "transmuted" in a reading enacts the very principle it legislates, even as it once again describes Zukofsky's sense of "duration" in reading, one poet's finding "what will suffice" in another's work. In keeping with his oft-repeated preference for "solid-state" language and his distaste for abstraction, Zukofsky glosses Stevens's "It Must Be Abstract" as a fundamentally trivial remark about the nature of language—*of course* the poem must be abstract, since "all words are abstract . . . things *after the* things." What Zukofsky's own sense of duration in reading Stevens finally confirms for him, then, is the reliance on the unmediated evidence of the senses, the "clear physical eye" that is at the base of both his Objectivist poetics and *Bottom: On Shakespeare,* which was written—as if one by this point could forget—to "do away with epistemology": "That instant of certainty [i.e., duration] affirms what the eyes see and the ears hear at least until proved wrong, when it is particularly hard not to feel the actual shocks of hearing and seeing" (*P* 27). That Stevens, convinced as he is that "What we see in the mind is as real to us as what we see by the eye" (*Opus Posthumous* 188), would by no means endorse a philosophy that so baldly rejects abstraction as Zukofsky's is for Zukofsky beside the point, when confronted with the immediate experience of duration.

While one might take Zukofsky's actual methods in this lecture of relating texts one to another—his seizing on individual words, phrases, and images at the expense of "larger" thematic concerns—to be mere idiosyncrasy, that would be ignoring the salience of such juxtapositional strategies throughout his work, especially in *Bottom* (one is reminded of his juxtaposition of Lear's

"Let me have surgeons; / I am cut to th' brains" and Homer's "a surgeon's worth many another man" [*B* 380]). These compositional strategies are in part indices of a larger shift within the practice of American poetry and poetics as a whole, a shift that, while it takes on a bewilderingly broad range of forms, might be roughly characterized as a movement away from the examination of the subject in poetry ("subject" in all senses of the word, both as "content" and as "person")—which in Stevens takes the form of a dissection of the relationship between a subjective "imagination" and an objective "reality"—toward the examination of the linguistic medium in which both subject and object are constituted. While Zukofsky's work, along with Stein's, stands as the most thorough and systematic working out of the premises of the modernist "revolution of the word," it also (as does Stein's) lays foundations for and at times participates in the later move toward "language" of which the Language poets are the most visible exponents.

Language writing represents itself, in the voluminous statements of poetics issued by its principle practitioners, as an exploration of the processes by which language, both in its contingent details and as a socially constituted system, works itself to constitute the subject as perennial "reader."[5] The Language poets, from the very beginning of their public careers, have acknowledged Zukofsky as a crucial precursor. *The L=A=N=G=U=A=G=E Book*, Charles Bernstein and Bruce Andrews's anthology of "critical" pieces from *L=A=N=G=U=A=G=E* magazine (1978–82), includes in its "Readings" section no fewer than four responses to Zukofsky's work, more than to any other author except Stein. "Language, Realism, Poetry," the preface to Ron Silliman's influential Language poetry anthology *In the American Tree*, a text in which one major aim is to demonstrate how Language writing swerves away from the speech-based poetics of the "New American Poetry," cites Zukofsky (along with Stein and Jackson Mac Low) as a writer in whose works can be found "a tradition of poetics not centered in speech" (*American Tree* xvi–xvii). Silliman's essay "Z-Sited Path" (*New Sentence* 122–46) and Bernstein's "Thought's Measure" (*Content's Dream* 61–86) remain among the most perspicacious readings of Zukofsky available—precisely to the extent, I believe, that they emanate from poets both profoundly influenced by his work. What is perhaps most indicative of the importance of Zukofsky's work to Language writing is the degree to which these poets feel free to quote, refer to, and argue about his work in their own writings and talks, often in a quite offhand manner. Zukofsky, to put it simply, is a central fixture of the background of Language poetry.

Unfortunately, academic criticism of the Language poets has been remiss in tracing such filiations. Linda Reinfeld's *Language Poetry* names Zukofsky a number of times—mostly because her subjects Bernstein and Palmer have named him first—but fails to pursue his significance to the writers she comments on. Sandra Stanley's ambitious account of Zukofsky's influence on the movement is weakened by her book's previous focus on the Zukofsky of the 1930s, a focus that makes the kinship she asserts between his writing and that of his poetic descendants seem somewhat surprising. George Hartley's *Textual Politics and the Language Poets* spends several pages on Zukofsky (16–18), mainly focusing on "A"-7, but practically dismisses him as holding to an epistemology that the Language poets will question and dismantle. True enough, yet Hartley's very focus on the early Zukofsky ("A"-7 was composed between 1928 and 1930, two decades before any of Hartley's principal subjects were born) blinds him to the significance of such texts as *Catullus* (the clear model, for instance, of David Melnick's *Men in Aida*, or various of Bernstein's short lyrics); "A"-18 (reminiscent of much of Silliman's *What*); or "A"-22, "A"-23, and *80 Flowers*, powerful *textural* influences on Language writing.

The very form of *"A"* as a whole, the logic by which these twenty-four sections are articulated one to another, has proved a profound influence on the various long projects undertaken by the Language poets. The other three most prominent modernist long poems preceding or coeval with *"A"*—Pound's *Cantos*, Williams's *Paterson*, and Olson's *Maximus Poems*—are all unfinished. *The Cantos* is of these three perhaps the most ostensibly similar to *"A"*. Pound, of course, had sunk into a tragic silence by the time the final "Drafts and Fragments" of *The Cantos* were published in 1969 (they had been written ten years earlier); as Massimo Bacigalupo curtly notes, "in Pound, the man survived the poet" (459). But the incomplete final form of *The Cantos* (as of

Paterson and *Maximus*, each in different ways) has deeper causes than the merely biographical. Balachandra Rajan, in his study of the unfinished in English poetry, concludes that Pound could not bring his poem to closure because he lacked a coherent theory of history, and beyond that, because of "the implacable logistics of a long poem composed over two generations. The rain of factual atoms from which knowledge is built up becomes a different rain falling from a different sky" (291).

"A", however, is complete as it now stands, and the Language poets have found compelling clues to that successful completion not in Zukofsky's biography but in the manner in which the poem moves, both between the realms of the historical and the personal and between its own sections. Silliman, Bernstein, and Barrett Watten have all written persuasively about *"A"*'s overall conception of form. "The poem," according to Watten, "is written specifically in a logic of development that creates the necessary conditions for its own 'next move in the game.' . . . The poem enacts a strategic argument of form, rather than a rhetoric of process, and this temporality occurs in a tension with time outside the poem, with history and with the events of the poet's life" (376). For Bernstein, *"A"*'s "carefully composed articulation of distinct movements, as in a symphony, permits maximum differentiation section to section without recourse to a single thematic or syntactic underpinning to create unification" (*Content's Dream* 361)—"maximum differentiation" indeed, as one can see comparing "A"-12's 135 pages to "A"-16's four words. Silliman sees in *"A"* "a new conceptualization as to the function of part-to-whole relations in the formation of a longpoem"; "each section," he notes, "is a totalization, capable of entering into larger structures as an autonomous fact. . . . This recognition that the sections of a large work must operate as a group, not as a series, empowers Zukofsky, in sharp contrast to Pound, Williams or Olson, to complete or, more accurately, close the poem" (*New Sentence* 128).

Silliman's own long project, *The Alphabet*, shows remarkable debts to Zukofsky's *"A"* in its overall formal structure, and in the very attitude toward form implied in that structure. *The Alphabet* has been in progress at least since the early 1980s and will when complete consist of twenty-six sections, each of whose titles begins with a letter of the alphabet. Its first installment, *ABC*, was published in 1983; among its latest are *N/O*, consisting of the poems "Non" and "Oz," and *Xing*. Just as the movements of *"A"* were not composed in numerical sequence, the sections of *The Alphabet* have not appeared in alphabetical order: for instance, *What* was published in 1988 and *Jones* in 1993. The sections are of radically different lengths and radically different forms. Whereas Zukofsky's *"A"* can be said to have begun as a modernist long poem on the model of *The Cantos* and later to have metamorphosed into a grouping of diverse formal experiments, Silliman's *The Alphabet* has taken that latter state as its starting point.

Zukofsky's thorough rethinking of the formal logic of the long poem is of course far from his only influence on the poetics of the Language writers. Also important are his experiments at "musical" form and his redefinition of translation. In Zukofsky's hands (and, in *Catullus*, Celia Zukofsky's hands) translation becomes something other than it is for poets before him. For Pound, poetic translation—always one of his primary modes of literary work—is an attempt to bring certain qualities, a certain virtu, of the original text over into English. As he writes in the introduction to his Cavalcanti, "I have in my translation tried to bring over the qualities of Guido's rhythm, not line for line, but to embody in the whole of my English some trace of that power which implies the man" (*Translations* 24). Of course translation is as well an important way of producing new poems in English. Part of Canto I, for instance, is a translation of a passage from Book XI of the *Odyssey*.

By relegating the "literal" meaning of source texts to a position of secondary importance and by rendering them into an English to which they are related primarily by *sound*, Zukofsky takes a far more radical step than Pound did when he inserted a "frigidaire patent" into his version of Propertius (*Personae* 206). Under one of its aspects, the fascination of the Zukofskys' *Catullus* lies in the complex interplay of Latin sound and English sound and in the tangled and mobile relationship between the lexical significance of the Latin—what one can obtain from a Penguin translation, for instance—and the meaning of the English words. But reading *Catullus* under another aspect—as poems in English—one cannot deny that these are highly unconventional, resistant texts: for instance, "Lesbia (my prize scent t'her hero) mauls and deplores me, '*dig it*': / he the lug fatuous Maximal Light titillates" (*CSP* 309). Yes, it makes American-English sense of a sort, but an enormous effort is required of a reader to untangle such a lexicon and syntax. The verse becomes not transparent meanings but words visible. The Latin, like the Hebrew of the opening of "A"-15, has become not a source text whose power is to be somehow carried over into English but a generative device, a formal template over which the poet composes a new English poem. The stringency with which Zukofsky adheres to his transliterative template—like the fidelity he shows to the formal scheme of Cavalcanti's "Donna mi priegha" in "A"-9 (even Pound had believed the Italian form unreproducible in English) accounts for the strangeness, the opacity, of the resulting poem.

This very opacity of language is perhaps what has most attracted the Language poets to Zukofsky. In an important polemical essay, "Disappearance of the Word, Appearance of the World," Ron Silliman decries the loss of the "felt" presence of language in the contemporary world. "What happens when a language moves toward and passes into a capitalist stage of development," Silliman claims, "is an anaesthetic transformation of the perceived tangibility of the word, with corresponding increases in its expository, descriptive and narrative capacities" (*New Sentence* 10). The result, in the reading practices of most contemporary readers, is a complete disappearance of the word as such: "the consumer of a mass market novel such as *Jaws* stares at a 'blank' page (the page also of the speed-reader) while a story appears to unfold miraculously of its own free will before his or her eyes" (*New Sentence* 13). The "perceived tangibility" whose loss Silliman laments is precisely the tangibility or objecthood that Zukofsky advocates, in his remarks on objectification, as "writing (audibility in two-dimensional print) which is an object or affects the mind as such" (*P* 13).

While Charles Bernstein is not as concerned as Silliman with assigning the "disappearance of the word" specifically to a capitalist era, he finds Zukofsky's work valuable precisely insofar as it manifests a "movement . . . toward opacity/denseness—visibility of language through the making translucent of the medium" (*Content's Dream* 70). Bernstein sees Zukofsky as desiring "to make language opaque so that writing becomes more and more conscious of itself as world generating, object generating" (*Content's Dream* 71). The value of such opacity, as I argue in this book's Conclusion, lies in the awareness it gives us of our embeddedness in language—the degree to which we participate in a communally shared world both created and recreated through language. While several of the Language poets are specifically concerned with the political implications of Zukofsky's exploration of the opacity of poetic language—Silliman, Watten, and Michael Davidson come to mind especially—the great majority of the poets associated with the movement have found the particular modes of Zukofsky's opacity a powerfully suggestive set of instigations toward their own practice. The radically "writerly" nature of Zukofsky's later work—the sections of *"A"* following "A"-12, *Catullus, 80 Flowers*—like that of Stein's *Tender Buttons*, offers the Language poets a clear model of a poetry that pushes toward the limits of conventional linguistic expression, soliciting its reader's participation in constructing a meaning that the text might suggest or condition but never enforces or imposes.

Zukofsky's reading of Stevens, although it discounts much of what the majority of Stevens scholars have found central to Stevens's work, still finds continuity between the two poets' work in contingent and paradigmatic coincidences of language. In this it bears an important relationship to similar strategies of appropriation in Language writing. Two short examples should suffice, each from a poet more or less closely associated with the Language group, and each taking as its starting point a Stevens poem. The first example is a poem by Bernstein—a poet whose polemics have in large part defined the public image of the Language school and who is consistently concerned with the political and ideological ramifications of poetry and interpretation. It is unsurprising, then, that he chooses the title of Stevens's "Like Decorations in a Nigger Cemetery" (*Collected Poems* 150–58) as his point of appropriative entry to the Stevens corpus. The implicit ideological critique mounted by Bernstein's "Like DeCLArationS in a HymIE CEMetArY" (*Sophist* 55–57) works on several levels, one of the more interesting being the purely formal protocols of capitalization and stanzaic form (the seemingly random capitalization of the title, for instance, continues throughout the poem).[6] On the face of it, there seems little obvious relationship between Bernstein's poem and the Stevens's poem whose title it parodies, although "DeCLAraTionS" contains several echoes of Stevens's language. The "PURPlE PeLICAn" (*Sophist* 55) echoes Section XXXIII of Stevens's "Decorations," in which "the purple bird" (clearly a figure for the poet) "must have / Notes for his comfort that he may repeat" (*Collected Poems* 155). Bernstein's "neW hARmonIUm" evokes, of course, the title of Stevens's famous first collection, *Harmonium* (1923).

Bernstein's most obvious moment of critique, however, is his poem's title. The title of Stevens's poem excited no criticism in 1935, when the poem was first published, and has attracted surprisingly little attention since, despite the extent to which it serves as an index of Stevens's own profoundly reactionary social attitudes.[7] Bernstein's revision of "Nigger" to "HymIE" raises the immediate question of whether an adjective as inflammatorily derogatory to Jews as "hymie" would have been as readily accepted in the literary community as the adjective "nigger." (Interestingly and proleptically enough, Stanley Burnshaw had in 1961 questioned whether the title "Like Decorations in a *Sheeney* Cemetary" might have been as amiably received [Filreis, *Modernism* 100].) Of course, the connotations of the word "nigger" have to some degree changed since 1935, when the word could have been seen as merely a demotic southern usage. As W. E. B. Du Bois commented on Carl Van Vechten's *Nigger Heaven* (1926), "my objection is based on no provincial dislike of the nickname. 'Nigger' is an English word of wide use and definite connotation" (Van Vechten, vii). But Langston Hughes, himself Van Vechten's collaborator, would comment in 1940, "The word *nigger* to colored people of high and low degree is like a red rag to a bull," and would call Van Vechten's title "an unfortunate choice" (Van Vechten, xvi–xvii).

Little critical attention, however, has been devoted to the word "nigger" as it appears in Stevens's title, and Stevens's critics, fascinated by the task of tracing his poems' act of the mind, have given little thought until recently to the ideology of poet or corpus. Bernstein's single word change opens up whole vistas of the racial politics of modernism, from Stevens's calling Gwendolyn

Brooks a "coon" (Brazeau 196), to the vicious anti-Semitism of Pound's wartime broadcasts. By changing "Nigger" to "HymIE," Bernstein both emphasizes the racism implicit in Stevens's original title and raises again the question of the Jew within modernism—both the Jew as a figure in modernist texts, from Eliot's Bleistein to Fitzgerald's Wolfsheim to Pound's Rothschild/Stinkschuld (not to mention Wharton's Sim Rosedale), and the Jew *as* modernist writer, the most prominent examples of which, for the Language writers, would be Gertrude Stein and Louis Zukofsky. Bernstein's title serves to emphasize the extent to which "Like Decorations" remains, in 1987, an unquestionably "canonical" work, a work for the most part uncritiqued in ideological terms. "Like DeCLAraTionS," then, appropriates Stevens's title for a none-too-subtle assault on the canon of modernist writing, at least to the extent that canon is constituted as a phalanx of white Gentiles—men who feel free to title a poem, in all seriousness, "Like Decorations in a Nigger Cemetery"—and to the extent that canon has been determined by an establishment of critics (both Gentile and Jew) to whom Stevens's racial views are of far less interest than the anti-Semitism of his prominent contemporaries.[8] Like Zukofsky, who finds his fruitful point of entry into Stevens's work to be the single word "Ariel," Bernstein makes the single word "Nigger" a basis for a canny, while deceptively simple-seeming, ideological critique of a whole range of problems within the literary phenomenon of modernism.

Michael Palmer is a less overtly political poet than Bernstein, and his revision of Stevens is correspondingly more oblique; nonetheless, he similarly follows Zukofsky in finding a single phrase—in this case, another title—to be a sufficient point of entry to Stevens's canon. Palmer's "Dutch Graves in Buck County" positions itself as a rewriting of Stevens's poem of the same title, but the shared title seems at first to be the only point of conjunction with Stevens's text. Stevens's poem is a two-voiced work in which five-line stanzas alternate with two-line stanzas. The longer stanzas describe the measured violence of the war that is presently (1942) devastating Europe and mobilizing America: "Men are moving and marching / And shuffling lightly, with the heavy lightness / Of those that are marching, many together. . . . There are circles of weapons in the sun" (*Collected Poems* 290).

Contrasted to this scene is the persistent address of the poet to his Pennsylvania Dutch ancestors, long dead: "And you, my semblables, in sooty residence / Tap skeleton drums inaudibly. . . . And you, my semblables, are crusts that lie / In the shrivellings of your time and place" (290–91). The violent contrast sustained through the first part of the poem between the frenetic activity above ground and the disinterested, self-absorbed rest of those below modulates into a questioning: is it true that the dead "in the total / Of remembrance share nothing of ourselves" (291)? The Dutch dead "know that the past is not part of the present," that "this time / Is not an early time that has grown late," and that "[their] children / Are not [their] children, not [their] selves" (291–92). The present is not merely a reprise of the past, and the sins of the fathers are not necessarily visited on the children, for the destiny of "These violent marchers of the present" (293) has not been determined by their heredity, by the violent acts of their ancestors. Nevertheless, even in the absence of a strict determination, generations repeat the cycle of war and death: "There were other soldiers, other people . . . defeated at last and lost / In an ignorance of sleep and nothing won" (291). Each generation is "free," undetermined, and each generation chooses in turn to slaughter itself:

> Freedom is like a man who kills himself
> Each night, an incessant butcher, whose knife
> Grows sharp in blood. The armies kill themselves,
> And in their blood an ancient evil dies—
> The action of incorrigible tragedy.
> [292]

The action of each succeeding generation is "incorrigible tragedy," a repetition of bloodshed like that of Yeats's *Purgatory*. Even though the present generation is not identical to that which lies in Bucks County graveyards, and "the past is not part of the present," the soldiers of 1942 follow the same path as their ancestors: "Time was not wasted in your subtle temples. / No: nor divergence made too steep to follow down" (293).

Palmer's "Dutch Graves in Bucks County" can also be read

as a poem that deals with generational difference, and does so by means of recognizably Stevensian images. What must be stressed at the outset, however, is that any reading that aims to approach the poem in terms of the intertextual filiations between it and Stevens's text has little to work with at first except the brute—and initially inexplicable—fact of its title:

Dutch Graves in Bucks County

She opens the letter and looks off stage

The theme of Christian sacrifice is prominent
in our dreams
as prominent as we please

There's less content here
but more activity
more rings on fingers

than in fashion magazines
more cocks and cunts showing
than in our dreams

The costume was unraveling
and the star thought to explain

in order to draw the audience's attention away
from their dreams

She opens the letter and glances off stage

Her costume is unraveling
and the star decides to explain
about the play
[*Without Music* 118–19]

What strikes one initially, despite their shared titles, is the almost total lack of continuity between Stevens's text and Palmer's. The "scene" of the poem, however, a single woman's reverie, is familiar from Stevens's "Sunday Morning," as is the "theme of Christian sacrifice":

Complacencies of the peignoir, and late
Coffee and oranges in a sunny chair,
And the green freedom of a cockatoo
Upon a rug mingle to dissipate
The holy hush of ancient sacrifice.
[*Collected Poems* 66–67]

"Sunday Morning" is of course a poem that confronts the loss of Christian faith, an immediate and important crisis to the poet of 1915; that "theme" has become less gripping in the late 1970s, merely an element "in our dreams / as prominent as we please."[9] The generational gap Palmer implies is one between the *Weltanschauung* of Stevens's generation and his own, or between Stevens's poetry and his own: "There's less content here / but more activity." Less *còn*tent, in the sense of intellectual argument, and simultaneously less con*tènt*, contentment. One's dreams of "Christian sacrifice," and the "fashion magazines" one reads lack the immediacy of the "here," "more rings on fingers," "more cocks and cunts showing." (We have clearly moved far beyond Stevens's notions of linguistic decorum, at the very least.)

The "audience," however, is powerfully attracted to the consolations of its dreams: her "costume . . . unravelling," the "star" must "draw their attention away." As the poem closes, she "decides to explain / about the play." This latter phrase could be an opening presentation for another of Stevens's most famous poems, "Of Modern Poetry," where the poet explains why the modern poem must be "The poem of the mind in the act of finding / What will suffice":

    It has not always had
To find: the scene was set; it repeated what
Was in the script.
                Then the theatre was changed
To something else. Its past was a souvenir.
[*Collected Poems* 239]

Palmer's "Dutch Graves" positions itself as a prolegomenon to another *ars poetica*, an "Of Post-Modern Poetry," perhaps. But even while it raises some of the issues a poet of the 1980s might find it necessary to confront, it gives no prescription of the sort Stevens provides: "It has to be living. . . . It has to think about war. . . . It has to construct a new stage" (*Collected Poems* 240), and so forth. By invoking the intergenerational drama of Stevens's "Dutch Graves," Palmer emphasizes a similar relationship between his own generation and that of Stevens. Each generation must "make it new" for itself, but that very act of renewal marks the continuity between one's "semblables" underground and one's own activity.

The radically fragmentary quality of Palmer's text, its purposeful inconclusiveness and repetition, and, most clearly, its total lack of prescriptivity—all of these elements serve to lay emphasis on the fundamental discontinuity between his work and that of Stevens. By invoking Stevens's "Dutch Graves in Bucks County," and by doing so in the bluntest possible manner, by appropriating its title, Palmer can evoke a number of Stevens's poetic gestures—the intergenerational contrast of "Dutch Graves," the post-Christian angst of "Sunday Morning," the poet as explanatory actor of "Of Modern Poetry"—and do so without at any point taking on Stevens's characteristic rhetoric or discursivity. The poem becomes a dialogue with Stevens by appropriating specific linguistic moments out of Stevens's corpus, but a dialogue in which Stevens himself is only a shadowy, marginal voice, a starting point for and barely heard counterpoint to Palmer's own characteristic gaps and starts.[10] Palmer's appropriation of the Stevens text, like Bernstein's, bears a striking resemblance to the manner in which Zukofsky reads not merely Stevens but all of the texts cited in *Bottom*, and all of the texts plundered and borrowed from in *"A"*.

By reason of his age, Zukofsky—along with the rest of the Objectivists—was excluded from Donald Allen's 1960 anthology, *The New American Poetry*, a work that is clearly the single most crucial document in shaping the poetic sensibilities of the Language poets. Charles Olson, born in 1910, is the oldest poet in that collection; most Language poets are members of the postwar baby boom generation. The thirty-five-year generational gap, then, might be seen as analogous to the two decades between Pound (born 1885) and Yeats (born 1865), especially when one considers that Olson did not begin writing poetry until his late thirties. But one must remember that Robert Browning (born 1812) was an even greater influence on Pound than Yeats and that Zukofsky's publishing career, which spans from 1927 to 1978, was perhaps most active and visible in those decades when the Language poets were arriving at their mature styles. Even though Zukofsky was not an official proponent of the "New American Poetry," these writers were far from unaware of Zukofsky's work. Robert Creeley, a close associate of Olson, was an indefatigable promoter of Zukofsky's poetry; Robert Duncan and Jonathan Williams (publisher of Jargon Press), both associated with Olson's Black Mountain School, knew his work and proselytized for it; and Cid Corman, editor of *Origin*, gave Zukofsky seemingly unlimited space in his pages, even as he would later publish the work of such young Language-oriented poets as Craig Watson and Ted Pearson.

As I shall detail in Chapter 11, the Language poets are far from the sole group of writers to be influenced by Zukofsky, although their partisanship on behalf of his work when that work was far from widely known outside poetic circles has perhaps given them an understandable desire to claim themselves as the true inheritors of his mantle of innovation. Such partisanship, I believe, indicates to us the importance of Zukofsky's work for younger generations. My own attitude toward arguments over literary lineage is a skeptical one (a "valid skepticism," I hope), for I see such contretemps as largely ex post facto turf struggles. Yet the very fact that Zukofsky has become the site for such struggles emphasizes that his work has maintained its capacity to inspire. That poets of our own day have found his writing a model for techniques and approaches and an inspiration to further innovations is a testimony to the enduring provocation it offers.

11

Zukofsky and After

Post-Objectivist Poetics in John Taggart and Ronald Johnson

> I don't like any of those *isms*. I mean, as soon as you do that, you start becoming a balloon instead of a person. And it swells and a lot of mad people go chasing it.
> —Louis Zukofsky (*LZMP* 265–66 [1968])

A definitive discussion of poetic "movements" is yet to be written. T. S. Eliot, in his 1944 essay "What is Minor Poetry," briefly discusses the importance of such groupings in fostering the work of young poets. His remarks, made no doubt with a glance backward toward the London-based "isms" of the first decades of the century, are useful in trying to determine the significance of a movement I have touched on several times—the event in twentieth-century literary history that is now widely identified as the Objectivist school. "Such groups," Eliot writes,

> frequently bind themselves together by formulating a set of principles or rules, to which usually nobody adheres; in course of time the group disintegrates, the feebler members vanish, and the stronger ones develop more individual styles. But the group, and the group anthology, serve a useful purpose: young poets do not ordinarily get, and indeed are better without, much attention from the general public, but they need the support and criticism of each other, and of a few other people. (*On Poetry and Poets* 36)

These remarks, which no doubt spring from crucial personal experience, are valuable, sociologically, to the extent that they help us analyze the impulses and attitudes that lead up to and accompany the formation of poetic movements. (At the same time Eliot's words exemplify the uneasy relationship between the literary historian and the practicing poet anxious, as Eliot so often was, to cover his own tracks.) But regardless of the roles such movements—or groups, or schools—play in the careers of individual poets, these more or less formal confluences of writers are crucial to the ways in which we construct our histories of literature. On the purely practical level at which literary history is retrospectively forged—the level of classroom syllabi and large-scale anthologies—it is easier to deal with poets and poetries in groups than it is to deal with them individually; this is as true of the Romantics as it is of the Beats, the New England Wits, or the New York School. There is a fundamental and very understandable impulse at work in Donald Allen's decision to group the poets in his ground-breaking 1960 anthology *The New American Poetry* into five separate "schools." In retrospect one can see exactly how arbitrary some of his placements were, and one can see to what extent those groupings have affected subsequent reception of some poets' work.

In Chapter 1 I sketched the bare outlines of the Objectivist "movement." Unfortunately, those outlines are pretty much all we have. Indeed, sixty-five years after the " 'Objectivists' 1931" issue of *Poetry*, it remains unclear whether the movement as such really existed in any form other than a marketing strategy.[1] When the ceaselessly instigational Pound persuaded Harriet Monroe to lend the editorship of that magazine to his young friend Zukofsky for the February 1931 issue, she insisted, Zukofsky claimed in his 1968 interview with L. S. Dembo, that "You must have a movement" (*LZMP* 266). Zukofsky is unequivocal in that conversation: there was never anything like a conscious movement called "Objectivism," and the tag "Objectivists" attached to the poets collected in that issue was merely a handle of convenience. Of course, Zukofsky speaks here retrospectively, and from a point in his life when he felt little affection for the other members of the "group" with which he now found himself perhaps uncomfortably associated. Dembo, as I have touched on earlier, had brought the four most prominent members of the Objectivist group to the campus of the University of Wisconsin in the spring of 1968 (it appears that no two of them were in Madison at the same time) and would publish the four interviews he conducted with them in *Contemporary Literature* as "The 'Objectivist' Poets: Four Interviews." It seems clear that current critical recognition of the Objectivists as a significant movement in modernist American poetry is largely the result of Dembo's gesture: his act of publishing these interviews together can be read as the *critical* inauguration of the Objectivist school. (Their marketing inauguration, of course, was in the 1931 *Poetry* issue. Neither inauguration should be confused with the beginnings of the careers of the individual poets.)

The first thing that strikes one when examining the four interviews that Dembo published is how little consensus there is among these poets as to what—if anything—the label "Objectivist" implied back in 1931–32. Zukofsky, of course, is able to provide a fairly detailed explanation of how the poem achieves objectification through the sincerity of the poet's compositional acts, thereby glossing the title terms of the most important document of Objectivist poetics. But he simultaneously refuses to limit the term to any one historical movement: "The objectivist, then, is one person, not a group . . . he is a craftsman who puts words together into an object" (*LZMP* 268). George Oppen, of the three others interviewed, seems most nearly to have understood the implications of Objectivist rhetoric. "I learned from Louis," Oppen says, "the necessity for forming a poem properly, for achieving form. That's what 'objectivist' really means. There's been tremendous misunderstanding about that. People assume it means the psychologically objective in attitude. It actually means the objectification of the poem, the making of an object of the poem" (Dembo and Pondrom 278). Charles Reznikoff, moving away from the implications of the terms Zukofsky developed in an analysis of Reznikoff's own poetry, describes the Objectivist poet as one whose work, in its impersonal statement of fact, resembles the courtroom testimony Reznikoff drew on for his own long poem *Testimony* (207–8). Carl Rakosi, while he admits that at the time he thought the term "Objectivist" "all right" (172), is remarkably vague as to how it pertains to his own poetry and is obliged to confess, "The term really originated with Zukofsky, and he pulled it out of a hat." (Rakosi, it appears, did not even *meet* Reznikoff or Oppen until some four decades after the " 'Objectivists' 1931" *Poetry* issue appeared [Pacernick 13].)

Even if one disregards this odd range of opinion as the result of faulty memory on the part of the four principals, or as a series of gestures aimed at dissociating their mature work from the associations of their youth, the ad hoc nature of any formulation of an Objectivist "movement" or "group" becomes even clearer when one examines the contents of that " 'Objectivists' 1931" issue of *Poetry.* While the four Dembo Objectivists are included here, Lorine Niedecker, who is more and more often claimed as the sole female Objectivist—as Laura (Riding) Jackson was for a while considered the only female Fugitive—was in fact instigated by the issue to begin her correspondence with Zukofsky. While there are included a number of prominent poets who might be considered at least temporary members of the Objectivist camp—Williams, Bunting, Kenneth Rexroth (whose work, after all, takes up more space in *An "Objectivists" Anthology* than anyone except Zukofsky himself)—there are also several minor writers who are remembered (if they are remembered at all) for reasons that have little to do with "Objectivism": John Wheelwright, Harry Roskolenkier, and Zukofsky's college buddy Whittaker Chambers. While the pool of poets is smaller in the 1932 *An "Objectivists" Anthology,* it again includes poets who clearly had no intention of being reckoned among a "group," prominent among them the expatriate Robert McAlmon, who receives three times as much space as Oppen, and T. S. Eliot himself, whose "Marina" Zukofsky reprints. Suffice it to say that precisely how we ought to assess the mutual association of the Objectivist poets, and how ultimately useful as a critical label "Objectivist" may be, are at best highly problematic matters.

Nonetheless, while they may be only marginally successful in defining the commonalities among the works of his fellow Objectivists, Zukofsky's polemical essays are of use in situating and evaluating the poetries of a small group of poets that might be described as "second-generation" Objectivists. I hesitate even to suggest that these poets, among whom one might include writers as diverse in style as Hugh Seidman, Michael Heller, Norman Finkelstein, Rachel Blau DuPlessis, and Armand Schwerner, might be considered to comprise anything as vaguely formal as a group, for their reception has been shaped in part precisely by the fact that they partake in no collective identity, no "school" even as amorphous as that of the Objectivists. In particular, I would like to look at the works of John Taggart and Ronald Johnson, two poets who have pursued resolutely individual aesthetics and, while never belonging to a particular group or school, have each extended, to what might seem a limit point, implications of Zukofsky's Objectivist rhetoric.

One can certainly observe the Objectivists' influence, as I have argued, on the Language writing of the 1970s and 1980s. In his essay "Z-Sited Path," Ron Silliman praises among other achievements Zukofsky's reconception of the part-to-whole relationship of the long poem, a reconception that has clearly influenced Silliman's *The Alphabet.* But Silliman, crucially, is as concerned with the social formations within which poetry is written and disseminated as he is with the formal innovations of a given poet. He is, if not our foremost theorist of the "movement," than at least one of its most vociferous proponents. In his critical commentaries on Language writing, Silliman is at pains always to emphasize the fact that these poets were a community, a group of writers with shared goals and interests who participated in a continuous exchange of ideas and techniques. Most notably, in the retrospective preface to *In the American Tree* Silliman traces the rise of Language poetry not through formal analysis or theoretical pronouncement—though heaven knows he indulges in these pursuits elsewhere—but through a blow-by-blow recounting of the little magazines, "talk" series, and poetry reading series within which the members of the movement found their mature poetics in dialogue with their peers.

Silliman's analysis of the Objectivist "movement" involves a narrative of how that movement, irrespective of the achievements of its individual members, failed qua movement, how Zukofsky himself, the prime theorist and anthologist of the group, was unable to keep these poets together for any significant length of time. While the Objectivist group began with the high promise of a new American avant-garde, it rapidly disintegrated over the course of the 1930s. The poets fell out of public view (and, more important, fell out of touch with one another). Rakosi and Oppen ceased writing altogether; Reznikoff and Zukofsky fell into obscurity. When New Directions, in collaboration with the *San Francisco Review*, began a program of publishing Objectivist poets in the 1960s,[2] Oppen returned (spectacularly) to public attention. But the poetry of this phase of Oppen's career, in sharp contrast to 1934's *Discrete Series*, represented a bridge between his uncompromisingly avant-garde work of the early 1930s and what Silliman calls the "middle-ground" of American poetic practice (*New Sentence* 141). Zukofsky, Silliman implies, came "bitterly" to his own late "isolation" in large part because of the failure of the Objectivist movement ultimately to "jell" ("Space" 290).

That failure, Silliman implies, should serve as a warning to post-Objectivist poets who have shied away from involving themselves in the close camaraderie and exchange of a defined group. In a 1978 review of Johnson's *Radi Os*, Silliman classifies Johnson and Taggart (along with Frank Samperi) as poets who "read Zukofsky not as the compacted source of suggestions as to which directions poetry, if it is to stay vital, must move, but as the limit of poetry itself" ("Space" 290). These poets, according to Silliman, "have chosen a certain isolation. Aware of one another, they neither constitute a 'group' nor align themselves with one, preferring an individualist's stance from which to work." Such a *chosen* isolation is in contrast to that of Zukofsky's later years, an enforced consequence of the failure of the Objectivist movement. The *communitas* of such a movement is centrally important to Silliman, impresario of the Language poets (such a position is at least implied in his editing of *In the American Tree*, which, unlike Douglas Messerli's 1987 *"Language" Poetries*, clearly aims to be both historical and definitive). In a community like that of Language writing—a group of working poets in continual communication and creative exchange—"the tension of conflicting beliefs gives rise to new moments, new ideas" ("Space" 290). Lacking such *communitas*, the works of Johnson and Taggart threaten to petrify, to become merely literary, and to fail to move beyond territory already explored by Zukofsky himself. Silliman has been passionately and consistently concerned with the roots of innovative poetries within communities of poets. As he writes (with evident scorn) in a 1997 email to the "Poetics" discussion group, a certain "non-group" of poets—among them Taggart—"all share enough features to compose a group of their own except that the Loner status with all its aching pretentiousness is one of its major preconditions."

Silliman's gesture of associating Taggart and Johnson with Zukofsky, and then questioning the individualistic routes their poetries have taken, is a critique to be reckoned with, even aside from its political implications. Silliman, while granting that Johnson's work is fascinating and bears close watching—"Whatever Johnson has been putting together in his lab this last half decade, we can be certain that it's a monster" ("Space" 290)—warns that both Johnson and Taggart, because of their failure to involve themselves in a poetico-critical community, have fallen into the trap of merely repeating the gestures of Zukofsky, their most important precursor. (Perhaps, to borrow Bloom's agonistic vocabulary, they have failed to read him "strongly" enough.) The overt message of Silliman's critique is clear: the poet is best served by allying her- or himself with a community of like-minded poets who can assure that all work produced within that community is properly innovative. Its subtext, however, is somewhat less salutary, for it implies that Language poetry itself—a correctly collaborative organization, or a similarly collaborative nexus of poets—is the only true inheritor and forwarder of the innovations of Zukofsky's poetics.

I am inclined, however, to set this implication aside for the moment and to take Silliman's review at its face value. Given that Johnson and Taggart are confessedly influenced by Zukofsky's work, to what degree have their own projects transcended that model, and to what degree have they merely repeated the achievements of their predecessor? If one accepts that the Language poets have fruitfully seized on the implications of Zukofsky's later work, as well as the small-scale tactical techniques evident in his quotational and citational practice, can one find other productive instigations in Zukofsky's poetics, other paths from which to learn and from which to extend his practice that do not reduce themselves to sterile emulation and aesthetic dead-end?

As is evident on even a cursory reading, Ronald Johnson's early work, collected in the celebrated *The Book of the Green Man* and (especially) *Valley of the Many-Colored Grasses*, bears close affinities with Charles Olson's "Projectivist" collages. One poem—"Landscape with Bears, for Charles Olson" (*Valley* 74–79)—is dedicated to the sometime rector of Black Mountain College. This filiation is unsurprising, given Johnson's close friendship with and tutelage under Jonathan Williams, publisher of the Jargon Society press and one of Olson's most partisan and dedicated Black Mountain students. Even in the early work of *A Line of Poetry, A Row of Trees* (written 1960–63), however, Johnson's collage poetic seems somehow to lack the dynamism, the momentum, of Olson's headlong concatenations. His work seems less concerned with the movement that Olson so valorizes in the "Projective Verse" essay—"get on with it, keep moving, keep in, speed, their nerves, their speed, the perceptions, theirs, the acts, the split second acts, the whole business, keep it moving as fast as you can, citizen" (*Human Universe* 53)—as with the careful and precise placement of his words and phrases. His syntax is for the most part straightforward, although his lineation works painstakingly to foreground specific words, and often large chunks of poems will consist of lineated passages of others' prose. "Shake, Quoth the Dove House," for instance, begins with a passage from an early essay of Alexander Pope's:

> 'A laurustine bear in blossom
> with a juniper hunter in berries,
> a lavender pig with sage growing in his belly
> & a pair of maidenheads in fir, in great
> forwardness'.
> [*Valley* 17]

Such lineation is evidence not of a headlong projectivist rush but of an almost fastidious concern for the placement of words upon the page and within the line. Such a concern owes much to Johnson's reading of Zukofsky. Johnson himself confirms his twinned influences: "More closely, Zukofsky and Olson, braving new schemes for language—The Minimalist and The Maximus—such opposing poles of influence: parities" (*ARK* [277]).[3]

The poetry of Johnson's middle period, which involves itself more and more heavily with various forms of "concrete" poetry, evinces his increasing inclination to take seriously—and even literally—the notion of the poem as a palpable object. Objectivist poetics are of course only one influence on Johnson's middle period works—works which have strong affinities with those of more strictly concrete poets like Emmett Williams and Ian Hamilton Finlay. Johnson's 1976 volume *Eyes & Objects*, a good example of such work, is a collection of pictures, still lives, carvings, and inscriptions that puts one strongly in mind of Finlay's labeled trees and inscribed stepping-stones. In contrast to the earlier two books, which leaned heavily on the quotation of previous works and a richly citational sense of literary history—in the "Notes" to *Book of the Green Man*, Johnson writes, "I lust after books with a certain 'Ohio soil,' a rich silt of bibliography, books which lead to other books" (83)—*Eyes & Objects* concerns itself with the immediately apprehensible and with the processes by which we perceive. In its concern with the mechanics of vision, it dovetails quite nicely with Zukofsky's own overwhelming concern with the *ethics* of vision and its interpersonal implications.

It is when Johnson embarks on his magnum opus, *ARK*, that the specifically Zukofskyan elements of his poetics come to the fore. Johnson began *ARK*, a two-and-a-half-decade project on the scale of the major modernist long poems, in 1970 and completed it in the early 1990s. *ARK* makes use throughout of the various quotational poetics that so pervasively structure Zukofsky's *"A"*—from the direct and fairly Poundian quotation of "A"-12; to piecemeal, "ventilated" quotations like that of *Paradise Lost* in "A"-14 (319–25); to the dense masses of uncited quotations that make up "A"-22 and -23. Like Zukofsky, Johnson is obsessively concerned with the aural qualities of his poetry, and the patterning of sound might well be *ARK*'s strongest aspect; in its sonic complexity, it is at times comparable to the best of Zukofsky or Bunting. Here, for instance, is Johnson's description of (I assume) Zukofsky's *"A"*, from "ARK 34, *Spire on the Death of L.Z.*":

> an edifice
> of matched snailshell
> faced to watch

Bach
in cherubim cliffed hayseed, rayed
cloud in plaster
forever
or near it
as consonance gets without
clef

[*ARK* (82)]

As a contemporary American long poem, *ARK* rests on singular and quite unique conceptual foundations. It is a cosmological poem, like Lucretius's *De Rerum Natura,* yet one that aims to celebrate not the Epicurean atomistic theory of the universe but the insights into the universe's fundamental unity and isomorphism gained by twentieth-century physics—and later, by chaos theory and the new science of fractals. Silliman reports Johnson claiming that the universe is "like an onion, layered" ("Space" 289). This insight, paired with Goethe's speculation that "unless the eye contained the substance of the sun how could we ever look on the light" (quoted in Johnson, *Green Man* 87), later rephrased in "BEAM 4" as "The eye may be said to be sun in other form" (*ARK* [9]), leads Johnson to his primary theme—that "Mind & Eye are a logarithmic spiral coiled from periphery" (*ARK* [10]). This foundational theme of the radical isomorphism of all of nature, as familiar to us from the transcendentalists as from David Bohm, leads Johnson into all manner of high-spirited linguistic play. *ARK* incorporates an impressive array of puns, visual wordplay, and concrete poetry. Like Zukofsky, Johnson radically reconceives the very notion of "composing" a poem, the very notions of originality and quotation. The volume *Radi Os,* published in 1977, consists of the first four books of Milton's *Paradise Lost*—but radically ventilated: Johnson has erased most of the words from Milton's work, leaving the remainder in their original positions on the page. This radical revision, Johnson writes, "when complete will mark ARK 100—conceived as a kind of Dymaxion Dome over the whole" (*ARK 50,* 56). (Since composing this endnote to *ARK 50,* Johnson seems to have had second thoughts: *Radi Os,* now retitled "Dome Excised Paradise Lost," will be published with a number of other poems as *The Outworks*, "a sort of garden surrounding *ARK*" [O'Leary 44].)

Such an architectural metaphor—even if the architect is as heterodox as Buckminster Fuller—shows to what extent Johnson conceives of *ARK* as an architectural structure. He calls his poem a "model for a monument," and its three major divisions reflect this spatial metaphor: 33 sections of "Foundations," 33 of "Spires," and 33 of "Ramparts." ARK 100, in turn, was to have been a "dome" over the whole, a crowning and covering shell like that over Monticello, the U.S. Capitol building, or the Roman Pantheon. The poem, then, is conceived of as in some sense a *literal* object, a literal *architecture*. Johnson gleefully quotes Robert Duncan in his note to a section of "Ramparts" published in the magazine *Conjunctions:* "yes, they'll compare you to *Maximus, The Cantos, A* [*sic*], even *Leaves of Grass*, but you're the only one to really make an Architecture of it" (189). The manner in which *ARK* is intended as a monument, a literal structure, is to my mind reminiscent of Wordsworth's description of his mammoth project *The Recluse*, to the whole of which *The Prelude* bears the same relation "as the Antechapel has to the body of a gothic Church." (Even Wordsworth's minor pieces fit into the scheme of this cathedral as "the little Cells, Oratories, and sepulchral Recesses, ordinarily included in those Edifices.") But for Wordsworth this architectural metaphor is merely a nonce description, which, while it might have clarifying force, is never a determinant factor within the compositional process. For Johnson, in the twenty-odd years during which he worked away at this eccentric and majestic project, the architectural metaphor became more and more the determining formal force of the poem.

Of course, his architecture is by no means neoclassical, like Jefferson's or Wren's, but, as he notes in *ARK 50*, "a kind of *naif* architecture on the lines of the Facteur Cheval's Ideal Palace, Simon Rodia's Watts Towers, or Ramond Isidore's mosaic house in the shade of Chartres" (56). He cites as well the Throne of the Third Heaven of the Nations Millennium General Assembly, an astonishing and dazzling visionary throne room put together in a rented garage by James Hampton, a Washington, D.C., janitor.

In a 1986 note, Johnson explains the relation of these men's visionary works to his own:

> These men . . . worked from an armature to an outer encrustation of curious rocks, broken colorful tiles or bits of glass, gold, and silver foil—anything they could get their hands on from detritus of a world which had not eyes to see. Just so, *ARK* composed itself from the everyday fragments of phrase, words plucked out of context, trouvailles to be worked and knitted and sawn [*sic*] or welded in. To make and mould and shape a dream, ineffable orders. ("Planting" 2)

As I have mentioned, Johnson's notion of poetic "composition" bears little resemblance to that of, for instance, Shelley (or Robert Lowell); the "regular 7″ × 5″ yellow ruled pad[s]" from which Johnson has precipitated his poem contain no extended perorations or lengthy drafts but "floating words, minute connections, unused directions," "bricks" that are later "mortared into song" on his electric typewriter ("Planting" 4). The line-by-line compositional methods that produce *ARK*—the jackdawlike accumulation of words and phrases, which are then woven into a "crazed" whole—have much in common with such folk art techniques as quilting or with the nineteenth-century scrapbook or portfolio. What is notable about Johnson's self-proclaimed pedigree of *bricoleurs* is that, with the exception of Hampton, all of these artists have essayed clearly architectural projects: Cheval's "Palais Idéal," favorite of the Surrealists, the mosaic house Isidore laid out in his backyard, and Rodia's Towers, whose dizzy spires seem a clear model for the center-justified lines of *ARK*, characterized as the blueprint for a "Ladder" centered over St. Jacob's Well, a "near legendary 'bottomless' pool" "between Ashland and Dodge City, Kansas" (*ARK 50*, 56). The complete *ARK*, as published by Living Batch in 1996, has a photograph of the Watts Towers on its cover.

Zukofsky conceived *"A"* as a 24-part poem long before he knew what would go into each of its sections. Johnson similarly worked out the overall "architecture" of *ARK* before the contents of its specific "foundations," "spires," and "ramparts" were clear to him: "I . . . saw [that] the obvious danger inherent in a long poem, written over decades, was to be its structure—the natural change in tone, style, and of course the quest for termination. So I devised a ground plan in my mind which could encompass growth" ("Planting" 3). (Of course, even this "ground plan," like Zukofsky's original movement titles for *"A"*, underwent some revision: sometime between *ARK 50* [1984] and this 1986 note, what were the "Outworks" became the "Ramparts"; and *Radi Os*, which was once to have been part of ARK 100, has now become part of a new *Outworks*, something of an appendix to the whole.) There is a temporal scheme in effect in the poem, as well as a spatial "blueprint": the Foundations begin at sunrise and end at noon, the Spires take until sunset, and the Ramparts last through the night until dawn.[4] But the temporal sequence does not really have much determining force over the poems that make up *ARK*. While "BEAM 1" does indeed begin at dawn, and "BEAM 33" ends with "High noon stand[ing] still as a just picked apple" (*ARK* [78]), "ARK 40, *Herm*" (by my calculations about 1:18 P.M.) is a slyly visual poem comparing art to masturbation (*ARK* [98]), and "ARK 47, *Plow Spire*" (around 2:49 P.M.) quotes large chunks of a traveler's description of Mount Vesuvius and then "ventilates" and reverses Henry James's description of Niagara Falls (in a section splendidly and anagrammatically titled *"The Majesnehry"*) to give Johnson's dustbowl hometown of Ashland, Kansas, a volcano—not of lava but of water (*ARK* [116–23]). The disposal of the various poems of the sequences as a whole, I believe, has little to do with temporal progression. Rather, Johnson's governing architectural metaphor provides him a broad frame into which he can arrange poems of widely divergent themes and approaches without a necessary narrative or thematic progression, a frame much like that of *"A"*.

There *are* thematic progressions evident in the poem, although tenuous. The early BEAMs for the most part celebrate the triad of eye, ear, and brain and revel in the transcendental "fitting" of universe and human perceiver. Again and again, Johnson announces the high goal of his poem, " 'To do as Adam did' / . . . and build a Garden of the brain" (*ARK* [71]), to weave a song out of the exquisite interplay of visionary physics and the human sensorium. But the high-spiritedness of *The Foundations* grows more muted in *The Spires*, until *The Ramparts* emerge as an altogether darker, more muted set of exultations. Night has indeed fallen, and Johnson, during the composition of these poems, has lived through the deaths of many of his greatest artistic models: Zukofsky, whose death is commemorated in ARK 34; Robert Duncan, who is saluted in ARK 71, *"Death of R.D.";* George Balanchine, the choreographer; and another dancer, Johnson's mother Helen Johnson (her initials are the same as those of Henry James, whom Johnson has called "my true Penelope" ["Planting" 1]). The second half of *ARK* was composed in San Francisco during the worst years of the AIDS epidemic, and the specter of death is always present at some level in the later movements of the poem. While the poem ends at its "dawn" on an emphatically hopeful note—"*as astra per aspera* / countdown for Lift Off" (*ARK* [275])—that heavenward reaching strikes a wistful note, qualified as it is by the elegiac tone of much that has preceded it.

ARK's thematic progressions and its temporal scheme, however, are ultimately secondary to its symmetrical and building-like structuring. It is precisely Johnson's insistent pursuit of the spatial metaphor of the poem as architectural structure that might render problematic his reception of Zukofsky's notion of the poem as an objectlike verbal construction. As *ARK* progresses, its emphasis shifts from *The Foundations*'s celebration of perception and natural process to an almost Renaissance emphasis on the poem as monument, not to a beloved or to an esteemed peer (although there are many epitaphs and dedications among the poems here) but to the very process of creation and poem making—a monument, in short, to the act of monumentalizing. That the poem has a form, shape, and life extending beyond its author—that the poem is an object that can be a monument—is of course an insight that has perennially provoked or welcomed moments of poetic self-reflexiveness, moments that can be found even in Zukofsky's work. But Zukofsky's notion of the poem as autotelic object is considerably more nuanced than Johnson's, for Johnson interprets the rhetoric of Objectivist poetics to imply that the poem must either *be* an object itself or must structurally mime an object (his preferred model, as we have seen, being an architectural one). In contrast, Zukofsky's "Sincerity and Objectification" stressed that "objectification" is as much a phenomenological principle, a moment in the reader's *reception* of the text, as it is a principle of composition or structure: "*the apprehension satisfied completely* as to the appearance of the art form as an object . . . [the poet's aim is] writing . . . which is an object *or affects the mind as such*" (*P* 13, emphases mine). Zukofsky's Objectivist poem is one that has a tangibility in the reader's perception analogous to that of a palpable object, not one that aims to achieve an objecthood over and above its existence as marks on a page representing a series of given sounds.

Any misgivings about *ARK*'s rhetoric of objecthood, and the self-reflexive quality of that rhetoric, must be dismissed as minor cavils in the face of what Johnson has achieved in the poem as a whole. Johnson begins his brief concluding "Note" to *ARK* by paying homage to Pound, Williams, Zukofsky, and Olson, each the author of one of the long poems whose "risks and shipwrecks" (*ARK* [277]) stood as intimidating models before him. In response, Johnson opted to write not a "poem including history" (Pound's definition of the epic) but "a poem *without* history . . . a poem which needs no reference except itself" ("Planting" 2). As Thom Gunn puts it, "Pound's didactic intentions are numerous, complex, and changing; Johnson's intentions are aesthetic" (21). While *ARK* is full of allusions, quotations, and references, it no more enforces our tracing of those references than do "A"-22 and -23. Johnson is well aware of the historiographical goals of Pound, Williams, and Olson, but he has chosen as his own model the generous significatory plenitude of later Zukofsky. In so doing, he has produced in *ARK* one of the most intellectually and aurally beautiful poems of our time. Johnson's work is an extraordinary achievement indeed. Silliman's implication that Johnson has read Zukofsky's work as "the limit of possibility itself" is understandable (if a trifle harsh) in context: of *ARK* as a whole, Silliman had seen only *Radi Os* (and perhaps some of the early versions of the "BEAMs" Johnson had published in journals) when he wrote his review. *Radi Os* is indeed a continuation and elaboration of what Zukofsky does to Milton in "A"-14 (although it is also an adaptation of what composer Lucas Foss does to Handel in the first of his *Baroque Variations*), just as the compositional methods of *ARK* itself owe much to the later movements of "A". But Johnson has taken Zukofsky's poetic modes and his poetic rhetoric and created something all his own—a post-Objectivist poem every bit as vital and alive as Silliman's *The Alphabet.* Guy Davenport has on several occasions pronounced Johnson "America's greatest living poet." I shy away from such obiter dicta myself, but in my heart I believe Davenport is right.

In 1974 John Taggart completed one of the very first doctoral dissertations addressing Zukofsky's work, "Intending a Solid Object: A Study of Objectivist Poetics." When he received his Ph.D., he had already left Syracuse University and was teaching at Shippensburg State College (now Shippensburg University, in Pennsylvania), where he is now professor of English. "Intending a Solid Object" takes its title from *Bottom* (*B* 423), and although it deals with the poetry of both Oppen and Zukofsky, its theoretical understanding of Objectivist poetics comes from Zukofsky's prose writings. As distinct from the "doctrinal minority" (*P* 31) of poets who had long praised Zukofsky's work, Taggart was one of its very first *critical* champions, editing a Zukofsky issue of his periodical *MAPS* (1973) that is still remarkable for the range and acuity of critics that it gathers, from David Melnick on *Bottom* to Kenneth Cox's splendid essay on "A"-19.

But Taggart is first and foremost a poet rather than a poet-critic or poet-theorist—to borrow the term Marjorie Perloff uses of him in her foreword to his *Songs of Degrees* (vi), where she groups him with David Antin, Susan Howe, and other prominent figures of his generation. The Objectivist dissertation as a whole was never published as a book, the usual route of academic dissertations, and Taggart brought out seven volumes of his own poetry before collecting his published essays in 1994 as *Songs of Degrees: Essays on Contemporary Poetry and Poetics*—another title, one notes, from Zukofsky. *Songs of Degrees* includes four essays on Taggart's own poetics, as well as essays on Robert Duncan and Charles Olson (one each), George Oppen (two), and three extended and to my mind indispensable considerations of Zukofsky. Taggart also writes on William Bronk and two lesser-known poets heavily influenced by Zukofsky, Theodore Enslin and the late Frank Samperi. Three pieces address two poets commonly considered members of the Language group: Susan Howe (two essays) and Bruce Andrews (one brief note). Taggart has almost unqualified praise for Howe's work, but it is significant that he values it for the "brilliant and dark" (132) vision that its fractured wordplay evokes, choosing to disregard completely the question of to what extent it may participate in a communal renovation of poetic language or form. His review of Andrews, indeed, calls into question many of the basic premises of the Language movement as a whole. Taggart asks whether the Language poets' work "hasn't turned the analytic preparation that is modernism into a self-contained (and contented) style of its own. . . . [Such writing] can force or encourage a more conscious experience of language, it can produce varieties of irony in the process. It is not clear that it can do anything else" (68–69). Such an assessment, however honestly it may be intended, is not calculated to win friends in the Language poetry camp.

Silliman's assessment of Taggart's position vis-à-vis the communities of practicing poets—if not his assessment of that position's results for Taggart's work—is on the whole accurate. Taggart has indeed refused to affiliate himself with any organized movement, and his work has in turn been passed over in the two most prominent avant-garde anthologies of the 1980s: Silliman's *American Tree* (1986) and Douglas Messerli's *"Language" Poetries* (1987). He has remained a liminal figure, publishing work in the same magazines as many of the Language poets (*Sulfur, Temblor,* and *Jimmy and Lucy's House of "K"*, for instance, and even in the periodical *L=A=N=G=U=A=G=E* itself) but refusing either to ally himself with those poets or to assent to the politicization of poetics that is such an integral part of much of their thinking. His work, I am convinced by any number of conversations with poets, is widely respected but regarded with a certain distance.

Silliman's more specific charge that Taggart's poetry has somehow failed to go beyond Zukofsky's example is, like the same charge applied to Johnson, well worth examining. Taggart's early work, especially the short poems of *To Construct a Clock* (1971) and *Prism and the Pine Twig* (1977), is in an explicitly Zukofskyan mode: brief-lined, chiseled, terse, specific, and taut. The final poem of *Clock,* indeed, openly tips its hat to Zukofsky in its epigraph and its title, "Liveforever: Of Actual Things in Expansion." It is clear from Taggart's critical writings that the Objectivist care with which Zukofsky produces such shorter poems as "Songs of

Degrees" (1953–55) represents a certain very persuasive ideal of the poet's task (see *Songs of Degrees* 88–107). If Taggart went no further than adapting the protocols of sincerity and objectification as exemplified in Zukofsky's short poems, then perhaps Silliman's charge would be a fair one. But Taggart clearly goes beyond this.

Where Johnson extends Zukofsky's rhetoric of the poem as a tangible object, Taggart has explored and extended the implications of Zukofsky's rhetoric of the audible, his notion of "musical form" in poetry. Zukofsky, as I have outlined, both makes music a rhetorical backdrop for his poems and models his poems on specific musical forms, in particular the Baroque fugue. In a 1978 interview, Taggart notes how he was initially attracted to Zukofsky by "the infinite care that was evident in the poem" (Interview 47) and by the possibilities Zukofsky offered for organizing a poem on musical principles. His 1974 volume *The Pyramid is a Pure Crystal,* which is dedicated to Zukofsky, is a large-scale canon (in the musical sense) that takes as its foundation, or cantus firmus, the single sentence "the pyramid is a pure crystal." In this work, and in its successor, *Dodeka,* Taggart makes fascinating and almost obsessive use of compositional techniques borrowed from classical music—techniques rivaling in complexity and reconditeness Zukofsky's numerical distribution of *n* and *r* sounds in "A"-8 and "A"-9.

As fundamental to Zukofsky's work as his obvious, mechanical adaptations of musical shape is his conceptual conflation of tangible, objectified shape and melodic form. "A"-6 does indeed inquire whether "The design / Of the fugue" can "Be transferred / To poetry" ("A"-6, 38), but it also asserts, rather boldly, "The melody! the rest is accessory" ("A"-6, 24). The aim of Zukofsky's principle of "sincerity" is writing that directs observed particulars "along a line of melody" (*P* 12). The tangible form the poet aims for—the objectification so crucial to the poem's realization—is here associated explicitly with "melody." For Zukofsky, poetry moves between the two limit points, "Lower limit speech / Upper limit music": the upper limit, the more sublime or enviable one, is a purely musical mode. Zukofsky is of course well aware that this is an unreachable limit, that words cannot *be* musical notes (unless they are actually sung). The poem is a "context associated with 'musical' shape, *musical with quotation marks* since it is not of notes as music, but of words" (*P* 16, emphases mine).

While Taggart's middle period work explores procedural compositional strategies that rival in complexity some of the systems underlying parts of Zukofsky's *"A"*, Taggart has, since 1981's *Peace on Earth*, obdurately pursued the implications of Zukofsky's rhetoric of poetry as an inherently musical art. *Peace on Earth* marks Taggart's emergence into his fully developed mature style, a mode that openly acknowledges its reliance on the models of jazz and American minimalist music. Zukofsky theorizes at various times that the printed poem is a score for the voice ("Typography—certainly—if print and the arrangement of it will help tell how the voice should sound" [*P* 17]) but never with the proselytizing vigor of Olson's 1950 essay, "Projective Verse." "It is the advantage of the typewriter," Olson writes, "that, due to its rigidity and its space precisions, it can, for a poet, indicate exactly the breath, the pauses, the suspensions even of syllables, the juxtapositions even of parts of phrases, which he intends. For the first time the poet has the stave and the bar a musician has had" (*Human Universe* 57). In his introduction to Taggart's mid-period work *Dodeka* (or so I classify it), Robert Duncan notes how for him and many of his contemporaries in the 1960s, "*'A'* and [Olson's] *Maximus*, for these two stood so in our minds in the aftermath of the work of Pound and Williams, could be posed as polarities of what poetic consciousness might be" (*Dodeka* v). (Compare Johnson's characterization of the two as "The Minimalist and The Maximus.") It is Duncan's joy to have discovered, even in the severely rule-constrained poems *The Pyramid* and *Dodeka*, that Taggart has managed simultaneously to tap into Olson's protean verbal energy and Zukofsky's overwhelmingly careful, sincere sense of poetic "placing."

Taggart's mature poetics, which have come to fruition in the years since 1979's *Dodeka*, are founded on both the Zukofskyan notion of the poem as melody, as musical composition, and Olson's Projectivist emphasis on the poet's voice as active performer of the poem. For the past fifteen years Taggart has written poems that are explicitly designed for reading aloud, poems in which, "if not enacted by the voice, the cadence makes no sense. Its shifting motion only confuses and irritates the eye" (*Songs of*

Degrees 77). What "defeat[s] the silent reading eye" in the poems of *Peace on Earth, Dehiscence, Loop,* and *Standing Wave* is a (mostly) long-lined poetry that seems to be rooted not directly in any Western literary tradition but to have more in common with jazz, rhythm and blues, and the so-called minimalist classical music. That is, this is a poetry whose most important components are rhythmical and aural and whose sense of repetition and repetition with variations owes as much to John Coltrane, Marvin Gaye, or Eric Dolphy as to Bach. The first few lines of "The Rothko Chapel Poem" serve as a germane enough example:

> Red deepened by black red made deep by black
> prolation of deep red like stairs of lava
> deep red like stairs of lava to gather us in
> gather us before the movements are to be made
> red stairs lead us lead us to three red rooms
> rooms of deep red light red deepened by black
> in this first room there is to be a wedding
> we are the guests the welcome wedding guests
> the groom welcomes us the bride welcomes us
> rooms full of deep red light room upon room
> [*Loop* 137]

While the shifting and overlapping repetitions of these lines put one in mind of the minimalist composers, Taggart's work differs from their music in the fact that he is at no point committed to the steady pulse that is at the heart of most of Steve Reich's, John Adams's, or Philip Glass's works (in poetry, such a pulse would be a principle of direct repetition, either metrical or lexical). Taggart explains how the notion of *cadence* operates in his poetry: "The line is prevented from falling in on itself by a recurrent, but never exactly repeating, cadence. This cadence undergoes a continuous motion (transformation). It is not quite accurate to say it shifts in and out of phase unless the phase of the cadence is understood to have no set identity. It is always identifiable in its overlapping *motion* of addition and decay" (*Songs of Degrees* 77).

The "cadence" of Taggart's poetry is of necessity a purely *verbal* one, but its extraverbal sources are clear: not only does Taggart, in his statements of poetics, draw attention to the composers and performers who have influenced his methods, but the poems themselves turn repeatedly, almost compulsively, to musical themes. *Peace on Earth*, for instance, Taggart's first work in this cadenced mode, borrows its title from a famous John Coltrane Japan concert, and its poem "Giant Steps" is based on a Coltrane tune. *Loop* includes poems explicitly deriving from the work of Jerry Lee Lewis ("For Jerry Lee Lewis," *Loop* 128) and Thelonious Monk ("Monk," *Loop* 178–80), and there are a multitude of references to musical works, performances, and composers, ranging from Jackie Wilson (*Loop* 236) to the Rolling Stones (*Loop* 101), Charles Wesley (*Loop* 13–15), and Olivier Messiaen (*Loop* 7–10).

This element of Taggart's work, its constant thematization of music and its reliance on musical compositions as structuring frame and even subject matter, might serve to raise some doubts about the overall validity of his musical poetics. In the first place, there is the matter of the poems' "cadence," a movement only realizable by the reading voice. To what extent is that cadence determined by Taggart's own benign, gently Midwestern voice? Can other readers, possessing their own distinctive voices and speech patterns, hope to realize a cadence approximating that which the poet has scored in his work? This question of the adequacy of the poem as reading score becomes most obvious when Taggart's lines include "scoring" that looks suspiciously like directions for actual singing rather than speaking, as in the "Marvin Gaye Suite" ("it's not who-who-who it's *oooooo—oooooo—oooooo* it's a hook / it's a hook made smooth made so very smooth *oooooo—oooooo—oooooo*" [*Loop* 218]) and in the more recent "Aria No. 17" ("Thrill is gone thrill is gone away-ay-ay-aay" [239]). Does one simply read these lines as printed, or does one sing them? And if they are sung, then to what tune? (In his public readings, Taggart sings the "*oooooo*"'s of "Marvin Gaye"; I have not heard him read "Aria No. 17.")

Closely intertangled with the question of the poems' performance, so manifestly at the heart of Taggart's art, is the fact that his poems often take recorded musical performances as their stepping-off point, or their formal frame. "Monk," for instance, is a fairly straightforward example: the words of the hymn "Abide With Me" are here subjected to a treatment similar to one of Thelonious Monk's improvisations on a tune; only a handful of the words remain, juxtaposed and repeated in a treatment reminiscent of what Johnson does for Milton in *Radi Os:*

A-bide a- a-
bide

fast falls
the tide

fast

the darkness deepens
[*Loop* 178]

(Readers not reared in Protestant families might find it helpful to recall the words "Abide with me, fast falls the even tide, / The darkness deepens, Lord with me abide.") But of what significance to the reader is the fact that Taggart had Aretha Franklin's performance of "The Thrill is Gone" in mind when writing "Aria No. 17"? And what resonance can the poem have for the reader who has indeed never heard the song at all? The nine poems of the "Marvin Gaye Suite" correspond in certain clearly determinate ways to the nine songs of rhythm and blues singer Gaye's classic 1973 album, *What's Going On.* And if one is familiar with the first track, the title track of that album, the opening lines of Section 1 will make immediate sense:

17 seconds of party formulaics by professional football players
intro of 17 second of hey man what's happening and right on
party of those gathered to be laid by the voice that lays
don't have to be a jock to be gathered brought together for the lay
Marvin mixed over the party Marvin calls out twice to mother
[*Loop* 216]

The record does indeed begin with what sounds like a party, in which voices can be distinctly heard saying "what's happening?" and "right on," followed by the entry of the rhythm section, and then Gaye's achingly pure voice singing, "Mother, mother." If, however, one has never heard the song, or if one does not know the tragic familial circumstances of Gaye's death, which figure so prominently in later sections of the poem—Gaye was shot to death by his own father—what sort of connections do Taggart's lines make?

It is ultimately not the specificity of the references that might be troublesome here: one can always look up and listen to a copy of *What's Going On,* just as one can listen to a recording of the *St. Matthew Passion* or consult a history of Renaissance Italy to find out what Pound's Malatesta is up to. Reservations center, rather, on Taggart's use, following Zukofsky, of musical analogies. Where Zukofsky takes music in a Paterian sense as the ideal—because contentless, nonrepresentational—formal art and constructs his poems on principles that follow those of music, Taggart goes further by pursuing an actual connection between music and poetry, to the extent that a large proportion of his work either directly refers to, or is based on, specific musical works. This focusing on the productions of another medium might appear as potentially narrowing as the monumentalizing self-reflexiveness evident in the later sections of Johnson's *ARK.* At moments, that is, it seems that Taggart has taken Zukofsky's description of poetry as a musical art all too literally and has thereby failed to go beyond the lessons of the older poet.

But Taggart's focusing on musical works is only a single aspect of his poetics as a whole, which is at its most fundamental level concerned with the act of reading, of interpretation. "The poet," as Taggart writes in his Duncan essay, "who is first a reader, makes no original discovery in reading. Instead, the poet becomes only more aware of the spider-web connectedness of his or her sources and of the innumerable ghostly speakers still beyond them" (*Songs of Degrees* 127). (In this concern with the poet as reader, I think Taggart's affinities with the Zukofsky of *Bottom* or of "A"-12 and "A"-23 should be evident.) The "reading" he speaks of here is in part a literal reading: his essay on Olson focuses on that poet's encounter with Melville, as his assessment of William Bronk concerns itself with Bronk's reliance on Stevens. But one can also "read" a musical work, and Taggart's poetry concerns itself as well with the contemplation of works of the visual arts, like the Mark Rothko paintings of "The Rothko Chapel Poem" (*Loop* 137–71), or the unnamed photograph of "Black and White Close-Up" (*Standing Wave* 33–44).

For Taggart, the act of poetry is bound up with the pursuit of the spiritual—the numinous—and that evanescent experience can be attained only through the prolonged contemplation of or meditation on an object or experience external to the poet. This process is most explicitly played out in Taggart's 1993 prose work *Remaining in Light,* an extended series of meditations on a single Edward Hopper painting. Taggart's contemplation of Hopper's "A Woman in the Sun" leads him on a potentially endless journey through a multitude of "texts" ranging from Francis Bacon paintings and Talking Heads recordings to writings by Michael Palmer, Edmond Jabès, and Jacques Derrida. At the same time, he develops the metaphor of the woman in Hopper's painting (nude, staring out a sunlit window off the right side of the canvas) as a figure of the reader, contemplating the numinous to the point of blindness. To contemplate such a painting, just as one contemplates an Aretha Franklin recording or a Marvin Gaye album, is not to somehow diminish the poet's "inspiration" through extrapoetic crutches. In response to the possible objection that his use of prior artworks might seem "terribly, maybe even incestuously, arty," Taggart asserts that such works "[exist] for me as the ring of Blue Mountains surrounding this valley. They simply *are.* Their art exists in the same continuous reality, the same continuous *day* of those mountains" (*Songs of Degrees* 73). Zukofsky registers his own recognition of commonalities between his own work and that of earlier poets, those moments of "duration," not with guilt or with a sense of Bloomian belatedness but with joy that "the shape of his ground seems to have been / A constant" ("A"-12, 175) for not merely him but all his predecessors. In a significant revision and furtherance of Zukofsky's project, Taggart finds in the achievements of earlier singers, musicians, artists, and writers not a crutch for his own writings or a foundation on which to build his own poetic creations but objects of contemplation and meditation through which he, and in turn his readers, can be to some degree in touch with the spiritual, the numinous, which Taggart represents in poem after poem as the "voice" that "eats away the face," that effaces the individuality of the listener/perceiver with its power and immediacy. As he writes in his Frank Samperi essay, "The history of poetry in our century is only superficially the history of the struggle to make it new.

More enduring is the struggle to regain the definition of poetry as spiritual ascesis" (*Songs of Degrees* 23).

The spiritual dimension of Taggart's work, a dimension utterly alien to most of the Language poets, has attracted a group of young poets associated with the journal *apex of the M*—poets whose primary basis of commonality seems to be their reaction against the perceived hegemony of what they see as an overtheorized, hypertechnical, and ultimately spiritually sterile Language poetry establishment. In his passionate manifesto *Swallowing the Scroll: Late in a Prophetic Tradition with the Poetry of John Taggart and Susan Howe* (a stylistic amalgam of Cotton Mather, Heidegger, and Richard Crashawe), Lew Daly, one of the editors of *apex*, lays particular stress on the Levinasian aspect of Taggart's poetics, its valorization of the poet's and reader's encounter with the human and extrahuman Other. Indeed, one of the most striking characteristics of Taggart's work is its explicitly communal aspect. Above all, as Taggart writes in "The Poem as a Woven Scarf," the poem must be "the voice's enactment of language, one interior calling out to another, so there may be presence and community" (*Songs of Degrees* 76). The printed poem as a script for reading invites a certain performance but does not impose it; where Taggart himself may sing certain lines, I may speak them, or sing them to a different set of notes. But the poem at all points makes manifest its status as both human artifact and human communication, its "responsibility to a community which, in part, the poet has helped come into existence" (*Songs of Degrees* 78). Taggart, I would argue, has indeed pursued an individualistic path in developing his poetics; but the goal of that poetics is ultimately not that different from what Silliman envisions as the proper starting point of innovative writing: community itself, individual voices entering into and partaking of the voices of others.

Taggart's and Johnson's mature poetics are radically different, and it seems almost to strain the definition of "tradition" to place them both within a single post-Objectivist tradition. Yet both the dazzling, playful architecture of Johnson's *ARK* and the sonically mesmeric and exhilarating musical structures of Taggart's *Loop* and *Standing Wave* are fundamentally indebted, not to any clearly defined Objectivist "movement" but to the poetics and poetic practice of Louis Zukofsky. It is true that these two poets have themselves steered clear of entangling alliances with groups or coteries, and this may in part account for their relative absence from critical studies and classroom syllabi—as opposed to, for instance, Charles Bernstein or Lyn Hejinian. But I cannot agree with Silliman that their chosen isolation has in any way impoverished their poetics, any more than the isolation of Zukofsky's later years mitigated the achievement of "A"-22 and -23 or *80 Flowers*. Zukofsky's poetic presence is capacious enough to serve as instigation and example for more than any one group of poets. Not merely the Language poets but Taggart and Johnson, and generations of poets younger than them, continue to look to his work as a peerless realization, fulfillment, and extension of the principles of the twentieth-century "revolution of the word" that is still being rigorously prosecuted all around us.

A Polemical Conclusion

(Toward) A Poetry of Knowledge

My heart rouses
          thinking to bring you news
            of something
that concerns you
          and concerns many men. Look at
                    what passes for the new.
You will not find it there but in
          despised poems.
                    It is difficult
to get the news from poems
          yet men die miserably every day
                    for lack
of what is found there.
—William Carlos Williams, *Pictures from Brueghel* 161–62

Much of my discussion of Louis Zukofsky's poetry has involved that poetry's formal characteristics, and I would close this book with an examination of form in one of his more celebrated shorter works. It is typical of Zukofsky, who often strikes one as a walking bundle of contradictions, that one of his most hortatory and politically committed poems, a work written in 1934 at perhaps the height of his involvement in left-wing politics, should as well be a formal exercise, and should be followed by an exegesis that concentrates not on the poem's ideological "message" but on its seemingly retrograde, traditional verse form.

" 'Mantis,' " like so much of Zukofsky's work, both reflects his tuition in the "school of Pound" and demonstrates the extent to which he brings a self-consciousness beyond Pound's to that tradition. Like Pound's "Sestina: Altaforte" (*Personae* 26–28), " 'Mantis' " is a sestina, a seven-stanza poem in a form invented by Dante's "miglior fabbro," the Troubadour Arnaut Daniel (fl. 1190). The requirements of the form are clearly specified and rigorously bind the poet. There is no conventional rhyme, but the line-end words of the first six-line stanza are reshuffled in each succeeding stanza until the sixth, when they reach the limit of their combinatory possibilities (the limit, that is, given the pattern of recombination that the form prescribes): a further combination would result in the repetition of the order of the first stanza. The sixth stanza is followed by a three-line coda, the *commiato* or *congedo* (or *tornada*), in which all six of the key words reappear, half in line-end positions and half somewhere within the lines.[1] The beginning of this movement can be seen in the first two stanzas of " 'Mantis' ":

> Mantis! praying mantis! since your wings' leaves
> And your terrified eyes, pins, bright, black and poor
> Beg—"Look, take it up" (thoughts' torsion)! "save it!"
> I who can't bear to look, cannot touch,—You—
> You can—but no one sees you steadying lost
> In the cars' drafts on the lit subway stone.
>
> Praying mantis, what wind-up brought you, stone
> On which you sometimes prop, prey among leaves
> (Is it love's food your raised stomach prays?), lost
> Here, stone holds only seats on which the poor
> Ride, who rising from the news may trample you—
> The shops' crowds a jam with no flies in it.
> [*CSP* 65–66]

Zukofsky's lines, though they are by no means blank verse, have approximately ten syllables each. The sestina form works to impose an extraordinary constraint on his semantic choice, on what Jakobson would call the "axis of selection": out of the approximately 390 syllables of the poem, over 10 percent (forty-two) are predetermined to be the six key words: "leaves," "poor," "it," "you," "lost," and "stone." An additional syntactic constraint is exerted by the relatively determined grammatical nature of half of these words; whereas "leaves" and "stone" can be either noun or verb and "poor" can be either adjective or noun, there is no such flexibility in constructing syntactic patterns around "it," "you," and "lost."

In choosing to write his "Altaforte" as a sestina, Pound is engaging in his favored activity of renovating the voices of the past (in this case the Provençal figure Bertran de Born) by reimagining them in English—but in foreign, archaic poetic forms. The sestina is a useful formal measure here because of its inherent association with Provençal verse, and by choosing the most vivid words possible as his line-ends ("peace," "music," "clash," "opposing," "crimson," and "rejoicing"), Pound can emphasize the violence and turbulence both of his persona and of the era in which he lives: "Dante Alighieri put this man in hell for that he was a stirrer up of strife," he notes, and asks his readers to judge, "Have I dug him up again?" (*Personae* 26). The sestina form, as well, mimes Bertran's obsessive nature through its constant repetitions. Zukofsky's poem, in contrast to Pound's historical enterprise, is involved with immediate events and contemporary society: the poet's chance encounter with a praying mantis in a subway station becomes the trigger for an exploration of the economic situation of the day (1934), a meditation that culminates in the coda with an impassioned address to the insect and a call to arms of the proletariat:

> Fly, mantis, on the poor, arise like leaves
> The armies of the poor, strength: stone on stone
> And build the new world in your eyes, Save it!
> [*CSP* 66]

Notwithstanding the affective power of the poem itself, and Zukofsky's obvious mastery of the sestina form (one evidence of the formal facility so overwhelmingly present in the double canzone of "A"-9), " 'Mantis' " would stand only as a tour de force—another vaguely dilettantish effort by a contemporary poet to breathe life into an exotic form—were it not for the poem that follows it: " *'Mantis,' An Interpretation*" (*CSP* 67–73). This commentary, over three times as long as " 'Mantis' " itself, attempts to justify Zukofsky's choice of the sestina form as a necessary compositional measure rather than a sterile formal exercise or reactionary gesture away from free verse. The dialectic of poetic history is marked by such retrograde gestures, the most famous of which is perhaps Pound's and Eliot's adoption, in *Hugh Selwyn Mauberley* and in the "quatrain" poems of *Poems* (1920), of a fairly rigid, rhymed quatrain form. As Pound puts it, "two authors, neither engaged in picking the other's pocket, decided that the dilutation of vers libre, Amygism, Lee Masterism, general floppiness had gone too far and that some counter-current must be set going. . . . Remedy prescribed 'Émaux et Camées' (or the Bay State Hymn Book). Rhyme and regular strophes" (quoted in Espey 25). Zukofsky at no point implies that his poem represents such a retrenchment, but even as *"An Interpretation"* ingeniously pleads on behalf of the ostensibly retrograde form of " 'Mantis,' " it makes evident an interesting and deep-seated contradiction within Zukofsky's very conception of the relationship of form and content, an ultimately insurmountable contradiction between the Romantic ideology of "organic form" and Zukofsky's own specifically modernist formal self-consciousness.

"An Interpretation" makes its argument on two levels that coexist uneasily. On the one hand it argues that the sestina, which Zukofsky characterizes in Dante's words as "la battaglia delli diversi pensieri . . . / the battle of diverse thoughts" (*CSP* 68),[2] bears an isomorphic relationship to "The actual twisting / Of many and diverse thoughts" evoked in the poet's mind by his experience of seeing the mantis. The relationship of form and content, then, is an organic one, and the sestina form itself is implicit in the manner in which the poet's insights appear to him:

> this thoughts' torsion
> Is really a sestina
> Carrying subconsciously
> Many intellectual and sensual properties of the
> forgetting and remembering Head
> One human's intuitive Head
> [*CSP* 68]

This is the New Critical Fallacy of Imitative Form with a vengeance; such a stance anticipates Robert Creeley's famous dictum, relayed through Olson's "Projective Verse" essay, that "FORM IS NEVER MORE THAN AN EXTENSION OF CONTENT" (*Human Universe* 52). But as well as anticipating the critical dogmas of the "New American Poetry," Zukofsky here strongly echoes the Romantic doctrine of organic form, most memorably stated in America by Emerson and Whitman. In "The Poet," Emerson writes, "it is not metres, but a metre-making argument that makes a poem,—a thought so passionate and alive that like the spirit of a plant or an animal it has an architecture of its own, and adorns nature with a new thing" (450). And Whitman, in the preface to the first (1855) edition of *Leaves of Grass*, argues that "the poetic quality is not marshalled in rhyme or uniformity. . . . The rhyme and uniformity of perfect poems show the free growth of metrical laws and bud from them as unerringly and loosely as lilacs or roses on a bush, and take shapes as compact as the shapes of chesnuts and oranges and melons and pears, and shed the perfume impalpable to form" (11). The sestina, in the light of this tradition and of Zukofsky's own comments, is not a frame to be filled but a "force" (like the fugue) that compels and shapes the writing: "as an experiment, the sestina would be wicker-work— / As a force, one would lie to one's feelings not to use it" (*CSP* 69).

The sestina " 'Mantis,' " however, with over one-tenth of its words determined by its form, is certainly no *Song of Myself* in terms of formal license. Zukofsky, writing *"An Interpretation,"* is fully aware that the sestina form, no matter how strikingly closely it may seem to model the "torsion" of the poet's thoughts, is at the same time an artificial form that bears with it a history of invention and usage.[3] Zukofsky comments acidly on the most immediately pre-modernist appearance of the sestina—its adoption in English by the Victorian Pre-Raphaelite poets:

> What is most significant
> Perhaps is that C—and S—and X—of the 19th century
> Used the "form"—not the form but a Victorian
> Stuffing like upholstery
> For parlor polish,
> And our time takes count against them
> For their blindness and their (unintended?) cruel smugness.
> [*CSP* 69]

This is the dilettantish use of the sestina that Zukofsky is anxious to disclaim—the sestina as "wicker-work" on which to hang already digested observation or rhetoric. What he does claim is that his own choice of the sestina, however organic or natural the form might seem for the thoughts he wishes to embody, is—however paradoxically—conditioned as well by the sestina's history and prior use.

A short way into *"An Interpretation,"* Zukofsky records his first attempt to "write up" the mantis, twenty-seven words of undistinguished free verse:

> "The mantis opened its body
> It had been lost in the subway
> It steadied against the drafts
> It looked up—
> Begging eyes—
>
> It flew at my chest"
> [*CSP* 67]

But the poet finds this unsatisfactory, initially because "The ungainliness / of the creature needs stating," and these six lines have not accomplished that goal: they are not ungainly but merely flat. Given the mental impetus of the poem—"Thoughts'—two or three or five or / Six thoughts' reflection (pulse's witness) of what was happening / All immediate, not moved by any transition"—the question in the poet's mind becomes "what should be the form / Which the ungainliness already suggested / Should take?" (*CSP* 68). The form that immediately occurs to Zukofsky (in his own account) is the sestina, a form that mirrors "Inevitable recurrence again in the blood / Where the spaces of verse are not visual / But a movement" (*CSP* 69). The sestina suggests itself not because of but *despite* its usage by the nineteenth-century poets. For Zukofsky, the preeminent practitioner of the sestina is of course Dante himself, whose *La Vita Nuova* is cited at the beginning of *"An Interpretation,"* and whose sestina "Al poco giorno" is quoted toward the end: "com'huom pietra sott' erba / as one should hide a stone in grass" (*CSP* 73). Dante's sestina represents for Zukofsky the perfect marriage of form and content, the poem's thought inseparable from the complex structuring in which it is embodied, as opposed to the "wicker-work" or "Victorian / Stuffing" of nineteenth-century English sestinas. Viewed in this historical perspective, the sestina is not a form per se but a force, a "fact" among other facts motivating and contributing to the writing:

> One feels in fact inevitably
> About the coincidence of the mantis lost in the subway,
> About the growing oppression of the poor—
> Which is the situation most pertinent to us—,
> With the fact of the sestina:
> Which together fatally now crop up again
> To twist themselves anew
> To record not a sestina, post Dante,
> Nor even a mantis.
> [*CSP* 69]

The poem aims to "record" neither a "sestina" nor a "mantis" but to embody a set of "facts" in the poet's mind, among which are his experience in the subway station, his firsthand or otherwise knowledge of the plight of the poor, and the poetic use-value of the sestina form.

The answer to the question "Is the poem then, a sestina / Or not a sestina?" (*CSP* 70) must then be both yes and no. It is yes, in the most basic sense, in that the turnings and "torsions" of the poem's language, reflecting the "twisting / Of many and diverse thoughts" (*CSP* 68), assume the seven-stanza pattern of recurrences identified with Daniel's and Dante's works. The answer is no in that the poem is not an exercise, an experiment, or a virtuosic display ("The word sestina has been / Taken out of the original title" [*CSP* 70]) in which the poet's primary aim is precisely to write a sestina, to produce a poem in a given form.[4] On a certain level, Zukofsky has inherited the sestina form from Dante, and from all other practitioners of the form who have preceded him. But he refuses to take this inheritance for granted, to accept it as a given (just as, one might argue, he refuses to accept the English language as merely an inheritance). Joseph Conte's allegory of the postmodern sestina is interesting; he proposes that Zukofsky's and John Ashbery's uses of the form resemble yuppie renovations of Victorian brownstone houses, in which only the shells of the houses remain intact, the interiors now containing "new hardwood, track lighting, framed lithographs, Boston ferns, and Italian furniture" (167). I propose an allegory more in line with the actual practices of postmodern architecture: by writing " 'Mantis' " as a sestina, Zukofsky is, as it were, reinventing the brownstone—building, in the form of the old, a new house that by its very existence critiques the old, functioning as an ironic commentary. Like Borges's Pierre Menard, a modern writer who schools himself to write—not *re*write—a chapter of *Don Quixote,* in the process recognizing the innumerable cultural forces that contributed to Cervantes' masterwork (*Labyrinths* 36–44), Zukofsky reinvents the sestina by recognizing in his own "thoughts' torsion" pressures identical to those that led Dante to write "Al poco giorno."

Such a reading, however, verges on mere apologetics. In all probability, " *'Mantis,' An Interpretation*" bears the same relationship to Zukofsky's poem " 'Mantis' " as Poe's "The Philosophy of Composition" does to its author's wildly popular "The Raven."[5] (With the crucial difference, of course, that Zukofsky is not attempting a money-making follow-up to a popular and profitable literary "hit," as was Poe.) Even if one were not to question the good faith of Zukofsky's description of how he arrived at the sestina form, it is extremely difficult to reconcile the competing claims of the sestina as an inevitable, organic outgrowth of the poet's thoughts and the sestina as a historically specific form, bearing with it a history of usage. Zukofsky can only imagine the compositional process that led Dante to write his sestinas; to claim that they are organic outgrowths of Dante's thought processes is to apply a historically posterior ideology of form—Romantic organicism—to a medieval composition for which it is, to say the least, ill-fitted. The compositional processes Dante himself describes in *Vita Nuova,* for instance, certainly bear little resemblance to what Zukofsky talks about.

By examining " 'Mantis' " itself, and Zukofsky's account of his poem, one begins to see how Zukofsky's ideology of form is inseparable from his ideology of information, the knowledge that the poem embodies and transmits to the reader. The "torsion" exemplified by the twistings and repetitions of the poem's six key words, a fairly mechanical species of counterpointing, is itself counterpointed by the poem's movement among the various themes and quanta of information in the poet's mind. In *"An Interpretation,"* Zukofsky provides something of a gloss on some of these data:

> For example—
> line 1—entomology
> line 9—biology
> lines 10 and 11—the even rhythm of riding under-
> ground, . . .
> line 12—pun, fact, banality
> lines 13 to 18—the economics of the very poor . . .
> lines 22 to 24—Provence myth
> lines 25 to 29—Melanesian self-extinction myth
> line 33—airships
> lines 35 and 36—creation myth (Melanesia), residue of
> it in our emotions no matter if fetched
> from the moon, as against l. 25 to 29.
> and naturally the coda which is the
> only thing that can sum up the
> jumble of order in the lines weaving
> [*CSP* 71–72]

What the poem accomplishes is the "weaving" together of a number of diverse perceptions and knowledges, ranging from the immediate experiences of the senses, to a more theoretical perception of economic realities, to recondite mythical and ethnological data of the sort one finds so often invoked in *The Cantos* and in *"A"*. The ultimate form that this weaving together takes is that of the sestina—not the sestina as an available form but the sestina as an inevitable outgrowth of the patterns in the poet's mind. The form is neither symbolic nor primarily mimetic but a structure in itself, a structure whose pattern is the pattern of the thoughts held in relation in the poet's "one head":

> Nor is the coincidence
> Of the last four lines
> Symbolism,
> But the simultaneous,

The diaphanous, historical
In one head.
[*CSP* 73]

As I have intimated, for Zukofsky poetic form is the primary incarnation of poetic knowledge. In this light, the sestina form of " 'Mantis' " conveys to its reader an immediate knowledge of how various "historic and contemporary particulars" (*P* 15) in the poet's mind are related one to another. One such particular, of course, is the literary-historical and human use-value of the form itself, both the uses made of it by Dante and Daniel and the more meretricious exploitations of nineteenth-century English poets. Implicit in the fact that " 'Mantis' " takes the form of a sestina is Zukofsky's intuition that the form, even in 1934, is more than "Victorian / Stuffing like upholstery"; if one regards the sestina as a structural force, a formal principle like the sonata or the fugue rather than a fixed form like the sonnet (or the limerick), then one can, according to Zukofsky, write a sestina with the same emotional authenticity and immediacy that he ascribes to Dante. The sestina binds the "particulars" of the poem—the poet's confrontation with the mantis, his conversation with the newsboy, his awareness of the plight of the poor in depression-era New York, his conviction that a proletarian uprising is the only possible solution to the economic situation, and so forth—into a "rested totality," a musical form in which these particulars may resonate both in turn and simultaneously in a reader's mind, imparting to that reader a knowledge that goes beyond that of elements presented sequentially to a knowledge of the relationships of those particulars with one another.

Whatever the historical accuracy of the compositional process delineated in *"An Interpretation,"* what is crucial here is the argument that Zukofsky mounts concerning the relationship of form and content in his poem, a position represented also, as we have seen, in other poems, such as "The lines of this new song." Emerson's comments concerning "metres" and "metre-making argument" are fundamental to the formal history of American poetry, and the argument of *"An Interpretation"* is squarely in line with Emerson's sense that poetic form cannot be simply received, inherited, or accepted but must be motivated by and rooted in the poem's argument. *"An Interpretation"* advances and further develops Zukofsky's long-standing conviction that the poem's form, while in some sense historically determined and therefore given, cannot bear a merely coincidental relationship with what one might (reductively) call the poem's meaning. The knowledge that the poem bears is a function of its relational structure rather than its referential reach. This position, at least, is not diminished by the glaring self-contradiction of Zukofsky's argument. Although the organicism of *"An Interpretation"* belongs to an ideology of form fundamentally at odds with the very formal structure it aims to explain—the sestina of " 'Mantis' "—the Objectivist rhetoric that characterizes the poem in terms of its structure, rather than its emotive movement, retains its explanatory and descriptive force.

The preceding chapters have explored Zukofsky's attitudes toward and treatments of traditional philosophical approaches to the question of human knowledge, that whole branch of philosophy we know as epistemology. This book has also examined the fundamental formalism of Zukofsky's work and how that formalism is bound up with both the concept of music and specific musiclike forms. In these discussions I have implied that for Zukofsky, the very particular knowledge to which poetry gives us access is somehow a function of its relationship with form and music. How then might one finally assess this relationship obtaining among music, poetry, and what one might somewhat awkwardly call "poetic" or "musical" knowledge? Once again, we return to Pater's claim in *The Renaissance* that "All art constantly aspires toward the condition of music" and to Pound's repetition of that claim in his *Gaudier-Brzeska* (82, 120). The latter work is a central document in understanding both Pound's own poetics and the whole "constructivist" strain of modernism (Marjorie Perloff's term). "One uses form," Pound writes, "as a musician uses sound. One does not imitate the wood dove, or at least one does not confine oneself to the imitation of wood-doves, one combines and arranges one's sound or one's forms into Bach fugues or into arrangements of colour, or into 'planes in relation' "

(*Gaudier-Brzeska* 125). Pound, in the context of his homage to the sculptor Henri Gaudier-Brzeska, is here speaking mainly of the visual and plastic arts, but the application of his rhetoric to the art of poetry should be evident. As Anthony Woodward puts it, music is crucial for Pound because, as the "least obviously mimetic of the arts," it is "a useful analogy for a literary artist bent on breaking with conventions of rhetorical progression and logical development" (21). For Pound, musical form provides a "useful analogy" for poetic form, just as the forms of painting and sculpture provide (somewhat less) useful analogies. Pound is usually too canny to represent the relationship between poetry and music as one of Pater's *Anders-streben*—that of one medium attempting to attain the condition of another. He seems to fall into this trap at one point in *Gaudier-Brzeska*, where he distinguishes between "lyric" and "imagistic" poetry: "There is a sort of poetry where music, sheer melody, seems as if it were just bursting into speech. There is another sort of poetry where painting or sculpture seems as if it were 'just coming over into speech' " (*Gaudier-Brzeska* 82). The key word in this passage, however, is "seems"; the *Anders-streben* here suggested is a moment in the reader's reception of the work rather than a constitutive principle of the poem itself, or an element in the poet's compositional process. The manner in which Pound draws the distinction among phanopœic, melopœic, and logopœic "kinds of poetry" makes it evident that musical (and pictorial) qualities in verse are potentialities inherent within the system of the language game itself rather than borrowings from other media.

In this light it becomes clear that Pater's "condition of music" represents for Pound not the interpenetration of two separate media but an ideal marriage of form and matter.[6] As Pater writes,

> That the mere matter of a poem, for instance, its subject, namely, its given incidents or situation—that the mere matter of a picture, the actual circumstances of an event, the actual topography of a landscape—should be nothing without the form, the spirit, of the handling; that this form, this mode of handling, should become an end in itself, should penetrate every part of the matter: this is what all art constantly strives after, and achieves in different degrees. (*Renaissance* 95)

In the portion of "An Objective" originally published in *An "Objectivists" Anthology*, Zukofsky describes poetry in terms that directly echo Pater's: "The order of all poetry is to approach a state of music wherein the ideas present themselves sensuously and intelligently and are of no predatory intention" (*P* 18). The Paterian ideal, one might argue, is the ultimate origin not only of the Objectivist conception of the poem as object, "the arrangement, into one apprehended unit, of minor units of sincerity—in other words, the resolving of words and their ideation into structure" (*P* 13), but of Yeats's 1936 formulation of poetic form as "full, sphere-like, single" (*Later Essays* 193) and of the New Critical paradigm of the poem as a self-contained, self-sufficient artistic construct not to be reduced by the heresy of paraphrase to a mere instrument of communication. As Cleanth Brooks writes, the poem's experience is communicable, if "we can come to know the poem as an object. . . . But the poet is most truthfully described as a *poietes* or maker, not as an expositor or communicator" (*Well Wrought Urn* 75). Zukofsky's critical writings and poetic practice constantly stress his similar conviction that the poem is not an outpouring or an expression but a *made* thing, a fundamentally formal construct, a language system whose very essence lies in the fact of its structure. This is not at all a revolutionary insight, of course, but it is one of the insights that most powerfully informs Pound's renovation of poetry in English: "To break the pentameter, that was the first heave" (*Cantos* 518) is a statement that fully encompasses the gravity involved in violating a poetic form so long established that its formal, artificial nature has been completely elided by the ideology of its naturalness, a seeming closeness to spoken English that somehow erases the form's artifactuality and renders it a neutral container for the lofty (or lowly) sentiments expressed by and the actions rendered within the poem (see Easthope).

To take Pater's "condition of music" as the ideal model of poetry's form/content relationship, however, as both Pound and Zukofsky do, in a crucial way simply repeats the gesture of Immanuel Kant's aesthetics. According to Jerome McGann, Kantian philosophy removes poetry from the business of truth telling and installs it in a purely aesthetic sphere. "According to classical tradition," McGann writes, poetry's ends were to please and instruct; Kant's aesthetic deliberately counters that position by removing instruction, or truth, from the realm of art and poetry. The modern uneasiness with "didactic" and "moral" poetry takes its origin in the Kantian view, which, as is well known, was formulated as a response and solution to the epistemological crisis generated by the rise and development of positive science. Kant's aesthetic is an effort to establish, in noncognitive sphere of reality, an accessible Form of ultimate order. (*Social Values* 36)

As McGann argues in a more recent essay, the Kantian aesthetic not only dispossesses poetry of its didactic, teaching function but problematizes its relationship to an extrapoetic world:

> The Kantian compromise, which "saved" the possibility of poetry by severing it from any obligations to referential truth, can now be seen as a clear signal that poetic discourse had come to face a deep cultural crisis. Poetry after Kant might look to have only the truth of its inner coherence. Being, however—as Coleridge said—"vitally metaphorical," its correspondence-truth was undermined. It could no longer easily lay claim to a relation (however ideal) between *res* and *verba.* Once a linguistic tool designed for "pleasure and instruction," poetry in the modern world thereby lost much of its teaching authority. At best it could be seen as a stately pleasure dome or Derridean *jouissance,* at worst an irrelevance or distraction. (*Black Riders* 122)

Pater's "condition of music," then, as applied by Pound and Zukofsky to poetry, would seem to represent the single most totalizing statement possible of this Kantian dilemma. And the conception of "poetic knowledge" that I have here outlined would seem simply to repeat the gesture that McGann indicts, the sequestering of the poem as an autotelic object, existing in a realm above that of human intercourse, whether interpersonal or political.

What "news," then (using Williams's term), can poetry bring us? And can poetry tell us anything other than its own endless formal tale—especially such a poetry as Zukofsky's, constantly weaving and woven up into its own self-mythologizing of musical form and musical analogy? On the one hand, one might praise a modernist poetics such as Zukofsky's for reopening poetry to a whole range of discursive modes that the dominance of the Romantic lyric had denied it—in Perloff's words, such modes as "narrative and didacticism, the serious and the comic, verse *and* prose" (*Dance* 181). Taking such a critical approach, one which refuses to accept the last century-and-a-half's common knowledge as to what constitutes the "proper" mode of poetry, one can argue that Zukofsky's poems do indeed fulfill the Augustan ethic of simultaneous pleasure and instruction and that they do so precisely *through* their formally musical structuring. Such structuring is motivated in large part by Zukofsky's relationship to actual music, a relationship much more intimate and committed than either Pater's or Pound's, for not only does Zukofsky see a necessary historical link between music and poetry, but he views a musical impulse as integrally bound up with the formal impulse basic to poetry itself. This is clear not only in his description of the poem as "a context associated with 'musical' shape" (*P* 16) but extends as well to the more overtly analogical uses he makes of specific musical forms in structuring his poems and to his broader conception of the poem as operating through sets of musically counterpointed themes and images. Zukofsky's concurrent stress on the informational aspect of poetry is integrated with his notion of the poem as musical context: just as a listener derives a knowledge of a musical composition's structure from listening, the most immediate knowledge a reader derives from a poem is of the poem's own formal movement. But since words, unlike musical notes, carry with them "communicative reference" (*P* 16), the reader gains a knowledge that goes beyond the pure form of music, even as it is embodied in that form. This knowledge is deeper and more immediate than the knowledge communicated through less overtly formal uses of language, since it is embodied not in the conceptual abstractions of a gas age but in the sensuous particulars of an objectified poem. Zukofsky's epistemology, which always stresses immediate sensory perception, reaches its fullest development in his conception of the poem as a musically structured artifact—a mode of language that conveys its information in an objectlike, tangible form.

The poem, then, is more than the sum of its form and its content. A poem such as " 'Mantis,' " for instance, goes beyond simply communicating an intimate knowledge of how the rhyme words of a sestina weave themselves back and forth in a pleasurable manner; " 'Mantis' " also communicates more than a bare relation of the poet's encounter with an insect in a subway station and a few impressions of the plight of the poor in Depression-era America. The poem, so to speak, gives pleasure and instructs through the synthesis of its pleasurable form and its instructive matter. Abstractions, in this poetry, are conveyed through tangible particulars, and when abstractions *do* appear—the rather bald "the poor" is perhaps the most obvious example—they are integrated into an objectlike, musical whole, a shape that can achieve "rested totality" in its reader's mind. Zukofsky's musical analogies provide the basis for the tangible wholes of his poems, thereby providing a shape in which the poet can embody extrapoetic truth, whether that truth concerns the Passaic Textile Strike ("During the Passaic Strike of 1926," *CSP* 26), a statue by the sculptor Zadkine ("for Zadkine," *CSP* 90), or a far more complexly woven congeries of political, cultural, and scientific informations ("A"-8, for instance).

Such a description of Zukofsky's poetics, of course, relies far too heavily on the form/content distinction, a distinction that remains at best uncomfortably slippery and that ultimately becomes simply untenable. It does little to address the difficulty posed by the Kantian separation of poetic truth and referential truth, a difficulty appearing not so much as a stumbling block to the poet in his compositional process as a moment in the readerly reception of the poem. McGann sums it up well when he refers to a "modern uneasiness with 'didactic' and 'moral' poetry," and Zukofsky himself distrusts such poetry as having "predatory intention"—as is most evident in the unhappy tale of his relations with *New Masses.* (Of course, the classic statement of such unease comes from Keats: "We hate poetry that has a palpable design upon us—and if we do not agree, seems to put its hand in its breeches pocket" [*Selected Letters* 121].) I suppose we as contemporary readers of poetry are most uneasy, as was Stevens, at the moment when the political and the poetic intersect, a moment at which both didacticism and moralizing seem almost inescapable. Cary Nelson, in his *Repression and Recovery,* has made a detailed and fascinating case for our rediscovering and revaluing the leftist poetry of the first part of this century, but my impression is that many readers, and readers quite in sympathy with Nelson's project as a whole, continue to find the majority of that poetry lacking: whatever the human value of the social and political interventions represented by the work of such poets as H. H. Lewis and Edwin Rolfe, their poetry lacks the aesthetic depth and complexity of some of their less committed contemporaries. That is, despite whatever successes it might have had in conveying the truth of the political realm—as Nelson phrases it, "Poetry in this time [i.e., the politicized 1930s] has become one of the most dependable sources of knowledge about society and one's place and choices within it (*Repression* 124)—it has failed to measure up in the realm in which we have been accustomed to judge poetry, the aesthetic realm where beauty remains at least as important as truth. In a manner analogous to Nelson's work, Jane Tompkins's *Sensational Designs* makes a compelling case for our valuing the sentimental fiction of the nineteenth century not in terms of contemporary standards of artistic complexity and intellectual depth but on its own terms, as social, cultural, and political interventions. I am moved and tempted by their arguments, but I am on some level convinced that our aesthetic values are more than mere false consciousness, are too deeply imbricated with our cultural identities as readers and writers to be simply set aside as politically naive.

Both Nelson and Perloff would have us set aside the paradigm of the personal Romantic lyric, but while Perloff seems to argue that we should be able to consider the didactic and the political as among the modes contributing to the poem's aesthetic whole, Nelson would remove our reading of poetry from the aesthetic realm altogether and reinstall it in the realm of social and political utility. Nelson views the poetry of the 1930s and its audience (or an idealized version of that relationship) as a temporarily lost ideal:

> At least in some points in our history, certainly almost pervasively in the 1930s and again in the 1960s and for many subcultures at other times, poetry was not only a valid place to comment on such [political] matters (itself a significant shift) but also one of the

places where political consciousness was forged. Locating themselves in poems, people thereby located themselves in relation to what they would change or preserve within their lives or in society as a whole. (*Repression* 128)[7]

This relationship of poem and reader—if it ever existed in anything like the form Nelson describes—seems an enviable ideal, but not one that Zukofsky could ever quite credit. Zukofsky's friend Oppen, famously, gave up poetry for some twenty-five years because he felt it would not advance the political cause to which he was committed. Wallace Stevens, the poet to whose work Zukofsky would come to feel such closeness, came out of the 1930s with political poetry definitely behind him, refusing to reprint his longest poetic exploration of the implications of leftism, *Owl's Clover,* during his lifetime. And Zukofsky, whose leftist beliefs were strong but who brooked very little Party discipline, would, with the fragments of "A"-8 published in *New Masses*, bid farewell to overtly political poetry with a whimper rather than a bang.

It is clear then that the knowledge that Zukofsky hopes to convey through his poetry is not a primarily political knowledge, a knowledge that would rouse people to act in the world, would alert them to their possibilities as social agents. What the poet gives to readers "to help [them] to live their lives," in Stevens's phrase (*Necessary Angel* 29), is not the same sense of life that one gains from a textbook or a propaganda leaflet. Poetry's knowledge is not the knowledge that can be traded on the world's markets; like the spiritual wisdom Paul invokes in the second chapter of 1 Corinthians, it is "foolishness" to the worldly. I believe it might clarify matters a bit to observe that knowledge, as I have been using the term, necessarily involves truth. Knowledge is, in McGann's words, "the historical form of truth," truth itself "an imaginable (as opposed to achievable) goal" (*Black Riders* 154).[8] McGann has for some years been investigating the manners in which poetry tells or shows the truth—from William Blake's embodying and casting off of error in his illuminated work, to the methods of prose truth telling that Laura (Riding) Jackson pioneered after finally abandoning altogether the resources of formal verse writing, casting off the name "poet" as "a lying word" (see *Black Riders* 124–34). Riding believed that poetry's formal features, its very linguistic patterning and verbal virtuosity, stood in the way of its revealing truth, which could only emerge in interpersonal dialogue. For McGann, poetry's "truth-telling" appears precisely at the moment when its formality and physicality are most evident. "When 'poetry,' " McGann writes, "is seen as the linguistic mode that calls attention to the activities of these codes [i.e., of language, which constitute not only the work but also the 'author and audience'], its truth-telling power appears in a new way. The physique and apparitions of poetry do not become, as they were for Riding, truth's obstacles and distractions. They become, rather, truth's own 'tellings' and eventualities" (*Black Riders* 140). The truth of poetry, then, unveils itself precisely when the language of poetry is the most visible: "Poetry's special privilege emerges at exactly this point [when we realize that 'language comprehends reality' and is 'self-authorizing'], for poetry is that form of discourse whose only object is to allow language to display itself, to show how it lives. What was once named 'God'—that being whose center is everywhere and whose circumference is nowhere—has died and been reborn in language" (*Black Riders* 143). McGann's own language verges on grandiloquence here, but I believe his point is well taken: the truth that poetry tells—the knowledge it gives a reader—is not merely embodied in a formal linguistic structure but involves, at least in part, the very fact *of* that structure, its very appearance *as* language.

The human being is above all a linguistic animal, a creature constituted by its language. Poetry, as the single most self-conscious use of language, is a self-reflexive art, but an art that shows us more than merely itself: by its very self-reflexiveness, it shows us ourselves *as constituted in language.* As "the young son" in Zukofsky's "All of December Toward New Year's" comments, as the book is turned toward the wall, "If it's turned / from us, we / are the shades" (*CSP* 144). This moment seems emblematic of the matter of poetry's knowledge: if we are turned from the world of language, the "print" of the atlas, we become mere wraiths, shadows, without weight or substance. Language—a fundamentally social, shared entity, as Wittgenstein showed in his discussion of the private language question—is the emblem and substance of our bond as fellow human beings: to acknowledge language is to acknowledge our commonality with other human beings, and to deny, elide, or pass over language is once again to fall into the trap of other-minds skepticism.

Zukofsky writes that "good poetry" "is precise information on existence out of which it grows, and information of its own existence, that is, the movement (and tone) of words" (*P* 20). *A Test of Poetry* repeats and elaborates this, describing good poetry as "the barest—most essentially complete—form of presenting a subject. . . . Good poetry is *definite information* on the subject dealt with, on the movement of the lines of verse, and on the emotion of verbal construction" (*TP* 89, my emphasis). By describing good poetry as "definite information," Zukofsky seems to present a remarkably dispassionate, nonpartisan description of the truth that poetry tells, the knowledge it communicates. Unpacking his formulation, however, we can see more clearly how his conception of the knowledge that poetry imparts squares with the version of truth telling I have just described. The "definite information" poetry embodies is of three types: information "on the subject dealt with," the extrapoetic event that the text might aim to describe, delineate, or otherwise mime; information on the language of the poem itself, "the movement of the lines of verse"; and information concerning the human entanglements of the poem's language, "the emotion of verbal construction." The language of the poem, then, comprehends at least three realms: that of the poet himself as human language user, that of the "subject" with which the poem would deal, and that of the poem's own formal, constructed nature. The poem can reveal the two former realms only by foregrounding the latter—that is, only by insisting on its own formality, its own literality, can the poem convey to us, as readers, knowledge of the poet who wrote the poem and the events, scenes, emotions, and thoughts that are the poem's "subject." Only by emphasizing its own literality can the poem be "the detail, not mirage of seeing . . . writing (audibility in two-dimensional print) which is an object or affects the mind as such" (*P* 12–13). The only truly *human* communication, the communication that acknowledges the common bond between poet and reader, is a writing acknowledging its own writtenness, its own embodiment in language, the common medium of human existence.

One immediate, concrete example of how such communication can work, and perhaps the most striking example in Zukofsky's oeuvre of the knowledge poetry conveys, is Zukofsky's phonetic translations. In the "Translators' Preface" to their *Catullus,* the Zukofskys write, "This translation of Catullus follows the sound, rhythm, and syntax of his Latin—tries, as is said, to breathe the 'literal' meaning with him" (*CSP* 243). This translation, through its radically unfamiliar language, makes us as readers intimately and uncomfortably aware of the language we are reading—its odd vocabulary, its gnarled syntax, and its strangely non-English sounds. At the same time, it aims to make us experience our commonality with the Roman poet Gaius Valerius Catullus, to make us breathe and speak a meaningful language that sounds something like the Latin he spoke and wrote (we should remember that silent reading is a relatively late development in the history of the written word; a silent reading, while not unheard of, would certainly have struck Catullus as an oddity). By breathing and phrasing as Catullus did, we gain "precise information" not only of the language itself, the "movement (and tone) of words" and "the movement of the lines of verse," but of the "existence out of which [the poem] grows," the specific linguistic medium within which Catullus's poems were composed.

On whatever level of generality we care to consider them, the poem and the poem's events, scenes, emotions, and thoughts are all constituted by language; as human entities in a "human universe" (Olson's phrase), they can only be realized, comprehended, recorded, or communicated through that most human organism, language. But these events are no less real for being linguistic events. To say that the human world is a world of language is not to diminish or discount the love, suffering, grief, pain, and exhilaration that the world offers or inflicts on us. It is rather meant as a neutral description of the human being's way of living in the universe—a way that is ultimately based on our constituting our world through language, and our constitution in turn by language. One implication of such a description, of course, is that poetry's treatment of a subject does not remove that subject into a realm above, an aesthetic realm apart from that of human intercourse. When we begin to conceive of language as fundamental to the human universe, and poetry as language's most profound self-revelation, we effect a Copernican shift: the Kantian separation of aesthetic and practical realms becomes immaterial because language itself is prior to both realms and constitutes the only reality human beings can know. Poetry, then, would seem the most absolutely suitable medium for exploring whatever concerns us closest as human beings. If, as McGann describes it, Kant's aesthetic reveals a disturbance in the previously assured relationship of *res* and *verba* in the realm of poetry, then that can only be a particular manifestation of a larger "crisis" of representation in language as a whole. (The very term *crisis* is of course misleading, since it implies a single definable event, a point of rupture at which language's moorings to the world become somehow loosened, rather than a gradual recognition on our part that language does not correspond to the world in quite the way we had once believed.) In the Kantian aesthetic, this crisis of representation is true merely of the aesthetic realm of art and poetry; language in the practical and scientific realms can still deal with existence on the old, solid footing. When we see language as the grounding medium of human experience, however, it becomes clear that such a crisis of representation is true of all human language: poetry is unique only in the degree to which it acknowledges this crisis, refuses to disavow the fundamental contingency and arbitrariness of its own medium.

While the high modernists from whom Zukofsky learned are (roughly) of the intellectual generation of Wittgenstein and Saussure, Zukofsky himself is among the products of the intellectual revolution they (and others) instigated. It is doubtful that Zukofsky knew Saussure's work (one can only speculate with what joy he might have regarded the linguist's late work on anagrams), but Zukofsky was deeply invested in Wittgenstein's philosophy. Despite Zukofsky's preference for the Spinozistic logic of the *Tractatus*, the actual arguments and modes of his poetry, as I have earlier argued, reflect a number of the fundamental insights of Wittgenstein's later work. Wittgenstein's *On Certainty* "does away with epistemology" by grounding human knowledge in a commonly shared, ultimately unquestionable—because to question it would make no sense—form of life: behaviors, in short, rather than beliefs. The *Philosophical Investigations* can be read to imply that such a ground is inseparable from language itself and involves the structures and assumptions embodied in language and conditioned by our common intercourse in language. The Wittgenstein of the *Philosophical Investigations* proceeds, in Guy Davenport's memorable phrase, "like an anthropologist from Mars" (*Geography* 333). Philosophy, for Wittgenstein, is "a battle against the bewitchment of our intelligence by means of language" (*Philosophical Investigations* 47e), the examination of the previously unexamined, the painstaking exploration of exactly what is involved in the language games by which we order our common lives. Zukofsky, similarly, wants us as readers to be as aware as humanly possible of the language that constitutes our human bond and birthright. We cannot elide language itself in a search for immediate "meaning"—that would be to allow the ritual dependability of linguistic communication to "bewitch" our intelligence, to distract us from attending to the mechanics and medium of that communication.

All of the devices that alienate us from Zukofsky's poetry, that make it seem strange and "difficult," contribute to our sense of its writtenness and our simultaneous sense of its divergence from a common norm, a common set of conventions through which meaning is generated, transmitted, and understood. Among those devices are his transliterations, his maddeningly complex and often indeterminate syntax, and the *apo koinou* that works not only from line to line and phrase to phrase but often from word to word. Most central of the elements that work to constitute Zukofsky's verse as self-conscious language structure, however, are the musical models that contribute so much to the objectified forms of his poems. Music itself, despite Zukofsky's arguments about "song," is not necessarily relevant to poetry. By arguing for its relevance and by making the poetry/music conjunction central to his own conception of the poetic task, the poet foregrounds the physicality of language that has throughout Western thought been discounted and disavowed in favor of an ideal of perfect transparency, perfect representation. The fugal form of various parts of *"A"* represents, aside from its inherent virtues and strengths (its elegant economy of means, its pleasing balance of repetition and change, its satisfying closure), a decisive break from previous modes of organizing the long poem—modes that, for Zukofsky, have the disadvantage of having been normalized and internalized to such an extent that they, like the iambic pentameter in the nineteenth century, seem somehow "natural" or "inevitable." Primary among these modes are the narrative, motivating works as diverse as *Aurora Leigh, The Faerie Queene,* and *Idylls of the King,* and the meditative, underlying such poems as *The Prelude, In Memoriam,* and (in a significantly altered form) *Song of Myself.* The significance of *"A"*'s musiclike form is fundamentally paradoxical. On the one hand, through its objectlike tangibility and its musical shapeliness it fulfills the requirements of Zukofsky's Objectivist rhetoric and simultaneously situates itself within a very ancient tradition of associating the written or spoken poem with the realm of aural, temporal music. On the other hand, because of its fundamentally analogical nature—a poem's words and lines, that is, are not musical notes or themes, and only through analogy can they be described in the same rhetoric—musical form makes strange and new the words and movements of the poem, awakening in its readers a recognition of the poem's language *as* language. Zukofsky's musical form, however ambiguous its pedigrees in the actual marriage of music and words, in the end works to impart to its reader a knowledge that goes beyond both positivistic information and emotional impression: it is a knowledge of language itself and of our common grounding in the walks of life, trials of life, and forms of life within which our language uses and language games are inextricably entwined.

Zukofsky's poetry of knowledge is to my mind one of the highest achievements of twentieth-century American literature, and indeed, in the foregoing pages I have aimed to argue precisely that point. But my words, and those of other critics of Zukofsky, ought always to be set beside those of the poets who have read, loved, and learned from Zukofsky. I will end by letting them speak, letting them address the inheritance that Louis Zukofsky has left to his art. The first is Ronald Johnson, from a brief note addressing Zukofsky's work:

> A poet, we say, has vision. Louis Zukofsky's vision came from excision of all but ears to the language itself, letter by letter: A. Like Nature, he was bent on ever more intricate goldfish. "Homer's Argos hearing / Handel's Largo as / The car goes". It is needless to state that this is first a telescope, before it is a poem. Behind the wheel, fiddling the syllables, the finest ears in the business is heading somewhere 100,000 years an hour (or so). Do you not hear them thunder? (Andrews and Bernstein 294–95)

Next is Michael Palmer, from a poem ("Notes for Echo Lake 3") mourning Zukofsky's death:

> Letters of the world. Bright orange poppy next to white rose next to blue spike of larkspur and so on. Artichoke crowding garlic and sage. Hyssop, marjoram, orange mint, winter and summer savory, oregano, trailing rosemary, fuchsia, Dutch iris, day lily, lamb's tongue, lamb's ears, blackberry, feverfew, lemon verbena, sorrel, costmary, never reads it as it is, "poet living tomb of his/games." (*Notes for Echo Lake* 16)

The final words are Robert Duncan's. While I have no firm knowledge that "With In," a poem from Duncan's open-ended sequence *Passages,* is a homage to Zukofsky, it is fit to be one:

> strict form
> alarms
> bound to
> and / or
> charm love's
> center
> out side
> work thru
> him / her
> undo
> knots yes
> in form

ties
releasing
me to you.
A
music
at rest
[*Ground Work* 71]

A Note on Texts

I would be remiss, in what amounts to an "advanced" introduction to Zukofsky's work, if I failed to include a note on the state of Zukofsky's texts. Most of Zukofsky's major works are now more or less available, with the notable exceptions of the play *Arise, arise,* the *Autobiography,* the pamphlet *First Half of "A"-9, The Writing of Guillaume Apollinaire,* and the essays and radio scripts written for the *Index of American Design.* The forms in which his texts are available, however, leave something to be desired. The textual history of *"A"* is complicated and involves, as with so many classics of modernist writing, an original composition by non-English-speaking typesetters; suffice it to say that even as the complete *"A"*—published by the University of California Press in 1978 and reprinted by Johns Hopkins University Press in 1993—corrects many of the problems of earlier editions, it introduces new ones of its own. Indeed, errors occurring in the first edition of *"A"-24* are preserved in the California *"A"*, since the "A"-24 of that latter edition is a simple photoreproduction of the earlier. (A list of some of the errata in this edition of *"A"*, as noted by Celia Zukofsky, can be found in *Paideuma* 8:3 (winter 1979): 585. There are no doubt more.)

Similarly, while the Johns Hopkins *Complete Short Poetry* supersedes the earlier *ALL: The Collected Short Poems 1923–1964,* provides an English text of the 1969 translation (with Celia Zukofsky) of Catullus, offers the first widely available edition of the 1978 *80 Flowers,* and includes a couple of fugitive short pieces, it is nonetheless difficult not to have reservations about this edition on at least two scores. First, the original Cape Goliard *Catullus (Gai Valeri Catulli Veronensis Liber)* includes a Latin text as an integral part of its presentation, and many readers familiar with the Zukofskys' translational methods would argue that the facing page text is essential to an assessment of the work; its absence from the Johns Hopkins text, although understandable in terms of space, is unfortunate. Second, Michele J. Leggott, in her study of *80 Flowers*, notes only one erratum in the first edition of Zukofsky's last book, an erratum that "alter[s] the sense of the line it was in" (27–28). That typographical error is reproduced in the new edition (*CSP* 345) and casts doubt on the overall quality of its textual editing. No textual editor is named, in fact, and the situation is similar with the University of California Press edition of *Bottom*, which claims to have "incorporate[d] corrections that Louis Zukofsky noted in his own handwriting on the flyleaf and first pages of his personal copy of this book" (*B* 6); those corrections, sent to the press by Paul Zukofsky, remain unspecified. We have most of Zukofsky's texts, but there are few clear indications of how "corrupt" or "accurate" those texts may be. Pending careful scholarly editions of Zukofsky's works, one must deal with the texts in the forms available. The situation, perhaps not ideal from the scholar's perspective, is surely better for readers of Zukofsky now than it was fifteen years ago, when both *Bottom* and the fiction were long out of print, and it would no doubt gratify Zukofsky himself, who worked on *"A"* for thirty-one years before seeing its first installment published in book form.

Aside from questions of textual purity or corruption, any thorough examination of Zukofsky's life's work (and this present project can hardly claim to even begin such a task) must take into account the bibliographical history of Zukofsky's texts—a history that is remarkably obscured in the texts as we now have them. Leggott's discussion of the printing history of the first section of "A"-22—first published as a three-line colored postcard, then as a 103-line chapbook, and finally as the opening of "A"-22 proper—is exemplary (Leggott 34–52). There exists as well, in the first British edition of *"A" 22 & 23*, a complex final device, "drawn by Geofroy Tory of Bourges and . . . published in his treatise on alphabets 'Champ Fleury.' " The fact that the British edition has this device, as well as an illuminated initial, might conceivably be trivial or accidental; but the work that Jerome McGann and others have done on the initials of Pound's early *Cantos* suggests to me that some serious consideration might be given to working out the relationship between these "ornaments" and the text they "illustrate" (McGann, *Textual Condition* 129–52).

In general, future Zukofsky criticism must take careful account of the historical fortunes of his poems—from their appearance in magazines, through their initial book publication (most often in tiny press runs from obscure presses), up to their current enshrinement between the covers of the Johns Hopkins University Press *"A"* or *Complete Short Poetry.* Such collections do their best to reify the poems and canonize the poet, obscuring the complex and often difficult history of their earlier publication. (This is especially true of *"A";* the earliest sections published sometimes appeared in forms considerably different from their final 1978 printing. "A"-3 and "A"-4, for instance, appear as a single poem in their 1931 publication.) Large "official" collections like these can make the critic lose sight of the fact that the poems were written, published, and sometimes withdrawn and revised before their final appearance. It is easy as well to lose sight of the poet as a historical human subject, influenced not only by other poets and literary movements but by his social and political positionings, his idiosyncratic likes and dislikes, and the circle of friends and loved ones nearest him. Clues to such connections, sometimes present in a poem's earliest publication, often disappear during the transition to hardcover.

"Collected" or "Complete" volumes seem inevitably to have the smell of death about them—that air of "great authors" series, all of whose members are long since deceased. It is easy to understand Wallace Stevens's reluctance to collect his poems: "I think that I should have difficulty in putting together another volume of poems, as much as I should prefer that to a collection. But I might as well face the fact" (*Letters* 829). His sentiments are seconded, perhaps more baldly, by Basil Bunting: "A man who collects his poems screws together the boards of his coffin. Those outside will have all the fun" (*Complete Poems* 3). There is certainly "fun" enough in Zukofsky's *"A"* and *Complete Short Poetry,* for those who make it past the books' forbiddingly serious covers. But in the end, there is no substitute for tracking the poems through their varied habitats—the manuscripts, the little magazines, the chapbooks, the annual anthologies—before their final capture within the collected edition's zoological garden. While this project has paid lamentably little attention to the transmission history of the texts it examines, I am well aware of the pressing need for that history to be written; I look forward not only to pursuing such work but to enjoying the fruits of other scholars' labors.

Notes

Introduction

1. For a tart reassessment of this period, see Caesar, *Dividing Lines*.

2. I use the much-debated term *postmodernist* for want of a better, but I shall (as much as possible) eschew it in the pages to come.

3. Two very fine studies are E. P. Thompson's *Witness Against the Beast* and Nicholas Roe's *Wordsworth and Coleridge: The Radical Years*.

Chapter 1

1. Aside from the ambiguously helpful *Autobiography*, the primary published source of biographical information on Zukofsky is Terrell, "Louis Zukofsky: An Eccentric Profile." This essay incorporates an interview with Celia Zukofsky, which is usefully supplemented by Ahearn's "Two Conversations with Celia Zukofsky." There is also abundant information, especially on Zukofsky's early years, in Ahearn, *Zukofsky's "A": An Introduction*, in *Pound/Zukofsky: Selected Letters of Ezra Pound and Louis Zukofsky*, and in Penberthy, *Niedecker and the Correspondence with Zukofsky*.

2. Speaking in 1971 of this poem, Zukofsky claimed, "they still exhume it as one of the best things I've written tho I've never reprinted it" (*P* 30).

3. Comens notes, for instance, that it "seems extraordinarily reductive to attempt to find some common denominator among Zukofsky, Reznikoff, Oppen, Niedecker, Rakosi, Williams, and the oth-

ers—even more so than is usually the case with literary movements" (*Apocalypse and After* 203n. 6).

4. See Quartermain, "Writing and Authority."

5. The two main chapters of this work were published in English as "The Writing of Guillaume Apollinaire: Le Flâneur, (I)—Il y a" and "The Writing of Guillaume Apollinaire: (II)—Le Poète Ressucité, (III)—& Cie."

6. On Zukofsky's *Index* writings, see Ahearn, "Zukofsky, Marxism and American Handicraft," and Nadel, " 'A Precision of Appeal.' " Kenneth Sherwood is editing the *Index* writings for publication.

7. See Schappes, "Historic and Contemporary Particulars," and Winters, "The Objectivists."

8. Niedecker's side of that correspondence is presented in Penberthy, *Niedecker and the Correspondence with Zukofsky*. See also Breslin, "Lorine Niedecker: Composing a Life."

9. In her interview with Terrell, Celia Zukofsky presents a chronicle of Zukofsky's employment history (*LZMP* 62–63).

10. These remarks on Zukofsky's academic environment are based in large part on Hugh Seidman's memoir of his teacher, "Louis Zukofsky at the Polytechnic Institute of Brooklyn."

11. Williams's efforts on his friend's behalf are recorded in his correspondence with Laughlin. See *William Carlos Williams and James Laughlin: Selected Letters*, esp. 86–87, 150.

12. I think Fielding Dawson's memoir of his friend Zukofsky is crucial to understanding the isolation of the poet's later years and the tragic dynamic that reinforced that isolation by repelling the younger poets who actively admired him.

13. See Paul Zukofsky's remark, *CF* 306; Dahlberg also had a famous falling-out with Charles Olson over matters culinary.

14. Creeley's most recent statement of gratitude is in his foreword to Zukofsky's *Complete Short Poetry* vii–xiv.

15. An illuminating discussion of the destabilization of authorship in "A"-24 is Parsons's "A More Capacious Shoulder: 'A'-24, Nonsense and the Burden of Meaning."

Chapter 2

1. In this reading I pass over the intertextual resonances of "Can a mote," especially its echoing of Thomas Campion's "Follow thy fair

Sun" (*TP* 131), which figures the dependent relationship of the shadow to the sun as that of an unhappy suitor to a disdainful lady. The shadow gains his being from the sun's light, and when the sun has finally set, both light and shadow are obliterated, "The sun still proved, the shadow still disdainèd."

2. Zukofsky quotes this passage, with evident approval, in *Bottom* (84). While the widespread view has it that Wittgenstein's views underwent a considerable revision between *Tractatus Logico-Philosophicus* and *Philosophical Investigations*, his *Tractatus* remarks on skepticism seem fairly representative of the view of skepticism presented in the *Investigations*, as well. See also Wittgenstein's *On Certainty;* and Haller's "Was Wittgenstein a Sceptic? or On the Differences Between Two 'Battle Cries,' " in *Questions on Wittgenstein* (100–113). For a provocative revision of the accepted views on the discontinuity between Wittgenstein's early and late philosophies, see Ackermann, *Wittgenstein's City*.

3. "About the Gas Age" is Zukofsky's "answer to a question from the audience following [his] reading at the American Embassy, London, May 21, 1969" (*P* 169).

4. Although this view is derived ultimately from Plato's *Cratylus*, it is more immediately related to similar ideas in Emerson; compare his 1836 book, *Nature:* "Words are signs of natural facts. . . . Every word which is used to express a moral or intellectual fact, if traced to its root, is found to be borrowed from some material appearance" (*Essays and Lectures* 20). Hugh Kenner's discussion of Fenollosa's transcendentalism is illuminating; see *The Pound Era* 157–58.

5. On the philosophical roots of modernist anti-abstractionism, see Schwartz, *The Matrix of Modernism* 12–49.

6. See also the excellent discussion of Hulme's thought in Levenson, *A Genealogy of Modernism* 37–47, 80–102.

7. In a short review of Santayana's *Dominations and Powers*, "The Effacement of Philosophy" (1951), Zukofsky advances a similar "phase-specific" theory of history. Unlike "About the Gas Age," however, "The Effacement of Philosophy" presents the process as a cyclical, rather than a strictly successive, one:

> The mathematician or the statistician is probably better equipped than the philosopher to draw the conclusion that history, especially unwrit-

ten history, works cyclically in expressing material phenomena. The unmathematical philosopher will probably be quick to see simply that in all times a proportion or style is mixed with story and with heartbeat. Different times seem to favor one or another of these phases. If it can be proved that they follow one another cyclically, he who likes story and is fated to style had at best make as much story of it as he can to be free in a materialistic sense. (*P* 55)

8. In his conception of "passion," Zukofsky generally follows Spinoza's use of that term in his *Ethics.* In that work, an emotion is a passion insofar as it involves a lack of clear knowledge about its object. As Seymour Feldman writes in his introduction to the *Ethics,*

> If an affect is understood clearly and distinctly, or in Spinoza's terminology, if we have an "adequate idea" of this emotion, then it is an *action,* i.e. we are the cause of it. . . . An emotion not adequately understood is a *passion,* because in this situation we do not act but suffer. . . . Here we are not properly agents, but reagents, i.e. we *react,* not act. (15)

9. The best introduction to the Poundian ideogrammic method is Kenner's *The Pound Era* 145–62. Géfin's *Ideogram: History of a Poetic Method* (3–46) provides an exhaustive account of the genesis of the method, and of Pound's (mis)interpretation of Fenollosa.

10. "By presenting for comparison several translations of the same passage from Homer, an elegy of Ovid and lines from Herrick that read like an adaptation of Ovid, or a fifteenth century poem about a cock and a recent poem about white chickens, and so on, a means for judging the values of poetic writing is established by the examples themselves" (*TP,* "Preface" n.p.).

11. As Pound writes Zukofsky in 1930, "Your problem coming after T.S.E. [Eliot] me an' Bill [Williams] is very dif. from what ours was coming after Yeats and Bliss Carman. Praps best for you not to worry about it at all, and cease considering it as a problem" (*P/Z* 85).

Chapter 3

1. Part of the pleasure of reading Cavell is the ease with which he reaches this conclusion—one at which Barry Stroud's otherwise

useful *The Significance of Philosophical Scepticism* spends some two hundred pages arriving.

2. This juxtaposition particularly incenses Melnick, who comments acidly, "It will always be true that 'a surgeon's worth many another man,' whatever his insufficiency in Lear's case. . . . If the reader cannot let hold of the feeling that Lear's defiant outcry rushes in on him with a truth that is not just mental blast or a pander to self-pity, then he must leave Zukofsky's whole setting behind. He has long since opted for a world that *Bottom* seeks to expose as shallow and valueless" (Melnick 64).

3. Much ink has been spilled in the philosophical community over the precise definition of a "form of life." Two useful discussions are Whittaker, "Language-Games and Forms of Life Unconfused" and Kripke, *Wittgenstein on Rules and Private Language* 96–98.

4. Anthony Hartley translates the stanza thus: "Yes, in an island that the air loads with sight and not with visions, every flower showed itself to be larger without our discussing it"; see Mallarmé, *Mallarmé* 63.

Chapter 4

1. On Olson and Objectivist poetics and thought, see Von Hallberg, *Charles Olson: The Scholar's Art* 82–125.

2. Roy Harris translates *signifiant* and *signifié* as "signal" and "signification" in order to avoid the common confusion of "signified" and "referent."

3. One might compare Mallarmé's polemical distinction between the newspaper and the book in "Le Livre, instrument spirituél" (1895) (*Œuvres complètes* 378–82). It seems clear that Zukofsky implies something like a newspaper when he speaks of writing that can be "harbored . . . solidly in the crook of an elbow."

4. Marnie Parsons supplies one fine reading of "I's (pronounced *eyes*)," locating what she calls its "synaesthesia" within her overall discussion of "nonsense" in twentieth-century poetry (*Touch Monkeys* 100–102).

5. A very useful discussion of lineation and its effects in nonmetrical verse can be found in Hartman, *Free Verse* 45–60.

6. Compare "Spook's Sabbath, Five Bowings," where Zukofsky uses *"grand détaché"* as the title of one of the five sections (*CSP* 136).

7. C. S. Lewis's *Studies in Words* includes a lovely discussion of the fortunes of the term "wit" (86–110). "A B C," in fact, sounds to me as if it could be a Zukofskyan rearrangement of fragments of passages from Shakespeare. Its opening line echoes *Love's Labor's Lost* II.i.59 ("he hath wit"), and the presence of the Elizabethan "withal," which appears in *Love's Labor's Lost* II.i.68, seems a clear indication that the words of the poem are somehow derived from Shakespeare. I have been unable to find a suitable passage, either cited in *Bottom* or indexed in a Shakespeare concordance; however, this by no means precludes the possibility that the passage is some sort of quotation. *Love's Labor's Lost,* one of whose primary themes is linguistic wit, wordplay, and the difficulty of precise verbal communication, would seem a fitting source for the words of "A B C."

8. See Barbara Johnson, *"Les Fleurs du mal armé."*

9. Zukofsky's awareness of mass media and "popular culture" is evident from the beginning of his career; note the Broadway musicals of "Poem beginning 'The' " (*CSP* 10, 13–14) and the "Camel" cigarettes and "Wrigley's" gum of "A"-1 and -2 (*A* 2, 8). In later sections of *"A"*, Zukofsky shows great interest in television and the national perception of news events (such as the Kennedy assassination in "A"-15) through the broadcast medium.

10. See Kripke (55–113) for his discussion of Wittgenstein and the "private language" argument, where Wittgenstein (roughly speaking) rejects the notion of a language spoken by only one speaker in favor of a conception of language as an inherently shared entity. See also Bloor, *Wittgenstein: A Social Theory of Knowledge.*

11. For the dating of individual poems by Zukofsky, see Celia Zukofsky's "Year by Year Bibliography."

12. While Zukofsky himself wrote a play, *Arise, arise,* and translated Plautus's *Rudens* as "A"-21, he seems singularly uninterested in the actual performance of Shakespeare's texts.

Chapter 5

1. Fred Kogos, in *A Dictionary of Yiddish Slang and Idioms,* defines "shaigetz" as "Non-Jewish boy; wild Jewish boy"; the epithet "shaigetz ainer!" is a "Berating term for irreligious Jewish boy, especially one who blatantly flouts Jewish law; fellow of great audacity" (69).

2. On Zukofsky's relationship with the *Menorah Journal*, see Finkelstein, "Jewish-American Modernism and the Problem of Identity."

3. In a 1930 letter to Pound, Zukofsky writes, " 'The' was a direct reply to The Waste Land" (*P/Z* 78). On the dating of Zukofsky's composition of the poem, which differs from that given in Celia Zukofsky's "Year by Year Bibliography," see *P/Z* 79. On the relationship between MacDiarmid's *A Drunk Man Looks at the Thistle* and *The Waste Land*, see Gish, "MacDiarmid Reading," and Crawford, *Identifying Poets* 42–63.

4. Where Julius's work is hard-nosed on Eliot's anti-Semitism but alert to the complexities of his poetry, Wilk's *Jewish Presence in T.S. Eliot and Franz Kafka* (11–81) is a blunter and less-nuanced version of the distasteful but absolutely necessary Augean stable–cleaning found in Casillo's relentless and comprehensive work on Pound's anti-Semitism, *The Genealogy of Demons*.

5. Here I differ with Sandra Stanley, who argues that while "Zukofsky would come to be impatient with the academic hegemony associated with Eliot in the decades ahead, he never really shared Bunting's or Williams's perception that Eliot was the leader of the enemy camp" (54). Indeed, the body of her discussion of Zukofsky and Eliot suggests rather that Zukofsky's admiration for Eliot's poetry coexisted with a deep distrust of its cultural agenda.

6. On the chronology of Williams's disillusionment with Eliot, see Mariani 191.

7. In his "Jewish-American Modernism," Finkelstein considers at length the respective positions of Yiddish Introspectivists and Anglophone Objectivists.

8. As Eric Sigg notes, "It takes a measure of chutzpah for the descendant of power and privilege to consider himself at a disadvantage vis-à-vis those he regards as his social inferiors. . . . Striving so irrationally to be low man on the totem pole must surely be one of the strangest manifestations of humanity's competitive instincts" (139).

9. I quote here the version presented in the 1978 publication of "A"-1; *An "Objectivists" Anthology* prints a version that differs in many particulars, although not in overall gist (115).

10. Or consider Pound's proclamation, on naming his son Omar Shakespeare Pound: "note the Crescendo!"

Chapter 6

1. See for instance the meeting between Henry James and Ezra Pound in the opening pages of Hugh Kenner's *The Pound Era*, which more than one critic has taken as historical narrative.

2. Ella Reeve ("Mother") Bloor (1862–1951) was a founding member of the CPUSA in 1919. She worked tirelessly throughout her life on behalf of Communist Party causes, eventually "achiev[ing] heroic status within the Communist Party of the USA and serv[ing] as its model of Communist womanhood" (Buhle, Buhle, and Georgakas 100).

3. For a detailed, career-long analysis of the political in Zukofsky's early poetry, see Mottram.

4. See Longenbach, *Wallace Stevens: The Plain Sense of Things* (143) for a handy summary of the review. Filreis's *Modernism from Right to Left* examines this review and Stevens's reactions to it in painstaking detail (180–247).

5. On small leftist magazines, see Nelson 206–33; on *Partisan Review*, see Wald, *New York Intellectuals* 75–97.

6. On Gold, *New Masses*, and the notion of a proletarian literature, see Klein 70–86, Buhle 171–83, and Kalaidjian 35–58. For a provocative reassessment of Gold's career, see James Bloom.

7. Alan Filreis paraphrases a 1933 typescript of Zukofsky's in which he describes Lenin as "having an admirable talent for 'verbal contrasts' and, despite his revolutionary seriousness, an ability to enjoy the surprise caused by contrary 'facts' offered merely for their contrariness" (*Modernism from Right to Left* 19).

8. An allusion too subtle for Morris U. Schappes, alas, who finds the poem "impoverish[ing]" the "reader's rich experience" ("Historic" 341).

9. I quote here from the version of " 'Recencies' " in *An "Objectivists" Anthology*. While Zukofsky reprints much of this essay in his collection *Prepositions* (14–18), he has purged it of all its overtly political and topical material.

10. Burton Hatlen ("Art and/as Labor") traces dialectical patterns through the first ten sections of *"A"*, and Michael Davidson asserts that Zukofsky, in " 'Mantis' " and "A"-9, "use[s] formalism not to aestheticize social tensions but to return a degree of use-value to

a poetry increasingly instrumentalized by social agendas" ("Dismantling" 523).

11. Zukofsky was intensely interested in the cinema during the 1930s. He reviewed Chaplin's *Modern Times* in 1936 in a fascinating and perspicacious essay, unpublished at the time (*P* 54–64), and in the early 1930s had a hand in a (never to be published or produced) screenplay of Joyce's *Ulysses.*

12. This is a lesson that both Cary Nelson and Jerome McGann have been propounding for some time.

13. For a historically fascinating account of Wheelwright and Mangan's careers, see Wald, *Revolutionary Imagination.*

14. Zukofsky, in a letter to Lorine Niedecker dated around 1953, would downplay the political thrust of the early sections of *"A"*, warning her especially not to take Laughlin's description too seriously; the political elements in "A"-8 are to be understood as historical materials for a poem, not as messages meant to have a proactive effect in the extrapoetic world. Needless to say, one must approach Zukofsky's postwar comments carefully: there is hindsight involved here. See Stanley 107.

15. Barry Ahearn has confirmed Zukofsky's association with *New Masses* to me in conversation. In a 1936 letter to Pound, Zukofsky mentions working his WPA job "till 6, & then [Communist] party shits etc." (quoted in Ahearn, "Zukofsky, Marxism and American Handicraft" 81).

16. According to Marcella Booth's catalogue of the Zukofsky manuscripts at the University of Texas (52–53), "A"-8, including the *New Masses* text of "March Comrades," was drafted between August 1935 and January 1937; it was revised, heavily in sections, in October 1957 in preparation for its 1958 publication.

Chapter 7

1. Peter Quartermain's reading of the "A-Bomb and H-" section of *Bottom* (*B* 97–99)—"a curious breed of apparently ample and expansive discursive prose that is actually highly concentrated"—is exemplary in demonstrating how *Bottom*'s prose, while miming the abstractions and argumentative strategies of philosophical writing,

"explodes" that writing (in this case, literally) by dint of a concerted metaphoricity (*Disjunctive Poetics* 112–13).

2. By Zukofsky's "poetry" I mean the works (primarily verse) that have been published and presented as such. Zukofsky himself believes that "poetry" is a category that spans both verse and prose. In "About the Gas Age" he comments, "Sometimes you do a thing in verse, and sometimes you do it in prose. To me they're both poetry." He then reads a passage from *"A"*, followed by a passage from *Bottom*, which is "the same thing as we say in prose, meaning loosely speaking the same thought, but the structure is different. It's the words that interest me" (*P* 171).

3. Painting is particularly important for Williams and Stevens. See Dijkstra, *The Hieroglyphics of a New Speech*, and Costello, "Effects of an Analogy: Wallace Stevens and Painting." For more general accounts of the relationship between modernist poetry and visual arts, see Dasenbrook, *The Literary Vorticism of Ezra Pound and Wyndham Lewis;* Materer, *Vortex: Pound, Eliot, and Lewis;* Robinson, *Symbol to Vortex;* and (especially) Altieri, *Painterly Abstraction in Modernist American Poetry.* These works are germane to the present discussion insofar as a major implicit theme of this chapter is Zukofsky's rejection of a painterly model of composition in favor of a *musical* one.

For a perceptive account of how the concept of poetry's music, as set out by Dante and the troubadours, informs Pound's notion of melopœia, see Korn, *Ezra Pound* 66–73. Korn is especially useful on the "musical" implications of Pound's Imagist propagandizings. Less helpful but still informative is F. Murray Schafer's "The Music in Pound's Poetry," his introduction to *Ezra Pound and Music* 3–22.

4. "Lawes and Jenkyns" are relevant to this reading as well. Henry Lawes (1596–1662) was an English composer; John Jenkins (1592–1678) was a musician in the courts of Charles I and Charles II. The concluding lines of this lyric passage, "Then resolve me, tell me aright / If Waller sang or Dowland played" (*Cantos* 520), serve to remind one of Pound's enduring admiration for Edmund Waller (1606–87), who Pound sees as one of the last English practitioners of the art of composing expressly for music. Waller's "Go, Lovely Rose" is the basis for the "Envoi" in *Hugh Selwyn Mauberley* (*Personae* 195).

5. W. R. Johnson examines a similar moment in ancient lyric

when the Greek lyric, primarily a musical art, passes into the Latin tradition. Unlike Pound, Johnson believes that the essence of lyric lies not in its musicality but in its personal rhetoric and pronominal stance. (Whether "lyric" can be defined—or ought to be—in essentialist terms is another question altogether.) See *The Idea of Lyric* 126–29. A more comprehensive account of the relationship between lyric verse and actual music is Winn's *Unsuspected Eloquence.*

6. In a characteristic passage in *Bottom,* Zukofsky repeats Pound's and Bunting's account of the emergent Renaissance gap between poetry and music, at the same time distinguishing between the single-line dance "melodies" of Shakespeare's songs and an implied "counterpoint" in his iambic verse:

> Erasmus laughed at pre-Reformation music for setting one syllable to numerous notes—as Purcell did later in his songs for *The Tempest.* The divorce of music from words became "the modern fault." Morley, Dowland, Weelkes, Campion, Lawes cared more for the quantities of the spoken syllables (declamation), the homophonic and harmonic. The words of Shakespeare's songs keep the feeling of old dance, as against ear busy hearing more than one voice in the counterpoint of his stage iambics. (*B* 420–21)

7. I can only note, but am loath not to mention, the paradox inherent in the rhetoric of music's universality. It is notoriously difficult for subjects of one culture to be spoken to by another culture's music; even within our own cultural sphere, it is all too common to hear the rock fan dismissing classical music—or the classical fan, bebop; or the jazz fan, bluegrass—as all "sounding the same." The disjunctures between such communities of listening may well cast light on the social grounds of Zukofsky's "difficulty."

8. I take this phrase from the title of Susan Howe's *Articulation of Sound Forms in Time.* That "forms" can be taken as both noun and verb is an insight fundamental to the Zukofskyan method.

9. "A"-11 and "A"-9 are in part products of Pound's fascination with Guido Cavalcanti's work, a fascination he transmitted to a number of other poets. Pound himself translated the "Perch'io non spero" in his *Sonnets and Ballate of Guido Cavalcanti* (1912) (*Translations* 120–23), and the "Donna mi priegha" in that same volume and in Canto XXXVI (*Translations* 132–41, *Cantos* 177–79). It is difficult

to underestimate the importance of the "Donna mi priegha" to Pound as a touchstone of poetic excellence and an epitome of the Renaissance philosophy of love (see his essay "Cavalcanti," *Literary Essays* 149–200). Modernist adaptations of Cavalcanti include both the first section of Eliot's "Ash Wednesday," "Because I do not hope to turn again"—which echoes the "Perch'io non spero" (*Complete Poems and Plays* 60), as do, in closer adaptations, Basil Bunting's "Perche no spero," beginning "Now we've no hope of going back" (*Complete Poems* 128)—and, in addition to "A"-11, Zukofsky's "To my baby Paul (After Guido)" (*CSP* 102).

Zukofsky seems to be the only poet who surpassed Pound in his enthusiasm for the "Donna mi priegha." Pound's own versions attempted only to suggest the complicated formal scheme of the original, while Zukofsky's two "imitations" (the two sections of "A"-9) not only precisely reproduce the rhyme and meter of the original Italian but do so using phrases from Marx's *Capital* and Spinoza's *Ethics* respectively. There is also extant a version of "Donna mi priegha" by Zukofsky that not only retains the formal features of the original but translates its argument into Brooklyn Irish slang: it begins "A foin lass bodders me" ("Donna mi priegha"). See Kenner, "Loove in Brooklyn" (*Historical Fictions* 122–32).

10. Celia Zukofsky denies that Zukofsky had any particular partita in mind as the model for this movement of the poem, although she speculates that Bach's *Partitas for Solo Violin* (in particular the Second Partita, "which has the chaconne in it") informed Zukofsky's conception of the partita form (Ahearn, "Two Conversations" 114–15).

11. Paul Zukofsky, I might add, questions Cox's interpretation both of chaconne form and of violin bowing.

Chapter 8

1. Michael Riffaterre makes a similar argument about Mallarmé's sonnet "Ses purs ongles," which, he claims, is "a text referring to its own shape, absolute form" (*Semiotics of Poetry* 19).

2. Moore, of course, is the American poet who most thoroughly investigates the formal possibilities of purely syllabic verse. Zukofsky had an abiding interest in her work and cites two of her poems as rare examples of achieved "objectification" in his original "Sincer-

ity and Objectification" essay (276). Such simple counting systems of prosody are central to much of Zukofsky's work, although they more often take the form of word-per-line counts than syllabic counts. See, for instance, the seven-word lines of "Atque in Perpetuum A.W.," an elegy for Zukofsky's brother-in-law in which the poet finds "Counting sevens an ornament unto my wound" (*CSP* 231); the two- and three-words-per-line of "A"-19; and the five-words-per-line formal basis of "A"-21, -22, -23, and *80 Flowers*.

3. My discussion of "It's a gay li-ife" and "The lines of this new song" owes much to Charles Bernstein, *Content's Dream* 69–71.

4. John P. McWilliams Jr. argues, in his *The American Epic*, that in the United States the "epic," which had originally taken the form of long narrative poems, passes into a variety of different genres, including the prose histories of Prescott and Parkman and novels such as Melville's *Moby-Dick*. McWilliams relegates Whitman's *Leaves of Grass* and such successors as *The Cantos*, *Paterson*, and *Maximus* to the category of "personal epics": "long, loosely unified works, without narrative, without a culturally accepted hero, and written in a literary form valued by a miniscule fraction of the reading public. . . . the writing of a personal epic is at variance with the basic connotations of the term epos" (237). For a contrary argument concerning the epic "usefulness" of *The Cantos*, *Maximus*, and *Paterson*, see Michael André Bernstein, *The Tale of the Tribe* 3–25.

5. On "series," whether "infinite" (open-ended) or "finite" (closed), see Conte, *Unending Design* 13–44.

6. W. B. Yeats's *A Packet for Ezra Pound* (1927) reports Pound's explaining that *The Cantos* "will, when the hundredth canto is finished, display a structure like that of a Bach Fugue" (quoted in Sullivan, *Ezra Pound* 100). Pound responded to *A Packet* at least twice: "If Yeats knew a fugue from a frog, he might have transmitted what I told him in some way that would have helped rather than obfuscated *his* readers"; and "God damn Yeats' bloody paragraph. Done more to prevent people reading Cantos for what is *on the page* than any other one smoke screen" (*Selected Letters* 293, 321).

7. Pound, along with the violinist Olga Rudge, is an important figure in the twentieth-century revival of interest in Vivaldi (*Ezra Pound and Music* 328–30). While Bach is the Baroque figure to whom Zukofsky hearkens back most often, his fellow Objectivist Basil Bunting takes as his formal model the sonatas of Arcangelo

Corelli, Domenico Scarlatti, and Johann Christian Bach. Bunting's longer poems are gathered as "Sonatas," and a passage of *Briggflatts* sums up his regard for Scarlatti's harpsichord sonatas: "It is time to consider how Domenico Scarlatti / condensed so much music into so few bars / with never a crabbed turn or congested cadence, / never a boast or a see-here" (*Complete Poems* 58).

8. Pound is mistaken when he surmises in his 1939 letter that "Zukofsky's experiment" is directly influenced by his "having stated that the Cantos are in a way fugal." In fact, Zukofsky had pretty much completed the first four movements of the poem, whose structure is openly fugal, *before* he read *The Cantos* with any knowledge of their intended structure and scope (see quotations above). What seems most likely is that Zukofsky, already attuned to Baroque musical forms (as is evident in the 1926 "Poem beginning 'The' "—"If horses could but sing Bach, mother" [*CSP* 17]), arrived at the formal principle of the fugue independently of Pound, and only later recognized a similar structure operating within *The Cantos.*

9. My reading of "A"-1 is indebted to various earlier interpretations, including those of Géfin 55–57; Ahearn, *Zukofsky's "A"* 38–46; Byrd, "Zukofsky's Canon" 180–83; and Larrissy 103–4.

10. For another discussion of fugal form, particularly as it relates to *The Cantos,* see Davis 72–75.

11. In the fourth line of this quotation, the Johns Hopkins *"A"* misprints "are" as "were."

12. On the importance of the plant liveforever (a succulent of the *Sedum* genus) as an emblem in Zukofsky's work, see Leggott 141–64.

13. The Johns Hopkins *"A"* misprints "lamposts" for "lamp-posts" on page 5.

14. There have of course been experiments in writing poems in more than one voice using split pages and double columns: see John Ashbery's "Litany" (*As We Know* 3–68), Ronald Johnson's "The Different Musics" (*Valley of the Many-Colored Grasses* 84–88), and John Taggart's "Body and Soul: Poem for Two Readers" (*Loop* 22–29). These poems cannot of course be realized by a single reader. Taking a less literal tack (and one more germane to my own reading of "A"-1), Kenner reads Canto I as inherently polyphonic, incorporating at once the voices of Homer, his Latin translator Andreas Divus, and the Anglo-Saxon poet of the *Seafarer* (*The Pound Era* 349–54).

15. Peter Makin, writing on *The Cantos*, corroborates this account: "Fugue is only a texture—or perhaps one should say a 'ribbing,' as being stronger in outline than texture" (*Pound's Cantos* 72).

16. The quoted portion is from *The Way of All Flesh*; see *B* 210.

17. Bach himself constructed themes out of the letters of his own name, as Zukofsky notes: "As the countersubject of the fourfold 19th fugue / Signed on death lightly, / B, A, C, H" ("A"-12, 130). In German musical notation, B equals B-flat and H equals B-natural.

18. See Taggart, *Songs of Degrees* 199–201, for an examination of Zukofsky's methods of quotation and condensation here.

19. These twelve concerti are cited in "A"-12—such numerical correspondences are Zukofsky's stock-in-trade. "The Trial of Harmony and Invention" includes the popular "Four Seasons" concerti; as Ahearn points out, one of the organizing principles of "A"-12 is such patterns of four (*Zukofsky's "A"* 125–27).

20. Zukofsky's translation of this passage of *Odyssey* XI also appears in *TP* 4–5.

21. See Makin, *Pound's Cantos* 124–28.

22. See Paracelsus 205.

23. But compare Quartermain: "The text [of *"A"*] is carefully jointed . . . and thus articulate; transitions are carefully handled, and the impression is of a careful dovetailing rather than of weaving, the building of a structure rather than the making of a tapestry" (*Disjunctive Poetics* 65).

24. These two terms, which are crucial to Zukofsky's conception of the place of the poetic act, appear repeatedly throughout his writings. Spinoza's explanation of them appears in the Scholium to Proposition 29 of Part I of the *Ethics* (51–52). Seymour Feldman's introduction also provides a useful definition (*Ethics* 11).

25. The clearest analogy here is to the letters that Williams transcribes in *Paterson*, which likewise enter that poem on a wholly serious basis.

26. This moment is a locus classicus for critical discussions of Pound's innovations. Michael André Bernstein writes,

> The seemingly unobtrusive moment in Canto VIII, when the first series of historical letters is introduced into *The Cantos* and the personality of Sigismundo is shown by juxtaposing his prose instruction concern-

ing a painter he wishes to engage with a lyric poem he writes for Isotta degli Atti *without privileging either medium,* represents one of the decisive turning-points in modern poetics, opening for verse the capacity to include domains of experience long since considered alien territory. (*Tale of the Tribe* 40)

Kenner repeats this valuation in his "The Making of the Modernist Canon" (*Mazes* 31). Richard Sieburth's comments on Pound's quotations are valuable:

> The art of quotation . . . should not be confused with mimesis: it is a mode not merely of copying or reflecting but of including the real. . . . In a larger sense, quotation involves shifting the emphasis from language as a means of representation to language as the very object of representation. To quote is thus to adduce words as facts, as exhibits, as documents, to lift them out of context, to isolate them, to make them self-evident. (*Instigations* 121)

The single most illuminating discussion I have seen of the poetics and politics of Pound's citational practices, and the way in which the ideology underlying those citational practices has carried over to shape the critical reception of *The Cantos,* is Rainey's *Ezra Pound and the Monument of Culture,* especially 57–64, where Rainey makes plain his concern with not merely the "roots" of quotation but their "routes," their paths of transmission.

27. Compare Massimo Bacigalupo's description of the later *Cantos:* "[Pound's] verse is essentially a transcription of traces he reads in books, on leaves, in the sky, and—in his better moments—in the mind, 'dove sta memòra.' In turn the poem will yield its 'revelations' only if closely read as trace, matter, graffito" (*The Forméd Trace* ix).

28. The passage to which this corresponds can be found on page 124.

29. Among all of these listed works, only "It Was" and *Graph: Of Culture* eventually found their way into print, the latter as a section of *Bottom,* "Notes for Her music to *Pericles* and for a graph of culture" (*B* 33–94). For "It Was," see *CF* 181–84. "The Hounds" was part of Zukofsky's work on the WPA *Index of American Design,* as is *A History of American Design* (see Nadel).

30. Celia Zukofsky's setting of Shakespeare's *Pericles, Prince of Tyre* was published as the second volume of *Bottom: On Shakespeare.*

Chapter 9

1. Other readers are not so generous as Williams, finding the difficulty of Zukofsky's work an alienating and distancing element, one that drives readers away. Zukofsky's fellow Objectivist George Oppen, for one, felt that much of Zukofsky's obscurity was a self-serving device, and that conviction was a major cause of his eventual break with Zukofsky. Mary Oppen refers to her husband's belief that Zukofsky "used incomprehensibility and obscurity as a tactic" (*Meaning a Life* 209), and in a 1980 interview Oppen himself opines that Zukofsky had been cynical "from the beginning" as to whether whatever audience he might have cared whether his poetry was "clear or not" (Hatlen and Mandel 45).

2. The Center's holdings are catalogued in Booth, *A Catalogue of the Louis Zukofsky Manuscript Collection,* and Henderson, "Supplement to Marcella Booth's 'A Catalogue of the Louis Zukofsky Manuscript Collection.' "

3. Alison Rieke's suggestion that Zukofsky derives a revitalized notion of how quotation can be used from his reading (in preparation for "A"-13) of Emerson's essay "Quotation and Originality" is a provocative one, although I think she overstates her case (Rieke, "Quotation and Originality" 77–84).

4. This is a troublesome statement, especially in its latter details: while Zukofsky and his wife spent a considerable amount of time compiling the index to the University of California *"A"*, an idiosyncratic and fascinating document that itself represents a fully thought-through critique and revaluation of his work (and one whose significance has yet to be completely assessed), he clearly had no hand in designing the book's cover. The paperback edition, for instance, misspelled the poem's title as *A* (sans quotation marks) on both cover and spine.

5. David Levi Strauss's reading of *80 Flowers,* which relies on the *OED,* various reference works that Zukofsky might or might not have used, and a good deal of free association, is an interesting example of how a contemporary poet approaches Zukofsky's later work. His reading goes both *beneath* the text to its sources and *through* it,

reading the syntax of the poetry in a way that Leggott too often fails to do.

6. For the exact wording of what I have here paraphrased, see Corman, "In the Event of Words," *LZMP* 326.

7. While I agree wholeheartedly with this statement of Taggart's, his contention that "A"-22 and -23 represent "the separated-out material which has been deliberately left at an earlier stage as an offering of material—'a raft of stuff'—for others to compose, mix down, into their own songs" (*Songs of Degrees* 200) does not stand up to the picture of Zukofsky's careful and thorough sifting and recasting of his materials as documented by Rieke and Leggott. See especially Leggott 34–72; Rieke, "Quotation and Originality" 100–104; and Rieke, *Senses of Nonsense* 186–226.

8. According to one of Oppen's letters, "Z[ukofsky was] much interested in G.S. [Gertrude Stein] circa 1928–30 (in many conversations)" (*Selected Letters* 289).

9. I take this figure from Leggott (56–57); while the duration of the time covered is not specified in the text of "A"-22 and -23 (and thereby fundamentally insignificant), even the most casual reading of the movements makes the temporal progression evident.

10. *"A"-24* (in its original Grossman printing) opens with an acknowledgment of the degree to which Celia Zukofsky's "L.Z. Masque" has accurately delineated the major themes and concerns of Zukofsky's work as a whole: "the gift— / she hears / the work / in its recurrence / L.Z." (n.p.). While the University of California and the Johns Hopkins editions of *"A"* print this at the end of the movement ("A"-24, 806), it is clearly intended as an opening epigraph. See Quartermain, *Disjunctive Poetics* 207n. 18, 214n. 17.

11. Quartermain defines *apo koinou*, a term derived from classical Greek rhetoric, as "where the end-word of a line . . . ends one statement, but unpunctuated also starts the next, acting as the pivot on which the next line turns" (*Disjunctive Poetics* 93). The device is common in Zukofsky's later work, one of the means by which it enforces a "multiplicity of meaning."

12. Bacigalupo describes *Thrones de los Cantares* as "a text atonally composed of broken-off micro-elements" and notes its quality of "subtle polyphony" (259–60).

13. As Leggott comments on Zukofsky's assembling of material for the composition of "A"-22 and -23, "the real delight of the

reading . . . was the unearthing of contingencies, those places where one voice had been, or seemed to have been listening to another. Zukofsky-Chaucer-Cicero-Plato on cosmic perspective, for example" (55).

14. Foreword to *"A" 1–12* n.p. (Doubleday ed.).

15. This passage is from Elizabeth I's translation of Boethius; see Rieke, *Senses of Nonsense* 222. The identification of the Arapaho is from *Senses of Nonsense* 219.

16. The poem is quoted at length in *Bottom* (116–17).

17. Jacket notes, *Niccolò Paganini: The 24 Caprices for Solo Violin.*

18. Also present, among others more or less "submerged," are Henry James, Arnold Schoenberg, and Wittgenstein. These less obvious identifications are from Leggott (66–67).

19. The technologies of digital sound sampling have made obsolete the rappers' practice of "cuing" up actual LPs (a practice not yet developed in "A"-23's 1974) to obtain their musical "grafts," although the collagistic techniques of rap music are a clear analogue to Zukofsky's later poetics.

20. Zukofsky refers to his own labor on several occasions as "pothering": Celia addresses him in "A"-12, "—Still awake, still pothering?" ("A"-12, 260), and elsewhere he addresses the reader, "o you'll regret // I pothered but / you'll have bothered" ("A"-23, 344).

21. These lines are an oblique homage to Shakespeare, a quotation of Romeo's exclamation to Juliet: "Lady, by yonder blessed moon I vow, / That tips with silver all these fruit-tree tops—" (*Romeo and Juliet* II.ii.107–8).

22. My own hunch, buttressed by the interest that Zukofsky showed in Apollinaire's work, is that "A"-7's image of sawhorses, transmuted by the poet's imagination, was suggested by a precisely parallel passage of Apollinaire's "Chevaux de Frise," from his volume *Calligrammes:* these trench defenses (called "Friesland horses" in reference to their invention "during the Dutch war of independence as a protection against enemy cavalry") resembled large sawhorses covered with barbed wire. The poet exclaims, "Chevaux muets / Non chevaux barbes mais barbelés / Et je les anime tout soudain / En troupeau de jolis chevaux pies" (Mute horses / Not barbary horses but barbed / And I change them suddenly / Into a herd of pretty piebald horses) (*Calligrammes* 320–21, 492n).

Chapter 10

1. Paul Zukofsky testifies to the heaviness of his father's annotations in the two volumes of Stevens he consulted in preparing the lecture.

2. Exemplary in this respect are James Longenbach's *Wallace Stevens: The Plain Sense of Things* and Alan Filreis's two volumes, the first reading Stevens's postwar poetry in the context of the social and political events and changes of the postwar years, the more recent examining his relationship to politically radicalized American poetry of the 1930s—including that of the Objectivists.

3. Mark Halliday describes these "reading" poems of Stevens's as "accounts of reading which are happily undisturbed by difference, accounts in which the gap between poet and reader is somehow healed. . . . The view of poetry as reconciliation is espoused here with such thoroughgoing wistfulness as to include a reconciling of poet with readers that is not just a reaching agreement but a merging" (101).

4. Zukofsky makes use of one minor Stevens poem, "Another Weeping Woman," in *A Test of Poetry* (completed 1940) (*TP* 139–40). Interestingly enough, this poem is grouped with two passages from *King Lear* under the consideration of "duration." There are no references to Stevens in *Bottom*, however, and Zukofsky's last explicit critical comment on Stevens (before his lecture) dates to 1930, when he castigates Stevens for "clambering the stiles of English influence" and writing lines that are "too obviously Milton" (*P* 138–39).

5. For representative examples of Language poetics, see the essays collected in Bernstein, *Content's Dream;* Silliman, *The New Sentence;* Andrews and Bernstein, *The L=A=N=G=U=A=G=E Book;* Bernstein, *The Politics of Poetic Form;* and Perelman, *Writing/Talks.*

6. I read much of *The Sophist* as a complex set of homages to and parodies of twentieth-century American poetries. Both "Outrigger" (27–30) and "A Person Is Not an Entity Symbolic but the Divine Incarnate" (145–59) are titles strongly reminiscent of Ashbery. The title "The Years as Swatches" (31–33) is an MTV-like revision of Robert Duncan's "The Years as Catches." "Come, Shadow, Come" (159) is a quote from Shakespeare by way of *Bottom* (see *B* 393). "Rose the Click for 23" (160) is a species of "homophonic translation" similar to that of the Zukofskys' *Catullus.*

7. Stevens got the title for the poem from his friend Judge Arthur Powell, the poem's dedicatee: "We were walking in Key West . . . when I stopped to look through a fence. I explained that I thought it enclosed a graveyard, as some of the rubbish looked 'like decorations in a nigger cemetary.' He was interested when I explained the custom of negroes to decorate graves with broken pieces of glass, old pots, broken pieces of furniture, dolls heads, and what not. The poem itself is an olio, and the title is fitting" (quoted in Brazeau, *Parts of a World* 100–101).

8. Mark Halliday's remark on Stevens's racial politics is alas accurate: "His lazy-minded racism is a clear subject for an essay that could be written, an essay which I imagine as rather short and rather grim, since I doubt that there are interesting variations in Stevens's racism" (182n). That Stevens's racism is "lazy-minded" is no more morally mitigating than that Pound's anti-Semitism was a "stupid suburban prejudice," as he described it late in life (quoted in Sullivan, *Ezra Pound* 354).

9. Zukofsky's reaction to this same crisis of faith, in specific reference to his reading of "Sunday Morning" at age sixteen, is interesting: "For all I know it was the conflict that bothered all of us at the turn of the century. There had been Darwin and obstinate rationalists whose atheism or agnosticism became a religion. They wanted to impose it on everybody, and Stevens felt it. It carried over to trouble or deepen his poems. I freed myself of the problem sooner because of the 25 years difference between us in history. I suffered it maybe from the age of 10 to 13 and no more" (*P* 29).

10. Michael Davidson, in his "Notes Beyond the *Notes*," to my mind a very important essay, cites Palmer as a poet whose poetics have been made possible by Stevens.

Chapter 11

1. Michael Heller's *Conviction's Net of Branches* is the only critical work treating the Objectivists poets as a group, but that volume amounts to a series of essays on the individual poets. Tom Sharp's "The 'Objectivists' Publications" is more useful in discussing the "movement" as a collective enterprise.

2. The *San Francisco Review* was published by June Oppen Degnam, Oppen's half-sister. Objectivists' books copublished with

New Directions included Reznikoff's *By the Waters of Manhattan* (1962) and *Testimony: The United States 1885–1890: Recitative* (1965), and Oppen's *The Materials* (1962) and *This in Which* (1965).

3. Johnson's complete *ARK,* published in 1996, is unpaginated. I have numbered the pages, taking the title page of "The Foundations: 1–33" as page 1.

4. Another late revision: Johnson had once planned "The Ramparts" to last until midnight, with ARK 100—the excision of *Paradise Lost* of which *Radi Os* was the first part—forming a star-speckled dome over the whole from midnight until dawn: "The world all before" ("Planting" 3).

Conclusion

1. In full, the combinations are as follows: stanza 1: ABCDEF, stanza 2: FAEBDC, stanza 3: CFDABE, stanza 4: ECBFAD, stanza 5: DEACFB, stanza 6: BDFECA, *commiato:* BA/DF/EC. I take this particular word order for the *commiato,* which differs from that in the *Princeton Encyclopedia of Poetry and Poetics* (Preminger et al. 764–65), from " 'Mantis' " itself and from the sestina by Dante that Leslie Fiedler discusses and translates in his valuable "Thoughts in a Green Shade: Reflections on the Stony Sestina of Dante Alighieri" (*No! In Thunder* 23–45): "Al poco giorno e al gran cerchio d'ombra." This sestina was clearly one of Zukofsky's formal models, as is clear from its appearance in " *'Mantis,' An Interpretation.*"

While the best reading of " 'Mantis' " remains Taggart's "Zukofsky's 'Mantis' " (*Songs of Degrees* 51–66), there are some fine insights in Vanderborg, " 'Words Ranging Forms' " 195–201.

2. This phrase is from chapter 14 of Dante's *Vita Nuova* (25).

3. The sestina form's very artificiality makes it a useful focus for formal argument, of course, since it cannot be assimilated to the rhetoric of "natural speech" so often associated with the equally artificial form of blank verse (see Easthope 51–77).

4. See, for instance, David Lehman's note on the sestina in the "Brief Glossary" to his *Ecstatic Occasions, Expedient Forms:* "Modern poets have treated the sestina as a test of their virtuosity and technical dexterity or, alternatively, as an invitation to surrender their initiative to the words themselves, allowing chance to become a determining element in the composition" (234). While it is

clear Lehman is right about the element of tour de force evident in most contemporary sestina writing, the appropriateness of invoking "chance" is questionable; since the line-end words are determined by the poet, there are no aleatoric elements involved. It is a confusion of terms to assign to the realm of hazard any prior structuring devices the poet may opt for.

5. The similarities between "The Raven" and "The Philosophy of Composition" and " 'Mantis' " and " *'Mantis,' An Interpretation*" are striking: in each poem, the poet confronts an emblematic but ultimately symbolically ambiguous animal, and in each commentary the poet attempts to justify the formal and semantic choices of his poem in a patently ex post facto manner.

6. Pound does, however, sometimes describe melopœia in terms of separate media: "In *melopœia* we find a contrary current, a force tending often to lull, or to distract the reader from the exact sense of the language. It is poetry on the borders of music and music is perhaps the bridge between consciousness and the unthinking sentient or even unsentient universe" (*Literary Essays* 26).

7. There is an odd resemblance between this description of readers reading proletarian poets and Charles Altieri's description of how readers of high modernist poets—poets whose work is antithetical to everything Nelson valorizes—find in their work "models of agency and versions of emotional economy that provide significant alternatives to those of the mainstream culture" and learn to "connect [modernist] formal structures to aspects of psychic powers embodied in new modes of human agencies. . . . Modernist art demonstrate[s] the capacity of formal energies to reject mimetic structures and still retain extraordinary semantic force by relying directly on the production of exemplary attitudes that an audience might project into extraartistic contexts" (*Painterly Abstraction* 6–7).

8. I offer this definition in order to distinguish the knowledge I am speaking of here from firm but falsifiable conviction (for instance, "I just *knew* that I was going to win the lottery.")

Works Cited

Works by Louis Zukofsky

55 Poems. Prairie City, IL: Decker, 1941.

80 Flowers. Lunenberg, VT: Stinehour P, 1978.

"A". 1978. Reprint, Baltimore: Johns Hopkins UP, 1993.

"A" 1–12. Kyoto: Origin, 1959.

"A" 1–12. New York: Doubleday, 1967.

"A" 13–21. New York: Doubleday, 1969.

"A" 22 & 23. London: Trigram, 1977.

"A"-24. New York: Grossman, 1972.

" 'A': Third and Fourth Movements: 'out of the voices.' " *New Review* 2 (May–July 1931): 83–88.

After I's. Pittsburgh: Boxwood P/Mother P, 1964.

ALL: The Collected Short Poems 1923–1958. New York: Norton, 1965.

ALL: The Collected Short Poems 1923–1964. New York: Norton, 1971.

Anew: Poems. Prairie City, IL: Decker, 1941.

Arise, arise. New York: Grossman, 1973.

Autobiography. New York: Grossman, 1970.

Bottom: On Shakespeare. Austin, TX: Ark P of the Humanities Research Center, U of Texas, 1963. Reprint, Berkeley: U of California P, 1987.

Catullus (Gai Valeri Catulli Veronensis Liber). [With Celia Zukofsky.] London: Cape Goliard, New York: Grossman, 1969.

Collected Fiction. Elmwood Park, IL: Dalkey Archive, 1990.

Complete Short Poetry. Baltimore: Johns Hopkins UP, 1991.

"Contributors' Notes." *Poetry* 37:5 (February 1931): 294.

Interview with L. S. Dembo ["Sincerity and Objectification"]. In Terrell, ed., *Louis Zukofsky: Man and Poet,* 265–81.

I's (pronounced eyes*)*. New York: Trobar, 1963.
Little; for Careenagers. New York: Grossman, 1970.
"March Comrades (*Words for a workers' chorus, from ' "A"-8'*)." *New Masses* 27:4 (3 May 1938): 14.
"Objectivists Again." [With Morris U. Schappes.] *Poetry* 42:2 (May 1933): 117–18.
"Of Dying Beauty." *Poetry* 23:4 (January 1924): 197.
Pound/Zukofsky: Selected Letters of Ezra Pound and Louis Zukofsky. Ed. Barry Ahearn. New York: New Directions, 1987.
Prepositions: The Collected Critical Essays. New York: Horizon, 1968. Expanded ed., Berkeley: U of California P, 1981.
" 'Recencies' in Poetry." *An "Objectivists" Anthology,* 9–25.
"Sincerity and Objectification: *With Special Reference to the Work of Charles Reznikoff.*" *Poetry* 37:1 (February 1931): 272–85.
Some Time / Short Poems. Highlands, NC: Jargon, 1956.
Le Style Apollinaire [The writing of Guillaume Apollinaire]. Trans. René Taupin. Paris: Les Presses Modernes, 1934.
A Test of Poetry. 1948. New York: C.Z. Publications, 1980.
"The Writing of Guillaume Apollinaire: Le Flâneur, (I)—Il y a." *Westminster Magazine* 22:4 (winter 1933): 9–50.
"The Writing of Guillaume Apollinaire: (II)—Le Poète Ressucité, (III)—& Cie." *Westminster Magazine* 23:1 (spring 1934): 7–46.

Works Edited by Zukofsky

"Objectivists" 1931. Poetry 37:1 (February 1931): 235–98.
An "Objectivists" Anthology. Le Beausset, Var, France, and New York: TO Publishers, 1932.

Other Works

Aaron, Daniel. *Writers on the Left: Episodes in American Literary Communism.* 1961. Reprint, New York: Columbia UP, 1992.
Ackermann, Robert John. *Wittgenstein's City.* Amherst: U of Massachusetts P, 1988.
Adams, Henry. *Novels, Mont Saint Michel, The Education.* Ed. Ernest Samuels and Jayne N. Samuels. New York: Library of America, 1983.

Ahearn, Barry. "Two Conversations with Celia Zukofsky." *Sagetrieb* 3:1 (spring 1983): 112–31.

——. "Zukofsky, Marxism and American Handicraft." In Scroggins, ed., *Upper Limit Music*, 80–93.

——. *Zukofsky's "A": An Introduction.* Berkeley: U of California P, 1983.

Altieri, Charles. *Painterly Abstraction in Modernist American Poetry.* Cambridge: Cambridge UP, 1989.

Andrews, Bruce, and Charles Bernstein, eds. *The L=A=N=G=U=A=G=E Book.* Carbondale, IL: Southern Illinois UP, 1984.

Apel, Willi. *The Harvard Dictionary of Music.* 2d. ed. Cambridge, MA: Belknap P of Harvard UP, 1969.

Apollinaire, Guillaume. *Calligrammes.* Trans. Anne Hyde Greet. Berkeley and Los Angeles: U of California P, 1980.

Ashbery, John. *As We Know.* Harmondsworth: Penguin, 1979.

Auden, W. H. *Selected Poems.* Ed. Edward Mendelson. New York: Vintage, 1979.

Bacigalupo, Massimo. *The Forméd Trace: The Later Poetry of Ezra Pound.* New York: Columbia UP, 1980.

Barthes, Roland. *S/Z.* Trans. Richard Miller. New York: Hill and Wang, 1974.

Bernstein, Charles. *Content's Dream: Essays 1975–1984.* Los Angeles: Sun & Moon, 1986.

——, ed. *The Politics of Poetic Form: Poetry and Public Policy.* New York: Roof, 1990.

——. *The Sophist.* Los Angeles: Sun & Moon, 1987.

Bernstein, Michael André. *The Tale of the Tribe: Ezra Pound and the Modern Verse Epic.* Princeton: Princeton UP, 1980.

Bloom, Harold. Interview by Imre Salusinszky. In Salusinszky, *Criticism in Society*, 44–73. New York: Methuen, 1987.

——, ed. *T.S. Eliot: Modern Critical Views.* New York: Chelsea House, 1985.

Bloom, James D. *Left Letters: The Culture Wars of Mike Gold and Joseph Freeman.* New York: Columbia UP, 1992.

Bloor, David. *Wittgenstein: A Social Theory of Knowledge.* New York: Columbia UP, 1983.

Booth, Marcella. *A Catalogue of the Louis Zukofsky Manuscript Collection.* Austin: Humanities Research Center, U of Texas, 1975.

———. "The Zukofsky Papers: The Cadence of a Life." In Terrell, ed., *Louis Zukofsky: Man and Poet*, 393–400.

Borges, Jorge Luis. *Labyrinths: Selected Stories and Other Writings.* Ed. Donald A. Yates and James E. Irby. New York: New Directions, 1964.

Brazeau, Peter. *Parts of a World: Wallace Stevens Remembered, An Oral Biography.* San Francisco: North Point, 1985.

Breslin, Glenna. "Lorine Niedecker: Composing a Life." In Susan Groag Bell and Marilyn Yalom, eds., *Revealing Lives: Gender in Autobiography and Biography,* 141–53. Albany: SUNY P, 1990.

Brooks, Cleanth. *The Well Wrought Urn: Studies in the Structure of Poetry.* New York: Harcourt, Brace, & World, 1947.

Buhle, Mari Jo, Paul Buhle, and Dan Georgakas. *Encyclopedia of the American Left.* Urbana, IL: U of Illinois P, 1992.

Buhle, Paul. *Marxism in the USA: Remapping the History of the American Left.* London: Verso, 1987.

Bunting, Basil. "Basil Bunting Obiter Dicta." Ed. Dale Reagan. In Terrell, ed., *Basil Bunting: Man and Poet,* 229–74.

———. *Complete Poems.* Assoc. ed. Richard Caddel. Oxford: Oxford UP, 1994.

Butterick, George F. *A Guide to The Maximus Poems of Charles Olson.* Berkeley and Los Angeles: U of California P, 1978.

Byrd, Don. "Getting Ready to Read 'A'." *Boundary 2* 10:2 (winter 1982): 291–308.

———. "The Shape of Zukofsky's Canon." In Terrell, ed., *Louis Zukofsky: Man and Poet,* 163–86.

Caesar, Adrian. *Dividing Lines: Poetry, Class and Ideology in the 1930s.* Manchester: Manchester UP, 1991.

Campbell, P. Michael. "The Comedian as the Letter Z: Influence and Effluence in Zukofsky's Comic Poetry." In Scroggins, ed., *Upper Limit Music,* 175–91.

Carpenter, Humphrey. *A Serious Character: The Life of Ezra Pound.* Boston: Houghton Mifflin, 1988.

Casillo, Robert. *The Genealogy of Demons: Anti-Semitism, Fascism, and the Myths of Ezra Pound.* Evanston, IL: Northwestern UP, 1988.

Cavell, Stanley. *The Claim of Reason: Wittgenstein, Skepticism, Morality, and Tragedy.* Oxford: Oxford UP, 1979.

——. *Disowning Knowledge: In Six Plays of Shakespeare.* Cambridge: Cambridge UP, 1987.

——. *In Quest of the Ordinary: Lines of Skepticism and Romanticism.* Chicago: U of Chicago P, 1988.

——. *The Senses of Walden.* Expanded ed. San Francisco: North Point, 1981.

Coleridge, Samuel Taylor. *Biographia Literaria.* Ed. George Watson. London: Dent, 1956.

Comens, Bruce. *Apocalypse and After: Modern Strategy and Postmodern Tactics in Pound, Williams, and Zukofsky.* Tuscaloosa: U of Alabama P, 1995.

——. "Soundings: The 'An' Song Beginning 'A'-22." *Sagetrieb* 5:1 (spring 1986): 95–106.

Conn, David. *The Divided Mind: Ideology and Imagination in America, 1898–1917.* Cambridge: Cambridge UP, 1983.

Conquest, Robert. "The Abomination of Moab." Review of Louis and Celia Zukofsky's *Catullus. Encounter* (May 1970): 56.

Conte, Joseph M. *Unending Design: The Forms of Postmodern Poetry.* Ithaca, NY: Cornell UP, 1991.

Corman, Cid. "In the Event of Words." In Terrell, ed., *Louis Zukofsky: Man and Poet,* 305–41.

Costello, Bonnie. "Effects of an Analogy: Wallace Stevens and Painting." In Gelpi, ed., *Wallace Stevens,* 65–85.

Cox, Kenneth. "The Poetry of Louis Zukofsky: *'A'*." *Agenda* 9:4/10:1 (autumn 1971/winter 1972): 80–89.

——. "Zukofsky and Mallarmé: Notes on *'A'*-19." *MAPS* 5 (1973): 1–11.

Crawford, Robert. *Identifying Poets: Self and Territory in Twentieth-Century Poetry.* Edinburgh: Edinburgh UP, 1993.

Culler, Jonathan. *Structuralist Poetics: Structuralism, Linguistics, and the Study of Literature.* Ithaca, NY: Cornell UP, 1975.

Dahlberg, Edward. *The Confessions of Edward Dahlberg.* New York: Braziller, 1971.

Daly, Lew. *Swallowing the Scroll: Late in a Prophetic Tradition with the Poetry of John Taggart and Susan Howe.* Buffalo, NY: M Press, 1994.

Dante (Dante Alighieri). *Vita Nuova.* Trans. Mark Musa. Oxford: Oxford UP, 1992.

Dasenbrook, Reed Way. *The Literary Vorticism of Ezra Pound and*

Wyndham Lewis: Towards the Condition of Painting. Baltimore: Johns Hopkins UP, 1985.

Davenport, Guy. *Every Force Evolves a Form: Twenty Essays.* San Francisco: North Point, 1987.

——. *The Geography of the Imagination: Forty Essays.* San Francisco: North Point, 1981.

Davidson, Michael. "Dismantling 'Mantis': Reification and Objectivist Poetics." *American Literary History* 3:3 (fall 1991): 521–41.

——. "Notes Beyond the *Notes:* Wallace Stevens and Contemporary Poetics." In Gelpi, ed., *Wallace Stevens,* 141–60.

Davis, Kay. *Fugue and Fresco: Structures in Pound's Cantos.* Orono, ME: National Poetry Foundation, 1984.

Dawson, Fielding. "A Memoir of Louis Zukofsky." In Terrell, ed., *Louis Zukofsky: Man and Poet,* 103–12.

Dembo, L. S., and Cyrena N. Pondrom, eds. *The Contemporary Writer: Interviews with Sixteen Novelists and Poets.* Madison: U of Wisconsin P, 1972.

Derrida, Jacques. *Dissemination.* Trans. Barbara Johnson. Chicago: U of Chicago P, 1981.

——. *Limited Inc.* Trans. Samuel Weber and Jeffrey Mehlman. Evanston, IL: Northwestern UP, 1988.

Dickinson, Emily. *Selected Letters.* Ed. Thomas H. Johnson. Cambridge, MA: Belknap P of Harvard UP, 1971.

Dijkstra, Bram. *The Hieroglyphics of a New Speech: Cubism, Stieglitz and the Early Poetry of William Carlos Williams.* Princeton: Princeton UP, 1969.

Donoghue, Denis. *Ferocious Alphabets.* Boston: Little, Brown, 1981.

Duncan, Robert. *Ground Work II: In the Dark.* New York: New Directions, 1987.

——. *Selected Poems.* Ed. Robert Bertholf. New York: New Directions, 1993.

Easthope, Antony. *Poetry as Discourse.* London and New York: Methuen, 1983.

Eliot, T. S. *After Strange Gods: A Primer of Modern Heresy: The Page-Barbour Lectures at the University of Virginia, 1933.* London: Faber & Faber, 1934.

——. *The Complete Poems and Plays, 1909–1950.* New York: Harcourt Brace Jovanovich, 1971.

——. *On Poetry and Poets.* New York: Noonday, 1961.

———. *The Sacred Wood: Essays on Poetry and Criticism.* 2d ed. London: Methuen, 1928.
———. *Selected Prose.* Ed. Frank Kermode. London: Faber, 1975.
Emerson, Ralph Waldo. *Essays and Lectures.* Ed. Joel Porte. New York: Library of America, 1983.
Empson, William. *The Royal Beasts and Other Works.* Ed. John Haffenden. Iowa City: U of Iowa P, 1988.
Espey, John. *Ezra Pound's Mauberley: A Study in Composition.* Berkeley and Los Angeles: U of California P, 1955.
Faulkner, William. *Novels 1930–1935.* Ed. Joseph Blotner and Noel Polk. New York: Library of America, 1985.
Fenollosa, Ernest. *The Chinese Written Character as a Medium for Poetry.* Ed. Ezra Pound. 1936. Reprint, San Francisco: City Lights, n.d.
Fiedler, Leslie. *Fiedler on the Roof: Essays on Literature and Jewish Identity.* New York: Godine, 1991.
———. *No! In Thunder: Essays on Myth and Literature.* New York: Stein and Day, 1971.
Filreis, Alan. *Modernism from Right to Left: Wallace Stevens, the Thirties, and Literary Radicalism.* Cambridge: Cambridge UP, 1994.
———. *Wallace Stevens and the Actual World.* Princeton: Princeton UP, 1991.
Finkelstein, Norman. "Jewish-American Modernism and the Problem of Identity: *With Special Reference to the Work of Louis Zukofsky.*" In Scroggins, ed., *Upper Limit Music,* 65–79.
———. *The Utopian Moment in Contemporary American Poetry.* Rev. ed. Lewisburg, PA: Bucknell UP, 1993.
Géfin, Laszlo. *Ideogram: History of a Poetic Method.* Austin: U of Texas P, 1982.
Gelpi, Albert, ed. *Wallace Stevens: The Poetics of Modernism.* Cambridge: Cambridge UP, 1985.
Ginsberg, Allen. *Collected Poems 1947–1980.* New York: Harper & Row, 1984.
Gish, Nancy. "MacDiarmid Reading *The Waste Land:* The Politics of Quotation." In Gish, ed., *Hugh MacDiarmid: Man and Poet,* 207–30. Orono, ME: National Poetry Foundation, 1992.
Gold, Michael. *Mike Gold: A Literary Anthology.* Ed. Michael Folsom. New York: International, 1972.

Golding, Alan. "The 'Community of Elements' in Wallace Stevens and Louis Zukofsky." In Gelpi, ed., *Wallace Stevens*, 121–40.

Gregory, Horace. Letter to the Editor. *Poetry* 38:1 (April 1931): 51–53.

Grove's Dictionary of Music. Vol. III. 5th ed. Ed. Eric Bloom. New York: St. Martin's P, 1954.

Gunn, Thom. "Starting to Read *ARK*." *Chicago Review* 42:1 (1996): 21–22.

H. D. [Hilda Doolittle]. *Ion: A Play After Euripides*. Redding Ridge, CT: Black Swan, 1986.

Haller, Rudolf. *Questions on Wittgenstein*. Lincoln: U of Nebraska P, 1988.

Halliday, Mark. *Stevens and the Interpersonal*. Princeton: Princeton UP, 1991.

Hartley, George. *Textual Politics and the Language Poets*. Bloomington: Indiana UP, 1989.

Hartman, Charles O. *Free Verse: An Essay on Prosody*. Princeton: Princeton UP, 1980.

Hatlen, Burton. "Art and/as Labor: Some Dialectical Patterns in 'A'-1 through 'A'-10." *Contemporary Literature* 25:2 (summer 1984): 204–34.

——. "From Modernism to Postmodernism: Zukofsky's 'A'-12." In Scroggins, ed., *Upper Limit Music*, 214–29.

——. "Zukofsky as Translator." In Terrell, ed., *Louis Zukofsky: Man and Poet*, 345–64.

Hatlen, Burton, and Tom Mandel. "Poetry and Politics: A Conversation with George Oppen." In Hatlen, ed., *George Oppen: Man and Poet*, 23–50. Orono, ME: National Poetry Foundation, 1981.

Heller, Michael. *Conviction's Net of Branches: Essays on the Objectivist Poets and Poetry*. Carbondale, IL: Southern Illinois UP, 1985.

Hemingway, Ernest. *A Farewell to Arms*. New York: Scribners, 1929.

Henderson, Cathy. "Supplement to Marcella Booth's 'A Catalogue of the Louis Zukofsky Manuscript Collection.' " In Oliphant and Dagel, eds., *Lawrence, Jarry, Zukofsky*, 107–81.

"His Main Enemy! The People." *New Masses* 27:4 (3 May 1938): 10.

Hollander, John. "Romantic Verse Form and the Metrical Contract." In Harold Bloom, ed., *Romanticism and Consciousness: Essays in Criticism*, 181–200. New York: Norton, 1970.

———. *Vision and Resonance: Two Senses of Poetic Form.* Revised ed. New Haven: Yale UP, 1975.

Homberger, Eric. *American Writers and Radical Politics, 1900–1939: Equivocal Commitments.* New York: St. Martin's P, 1986.

Homer. *The Odyssey.* Trans. E. V. Rieu. Harmondsworth: Penguin, 1946.

Howe, Susan. *Articulation of Sound Forms in Time.* Windsor, VT: Awede, 1987.

Hulme, T. E. *Further Speculations.* Ed. Sam Hynes. Lincoln: U of Nebraska P, 1962.

Hynes, Samuel. *The Auden Generation: Literature and Politics in England in the 1930s.* Princeton: Princeton UP, 1976.

Jameson, Fredric. *The Prison-House of Language: A Critical Account of Structuralism and Russian Formalism.* Princeton: Princeton UP, 1972.

Johnson, Barbara. "*Les Fleurs du mal armé:* Some Reflections on Intertextuality." In Chaviva Hosek and Patricia Parker, eds., *Lyric Poetry: Beyond New Criticism,* 264–80. Ithaca, NY: Cornell UP, 1985.

Johnson, Ronald. *ARK.* Albuquerque: Living Batch, 1996.

———. *ARK 50.* New York: Dutton, 1984.

———. "*ARK:* The Ramparts (Arches I-XVIII)." *Conjunctions* 15 (1990): 148–89.

———. *The Book of the Green Man.* New York: Norton, 1967.

———. *Eyes & Objects (Catalogue for a Exhibition: 1970–72).* Highlands, NC: Jargon, 1976.

———. "Planting the Rod of Aaron." *Northern Lights* 2 (1985–86): 1–14.

———. *Valley of the Many-Colored Grasses.* New York: Norton, 1969.

Johnson, W. R. *The Idea of Lyric: Lyric Modes in Ancient and Modern Poetry.* Berkeley: U of California P, 1982.

Julius, Anthony. *T.S. Eliot, Anti-Semitism and Literary Form.* Cambridge: Cambridge UP, 1995.

Kalaidjian, Walter. *American Culture Between the Wars: Revisionary Modernism and Postmodern Critique.* New York: Columbia UP, 1993.

Keats, John. *Selected Letters.* Ed. Lionel Trilling. New York: Anchor, 1951.

Kenner, Hugh. *Historical Fictions: Essays on Literature.* San Francisco: North Point, 1990.

——. *Mazes: Essays.* San Francisco: North Point, 1989.

——. "Oppen, Zukofsky, and the Poem as Lens." Ralph Bogardus and Fred Hobson, eds., *Literature at the Barricades: The American Writer in the 1930s.* University, AL: U of Alabama P, 1982.

——. *The Pound Era.* Berkeley: U of California P, 1971.

Klein, Marcus. *Foreigners: The Making of American Literature, 1900–1940.* Chicago: U of Chicago P, 1981.

Kogos, Fred. *A Dictionary of Yiddish Slang and Idioms.* New York: Citadel, 1967.

Korn, Marianne. *Ezra Pound: Purpose/Form/Music.* London: Middlesex Polytechnic P, 1983.

Kripke, Saul A. *Wittgenstein on Rules and Private Language.* Cambridge, MA: Harvard UP, 1981.

Kuberski, Philip. *A Calculus of Ezra Pound: Vocations of the American Sign.* Gainesville: UP of Florida, 1992.

Larrissy, Edward. *Reading Twentieth-Century Poetry: The Language of Gender and Objects.* Oxford: Basil Blackwell, 1990.

Laughlin, James. "Notes on Contributors." *New Directions, 1938.* Ed. James Laughlin. Norfolk, CT: New Directions, 1938.

Lawrence, Karen. *The Odyssey of Style in Ulysses.* Princeton: Princeton UP, 1981.

Leggott, Michele J. *Reading Zukofsky's 80 Flowers.* Baltimore: Johns Hopkins UP, 1989.

Lehman, David, ed. *Ecstatic Occasions, Expedient Forms: 65 Leading Contemporary Poets Select and Comment on Their Poems.* New York: Collier, 1987.

Levenson, Michael H. *A Genealogy of Modernism: A Study of English Literary Doctrine 1908–1922.* Cambridge: Cambridge UP, 1984.

Levi Strauss, David. "Approaching *80 Flowers.*" *Code of Signals: Recent Writings in Poetics.* Ed. Michael Palmer. Berkeley: North Atlantic Books, 1983.

Lewis, C. S. *Studies in Words.* 2d ed. Cambridge: Cambridge UP, 1967.

Lipman, Samuel. *Music After Modernism.* New York: Basic Books, 1979.

Longenbach, James. *Wallace Stevens: The Plain Sense of Things.* New York: Oxford UP, 1991.

MacDiarmid, Hugh [Christopher Murray Grieve]. *Selected Poetry.*

Ed. Alan Riach and Michael Grieve. New York: New Directions, 1992.
Makin, Peter. *Bunting: The Shaping of His Verse.* Oxford: Clarendon P, 1993.
———. *Pound's Cantos.* 1985. Baltimore: Johns Hopkins UP, 1992.
Mallarmé, Stéphane. *Mallarmé.* Trans. Anthony Hartley. Penguin Poets series. Harmondsworth: Penguin, 1965.
———. *Œuvres complètes.* Ed. Henri Mondor and G. Jean-Aubry. Paris: Gallimard, 1954.
Mariani, Paul. *William Carlos Williams: A New World Naked.* New York: Norton, 1981.
Materer, Timothy. *Vortex: Pound, Eliot, and Lewis.* Ithaca, NY: Cornell UP, 1979.
McGann, Jerome J. *Black Riders: The Visible Language of Modernism.* Princeton: Princeton UP, 1993.
———, ed. *The New Oxford Book of Romantic Period Verse.* Oxford: Oxford UP, 1994.
———. *Social Values and Poetic Acts: The Historical Judgment of Literary Works.* Cambridge, MA: Harvard UP, 1988.
———. *The Textual Condition.* Princeton: Princeton UP, 1991.
McWilliams, John P., Jr. *The American Epic: Transforming a Genre 1770–1860.* Cambridge: Cambridge UP, 1989.
Melnick, David. "The 'Ought' of Seeing: Zukofsky's *Bottom.*" *MAPS* 5 (1973): 55–65.
Messerli, Douglas, ed. *"Language" Poetries.* New York: New Directions, 1987.
"The Moscow Trials: A Statement by American Progressives." *New Masses* 27:4 (3 May 1938): 19.
Mottram, Eric. "1924–1951: Politics and Form in Zukofsky." *MAPS* 5 (1973): 76–103.
Nadel, Ira B. " 'A Precision of Appeal': Louis Zukofsky and *The Index of American Design.*" In Scroggins, ed., *Upper Limit Music,* 112–27.
Nelson, Cary. *Repression and Recovery: Modern American Poetry and the Politics of Cultural Memory, 1910–1945.* Madison: U of Wisconsin P, 1989.
O'Leary, Peter. "An Interview with Ronald Johnson." *Chicago Review* 42:1 (1996): 32–53.

Oliphant, Dave, and Gena Dagel, eds. *Lawrence, Jarry, Zukofsky: A Triptych-Manuscript Collections at the Harry Ransom Humanities Research Center.* Austin: Harry Ransom Humanities Research Center, U of Texas at Austin, 1987.

Olson, Charles. *Human Universe and Other Essays.* Ed. Donald Allen. New York: Grove, 1967.

Oppen, George. *The Selected Letters of George Oppen.* Ed. Rachel Blau DuPlessis. Durham, NC: Duke UP, 1990.

Oppen, Mary. *Meaning A Life.* Santa Barbara: Black Sparrow, 1978.

Pacernick, Gary. "An Interview with Carl Rakosi." *American Poetry Review* 26:1 (January/February 1997): 13–19.

Palmer, Michael. *Notes for Echo Lake.* San Francisco: North Point, 1981.

——. *Without Music.* Santa Barbara: Black Sparrow, 1977.

Paracelsus. *Selected Writings.* Ed. Jolande Jacobi. Princeton: Princeton UP, 1979.

Parsons, Marnie. "A More Capacious Shoulder: 'A'-24, Nonsense and the Burden of Meaning." In Scroggins, ed., *Upper Limit Music,* 230–56.

—— *Touch Monkeys: Nonsense Strategies for Reading Twentieth-Century Poetry.* Toronto: U of Toronto P, 1993.

Pater, Walter. *The Renaissance: Studies in Art and Poetry.* Ed. Donald L. Hill. Berkeley: U of California P, 1980.

Penberthy, Jenny. *Niedecker and the Correspondence with Zukofsky, 1931–1970.* Cambridge: Cambridge UP, 1993.

Perelman, Bob. *The Trouble With Genius: Reading Pound, Joyce, Stein, and Zukofsky.* Berkeley: U of California P, 1994.

——, ed. *Writing/Talks.* Carbondale and Edwardsville, IL: Southern Illinois UP, 1985.

Perloff, Marjorie. *The Dance of the Intellect: Studies in the Poetry of the Pound Tradition.* Cambridge: Cambridge UP, 1985.

——. *Poetic License: Essays on Modernist and Postmodernist Lyric.* Evanston, IL: Northwestern UP, 1990.

Poe, Edgar Allan. *Essays and Reviews.* Ed. G. R. Thompson. New York: Library of America, 1984.

Pound, Ezra. *ABC of Reading.* 1934. Reprint, New York: New Directions, 1960.

——. *The Cantos.* New York: New Directions, 1970.

——. *Collected Early Poems.* Ed. Michael John King. New York: New Directions, 1976.

——. *Ezra Pound and Music: The Complete Criticism.* Ed. F. Murray Schafer. New York: New Directions, 1977.

——. *Gaudier-Brzeska: A Memoir.* New York: New Directions, 1970.

——. *Literary Essays.* New York: New Directions, 1968.

——. *Personae: The Shorter Poems.* Revised ed. Ed. Lea Baechler and A. Walton Litz. New York: New Directions, 1990.

——. *The Selected Letters of Ezra Pound, 1907–1941.* Ed. D. D. Paige. New York: New Directions, 1971.

——. *Selected Prose.* Ed. William Cookson. New York: New Directions, 1973.

——. *Translations.* Enlarged ed. New York: New Directions, 1963.

Preminger, Alex, et al., eds. *Princeton Encyclopedia of Poetry and Poetics.* Princeton: Princeton UP, 1965.

Quartermain, Peter. *Disjunctive Poetics: From Gertrude Stein and Louis Zukofsky to Susan Howe.* Cambridge: Cambridge UP, 1992.

——. "Writing and Authority in Louis Zukofsky's *Thanks to the Dictionary.*" In Scroggins, ed., *Upper Limit Music,* 154–74.

Rainey, Lawrence S. *Ezra Pound and the Monument of Culture: Text, History, and the Malatesta Cantos.* Chicago: U of Chicago P, 1991.

Rajan, Balachandra. *The Form of the Unfinished: English Poetics from Spenser to Pound.* Princeton: Princeton UP, 1985.

Reinfeld, Linda. *Language Poetry: Writing as Rescue.* Baton Rouge: Louisiana State UP, 1992.

Ricks, Christopher. *T.S. Eliot and Prejudice.* Berkeley: U of California P, 1988.

Riddel, Joseph N. *The Clairvoyant Eye: The Poetry and Poetics of Wallace Stevens.* 2d ed. Baton Rouge: Louisiana State UP, 1992.

Rieke, Alison. " 'Quotation and Originality': Notes and Manuscripts to Louis Zukofsky's *'A'.*" In Oliphant and Dagel, eds., *Lawrence, Jarry, Zukofsky,* 77–105.

——. *The Senses of Nonsense.* Iowa City: U of Iowa P, 1992.

Riffaterre, Michael. *Semiotics of Poetry.* Bloomington: Indiana UP, 1978.

Robinson, Alan. *Symbol to Vortex: Poetry, Painting and Ideas, 1885–1914.* New York: St. Martin's P, 1985.

Roe, Nicholas. *Wordsworth and Coleridge: The Radical Years.* Oxford: Clarendon P, 1988.

Rosenthal, M. L. "Zukofsky: 'All My Hushed Sources.' " In Terrell, ed., *Louis Zukofsky: Man and Poet,* 227–34.

Saussure, Ferdinand de. *Course in General Linguistics.* Trans. Roy Harris. La Salle, IL: Open Court, 1986.

Schappes, Morris U. "Historic and Contemporary Particulars." *Poetry* 41 (1933): 340–43.

Schelb, Edward. "The Exaction of Song: Louis Zukofsky and the Ideology of Form." *Contemporary Literature* 31:3 (1990): 335–53.

Schimmel, Harold. "Zuk. Yehoash David Rex." In Terrell, ed., *Louis Zukofsky: Man and Poet,* 235–45.

Schwartz, Sanford. *The Matrix of Modernism: Pound, Eliot, and Early Twentieth-Century Thought.* Princeton: Princeton UP, 1985.

Scott, Peter Dale. "The Social Critic and His Discontents." In A. David Moody, ed., *The Cambridge Companion to T.S. Eliot,* 60–76. Cambridge: Cambridge UP, 1994.

Scroggins, Mark, ed. *Upper Limit Music: The Writing of Louis Zukofsky.* Tuscaloosa: U of Alabama P, 1997.

Seidman, Hugh. "Louis Zukofsky at the Polytechnic Institute of Brooklyn (1958–1961)." In Terrell, ed., *Louis Zukofsky: Man and Poet,* 97–102.

Shakespeare, William. *The Riverside Shakespeare.* Ed. G. Blakemore Evans, et al. Boston: Houghton Mifflin, 1974.

——. *The Tempest.* Ed. Stephen Orgel. Oxford: Clarendon P, 1987.

Sharp, Tom. "The 'Objectivists' Publications." *Sagetrieb* 3:3 (winter 1984): 41–47.

Sieburth, Richard. *Instigations: Ezra Pound and Remy de Gourmont.* Cambridge, MA: Harvard UP, 1978.

Sigg, Eric. *The American T.S. Eliot: A Study of the Early Writings.* Cambridge: Cambridge UP, 1989.

Silliman, Ron. *The New Sentence.* New York: Roof, 1987.

——. "Space May Produce New *Wor(l)ds.*" Review of Ronald Johnson, *Radi Os. Montemora* 4 (1978): 289–91.

——, ed. *In the American Tree: Language, Realism, Poetry.* Orono, ME: National Poetry Foundation, 1987.

Simon, Linda. "A Preface to Zukofsky." *Sagetrieb* 2:1 (spring 1983): 89–96.

Spinoza, Baruch. *The Ethics and Selected Letters.* Trans. Samuel Shirley, ed. Seymour Feldman. Indianapolis, IN: Hackett, 1982.

Stanley, Sandra Kumamoto. *Louis Zukofsky and the Transformation of a Modern American Poetics.* Berkeley: U of California P, 1994.

Steiner, George. *On Difficulty and Other Essays.* New York: Oxford UP, 1978.

Stevens, Wallace. *Collected Poems.* New York: Knopf, 1955.

———. *Letters of Wallace Stevens.* Ed. Holly Stevens. New York: Knopf, 1966.

———. *The Necessary Angel: Essays on Reality and the Imagination.* New York: Knopf, 1951.

———. *Opus Posthumous: Poems, Plays, Prose.* New ed. Ed. Milton J. Bates. New York: Knopf, 1989.

Stroud, Barry. *The Significance of Philosophical Scepticism.* Oxford: Clarendon P, 1984.

Sullivan, J. P., ed. *Ezra Pound: A Critical Anthology.* Harmondsworth: Penguin, 1970.

Swift, Jonathan. *The Complete Poems.* Ed. Pat Rogers. New Haven, CT: Yale UP, 1983.

Taggart, John. "Aria No. 17." *Conjunctions* 16 (1991): 237–39.

———. *Dodeka.* Milwaukee, WI: Membrane, 1979.

———. "Interview." [With Gill Ott and Toby Olson.] *Paper Air* 4 (spring 1978): 46–50.

———. *Loop.* Los Angeles: Sun & Moon P, 1991.

———. *Remaining in Light: Ant Meditations on a Painting by Edward Hopper.* Albany: SUNY P, 1993.

———. *Songs of Degrees: Essays on Contemporary Poetry and Poetics.* Tuscaloosa: U of Alabama P, 1994.

———. *Standing Wave.* Providence, RI: Lost Roads, 1993.

Terrell, Carroll F. "Basil Bunting: An Eccentric Biography." In Terrell, ed., *Basil Bunting: Man and Poet,* 25–61.

———, ed. *Basil Bunting: Man and Poet.* Orono, ME: National Poetry Foundation, 1981.

———. *A Companion to the Cantos of Ezra Pound.* 2 vols. Berkeley: U of California P, 1980, 1984.

———. "Louis Zukofsky: An Eccentric Profile." In Terrell, ed., *Louis Zukofsky: Man and Poet,* 31–74.

———, ed. *Louis Zukofsky: Man and Poet.* Orono, ME: National Poetry Foundation, 1979.

Thompson, E. P. *Witness Against the Beast: William Blake and the Moral Law.* New York: New P, 1993.

Tomlinson, Charles. “Objectivists: Zukofsky and Oppen, a Memoir.” In Terrell, ed., *Louis Zukofsky: Man and Poet,* 79–96.

Tompkins, Jane. *Sensational Designs: The Cultural Work of American Fiction, 1790–1860.* Oxford: Oxford UP, 1985.

Twitchell, Jeffrey. Review of Sandra Kumamoto Stanley, *Louis Zukofsky and the Transformation of a Modern American Poetics. South Atlantic Review* 60:1 (January 1995): 186–89.

“Unity on May Day.” *New Masses* 27:4 (3 May 1938): 8.

Vanderborg, Susan. “ ‘Words Ranging Forms’: Patterns of Exchange in Zukofsky’s Early Lyrics.” In Scroggins, ed., *Upper Limit Music,* 192–213.

Van Vechten, Carl. *Nigger Heaven.* 1926. Reprint, New York: Harper, 1961.

Von Hallberg, Robert. *Charles Olson: The Scholar’s Art.* Cambridge, MA: Harvard UP, 1978.

Wald, Alan. *The New York Intellectuals: The Rise and Decline of the Anti-Stalinist Left from the 1930s to the 1980s.* Chapel Hill, NC: U of North Carolina P, 1987.

———. *The Revolutionary Imagination: The Poetry and Politics of John Wheelwright and Sherry Mangan.* Chapel Hill, NC: U of North Carolina P, 1983.

Watten, Barrett. “Social Formalism: Zukofsky, Andrews, & Habitus in Contemporary Poetry.” *North Dakota Quarterly* 55:4 (fall 1987): 365–82.

Weinberger, Eliot. *Works on Paper.* New York: New Directions, 1986.

Whitman, Walt. *Poetry and Prose.* Ed. Justin Kaplan. New York: Library of America, 1982.

Whittaker, John H. “Language-Games and Forms of Life Unconfused.” *Philosophical Investigations* 1:4 (1978): 39–48.

Wilk, Melvin. *Jewish Presence in T.S. Eliot and Franz Kafka.* Atlanta: Scholars P (Brown Judaic Studies 82), 1986.

Williams, Jonathan. *In the Azure Over the Squalor: Ransackings & Shorings.* Frankfort, KY: Gnomon, 1985.

Williams, William Carlos. *Autobiography.* New York: Random House, 1951.

———. *Collected Earlier Poems.* New York: New Directions, 1961.

———. *Imaginations.* Ed. Webster Schott. New York: New Directions, 1970.

———. *Pictures from Brueghel and Other Poems.* New York: New Directions, 1962.

———. *Selected Letters.* Ed. John C. Thirlwall. New York: McDowell, Oblensky, 1957.

———. *Something to Say: William Carlos Williams on Younger Poets.* Ed. James E. B. Breslin. New York: New Directions, 1985.

———. *William Carlos Williams and James Laughlin: Selected Letters.* Ed. Hugh Witemeyer. New York: New Directions, 1989.

Winn, James Anderson. *Unsuspected Eloquence: A History of the Relations Between Poetry and Music.* New Haven, CT: Yale UP, 1981.

Winters, Yvor. "The Objectivists." *Hound and Horn* 6:1 (1932–33): 158–60.

Wittgenstein, Ludwig. *On Certainty.* Ed. G. E. M. Anscombe and G. H. von Wright. New York: Harper & Row, 1969.

———. *Philosophical Investigations.* 3d ed., trans. G. E. M. Anscombe. New York: Macmillan, 1968.

———. *Tractatus Logico-Philosophicus.* Trans. C. K. Ogden. London: Routledge, 1922.

Woodward, Anthony. *Ezra Pound and "The Pisan Cantos."* London: Routledge, 1980.

Wordsworth, William. *William Wordsworth.* Ed. Stephen Gill. The Oxford Authors series. Oxford: Oxford UP, 1984.

Yeats, W. B. *Later Essays.* Vol. V of *The Collected Works of W. B. Yeats.* Ed. William H. O'Donnell. New York: Scribner's, 1994.

Yovel, Yirmiyahu. *The Marrano of Reason.* Vol. I of *Spinoza and Other Heretics.* Princeton: Princeton UP, 1989.

Zukofsky, Celia. "Year by Year Bibliography of Louis Zukofsky." In Terrell, ed., *Louis Zukofsky: Man and Poet,* 385–92.

Zukofsky, Paul. Jacket notes to *Niccolò Paganini: The 24 Caprices for Solo Violin (Complete).* Vanguard Cardinal Series, VCS-10093/4, 1970.

Index

About the Author

Mark Scroggins is assistant professor of English at Florida Atlantic University. He is a poet and has published essays and reviews on various modern and contemporary poets, including Nathaniel Mackey, Louis Zukofsky, and Ian Hamilton Finlay. He is the editor of *Upper Limit Music: The Writing of Louis Zukofsky* (1997).